D0881180

POWER IN AFRICA

Also by Patrick Chabal

AMÍLCAR CABRAL
POLITICAL DOMINATION IN AFRICA

POWER IN AFRICA

An Essay in Political Interpretation

Patrick Chabal
King's College London

St. Martin's Press   New York

First published in the United States of America in 1992

Printed in Hong Kong

ISBN 0–312–07509–X

Library of Congress Cataloging-in-Publication Data
Chabal, Patrick, 1951–
    Power in Africa : an essay in political interpretation / Patrick
Chabal.
        p.   cm.
    Includes bibliographical references and index.
    ISBN 0–312–07509–X
    1. Africa—Politics and government—1960–   2. Power (Social
sciences)   I. Title.
JQ1872.C48   1992
320.96—dc20   91–28651
                                                         CIP

To my parents

Contents

Preface

Power in Africa is an old-fashioned book in that it is first and foremost an *essay*, that is a sustained analytical and interpretative text on contemporary African politics. The two essential qualities of the essay which have most influenced my writing are, first, the need to develop a broad argument on a well-defined topic and, second, the willingness to speculate.

Power in Africa thus engages in a systematic but necessarily personal reflection on the complex set of political issues which I call power in Africa. At the same time, it aims to stimulate a debate about the interpretation of politics in post-colonial Africa. By its very nature, therefore, this book is bound to be considered subjective, provocative and perhaps over-ambitious. This is as it should be, for the usefulness of the old-fashioned political essay, as I see it, is to be creatively and constructively 'polemical'.

Even, or perhaps particularly, in the age of 'scientific' and narrowly focused political science, I believe there is a place for such a political essay, as it is useful for us, political analysts, to reflect on the purpose, method and interpretative sharpness of our discipline. In the present climate of simple (if not facile) political certainties, this book sets out both to reconsider the analytical premises on which we Africanists operate and to offer one possible interpretation of contemporary African politics.

Power in Africa has grown out of the twenty years during which I have studied African history and politics – several of which were spent working and doing research in Black Africa. It is also the product of innumerable discussions with Africans both in Africa and elsewhere. I have benefited greatly from being taught and from teaching African studies in Europe, Africa and North America. It is here neither possible nor desirable to furnish a list of all those, teachers, students, colleagues and friends, who have nourished my interest in Africa and challenged me to clarify my thinking. They have all helped me although they may not agree with the ideas presented in this book.

I should, however, like to thank specifically Donal Cruise O'Brien, John Dunn, Prosser Gifford, Franz-Wilhelm Heimer, Bogumil Jewsiewicki, Murray Last, Achille Mbembe, Richard Rathbone, Paul Richards and Lars Rudebeck for inviting me to present some of the ideas contained in this book at conferences or seminars which they organised. I am also grateful to Jean-François Bayart and Jean Copans for the alacrity with which they agreed to read an early draft of the book and to my brother Pierre for his useful comments on one chapter. I want to thank my colleagues at King's

College London for allowing me the sabbatical leave during which I completed the manuscript and Jessica Kuper for her advice on publication. I am grateful to the Rockfeller Foundation for letting me revise the final manuscript in the magnificent luxury of their Bellagio Study Centre. Finally, I wish to thank my editor, T. M. Farmiloe, who has made every effort to facilitate the production, publication and distribution of *Power in Africa*.

I should like to record my debt to Farzana, ever-supportive companion as well as fierce intellectual critic and to Emile, whose very presence is the greatest and most constant stimulant to my work.

PATRICK CHABAL
December 1990

Part I
The Meanings of
Political Interpretation

Introduction

> Could the old saying be true, that in Africa no known system of government works? In the last 30 years the twentieth century has tightened its hold on the world, even on many parts of the Third World, but this one large part of the globe, defying the unities of space and time, has moved in the opposite direction. It is hard to think of a country in sub-Saharan Africa where life for most people is better today than it was in 1957, when Ghana became the first British colony to gain independence . . . Nowhere on the continent is there a flicker of hope.[1]

This book asks a simple, though not simply answered, question: how best to understand the politics of contemporary Africa? But what does this question mean and is it appropriate? Are there grounds for thinking that understanding politics in Africa is any more onerous or any more urgent a task than understanding politics anywhere else? What do we mean by understanding? Is is plausible to assume that African countries can profitably be compared simply because they are African? Is not the whole notion of African politics parochially tautological? Do we not, perhaps, ask questions differently when we try to explain the politics of Africa? And if we do, do we understand the implications of so doing?

An attempt to understand contemporary African politics is both appropriate and necessary, even if it is not easily achieved. It is appropriate because much of what has hitherto passed for an explanation of African politics has often failed meaningfully to account for what has actually happened in Africa since independence. It is necessary because failures of understanding have practical consequences. Where understanding dissolves, prejudice thrives. Where prejudice thrives, the lives of ordinary people become opaque.

The consensus today is that Africa is in crisis. Certainly, no one would deny that an excessively large number of men and women suffer in Africa. Africa has virtually been reduced to the television images of the emaciated refugee child starving in the arms of an almost lifeless mother – or of the Liberian civil war. Yet, for all the pathos contained in this endless series of apocalyptic pictures, and for all the charity displayed by large sections of Western societies, there is an almost total absence of understanding. Surely something is wrong. Undoubtedly, what is wrong has to do with 'politics'. But how do we explain it?

Outside observers seem to be baffled. Where once they confidently displayed blueprints for the advancement of Africa, they now resort to incantation and exhortation. Where once they claimed to understand 'African' politics they now decry its 'Africanness'. Where once they saw 'progressive' parties, ideologies or class alliances they now see parties of exploitation, ideologies as smokescreens and parasitic ruling classes. Where once they advocated the rapid modernisation of the economy they now call for a return to peasant agriculture. Where once they sang the virtue of self-sufficiency they now call in the World Bank and the International Monetary Fund (IMF). And everywhere they see the spread of AIDS.

Furthermore, in the litany of wrongs there is now reproach: Africa is making war on itself; African rulers are despots; politicians are venal, corrupt and violent; the state is a predatory monster; the people are fatalistic; Africans destroy the natural habitat, provoking droughts and plagues; etc. Is Africa's crisis self-inflicted? Whatever the origins and nature of the present crisis in Africa, there is certainly a crisis in understanding when it becomes necessary to invoke the hand of destiny or the spectre of original sin to explain African politics.[2]

Any understanding of politics is rooted in the conditions in which we live, for the purpose of understanding is essentially to make coherent to ourselves specific historical problems. When these conditions change, and in the past thirty years they have changed in Europe as they have in Africa, understanding also changes. The immediate post-colonial period had different needs for coherence from those of the present. The context changes but the need for understanding remains.[3]

The time has come therefore to rethink Africa's politics, that is in terms not so much of 'African' politics but of politics in Africa. The distinction is important.[4] For too long, analysts (of whatever persuasion and persuasiveness) have focused on the uniqueness of Africa. My starting point is the opposite. To understand politics in Africa we need to take Africans seriously, that is we need to accept that the process of understanding their politics is conceptually and in practice similar to the process of understanding politics anywhere else.[5]

There is nothing specifically African about politics in Africa, or rather there is nothing which is more specifically African in the politics of Africa than is specifically European in the politics of Europe. The search for the specifically African quality of African politics must not be at the expense of what is more properly the object of political analysis: understanding power.[6]

This book, therefore, is about power in contemporary Africa. But is it plausible to study Africa as a whole? I believe it is, with the crucial proviso that what is meant here is Black Africa (excluding North Africa, South Africa and Ethiopia), that part of Africa which was colonised by the European powers at the end of the nineteenth century. The fact that it was parcelled out between different European powers is far less important in this respect than the fact that it was colonised at all. For the starting point in the analysis of independent Africa must be pre-colonial and colonial Africa rather than merely the national entities created in the process of decolonisation.

What, then, is politics? Politics is about power – in Africa as anywhere else. Power, whatever its precise definition, is minimally about the balance between control and consent which governs the relation between ruler and ruled. Relations of power exist as soon as men and women are gathered in communities, whatever the level of their productive development. To understand politics is thus to understand relations of power in their historical settings.

In the real world, however, power and production are inextricably linked. There can be no power exercised in a productive void, nor can there be production other than in a context of power relations. The object of political analysis must be to understand the link, causal or otherwise, between the two. There is nothing specifically African about this aspect of politics either. Power and production are the two axes of politics in any society.

The argument presented thus far is simple. The task of understanding politics in Africa today must start at the beginning, historically and conceptually[7]: historically, that is in the process by which Africans were brought under colonial control and aggregated in colonial territories eventually to become independent countries; conceptually, that is in the analysis of the evolution of the relation between power and production which defined the evolution of what are African countries today.

A further assumption is that the politics of Africa is best understood comparatively. To proceed otherwise would be to reify the notion of post-colonial nation-states. We must understand rather than assume the division of Africa into nation-states. Two observations derive from this assumption: first, a comparative analysis of the politics of African countries must transcend colonial boundaries, that is the division between former British, French, Portuguese, Belgian or Spanish colonies; second, what is most profitably compared must be determined by historical context.[8]

The study of contemporary politics in Africa is *ipso facto* about interpretation. Political interpretation, whatever its character, does not arise in a vacuum. It is intimately linked to the historical context within which it appears. We are all products of our age. In any discussion of African politics, therefore, it is important to bear in mind the intellectual and generational pedigree of particular interpretations. There has been an evolution in the interpretation of post-colonial African politics which it is important to consider in some detail.

Three general remarks are appropriate here. First, the context of world morality has changed considerably since the end of the Second World War, influencing thereby the intellectual climate within which scholars have studied politics in Africa. Second, there has been a shift of emphasis between and within the various academic disciplines concerned with the study of African societies. Third, the attitude of African scholars and intellectuals has evolved considerably in response both to the internal evolution of their own societies and to the ways in which outsiders interpret Africa.[9]

The impact of the Second World War on the morality of colonial rule was considerable. Both the colonial peoples and their masters came to realise that the moral ground had irretrievably shifted. There was little justification for continued colonial rule. The period which preceded and followed independence (whenever it came) was often one of optimism. In the spirit of the new democracy, colonisers and colonised alike expected much of independence. Pride as well as self-interest conspired to create a climate in which the successful political and economic progress of the former African colonies was largely taken for granted.[10]

Within ten years of independence disillusionment had set in. The perceptible lack of political order and the absence of the expected economic development changed the outside perception of Africa. The Western world, now in the grip of the first oil crisis (1973/4), perceived world morality in different terms. The optimism of the 'Decade of Development' was replaced by a more calculating approach steeped in more narrowly defined national self-interest and Cold War politics. This in turn gave way to the 'spirit of the eighties', characterised by a backlash against liberal values and the emergence of a new morality of greed. [11]

Africa's political and economic crisis is nowadays usually seen as the outcome of the follies of its governors who, having used and abused power for their own ends, have dissipated their colonial inheritance and shackled the initiative of their subjects.[12] The message from the West now is: get your own house in order. The two faces of the West today are the IMF/World Bank and its necessary concomitant, Band Aid.

The Western image of Africa derived primarily from the interpretation of its societies by Western scholars, researchers, academics or simply intellectual quacks.[13] The colonial period was essentially seen through the eyes of, chronologically, the explorer, the missionary, the anthropologist and the administrator.[14] Decolonisation and the early period of independence were, for reasons which I discuss later, largely the preserve of political scientists.[15] Then, it was the turn of the political economists to re-interpret the condition of Africa from the perspective of underdevelopment. Many were influenced by the Latin American dependency school and by African (neo)Marxists.[16]

More recently, two widely different types of 'knowledge' about Africa have altered the West's perception of the continent. On the one hand, the incessant activity of 'technical experts' has led to a growing body of information and opinion about the workings of African (particularly rural) society. Much of the current wisdom on peasant production, for example, derives from the information gathered by 'experts' working in villages.[17] The changing IMF/World Bank strategies for development, from the green revolution approach to today's concern with rural poverty, also reflect the changing views of technical experts and economists.[18]

On the other hand, and growing in importance all the time, there is the output of historians of Africa. From the particular to the synthetic, historians have extended the boundaries of our knowledge about pre-colonial, colonial and even independent Africa. Their work has provided the depth and texture which was lacking from almost all previous Western interpretations of Africa. For the first time, we have some of the historical material which is considered essential by scholars of, say, European societies. The historiography of Africa is deservedly acquiring a high reputation and it ought to be relevant to our understanding of its contemporary politics.[19]

Finally, the current Western perception of Africa is under the powerful spell of two generations of prophets. The first, vocal since the seventies, is essentially neo-Malthusian. Africa is doomed because its population growth is far outstripping its food production. Food production is sacrificed because of export needs but exports cover a decreasing proportion of import needs, including food. The second generation of prophets is gloomier yet. Into this scenario of doom it introduces the ecological dimension. African agricultures are suffering so much from man-made and natural ecological calamities that the prospect for self-sufficiency in food, let along development, is virtually non-existent.[20]

At the same time, the influence of African scholars, writers and intellectuals on our perception of post-colonial Africa is growing. If the colonial period was seen (wrongly) by the West merely to have been the age of the collaborator and the nationalist, the period since independence has (rightly) been perceived as far richer.

True, the nationalist revolution has (over)determined both the position of African intellectuals and our perception of them. The first generation of intellectuals were the great nationalist leaders, at once writers, ideologues and activists. Some of them (e.g., Senghor) were scholars; most (e.g. Nkrumah, Nyerere) had scholarly ambitions. They dominated the early intellectual life of their countries. Even those (e.g., Houphouët-Boigny,

Amadou Ahidjo) who had no intellectual pretensions still had a vision of Africa which informed their discourse, if more rarely their action.[21]

After independence most African scholars, trained in Western universities where there was empathy for the great nationalist vision, shared in the optimism for progress. Some, however, particularly those influenced by (neo)Marxist thought, berated bourgeois independences and warned against the dangers of economic and cultural neo-colonialism.[22] But perhaps the most lucid and trenchant critique of the early years of independence came from fiction writers, playwrights and poets. Wole Soyinka, Chinua Achebe, Ngugi, Mongo Béti and many others did more to reveal the reality of post-colonial Africa than most African scholars.[23]

There were perhaps three trends in this African critique. The first argued that Africa had lost its soul and needed to recover its Africanness if it was to survive and develop along its 'natural' path. This argument turned more and more towards a rethinking of the notion of African identity and the concepts extant in African social and political thought. The second returned to Marxist analysis in order to explain economic and political exploitation in African countries. But it too now defined a specifically African problematic. The third argued from a 'democratic' perspective and adumbrated many of the themes now common to democratic theory. All worked within a much firmer and more self-assured sense of African identity.[24]

The historians for their part wrote at first from a clear nationalist perspective. But they too eventually responded to the changing circumstances of independence and sought to bring a more critical African perspective to the study of pre-colonial and colonial Africa. They, perhaps, found it easiest to establish and maintain a meaningful dialogue with their Western counterparts in that they, like them, often attempted to draw lessons from the history of Europe.[25] There is in the UNESCO *General History of Africa* (largely written by Africans) a parallel to the *Cambridge History of Africa* (largely written by Europeans) which extends this debate.

Having briefly outlined the historical context of these multiple interpretations of politics in Africa, I want now to stress the importance of method. Political analysis is about understanding the real world, not about the ideological or aesthetic merit of a given discourse. The application of theoretical frameworks, the generation of concepts, the production of analytical categories can have only one relevant justification, that of explaining historical events and political processes. The validation of political theory lies in its relevance to understanding.

Historians, like political scientists, need concepts. But if historians have at times operated as though common sense was the single most important (or even the only) criterion of analysis, political scientists of Africa have even more often behaved as though the validation of *a priori* theory was the only reason why they deigned to examine the real world of African politics. Detached and supposedly objective historical narrative can often be as limiting as excessively theoretical discourse.

To a large degree, the crisis of credibility which struck African studies in the mid-seventies (and from which it has yet to recover) was caused by the palpable incapacity of political analysis meaningfully to interpret political events in Africa. This was often due to the development of models and frameworks of political analysis which so abysmally failed the test of plausibility as totally to undermine confidence in the ability of political analysts.[26] For this reason, Africa became once again an enigma, a void, a continent of dark shadows and inexplicable events.

Power in Africa is one attempt to overcome this crisis in understanding. The book follows two programmatic injunctions: first, politics in Africa must be conceived in universal rather than parochial terms and, second, interpretation must be rooted in the deep history of Africa. I believe that thus to approach politics in Africa is to begin to take seriously its political life. It is to begin to move away from the overwhelmingly powerful image of Africa as other, different, unique, that is incomprehensible, which has so narrowly restricted our understanding of the continent over the past century.[27] It is, finally, to begin to understand the politics of contemporary Africa in terms which ought to be immediately familiar to anyone with an interest in politics.

An essay in the political interpretation of power in Africa, such as this aspires to be, is only made possible by the work which has already been done by others. Interpretation rests on the use of certain ideas and concepts which necessarily derive from the re-examination of the existing conceptual and analytical *corpus*. My enterprise itself, therefore, must also be set in the appropriate historical and theoretical context. The first point to be made is that the reflection undertaken in this book would scarcely have been feasible earlier. For it is the accumulated scholarship of several decades of African studies which provides us today with the means to rethink politics in Africa.

The process by which interpretation moves is not, however, either linear or straightforward. Hermeneutics is not a science *per se*. We political analysts are the products of our age. The concepts which we favour are likely to bear some relation to the specific environment in which we live. There is no such thing as an 'objective' analysis of an 'objective' reality and it would be otiose to deny that as reality changes so does our analysis. This is as it should be, since the point of analysis is to relate political understanding with the concerns of our times.

Whatever the arguments and tone of this book, I do not claim that its perspective or hermeneutic quality are any less historically bound than that of other possible interpretations. Nor do I claim for this essay any high moral or political ground. Its putative success in explaining politics in Africa does not derive from any *a priori* notion of what explanation ought to mean in the abstract. The book's merit must rest in its capacity to reveal, to make clearer, the realities of the politics with which it is concerned.

Political analysis ought to benefit from the accumulation of historical knowledge. In the interplay between the historical and political analysis of modern Africa, historians have recently shown greater boldness and greater inventiveness than political scientists.[28] They have been more readily prepared to make use of (some of) the concepts evolved by political scientists than the latter have been willing (or able) to use the history thus revealed.[29] This has been to the detriment of political analysis.

Power in Africa is thus an attempt to begin to construct a political interpretation of contemporary Africa on firmer historical foundations. Because it does not aim to provide a political history of the post-colonial period, it will be most profitably read in conjunction with existing political histories of individual African countries.[30]

Since the entire book is in a sense an attempt to address the issues raised by existing conceptual frameworks, I try in the remainder of Part I to provide a systematic review of the political theory underpinning what I take to be the main interpretative approaches of the past thirty years: that is (in my appellation), development theory, class theory, underdevelopment theory, revolutionary theory and democratic theory.

By systematic, I do not mean that I provide an exhaustive treatment of these approaches but rather that I try to reveal the connections between the assumptions on which they are constructed and the interpretation which they offer. I endeavour both to give a fair summary of their strengths and weaknesses and to explain the limits of their interpretative qualities from the perspective of *Power in Africa*.

The point is not to demonstrate the inadequacies of previous approaches from a given 'other' theoretical viewpoint. It is rather to show how, from my perspective, these 'schools' of interpretation have tended to examine African politics through excessively opaque theoretical lenses and thus frequently neglected to look at contemporary African politics as it is. Hence, what follows is not simply a summary of the existing literature but an attempt to relate concept to context, to reflect on the premises and practices of African studies in the past thirty years.

1 Paradigms Lost

1. DEVELOPMENT THEORY

Development theory sought to analyse post-colonial African politics from the perspective of a general theory of the political development of 'under-developed' countries. Aimed in part at providing an alternative to Marxism, it rested on the assumption that African polities would follow a relatively well-defined unilinear path of economic, social and political development – i.e., Westernisation – which, in due course, would bring them closer to the Western European and North American 'models'. The task of development theorists was to identify the processes which advanced or retarded the movement forward of African polities.[1]

Development theory derived from an attempt (largely by American political scientists) to provide a systematic conceptual framework for the new discipline of comparative politics. Their political and moral imperative was to meet the challenges of communism/Marxism and that of world poverty. As the Cold War descended on international relations and decolonisation gathered pace, they endeavoured to establish a non-Marxist science of politics which would both reveal the superiority of Western polities and explain the politics of the newly independent nation-states.[2]

At the heart of development theory was a determination to evolve a model of how nation-states progress over time. Because American political science was concerned to refute the Marxist theory of the development of societies, it necessarily looked to a similarly teleological model of political development – one, that is, which would account for the experience of all countries, advanced and underdeveloped. Hence, development theory was an attempt to devise a framework of analysis to compare nation-states at different stages of their development.

This led to the construction of a functionalist model of politics which tied in with a structural account of political development. The model, perhaps most elegantly outlined by Karl Deutsch, made it possible to focus analysis on the functional and structural components of political change deemed to be similar in all polities.[3] Heavily influenced by the biological analogy, this model appeared to be a neat scientific alternative to class analysis.[4]

Development theory was an answer to Marxist analysis in that it too provided an account of the political evolution of societies over time. Both related economic to political development. Marxist theory rested on the assumption that class formation and class struggle determined the development of societies. Development theory envisaged a unilinear and progressive movement of self-sustained economic growth, eventually leading to a state of development similar to the most advanced capitalist countries.

There was thus in development theory an attempt to provide a political alternative to the Marxism which, with the Chinese, Cuban and Vietnamese experiences, seemed increasingly to appeal to 'Third World' leaders the world over. For even if development theory was conceived by its exponents as a scientific theory, it emerged out of a climate of fierce ideological contest between the 'Free World' and 'Communism', a struggle between 'good' and 'evil'.[5]

The establishment of a separate discipline of comparative politics, to which development theory was central, coincided with the decolonisation of the French, British and Belgian colonies of Africa. It provided political scientists with a unique opportunity to study instances of political development from the inception of the nation-state.[6] Hence, they were often more interested in finding out how the evolution of the new African nations fitted the theory of political development than in understanding African politics *per se*.

Development theory rested on the following assumptions. First, whatever their origins and genesis, the structures and functions of the newly independent and sovereign African post-colonial polities were amenable to comparison with those of Western polities. Second, the process of political development, like that of economic development, was seen to be unilinear and cumulative. Countries started life at a low level of (economic and political) development and progressively advanced on the path trodden by those who were already more advanced. The process might be delayed, even reversed, but its course was clearly charted.[7]

Third, there was a reciprocal causal relation between economic and political development. Economic development provided the material basis for political development; conversely, political development created the organisational structure for economic development. Both were seen to be state-driven. Fourth, political development consisted in the progressive institutionalisation of key political functions, the establishment of a rational bureaucracy (in the Weberian sense) and the routinisation of the reproduction of power. Hence, political development could be measured by means of structural and functional criteria.

Fifth, development theory also assumed a reciprocally causal relation between political development and the rise of a 'modern' political culture. Political development was predicated upon the acquisition by citizens of the cultural attributes of 'modern' man: rationality, literacy, secularism, individualism, industry, etc. This entailed, conversely, that 'traditional' cultural attributes were either irrelevant or else impediments to political develop- ment and would in due course be erased by 'modernity'.[8] Sixth, develop- ment theory assumed that political development was synonymous with political order. This implied that, as countries developed, greater political order prevailed and, conversely, that political disorder was an indication of insufficient political development.[9]

It will immediately be apparent that the two most fundamental shortcom- ings of development theory were that it was teleological and ahistorical. Despite or perhaps because of its aversion to class analysis, its teleology became a virtual mirror image of Marxist teleology. Where class analysis had posited that modern societies would follow a historical pattern of development mooted in the transition from the feudal to the socialist, development theory posited that 'Third World' societies would develop along the lines of Western capitalist nations.

The hallmark of the political analysis produced within the perspective of development theory was an astonishing neglect of the colonial and pre- colonial history of Africa. Political scientists analysed the politics of inde- pendent Africa as though their historical antecedents mattered little. Attention was paid to the process of decolonisation only insofar as it provided the backdrop against which post-colonial politics was played. For the rest, there was little history.[10]

Political scientists of Africa were rarely aware of the historiography of colonial and pre-colonial Africa. Nor did they care to find out, for such historiography was seen to be tainted by the colonial mentality of their authors (often missionaries or colonial officials). More profoundly, how- ever, these political scientists genuinely believed that a science of the politics of the newly independent countries could be constructed inde- pendently from a knowledge of their histories. Insofar as they took history into account, however, they tended (because of their sympathies for African nationalism) to rely on nationalist historiography.

The conceptual framework of development theory also led political scientists to concentrate research on 'high' politics, that is the politics of the state and of the main political actors.[11] For obvious historical reasons, this meant in effect that much attention was devoted to the quality of political leadership and the workings of the (single) nationalist party.[12] This is un- derstandable: the nationalist revolution had thrown 'historic' leaders into prominence and focused attention on the political successes of nationalist parties. And Africanists, so relentlessly 'scientific' in their presentation of the political 'system', were often swept by the momentum and glamour of the post-nationalist euphoria.

Nevertheless, the analytical consequences of this enthusiasm for the nationalist revolution were serious. First, the focus on nationalist sources to the exclusion of almost any other was bound to distort perspective. Second, the belief in the developmental commitment of the leaders of the new countries led to an excessive reliance on their pronouncements.[13] Third, the focus on high politics diverted attention from the examination of *realpolitik* – that is the political realities of post-colonial Africa. Finally, the search for developmental success distracted them from the analysis of the serious problems besetting African countries soon after their independence.

More generally, development theory induced political scientists to look at African politics from the perspective of a theory of political progress which in the end had exceedingly little connection with reality. However accurate the analysis of political institutionalisation had been in respect of the political development of Western countries (and there is doubt about that), it patently did not account for what was happening in Africa; nor did the notion of the 'modernisation' of political culture, another dubious concept. Although there was evidence of political institutionalisation and a 'modern' political culture, there seemed to be little immediate causal relation between such evidence and contemporary African politics.

Because development theory failed to account for so many of the processes at work in post-colonial Africa (e.g., ethnicity, coups, violence, corruption, dictatorship), its exponents were left to grasp at straws. They were often forced to introduce new concepts with which to explain the lack of political progress. Thus were born the notions of the shrinking political arena, arrested development, de-institutionalisation, etc.[14] Indeed, by the mid-sixties, the evidence of political disorder was as overwhelming as the evidence of the absence of economic development. The combined force of such evidence greatly eroded the credibility of development theory and seriously discouraged political scientists.[15] Africa's post-colonial politics had turned out to be mean, violent, chaotic, corrupt and, ultimately, incomprehensible.

Nevertheless, the great merit of development theory was that it attempted to build up a conceptual framework to compare the politics of post-colonial Africa with that of the rest of the world. In doing so it sought to move away from the theory of the exotic and the particular which had so marked colonial accounts of Africa. Political scientists of Africa took Africans seriously and genuinely believed that the nationalist revolution would usher in the development which colonial rule had prevented. Equally, there were willing to take seriously the commitments of the new African rulers to the proper operation of the political institutions created at independence. The work of development theorists greatly advanced African studies even if it did not fulfil their most cherished theoretical ambitions.

The greatest failure of development theory lay in the theory rather than in the concepts themselves. It was the teleological quality of the theory which made it impossible for the concepts to be tested against the reality of post-colonial politics. Once it became obvious that political development, as defined in theory, was not taking place, there was little further use for the conceptual apparatus. Indeed, the best political scientists managed to provide us with genuine insights into post-colonial African politics despite, rather than through, the concepts which they deemed necessary to utilise. Or rather, they recast the concepts without the theory and found that some of them were useful.[16]

2. CLASS THEORY

Class theory was in part a reaction against development theory and in part a serious attempt to apply Marxist analysis to a continent hitherto neglected by Marxist political scientists. Class analysts sought to identify in the post-colonial period the modes of production and class developments which best explained the politics of independent Africa. Their work concentrated heavily on the definition of the capitalist order in Africa, its emerging ruling classes and the hegemonic role of the post-colonial state.[17]

Class analysis of post-colonial African politics had two filiations. The first drew from the work of Marxist social anthropologists and historians working on pre-colonial and colonial Africa. Theirs was an attempt to study the history of social formations in Africa and to define the relationship between mode of production and social change.[18] The second issued out of the leftwing political belief held by a number of Africans and Africanists that the future of the continent depended on the capacity of its political leaders to carry out a genuine economic and social revolution.[19]

The attempts by Marxists to conceptualise the politics of the African continent date back to the colonial period. This first group of (chiefly French) Africanists had two main ambitions. They wanted to situate the evolution of African pre-colonial societies within the general Marxist theory of the development of all human societies and to provide a convincing Marxist analysis of colonial rule. Their debate about an 'African' mode of production generated much intellectual ferment.[20]

The Marxist analysis of colonialism took its cue from the analysis of imperialism. While there was disagreement on the practical effects of colonial rule, there was consensus on the historical function of colonialism in the development of capitalism. Colonialism was the outcome of imperialist competition among Western capitalist societies for overseas raw materials and markets. Whether colonialism had turned out to be 'profitable' for imperial exchequers was deemed to be less important than the fact that it had been profitable enough for the capitalists who has invested in Africa.[21]

Marxists disagreed on how historically 'progressive' colonialism had been for Africa. Some, following Marx's discussion of India, maintained that colonialism was the historically necessary process by which undeveloped parts of the world were brought into a capitalist world economy. Hence, the penetration of capitalism into Africa was *ipso facto* 'progressive'. Others felt that colonialism had amounted to pillage and resulted in very little capitalist development. They viewed the colonial economy as a machine for the exploitation of the people and resources of the colonies, exploitation which decolonisation would have to break.[22]

Neither did Marxists agree on the class implications of colonialism. It was simple enough to see railway workers, employees and civil servants in class terms. It was possible, though not always easy, to point to the proletarianisation of Africans who took employment in factories or on plantations. It was, however, considerably more difficult to situate in class terms the mass of Africans who lived and worked on the land.[23]

Class analysis is grounded in the study of the historical development of specific societies. Unlike development theory, then, class analysis sought from the beginning to understand how African societies had evolved historically since the pre-colonial period. The diversity and complexity of pre-colonial Africa did not lend itself to simple answers. Marxists produced some first-class anthropological research but could not, in the end, come to cast-iron conclusions about the nature of pre-colonial modes of production.[24] Some argued for a specific 'African' mode of production. Others found it more useful to recognise the plurality of modes of production. Yet another inconclusive debate centred on the possible existence of feudalism in pre-colonial Africa.[25]

The failure to reach a consensus was not surprising. Marx himself, and many Marxists after him, had remained vague on the precise historical meaning of the Asiatic mode of production (a concept which did not readily apply to Africa), the only explicit non-European pre-feudal stage of development they had identified.[26] Nevertheless, even if Marxist anthropologists failed to agree, their research served to emphasise that an understanding of contemporary Africa required an understanding of the development of its societies from pre-colonial times. Furthermore, some of their insights, such as the importance of trade, the role of slavery and of the 'artisan caste' systems in pre-colonial Africa, became common currency.[27]

Economists focused their attention on colonial and post-colonial Africa. Although they disagreed on the definition of a 'colonial' mode of production and on the nature of colonial class formation, their work contributed significantly to our understanding of the mechanisms of the colonial and post-colonial economy. The analysis of the penetration of capitalism, the examination of the system of economic exploitation set up by the imperial powers, the study of the development of indigenous capitalism and of class formation extant in the colonies, all shed some considerable light on the economic impact of colonialism.[28]

Perhaps one of their most important insights was the notion of dual economy – by which they meant the co-existence of capitalist and pre-capitalist modes of production in Africa. Africans who entered the capitalist sector as (agricultural or even industrial) workers remained connected with the pre-capitalist economy of which they had hitherto been part. Because they derived some revenue (e.g., minimally, food) from the 'traditional' sector, they could be paid wages below the cost of reproduction. This worked against their full proletarianisation. While this conclusion has been disputed by those who argue that the wages paid to workers merely reflect market forces, there is no doubt that the notion of dual economy provides a useful insight into the workings of the colonial and even post-colonial economy. It also explains why capitalist development need not always be at the expense of the pre-capitalist sector of the economy.[29]

Marxists helped to refine our understanding of the colonial economy. Their work on the process by which commodity production was introduced, on the consequences of the development of a labour market and on the transformation of 'communally' held land into a commodity produced a clearer picture of the effects on individual Africans of the colonial economy. Even if Marxists failed to provide convincing class causalities for nationalist politics, they made it easier to understand the historically crucial connections between the colonial and post-colonial political economy.

However, class analysis of post-colonial African politics was less convincing. The chief object of Marxist political scientists was to search for connections between class struggle and political action. But their work suffered from a lack of historical depth and excessive theorising. Not a few prefaced their studies with long and abstract debates on the role of classes in capitalist societies, debates which in truth had very little to do with Africa. This theoretical bias allied with a surprising neglect of the (Marxist and non-Marxist) historiography of Africa led many into highly esoteric analysis. The focus was on the identification of classes, subclasses, fractions of class, etc. Since the process of identification derived more from theory than from the examination of African reality, class analysis tended to be reductive in linking given class (or class fractions) with particular political actions.[30]

The focus on a class-based explanation of post-colonial African politics was in part a reaction against the notion of a classless Africa expounded by some African politicians. Leaders as different as Senghor, Sékou Touré, Nyerere and Kaunda had emphasised the communal nature of African societies and frequently depicted the Africa of the future in terms of its supposed classless pre-colonial past.[31] The merit of Marxist analysis was to remind us that nationalist politics was anchored in the socio-economic context out of which it issued.

Equally, it was a reaction against development theory which had flushed class out of the political equation. Where development theory emphasised the failures of institutionalisation and the insufficient development of a 'modern' political culture, class analysis stressed the class nature of political action. Where one saw disorder as the malfunctioning of the political system, the other interpreted it as evidence of class struggle. Where, finally, one deemed the failure of economic development to be a failure of the spirit of enterprise, the other ascribed it to class exploitation.

While Marxist analysis usefully punctured the illusion of a classless African society, it did not provide a very plausible account of the vagaries of post-colonial politics. Like development theory it was teleological and teleological approaches are usually hampered by their inability to adjust analysis to changes in the realities under study. Class analysis suffered severely in this respect because of the volatility of African politics. It could not easily account for rapid political change, disorder, violence and even chaos other than in terms of infinitely multiple and complex struggles between fractions (or fractions of fractions) of classes. The case of Uganda provides a revealing example of the failure of class analysis to explain the country's (admittedly baffling) post-colonial political history.[32] Although class factors were not irrelevant, they were not crucial.

The same is true for most African countries. Class factors can only be dominant when classes possess a relatively homogeneous and self-conscious existence. This is exceedingly rare in post-colonial Africa. Some African workers (e.g., miners, dock-workers, railwaymen) are sometimes organised in trade unions and, when they are, they sometimes do influence politics significantly.[33] They are, however, virtually the only group of labourers who might qualify as a 'class'. All others, particularly those working the land, are heterogeneous, unorganised and rarely self-conscious as a class. All attempts to define African rural producers as a class of peasants have been unsatisfactory.

For their part, agricultural, commercial or industrial entrepreneurs in Africa are only poorly 'organised as classes'. Their interests are too diverse and their links with the non-capitalist sector too important. Nor, for that matter, is the class position of ruling élites clear. Such concepts as bureaucratic bourgeoisie, *comprador bourgeoisie* or state capitalists are too *portmanteau* to help in the understanding of their political action. Furthermore, the relation between ruling élites and 'recognised' capitalists is rarely simple or straightforward. The relations between economic and political power in Africa are too complex to be consistent with class analysis.

The uneven and limited degree of capitalist development, the fact that African nation-states were states before being nations and that the post-colonial order was politically overdetermined, all militate against a class explanation of politics. As I shall show later, it is political, rather than economic, power which determines the configuration of ruling élites in contemporary Africa. Or rather, it is access to the state, which is the single most crucial factor in the (individual and collective) hegemonic drive.[34]

The recognition that orthodox class analysis has not been very successful in explaining post-colonial African politics is only partly a reflection of the limitations of class analysis *per se*. It is rather more an indictment of the somewhat mechanistic approach adopted by many Marxist Africanists. Kitching's impressive *Class and Economic Change in Kenya* shows that, where Marxists deploy their analytical skills upon historically grounded research of specific geographical areas, they do succeed in shedding light on the relevance of economic change to contemporary African politics.[35] Kitching's work on Kenya is likely to stand the test of time even if interest in its theoretical claims subsides.

3. UNDERDEVELOPMENT THEORY

Underdevelopment theory combined a critique of standard development economics with a re-interpretation of the development of the world-wide capitalist system. Originally developed to account for the economic and political *under*development of Latin America after the Second World War, it was later applied to other 'Third World' countries, including Africa, which were on the capitalist periphery. The aim was to explain how the economic development of the core capitalist countries (Europe, North America, Japan) had been achieved by *under*developing the periphery. Underdevelopment theory thus focused on the extraversion of African countries and explained their post-colonial politics in terms of their dependent economic structure and parasitic class development.[36]

Underdevelopment theory was at first a response to the claims of classi-cal development economics that international trade would result in the gradual and complementary development of all countries. These claims rested on four postulates: first, that within a world capitalist system less advanced countries would develop by means of free trade; second, that the sale of primary, mineral and agricultural resources which other countries did not posses would (through comparative advantage) generate sufficient capital for development in the poor counties; third, that their path to eco-nomic development would follow that of the more advanced countries; finally, that capitalist development could become self-sustaining even if it did not originally arise from the internal economic development of less advanced countries.[37]

It was this theory which Latin American economists began to challenge after the Second World War.[38] They claimed that the economic history of the major Latin American countries provided evidence to refute these assumptions. They pointed out that, well after a century of independence, Latin American countries had not developed economically along the lines intimated by development theory. Although rich in natural and agricultural resources and actively trading on the world market, the countries of South America had not 'taken off' economically. Their economic development was seriously distorted and did not seem to follow the path of the more advanced capitalist countries.

Instead, international trade and capitalist penetration of South America had generated economies which were dependent, incapable of self-sus-tained development and massively unable to meet the needs of the local population.[39] The statistical data examined by these pioneer Latin American economists (of whom Raúl Prebisch was the earliest and most influential) revealed a reality so seriously at variance with what the theory of economic development would have predicted as to invalidate the theory altogether.

Their argument ran as follows. First, Latin American countries did not benefit from comparative advantage. The overall trend in the terms of trade was one in which primary material consistently lost value relative to the manufactured goods which less advanced countries needed to import. Sec-ond, the transformation of primary material – that part of the process which most adds value – was controlled by foreign capitalist interests. Little of the profits accrued to the countries of Latin America. As a result, third, there was insufficient capital accumulation to sustain self-generating capitalist development in Latin America.

Capitalist development took place in economic enclaves controlled by foreign (or local dependent) interests and divorced from the rest of the country's economy. Profits were not re-invested locally but exported. Most importantly, however, such economic development as took place in those capitalist enclaves was only made possible by the exploitation of cheap labour in the non-capitalist sector. In other words, the success of local (dependent) capitalist development, such as it was, was based on the continued availability of cheap local labour often paid below reproduction costs. Their continued availability was dependent on the continued failure of the non-capitalist sector to provide employment.

The exponents of underdevelopment theory thus concluded that their countries' integration into the world capitalist system, far from having spurred their development, had actually led to their *under*development.[40] Countries which originally had merely been *un*developed had now become *under*developed. Conversely, they argued that the development of the core capitalist countries had only been made possible by the *under*development of the countries of the periphery. Classical development theory merely obscured the process by which the core countries had been able to exploit the periphery. There was not the remotest chance that the periphery would ever be able to develop in the same way.

To them, then, underdevelopment was a process not a state of being. Countries were not born but became *under*developed. They argued that *under*development was the process by which a country became economically dependent on a pattern of international trade ever more unfavourable to their economies and in which the success of local capitalist enclaves was at the price of the further *under*development of the rest of the economy. Although the dependent local capitalists (who controlled power) benefited from this arrangement, it was the core capitalist countries which reaped (relatively and absolutely) the most profit.

This argument was fundamental for it totally undermined the assumptions of linear economic progress on which classical development economics was built.[41] It gave an account of how dependent countries became less and less developed (in the classical sense). It made explicit the process by which the economies of post-colonial countries were subjected to the continued dominance of the core imperial countries. And it seemed to account for the fact that many poor countries appeared to become poorer.

Underdevelopment theory also provided a conceptual framework for the understanding of the politics of dependent countries.[42] Power was in the hands of ruling classes whose economic hegemony derived from their role as the handmaidens of the capitalists from the core countries. It was in the interest of these dependent capitalist classes to ensure that the system of *under*development thrived. Since this resulted in the growing poverty of the non-capitalist sector, it required a repressive political system to maintain law and order. For this reason, the armed forces played a prominent political role in underdeveloped countries.[43]

In Africa, underdevelopment theory led to a vigorous reinterpretation of African politics. If Walter Rodney's *How Europe Underdeveloped Africa* was the most widely read book on the subject, it was perhaps the work of the political economist Samir Amin which most contributed to this re-interpretation.[44] What underdevelopment theory brought to the political analysis of Africa was an interpretation of the colonial economy as the matrix within which the continent had become dependent. Whatever reasons why Europe had colonised Africa, the consequence of having done so was the establishment of a system of economic extraversion which made possible the exploitation of Africa's natural and labour resources.

Decolonisation was seen not as the prelude to economic self-determination but merely as a process by which political control passed from colonial masters to dependent African rulers – a process dubbed neo-colonialism.[45] The new rulers who took power at independence were thus the instruments of neo-colonialism. The state structure of the newly independent countries ensured that they became the local managers of the dependent economy. It was the structural economic mechanism by which capitalist countries exploited African countries, largely through the exploitation of dependent labour within dual economies, which Arghiri and Samir Amin conceptualised respectively as unequal exchange and unequal development.[46]

The class implications of this interpretation were important. Dependent capitalist development lay in the hands of dependent capitalist classes – the so-called *comprador bourgeoisie*. Their economic hegemony depended on their political hegemony, for in neo-colonial countries it is the state which controls access to the main economic levers. These ruling classes were pitted against civil society, that is, those who did not have access to the state and who were thus deprived of the political means to share in the economic profits which neo-colonialism provided to its dependent classes.[47]

In underdevelopment theory, therefore, the fundamental class division was that which opposed the (core and dependent) capitalists to the classes which neo-colonialism exploited. Class struggle was thus played out not on a national but international scene. It was not possible to identify class formation and class struggle within individual African nation-states without taking into account the socio-economic implications of dependence. Hence, understanding post-colonial politics required understanding the specific ways in which individual nation-states were integrated into the world capitalist system.[48]

The dominant reality of the post-colonial period was seen to be the division between advanced capitalist countries and the 'Third World'. The experience of the (nationalist) revolutions of the second half of the twentieth century (e.g. China, Vietnam, Cuba, Algeria) was viewed as evidence that class struggles were played out on a world scale. Applied to Africa, this vision of world class politics reinforced the view (best articulated by Samir Amin) that the key political issue of the post-colonial period was to resist neo-colonialism by means of a policy of economic autonomy.[49]

The interpretation of independence as the triumph of neo-colonialism was first put forward by Frantz Fanon.[50] Although proponents of underdevelopment theory later dismissed Fanon's faith in the revolutionary potential of the so-called lumpenproletariat (the 'wretched of the earth') and proposed alternative class alliances to fight the neo-colonial classes, the difficulty of relating the general model of dependence with a class analysis of specific countries remained. For even when there was agreement on the parasitic and extraverted nature of the ruling classes, there was little consensus on the precise class implications of dependence. The theory seemed incapable of refining political analysis beyond the great divide between the ruling classes and the exploited classes. Given the instablility of post-colonial politics in Africa and given the obvious manifold links between 'ruling' and 'exploited' classes, this seemed at best a crude theory.[51]

Underdevelopment theory runs into the same problems as class analysis: the difficulty of establishing causal links between class struggles and political change. The fact that its conceptual model of politics is overdetermined by a prior teleological general macro-economic theory makes it difficult to provide a useful interpretation of contemporary politics in Africa. Its analytical framework is poorly equipped to account for processes other than state politics, particularly the politics of civil society. Furthermore, it neglects to consider those specifically 'African' aspect of politics – e.g., ethnicity, kinship, clientelism, witchcraft – which are self-evidently important to understanding politics in Africa.[52]

In sum, the strength of underdevelopment theory is that it points to the political implications of the very real condition of economic dependence which formal independence left untouched. Its weakness is that it does not possess the conceptual apparatus plausibly to link its economic model with the domestic politics of specific individual countries.[53]

4. REVOLUTIONARY THEORY

Revolutionary theory derived in part from the assumption that socialism was the way forward for Africa and in part from a particular interpretation of the wars of national liberation in the Portuguese colonies and Zimbabwe (and of the revolution in Ethiopia).[54] It was also a reaction against the notion of an *Ur*-African socialism fashionable in the sixties but which was seen in the late seventies as having failed to prevent 'neo-colonialism'. Revolutionary theory postulated that 'neo-colonialism' could only be broken by the formation of a revolutionary class alliance of peasants, workers and progressive intellectuals on the model of twentieth-century revolutions and of the African nationalist wars of the seventies.[55]

Revolutionary theory emerged out of an on-going debate on socialism in Africa, a debate put into much sharper focus by the experience of the nationalist wars in the Portuguese colonies. This debate had a dual ancestry. On the one hand, it was a continuation of the age-long Marxist debate on the viability of socialism in pre-capitalist societies, first discussed in the context of the Russian and Chinese revolutions. Could socialism be appropriate to Africa, the last continent to decolonise, when it had failed as a model of development in, say, Vietnam or Algeria?

On the other hand, the genesis of the socialist ideal in Africa had a purely indigenous strand in the notion that pre-colonial Africa was somehow already 'socialist' – admittedly not in the sense understood by Marx and the Marxists who followed him but, rather, socialism in the more instrumental sense of what a socialist society would be like. Socialism was conceived here as a 'classless quality of life' closer to the pre-Marxist French socialist ideas than to post-Marxist twentieth-century Russian or Chinese variants.[56]

The nature of the socialism envisaged thus turned on the interpretation of the historical development of the continent. The early post-colonial debate revolved around the question of class. Marxists worked from the premise of the centrality of class and tended to construct socialist scenarios on the 'Chinese model' of an alliance of workers, peasants and progressive petty bourgeois. Non-Marxist socialists insisted on the absence of class in 'traditional' Africa and emphasised instead a communal notion of socialism.

In the immediate post-independence period, most African leaders (e.g. Senghor, Nkrumah, Sékou Touré, Nyerere, Kaunda) leaned towards a non-Marxist position. There were well-founded intellectual reasons for such a position – reasons which had to do with the redeeming of African civilisation in world history. Nevertheless, this 'indigenous' notion of socialism can also be explained in more simple contingent terms by the fact that the demands of nationalist politics and of the construction of the post-colonial order induced African leaders to seek in pre-colonial Africa a unifying model of society.[57]

The political experience of the first decade of independence, however, dissipated any illusion about the political consensus which the apparent unity of the nationalist movement might have endangered. Equally, it revealed deep economic divisions between the citizens of the newly independent African nations. It thus dispelled any hope that the by now ubiquitous one-party state could be construed simply as the modern embodiment of some *Ur*-African communalism.[58]

Furthermore, historical research into pre-colonial Africa unsurprisingly revealed economic, social and political inequalities as deep as those found in other pre-capitalist parts of the world.[59] Whatever one's view of class in post-colonial Africa, by the late sixties the African model of 'communal socialism' had been discredited. The post-1966 socialist experiments attempted in many African countries (e.g., Mali, Guinea, Ghana, the Congo, Uganda) were made of an altogether sharper Marxist mettle. Class was now firmly at the centre of African politics.

As African socialism rejoined the Marxist–Leninist model and African socialists reclaimed scientific socialism, the experience of the wars of national liberation in the Portuguese colonies of Guinea, Angola and Mozambique revealed the possibility of a new revolutionary theory for Africa. While Marxist regimes in Africa (like the Congo's) ossified into bureaucratic dictatorships, the process of political mobilisation underpinning these nationalist struggles seemed, for the first time in Black Africa, to make possible the formation of a true 'socialist class alliance'. Whereas earlier socialist experiments in Africa had been the outcome of 'revolutions from above', wars of national liberation offered the prospect of a transition to socialism grounded in a mass popular movement.[60]

Revolutionary theory was thus born of an interpretation of these nationalist struggles as political movements carried towards socialism by a unique combination of historical factors. The argument was as follows.[61] Independence had been achieved by an armed struggle grounded in the political mobilisation of the rural areas. The process by which the countryside was mobilised turned the nationalist struggle into a people's war, radicalised the largely *petit bourgeois* nationalist leadership and thus forged a socialist class coalition of 'progressive nationalists, workers and peasants'.

Revolutionary theory rested on the premise that the autonomous development of a nationalist people's war put into motion a process of political, social and economic change which made it possible to envisage a genuine transition to socialism after independence. Politically, it was argued that the need for the *petit bourgeois* leadership to achieve political mobilisation by consent anchored them to a 'progressive' class coalition. Because their constituency was popular rather than bourgeois, their political project for the construction of the post-colonial order would be conditioned by the needs of the people – that is, it was assumed, socialism.

In terms of social change, the argument was that mobilisation for a modern guerrilla war would break down 'traditional' structures and release social forces committed to the (socialist) modernisation of society. Because the struggle relied primarily on the participation of the young and those committed to change, it would erode the supremacy of 'traditional' conservative élites. Furthermore, the war would also reduce the salience of ethnic and other ascriptive attributes which tended to divide Africans. The struggle itself would accelerate social change in the countryside – historically the section of society slowest to modernise.[62]

Finally, revolutionary theory assumed that the nationalist wars had achieved substantive and irreversible structural economic changes in the liberated areas (the areas wrested from colonial control and administered by the nationalists). This model was conceptualised as one of cooperative agricultural production and distribution, the first stage in the modernisation of the 'traditional' family and village mode of production towards a more fully collective agriculture. This modernisation of agriculture would be the base for the development of a modern socialist industrial economy.

Although it had little historical connection with the nationalist struggles in the Portuguese colonies, the Ethiopian revolution, exploding as it did just as Portugal conceded defeat (1974), gave further impetus to revolutionary theory. For the first time a revolution had taken place in Africa on the model of the classical revolutions (e.g. French, Russian, Chinese), that is, as the outcome of the collapse of a long-established feudal order which had adapted too slowly to the challenge of modernisation. In Ethiopia, as in France, Russia or China before, the revolution was nourished by a 'peasant' revolt against the intolerable injustices engendered by a decaying feudal order. The established dynasty was felled by the social and political forces which its belated attempt at modernisation had unleashed.[63]

It was, however, the success of the Zimbabwean nationalist struggle (1979) which seemed to confirm the model of revolution first derived from the Lusophone people's wars.[64] For here too, the transition to socialism was seen as the natural outcome of a nationalist war based on the mobilisation of the rural areas. The experience of Zimbabwe gave yet fresher hopes for the future of socialism in Africa. Mugabe's greater pragmatism, a successful transition from white to majority rule and a determination to repair the injustices inflicted on Zimbabwe by a settler economy, all seemed to buttress revolutionary theory.

By the eighties, events in Zimbabwe, Angola, Mozambique and Guinea-Bissau showed that most of the assumptions on which revolutionary theory was constructed were not warranted. In the first instance, although it is true that the process of political mobilisation underpinning people's war in the four countries generated political dynamics and political movements hitherto unseen in Africa, it did not usher in a revolution. The prospects for revolution, in Africa as elsewhere, depend first and foremost on whether there exist objective conditions propitious to revolution – by which I mean a combination of regime decay and deep socio-economic crisis which makes it possible for revolutionary counter-élites to channel large-scale social discontent into the wholesale reconstruction of society. Such conditions did not obtain in Black Africa as they did in Ethiopia.[65]

Second, while it is true that the control and administration of the liberated areas depended on the nationalist party's capacity to meet the needs of the local population, what happened in the liberated areas (on which there is no consensus) did not constitute a 'socialist model' of society. Revolutionary theory assumed that the party had reshaped the liberated areas into an embryo 'socialist' state. If anything, the reverse had occured. In order successfully to mobilise the countryside, the nationalist party had had to adapt its politics to the realities of the village political economy. The policies of the newly independent regimes in Angola, Mozambique, Guinea-Bissau and even Zimbabwe revealed that their models of development did not issue from, nor did they reinforce, the experiments in 'people's power' long held to characterise the liberated areas. Not only was the experience of the liberated areas not taken as a model to follow for a rural-based revolution but the socialism adopted in the first three of these countries radically turned its back on 'people's power' and moved firmly in the direction of collective farming, state control of agriculture and an attempt at primitive socialist accumulation.[66]

Third, the political structures established in Ethiopia, Angola, Mozambique, Guinea-Bissau and Zimbabwe, though they bore superficial resemblance, were very differently 'revolutionary'. Only in Ethiopia did the 'military revolution' from above and the social revolution from below connect (even if briefly and unsatisfactorily). Only there could the historian find an echo of what had happened in the earlier 'classical' revolutions. In the other four countries, the new state essentially concerned itself with the consolidation of its power and the construction of a unified political order rather than with revolution – however it is defined. Their politics rapidly came to mirror those of most other African countries whether 'socialist' or not.

Revolutionary theory failed to illuminate the trajectory of those countries which liberated themselves through armed struggle because it constructed a model of post-colonial politics upon an imaginary causality between the process of a nationalist people's war and 'socialist revolution'. Instead of conceptualising the nationalist war of liberation as one instance of nationalism, it read in its instrumentalities the promise of a transition to socialism. In so doing, it neglected to insert the experience of those countries within the broad historical development of modern Africa. It took an excessively ahistorical view of their decolonisation.[67]

5. DEMOCRATIC THEORY

Democratic theory is a reaction to all of the above. It starts from the conclusion that statist politics have failed and dismisses the idea that there is a trade-off between democracy and development. It argues instead that democracy alone will release the creative and productive energies of Africans and enable them to move out of underdevelopment. Democratic theory holds African rulers responsible for the present crisis in Africa and focuses analysis on the means by which a democratisation of the political system and a liberalisation of the economy can combine to promote sustained development beneficial to all. The call for multi-party democracy in many African countries is seen as confirmation that one-party statism is no longer appropriate as a model for Africa.[68]

Democratic theory is also a reaction to the present crisis in Africa. It is a response to the clamour of countless Africans for more political accountability and less arbitrariness.[69] It is, too, a response to the current political climate in which the domination of the state is being challenged throughout the world by those who feel they labour unfairly under its shadow. For the eighties has been the decade when the welfare state was pronounced obsolete in the West, when socialist ideology was abandoned in Eastern and Western Europe and when 'people's power' toppled dictatorships in many parts of the 'Third World' – the decade in which it seemed that democracy had finally triumphed over its enemies.[70]

At the same time democratic theory is an approach which seeks to stand back from the search for the particulars of African politics and address instead the fundamental question of power in Africa. No longer satisfied with the justifications for the present crisis in Africa, the exponents of democratic theory ask instead whether political unaccountability and economic failure are not in fact causally linked. They ask too whether the focus on the structural impediments to democratisation has not been at the expense of understanding the mechanisms by which the African ruling élites have sought political and economic hegemony on the back of their citizens.[71]

Democratic theory is thus a decisive step away from the strong parochialist tendencies of African studies and a move towards the analysis of African politics in more universal terms. For the argument that democracy is the best way forward for Africa implies a rejection of the argument long dominant in African studies that Africa was not politically 'mature' enough for democracy. It implies that the need for democracy is as strong in Africa as in the rest of the world. From this perspective, then, democratic theory implicitly or explicitly restores Africa to the community of nations.

Democratic theory is, finally, an indictment of the vision of Africa which has fuelled prejudice since pre-colonial times: Africa as the heart of darkness, a continent not susceptible to rationality, one to fear or to patronise but rarely to comprehend.[72] Equally, it challenges liberal Africanists who often worked too hard at countering this age-old prejudice and sought for the African too many historical dispensations on the ground of the uniquely awfulness of the colonial legacy. For democratic theory, the search for such an *African* approach was itself the legacy of a paternalist approach.

Unlike all the other approaches, democratic theory focuses on the individual. By looking at the citizens of the polity rather than merely at those who speak on their behalf or at the classes into which they are supposed to be aggregated, it redresses the analytical balance between high politics and low politics, between the state and civil society. In so doing it asks questions about everyday politics which the other theories were often ill-equipped to address. In particular, it calls attention to the ways in which political accountability operates in practice at different levels (e.g., local/national) in society and to the multi-layered relationships between politics and economics.[73]

Democratic theory is also a response to the realisation that African states have largely failed to 'capture' their domestic economies.[74] The growing importance of parallel economies in Africa is a damning indictment of the failure of the rulers' official economy and a true measure of the ruled's productive labour.[75] The economic crisis in Africa is thus not just a reflection of the impoverishment of the continent but also the product of a contest between the state and civil society which the state has in some fundamental way been steadily losing.[76]

Democratic theory is thus a turning point in the political analysis of post-colonial Africa. It marks the acceptance of the need to conceptualise the politics of Africa in the terms that we would use, for example, to conceptualise the politics of Europe. It implies a recognition that the notion of power in Africa is conceptually coterminous, not generically distinct, with that of power in Europe or elsewhere. This, the axiomatic principle of democratic theory, is a conceptual advance over previous approaches.

Like all other theories, however, democratic theory is only as useful as the assumptions on which its interpretation of African politics rests. The first and most important assumption is that of the discrete political role of the citizen in society. The polity is composed of individual, autonomous, political actors. It is undoubtedly a necessary corrective to think of Africans as autonomous individuals instead (as has so often been the case) of merely as tribal, kin-linked and communal human beings. Yet, in the end it is the way in which individuals perceive themselves and each other as individuals within their own societies, rather than the mere fact that they are individuals, which matters politically. There is a danger that the use of the ready-made Western liberal concept of the individual which is implicit in democratic theory will obscure the understanding of the complexity of the individual who lives in contemporary Africa.[77] The undoubted heuristic gains resulting from the recognition that human beings are similar everywhere must not be erased by assumptions of political homomorphism.

The second assumption concerns the relation between citizens and government. For democratic theory the central axis of politics is that between the constituent and the representative, as sanctioned by the ballot box. Its analysis of the body politic assumes that relationship to embody both the principle and the reality of political accountability between rulers and ruled. This is important, especially given the widespread tendency among Africanists to disregard electoral politics. Africans too are entitled to express their political preferences through the ballot box and analysts ought certainly to pay more proper attention to the nature of elections in Africa.[78] Furthermore, democratic elections would undoubtedly be a vast improvement in political accountability for most Africans.

There is, however, danger in assuming either that the notion of representation in Africa is fully contained within the formal democratic electoral process or that the process of political accountability is exhausted by the operation of the formal democratic order. To do so would be to ignore that the structures and instruments of democracy which obtain in the West today are the historical products of historically specific processes in historically specific settings. While it may be true that, in the West, the relationship between citizen and constituent is most fully expressed through representative multi-party politics, it would be historically naïve to assume that such can be true everywhere.[79]

The third assumption is that of the conceptual separation between the political realm and the rest of society, that is, *inter alia*, the economic, social and cultural spheres. Democratic theory constructs an interpretation of African politics strictly in political terms. Its model of politics focuses attention on the texture and workings of political accountability between rulers and ruled. It assumes that the quality of political accountability can be meaningfully assessed in the analysis of the instrumentalities which characterise its operation in practice.[80]

This, however, can become an ahistorical approach. While there is every reason for political analysts of Africa to give the fullest attention to political accountability, it would be wrong (both in theory and practice) to confine analysis to the 'manifest politics' of political accountability. We must instead seek to understand both the multiple layers of the body politic and the multiple connections between the political and non-political realms. We must understand and (as importantly) be able to enunciate how the political realm relates to the rest of society and how the politics of the social, economic and cultural spheres operate.[81]

The danger faced by democratic theory is the same which plagued development theory, that is, limiting the scope of political analysis to a notional "political system' derived from the political experience of Western democracies. What makes it possible to understand this 'political system' in the West is not so much that politics are wholly contained within it but that we understand the political implications for analysis of the links between that system and society at large. Because that understanding is implicit and unarticulated, however, we readily omit to think how deeply it affects our use of the model we employ for political analysis.

Democratic theory assumes, fourthly, that it is possible to combine analytical and prescriptive interpretation. It is indeed the hallmark of democratic theory (in this respect like Islamic political theory) to consider politics from the perspective of the desirability of the 'ideal polity' which the fully functioning democracy is seen to represent. Democratic theory thus combines normative and analytical categories. The best available system of political accountability, democracy, also represents the movement of society to a higher and morally superior political order.

Whether or not democracy is a morally superior political order, there is danger in the conflation of the analytical and normative.[82] For this conflation may lead the analyst either to focus on political processes which are not central to the contemporary African political order or to neglect political processes which most certainly are. The current emphasis on multi-partyism, for example, clearly shows how the Western democratic model can influence the use of democratic theory in Africa. However admirable the move to multi-partyism would be, the consequences of reducing political analysis to charting the progress of Africans towards that goal could obscure rather than illuminate the understanding of power in Africa. This is not because multi-partyism is a moot issue but because the reason why it has become salient in Africa today has more to do with its usefulness as a political weapon against regimes with little political accountability than with its suddenly revealed moral superiority.[83] Furthermore, the advent of multi-partyism in Africa would not in and of itself produce a Western-type liberal democratic order.

The argument that Africans too not only deserve but are fully capable of building a democratic political order is morally a strong one. Democratic theory is bound to gain ground given the present 'drive for democracy' in the Eastern bloc, the Soviet Union, China and many 'Third World' countries – not to mention the spurious and naïve but powerful 'end of history' idea.[84] Whether it also leads to a better understanding of contemporary African politics will depend on the ability of its exponents not to confuse moral crusade with political analysis, i.e., understanding power in its historical context. Otherwise, democratic theory may suffer the fate of development theory – a theory discredited when it becomes obvious that its normative imperative bears no relation to the political reality it purports to explain.

Part II
Concepts for the Analysis of Power in Africa

Introduction

I discussed in the previous chapter the strengths and weaknesses of the major paradigms used in the political analysis of post-colonial Africa over the last three decades. I now want to outline the book's conceptual framework.

To outline such a framework is not, however, to claim a theory, even less a paradigm. *Power in Africa* does not purport to provide a 'theory' by which to understand what is often called the political development of Black Africa since independence. Nor does it make any theoretical claim above and beyond the need to use concepts judiciously. Indeed, one of the premises of the book is precisely that excessive *a priori* theory has often obscured the understanding of contemporary African politics.

Yet, even if we could do without theory, we would still need concepts, for all political analysis rests on the concepts which inform its approach and underpin its interpretation. Any attempt to rethink contemporary African politics and reinterpret post-colonial history in Africa must make clear its conceptual foundations. For interpretation is not merely a matter of opinion. It is above all the attempt to show how the use of particular concepts can help to make better sense of what is actually happening, in the real world.

Concepts are prior to theories. All theories are built on a conceptual apparatus, whether explicit or implicit, but not all conceptual frameworks make up a theory. The failure to distinguish clearly between concepts and theories has often led to confusion in the political analysis of contemporary Africa. When concepts are used within a given paradigm (e.g. developmental, class analysis, dependency), their explanatory usefulness is tied to the overall heuristic quality of the theory which informs analysis. The usefulness of concepts such as class or political development, for example, is tied to the interpretative quality of, respectively, class analysis and development theory.

The concept of class, however is not invalidated by the failure of class analysis to account convincingly for post-colonial politics in Africa. The notion of class may (or may not) be useful to political analysis independently of a Marxist theoretical approach. For Marx did not invent the concept of class, even if he recast it with such force as to make it synonymous with the theory which is forever associated with his name. This is true of all other concepts, most of which can readily be associated with a particular theoretical framework. And it is precisely because concepts are so easily mistaken for theories that it is imperative to make explicit the conceptual framework on which any political analysis is based.

One of the dominant themes of this book is that a reinterpretation of post-colonial politics in Africa must start from the very beginning, conceptually and historically, without undue theoretical or ideological preconceptions, with as open a mind as possible. Another is that the analysis of post-colonial Africa does not require the invention of new concepts but rather the understanding of how the historically fundamental concepts of 'classical' political analysis apply to contemporary Africa.

This means, first, that no concept should be ruled out on *a priori* theoretical grounds – deemed heretical simply because it forms part of a theoretical apparatus with which we may not agree. Second, and more importantly, it means that a conceptual framework for the political analysis of contemporary Africa should seek above all to build on concepts which have proved historically significant in the political analysis of Europe or other parts of the world.

It is for all these reasons that I propose to begin to construct a political interpretation of the politics of post-colonial Africa by means of five concepts which, to my mind, stand at the core of political analysis: the political community, political accountability, the state, civil society and production.

It will be immediately apparent that these concepts are both first-order concepts and also extra-African. By first-order, I mean that they are the building blocks, the fundament of all modern political analysis. By extra-African, I mean that they are not Africa-specific and that they could readily be (and indeed are) used in the political analysis of other contemporary societies.

Nevertheless, it will also be immediately apparent that some of these concepts have found a more natural home in some paradigms than in others. While the concepts of political community and political accountability may not readily evoke specific paradigms, the notions of the state, civil society and production appear to belong to the Marxist conceptual apparatus. Whether they do or not is irrelevant to my purpose here, or rather my purpose is to focus on what the concepts imply for analysis regardless of their theoretical pedigree. Mine is not a quest for paradigm.

Furthermore, I am concerned here less with defining these concepts (although I do attempt to give as precise a working definition as I can) than with discussing their historical relevance to Africa. For it is another argument of this book that the most useful concepts of political analysis are those which make it possible to relate, to link, and indeed to compare, pre-colonial, colonial and post-colonial Africa.

In each of the next five chapters I try to set each one of the concepts within its appropriate historical context. This means, first, that I discuss the concept both in terms of its definition in 'classical' political analysis and then in terms of its appropriateness to African history, showing the relevance of the one to the other. Second, I discuss how the particular concept at hand has hitherto been used in African studies. Third, I attempt to reconsider some of the historical material extant from the perspective of that concept. Finally, and most importantly, I try to show how the use of that particular concept illuminates both the continuities and the ruptures in Africa's political history from the pre-colonial period to the contemporary era.

Thus, Part II is above all an attempt to link concepts with history, for it seems to me that this is the only way in which political analysis can move forward. Concepts are not valid or invalid *per se*; they are merely instruments and like instruments they are only useful in practice. The choice of the wrong instruments is, of course, prejudicial to practice. It is my argument here that the five concepts chosen are most appropriate to the task at hand (although I do not claim that they are the only appropriate such concepts) and it is the purpose of these five chapters to show how useful they can be for the political analysis of Africa.

2   The Political Community

Politics begins with men and women organising for common purposes. Such organisation requires, implies, the formation (if not the pre-existence) of a community. The notion of community is, therefore, the most primary of all political concepts. There are, of course, many other aspects contained within the notion of community but all communities are necessarily political, or, rather, all communities are defined (and governed) by certain rules about the exercise of power. What power means and what these rules are in a particular historical context are the fundamental questions of political analysis.

We all approach Africa with certain notions of what the (political) community is, or ought to be. These concepts derive partly from the intellectual and cultural climate in which we live, partly from our understanding of the notion of political community generally, and partly from our reading of previous generations of observers of Africa.

It would be instructive, and I suspect very revealing of the European mind, to examine the notion of community associated with the various generations of Europeans who went to Africa.[1] From the accounts of fifteenth-century Portuguese sailors to those of present-day World Bank experts on mission, there would emerge a rich tapestry of insights and prejudices many of which still inform our understanding of the 'dark continent'.[2]

Through the ages, Africa has appeared to the European to be what the European mind has needed to believe it was. Naturally, these notions have incorporated the concepts of community which Africans themselves appeared (or professed, or feigned) to reveal. What the Africans have said and what the Europeans have understood has thus largely depended on the power relations between the two, and those power relations have also changed over time.

My aim here is less ambitious. I merely want to examine the visions held of the African political community in the last hundred years or so, visions which have influenced the political analysis of Africa. In the first part of this chapter, I discuss the earlier notions of the pre-colonial and colonial community as articulated, respectively, by the missionary, the colonial official, the anthropologist and the nationalist. The concepts as I present them are obviously simplifications of complex sets of perceptions and experiences which could only be properly understood by a more systematic analysis of the relevant texts. I make no claim for an exhaustive treatment. I simply wish to highlight some of the main differences and similarities in

these notions of the African community and explain why they were consequential for our understanding of Africa.

In the second part of the chapter, I argue that it is useful to look at the
post-colonial nation-state as an imagined political community. To this end
I analyse the creation of the modern African nation-state in terms of the
continuities and ruptures with its antecedents. For it seems to me imperative
to discuss the reality of contemporary African countries within the context
of their pre-colonial and colonial past if we are ever to move beyond the
nationalist myth of their origins under which we have so often laboured.

The missionary vision of Africa was partly determined by the nature of
his religious beliefs. Here there were major differences not only between,
but also within, Catholic and Protestant mission societies. Missionaries
from both sides had reasons for seeing only what they wanted to see, just as
the Africans had reasons for revealing themselves differently to each.
Perhaps there were more Protestants who, for their own reasons, learnt,
transcribed, and made use of African languages. Understanding a language
necessarily requires some understanding of the community in which the
language is used. Ultimately, however, whether the missionaries were
Catholic or Protestant mattered less than whether they made genuine attempts
at understanding African communities.

The perception of missionaries is important to our understanding of
Africa simply because they often were the first 'modern' Europeans to live
with pre-colonial Africans.[3] Explorers took the credit for 'discovering' Africa
but, with few exceptions, they did not attempt to understand the societies
with which they came into contact. We have too few sources about pre-
colonial Africa not to take missionaries' accounts seriously.

Missionaries sought to convert. They highlighted those aspects of African
societies which most facilitated or hindered their mission. As a result, they
did not always understand the complexities of the relation between the
temporal and the religious in African societies. Nor did they always realise
that they were being manipulated by those they sought to convert. Also,
they shared the nineteenth-century European notion of civilisation. They
could only see African societies as primitive societies due, in time, to
evolve towards the European model. Within these limitations, however,
they gave us a picture of African communities which, with the benefit of
today's historical knowledge, appears less simplistic and more useful than
is often thought.[4]

Missionaries usually understood the complexities of the dominant modes
of production, the relationship of man to land, animals, nature, and productive
activities. They also had a fairly good idea of the nature of the relation
between economic and political power, even if they did not always perceive

the intricacies of the community's political economy. They were easily misled about notions of wealth and accumulation but less easily duped by the attempts to conceal economic ill-health or political infighting. But, above all, they were sensitive to the life rhythms of the communities in which they lived and they were aware of the changes taking place over time. They were capable of relating historical cause and effect with some insight even if they did not always understand the many ramifications of the changes they were witnessing.[5]

What missionaries tell us is that nineteenth-century African communities experienced rapid economic, social and political change. Some African societies were disintegrating, others were forming and a few were seeking to maintain themselves unchanged in a changing world. Production and trade were being subjected to manifold pressures engendered by the ever-encroaching world market, war, migration, disease, climatic changes and colonial conquest. Polities were disrupted: existing élites were often challenged or discredited, new élites appeared or threatened to take over, political beliefs were shaken, the social fabric was under strain and sometimes cracked.[6] The new religion brought by the missionaries insinuated itself into the interstices which appeared during such rapid changes and in turn contributed to further changes.

From the perspective of political analysis, the missionaries' most important observation perhaps concerns the sense of identity which nourished the community. Far from perceiving African society as monolithic and unchanging, the missionaries understood that Africans defined themselves in many different ways. Ethnic, religious, social, regional, and economic factors all contributed to the way each individual perceived the community and was integrated within it. The relationship between individual and community was different from that of nineteenth-century Europeans but it was complex and rich. The missionaries' notion of the political community, and by implication that of power, was conceived in what we might call today universal rather than purely in African terms. To missionaries, Africans, whatever their characteristics, were not unlike the early Europeans. This is an observation that was almost entirely lost during the colonial period.

The colonial official had other tasks and other pre-occupations but he too required an understanding of African communities. That understanding was almost entirely determined by the nature of his colonial experience and by the requirements of the job at hand. Concerned as they were with temporal matters, colonial officials (particularly policy-makers) were of necessity less disinterested observers than their religious contemporaries. They mostly sought an instrumental understanding of power and community – that is who orders whom and how, rather than why. However variegated, the official mind tended to think along some well-defined lines and his action tended to have a more profound impact on African societies than that of the missionary.[7]

It is often believed that colonial officials from different European countries had importantly different understandings of Africa derived from their different intellectual and bureaucratic traditions. Thus the British are seen to have been pragmatic as ever, the French centralist and Cartesian, the Belgians paternalist and the Portuguese feeble and corrupt. What strikes us today, however, is how much they had in common. Some 'colonials' were shrewder and more perceptive than others and saw that the accepted notion of the African community was at odds with reality. But this was an individual rather than a national quality.[8]

With some important caveats, the colonial mission essentially required a simplified and reductionist view of African society and a belief in the beneficial effects of colonisation. From the point of view of understanding the concept of community, the most important aspect of colonial rule was that the European no longer sought to *live with* the African, as the missionary had done, but to *rule over* him. The colonial revolution, for it was nothing less, introduced a new notion of political community which was superimposed over existing ones. It established rigid territorial and regional boundaries which cut across existing political, economic, social, ethnic and religious borders and it set up an administration to manage these new colonial communities. It did so for reasons of pride or expediency, but having done so it sought to legitimate its action.

Colonial rule thus invented new communities with or without historical roots.[9] This was not a new process in Africa, of course. Communities had been invented and re-invented at intervals, as dictated by the historical requirements of conquest and suzerainty. But hitherto there had been flexibility within and at the margins of the newly created communities, evolution rather than revolution. The colonial mind attempted a wholesale re-creation as though it were in its power to wipe the slate clean and write a new history.[10]

Colonial rule dictated the categories by means of which individuals and communities were to be defined. Some of these categories (e.g., region or economic activities) derived from a perception of reality which made sense to the African. Others (e.g., ethnicity) were based either on a mixture of accurate and accidental perceptions or on wilful misperceptions of reality. Yet others (like administrative districts and colonial territories) had no basis in pre-colonial Africa and merely served official purposes.

For understandable historical reasons, the colonial mind chose to invent an African torn between his 'traditional' ethnic, religious, regional and 'irrational' roots and his 'modern' social, political, 'rational' and economic attributes. For equally understandable reasons, the African chose to re-invent a set of 'traditional' roots readily admissible by colonial administration and to define himself according to the most profitable of the latest invader's new categories.[11]

Thus the colonial mind was prepared to accept that Africans had 'traditional' beliefs, that they were part of ethnic communities with traditional chiefs, held together by ancient social bonds and rituals, and engaged in kin-based economic occupations. It was prepared to tolerate the continued existence of the (real or imagined) 'traditional' community so long as it did not interfere with the creation of the new colonial community. Indeed, traditions were fine so long as they were compatible with colonial modernity.[12] But there was no sense in which modernity was the outcome of the transformation of tradition.

Not surprisingly, the African understood that the concept of community inherent in the colonial condition was one of sharp dichotomies. As power essentially derived either from new identities or from old identities as redefined by the colonial mind, the colonial community became one in which the traditional was fitted into the European vision of the African community.

Thus the colonial community could accommodate feudal chiefs such as the emirs of the northern parts of West Africa but it had little time for the deliberations of the governing bodies of 'stateless' villages. It could accommodate ethnic groups within a territory but had less patience with migrant, nomadic peoples or trading communities. Colonial officials could accept the pagan rituals of African religions but were not prepared to tolerate independent prophetic churches. Similarly, they could comprehend (if not always readily accept) modern structures of African representation (e.g., parties, trade unions, Christian churches) but not 'traditional' ones (e.g., age-groups, spirit mediums, African churches, oath-groups). The colonial era thus ossified many fluid 'traditional' attributes and spawned divisions where none had existed before.

The colonial legacy was, therefore, not so much the notion of a community where modern and traditional fitted within a modernising rationality but rather one in which the modern obscured the continued evolution of African communities artificially redefined. The greatest colonial myth was that of the rupture between the pre-colonial and the colonial worlds. A new community had indeed been invented but one whose rationality remained, whatever the colonial pronouncements, anchored more firmly to its African than to its European roots.[13]

Anthropologists, though contemporaries of colonial officials, had more in common with missionaries. Their influence on our understanding of African societies was equally profound. Their purpose was to understand the 'traditional' African community. To that end, modern anthropology sensibly proposed prolonged sojourn and total immersion within that community. The language must be learned but, otherwise, the anthropologist was to be an observer, rather than a participant. Anthropologists did not seek to convert or modernise. The aim of the anthropology of that period was to make sense of the society under observation on its own terms, that is to understand the symbolic and practical logic of a community from its own normative perspective.

Like all of us, however, anthropologists came to Africa with their prejudices, with assumptions about their profession and with some notion about the likely outcome of their research. Anthropology, in the first part of the century, was essentially concerned with the study of 'primitive' society: that is societies in their earliest stages of development.[14] The fundamental working assumption of the discipline was that an in-depth synchronic study would reveal the values and practices of such societies. Successful anthropological studies were those which made sense of the religion, rituals, social habits, customs and political economy of a particular community at a given moment in time.[15]

There was great self-assurance about the new anthropological methodology but scant reflection about the historical context within which field work was taking place. In particular, there was insufficient attention given to the fact that the supposedly primitive societies which anthropologists were observing were, with very few exceptions, societies under the influence of colonial rule. Primitive societies (in the meaning it had then) were not readily to be found in Africa as they were in Papua New Guinea. What anthropologists observed in Africa were societies which had long been part of the wider (even extra-African) world and which were seeking means of adapting to colonial conquest, the greatest of all the challenges ever thrown at them. The anthropologist's quest for the 'organising principle' of African societies was met by the African's attempt to understand the role of the anthropologist in the colonial world.[16]

What the European mind retained from the anthropologist's work was often a drastic over-simplification of what the anthropologist really said. Nevertheless, it had a profound influence on the colonial mentality. Thus the African (rural) community was taken to be homogeneous, ethnically determined, kin- and family-based, socially and economically rather undifferentiated, relatively static and unchanging, hierarchic and rigid though egalitarian and supportive of the less privileged, but above all little able to generate economic and social change from within. In sum, the African community was well-defined, well-ordered, cohesive, supportive but ultimately incapable of moving unaided to a 'higher' stage of civilisation.[17]

This view, which echoed Europe's need for the timeless exotic, was also congruent with the official perception of the traditional societies which they were trying to modernise. These ideas helped to solidify a certain notion of the African community which emphasised the traditional over the modern, the static over the dynamic, the homogeneous over the heterogeneous, the socially simple over the complex, the conservative over the innovative, the religious over the secular, and the discrete over the continuous.[18] It is this view which official and non-official historians of the period carved into the *image taillée* of a closed, traditional, ancestral, tribal, ritualised, backward, and undeveloping Black Africa. It is an image of such force that generations of Africans and Africanists have since done battle with it.

The nationalist had to fashion a view of the African community which was consonant with his opposition to colonial rule and with his desire for self-government. At the same time, it had to be an image which would make sense to Europeans and Africans alike. The European had to be convinced that the African possessed the qualities required of the modern man. The African had to believe in the nationalist's capacity to transform the colony into an independent country.[19]

The nationalist's notion of the African community was, at least in the beginning, largely a reaction to that of the European. The nationalists usually were those who had been educated, assimilated or in other ways acculturated into colonial society. Their claim to moral and political authority issued largely from their success in penetrating that society and/or in rising through the colonial hierarchy. The notion of success was different in each imperial system but the process was the same. The nationalists came from that section of society which had ben 'civilised'.

To the colonial mind 'civilisation' was proof that colonialism was working: civilising the African meant taking him out of his traditional community. To the Africans, they, the nationalists, were proof that Africans could compete with Europeans on their own terms and thus successfully challenge the racial legitimation of the colonial enterprise. The African community was perfectly capable of producing modern men.

The nationalist thought in terms of national rather than regional or ethnic communities and his primary concern was to relate what he knew of African society to what he envisaged the post-colonial nation-state would be.[20] His dispute with the colonial official was about ownership not modernity. Both agreed on the need to transform 'traditional' African society into a nation capable of joining the world of modern nation-states. Hence, the nationalist's concern was to show that he had assimilated the colonial lessons and that he was capable of replacing the colonial official.

His greatest rival was the chief, the organically recognisable authority within the African community. Whether the chief had collaborated with or opposed colonial rule, he retained formal or informal power. Most importantly, he was the link with the past. Because the colonial strategy was essentially to promote the modern while relying on the traditional, the old and new élites were necessarily in competition. The legitimacy of the nationalist thus depended on his ability to establish *his* link with the past. All successful nationalists managed to straddle the modern and the traditional, that is successfully to invent an African community to meet the historical demands of the time.[21]

This process, of which there is no better illustration than Kenyatta's *Facing Mount Kenya*, involved the redefinition of the notion of the African community to meet the colonial challenge.[22] The nationalist started from the concepts evolved by missionaries, colonial officials and anthropologists, which he knew best, and sought to provide the missing link between the pre- and post-colonial periods. The nationalist accepted that there was a dynamic traditional African community with well-defined social, religious, political and economic characteristics. Africa was rich in traditions which had served the Africans relatively well until the colonial conquest.[23] Yet, to him, the African community was in some respects backward, adapting too slowly to modern life.

At the same time, the nationalist challenged the colonial *image taillée* in several key respects. The African community had resources and strength which enabled it to adapt and change. Looked at historically, African societies displayed everywhere the capacity to meet the demands of the colonial world. It was colonial rule which retarded change by insisting that the African community continue to live and work according to the supposed old ways. In this respect, colonial officials were often the allies of the chiefs who hindered change because they feared losing power.

Equally important the nationalists re-invented the African past to prepare Africans for independence. The African community possessed attributes which were important for the future. The nationalist vision emphasised the strength of identity, the qualities of homogeneity, equality, solidarity and communality which marked the Africans from the atomised, uprooted (when not anomic), unequal, individualist world of the European. Thus the concept of the African community espoused by Kenyatta, Senghor, Houphouët Boigny, Nyerere and many others may have differed in detail, but its

fundaments were similar. For in the process of inventing the African community of the past which best served the future task of constructing a
modern nation-state, all successful nationalists recognised the importance
of identity, pride, will and industry. Potentially useful (real or invented)
traditions were clearly identified. In this way, the nationalist myth of the
African community was created.[24]

The nationalist discourse was modernising. Independence would give
body to the modern African community. The new nation would find strength
in its traditions to create a modern society capable of developing in the
direction mapped out by Western societies. The norms of modernity (e.g.,
literacy, urbanisation, employment, industrialisation) would confine traditional values to the cultural realm. The attributes of tradition (e.g., ethnicity,
rituals, witchcraft, regionalist allegiance) would be superseded by the
characteristics of modernity. Africans had made the great leap forward and
cast away the fetters of traditions. Ibos were now Nigerians, marabouts
were Senegalese, Maasai were Kenyans, Sékou Touré was the modern re-
incarnation of Samory Touré, the Baganda king was an elected ruler, the
Ashanti king was a traitor, the Emir of Kano was a democrat and Nyerere
was *mwalimu*.[25]

As the assumption that modernisation meant Westernisation was shattered
in post-colonial Africa, so the nationalist discourse was revised. The traditions
of African polities were re-examined in the search for a key to an understanding of the vagaries of modern politics. The colonial system was now
claimed by the post-nationalist to have bequeathed a legacy of unworkable
political practices which went against the African 'genius'. If consensus
was the African way, one-party states were natural and elections mere
formalities. If traditional solidarity still prevailed, trade-unions could only
be divisive. The traditional now explained the modern. So he, as well as the
Africanist, began to question the nationalist discourse and to re-examine the
African past. The meaning of that past was neither simple nor straightforward. The notion of the African community was yet again being reinterpreted.

In Africa, as in some other parts of the world, the modern nation-state is
a more deeply imagined community than it was in Europe, simply because,
with very few exceptions, there was no pre-colonial basis for such a construct.
The imperial powers constructed territories which they called colonies. At
independence, the nationalists reconstructed them into nation-states.[26]

The political process whereby men and women (or rather those who rule
on their behalf) imaginatively construct a political community is as old as
the history of mankind. There is in the systematic study of this imaginative
process, along the lines of Benedict Anderson's book, an agenda for future

research which would illuminate much of what has hitherto come under the rubric of nationalism. Here I merely want to draw the outline of what I mean by the nation-state as imagined community and discuss how the concept is relevant to the political analysis of contemporary Africa.

What was peculiar to post-colonial Africa was not that the nation-state was imagined by the nationalists. All nation-states have to be constructed through imaginative labour. What marked out Africa (and many of the world's colonies) from most European states is that the state preceded the nation. This had profound consequences for the genesis as well as for the identity of the new political community.[27]

The African nation-builders had two models: the pre-colonial and the colonial. The former issued from the nationalist perception of the African community and from his understanding of the colonial impact on it. The latter derived from the particular type of European nation-state which the colonial power embodied and the particular vision that that colonial power itself had of the African community.

The nationalists sought to oust the colonial power and take power themselves. The way in which they went about ousting the colonial power and the manner in which they took power varied in the different colonies and at different periods. What never varied was the process by which they attempted to create a modern political community. This process involved at least three steps: the creation of a national vision; the nationalist myth; the setting up of a national organisation, the nationalist party; and the aggregation of local support for the nationalist project, that is, the invention of unity. The ultimate aim of that process was to win independence and to create a viable nation-state at the end of decolonisation (however long or protracted it was).[28]

It was the first step which required the greatest imaginative labour. All nations need nationalist myths but not all nationalist myths are equally effective or simple to invent. Where the nation-state is the outcome of the gradual march of a recognisable nation towards statehood, as it was in much of Europe, the myths emerge *sui generis* as it were. Where, as in Africa, the (colonial) state forced the construction of an artificial nation-state, the constraints were greater and the resources fewer. It is not surprising that all African nationalists resorted to similar artifices. First, the political community of the past had to be conceived in terms of the demands of the present. The past had to be re-interpreted with a view to the creation of the modern nation-state. Then, the legitimacy of the nationalist myths had to be established and asserted in contemporary political language.[29]

Negritude, Consciencism, African Humanism, African Socialism, etc., were all attempts to re-interpret the past in order to fashion the foundations of the future nation-state.[30] The process, which (at an individual level) was intimately connected with the alienation of the assimilated élite, had more to do with the invention of a language understandable to the colonial masters than with the creation of war cries for the people. As Soyinka is alleged to have once said, a tiger does not need to proclaim its 'tigritude'. The Kikuyus hardly learnt from Kenyatta's *Facing Mount Kenya* that they were Kikuyu. What they learnt from Kenyatta is that they were now Kenyans. But the process by which the Kikuyu were re-invented was an integral part of the process by which the Kenyans were invented.[31]

The extent to which the nationalist myths penetrated the consciousness of the inhabitants of the colonies depended partly on their plausibility. Their plausibility depended partly on the attitude of the colonial masters towards the nationalists and partly on the extent to which different groups recognised themselves in the nationalist myths. Some groups were more convinced than others by the new national symbols. Equally, some national(ist) creations required more convincing than others. Kikuyus were more firmly Kenyan than the Luos or Somalis, Bagandas more firmly Ugandan than the Dinkas, Wolofs more firmly Senegalese than the Mandjaks, etc. In short, almost all nationalist myths were meant to appeal to the larger or more powerful of the ethnic groups, even if they were broad and general enough to speak to the majority of the colony's peoples.[32]

The legitimacy of the new political comunity being created depended in part on the discourse which characterised it. The primary matrix of that discourse was the colonial ideology itself. Where assimilation was deemed possible (as in the French or Portuguese colonies), a modernist discourse would carry more weight. Where assimilation was not envisaged (as in the British and, differently, the Belgian colonies), or where separate development was seen as the way forward, the conservative discourse could be more appropriate. For this reason, the British notion of self-government and the French concept of *autonomie*, both seen by the colonised as way-stations towards ultimate independence, formed the basis of the nationalist discourse. The nationalist myths, therefore, were shaped out of the confrontation between the nationalist interpretation of the pre-colonial and colonial past and the colonial encoding of the characteristics of the modern political community.[33]

The establishment of a nationalist organisation was the most crucial step in the invention of the modern political community;[34] for if the nationalist myth provided the vision, it was the organisation which, in concrete terms, created and embodied the nation. The ideology and the structure of the party largely determined the ideology and the structure of the nation to come. The nationalist organisation was shaped in part by the ideology and structure of the colonial state and in part by the nationalist perception of the African community.[35]

If one of the primary purposes of the establishment of a nationalist party was to demonstrate to the colonial overlord that there existed a legitimate territorial political organisation representing the 'native' population, the other was to show the Africans that they could organise in a modern political community. And where there was nationalist competition, what was at stake was not just the representativeness of each organisation but rather the nature of the modern political community they sought to project.

There were, broadly, three issues which marked out the different nationalist projects: identity, modernity, and ideology. The three were often interrelated and are distinguished here purely for analytical purposes. The debate about identity was a debate about the relation of the individual to the community, a debate about how best to define the new African in political terms. At the centre of the debate was the key question of the importance of ethnicity to African identity. Colonial ideology had decreed that Africans understood themselves essentially in ethnic terms and colonial bureaucracy had organised its subjects in ethnic categories.

The nationalists thus tended to divide on the issue of whether the nationalist party was primarily an aggregation of ethnic blocs or a supra-ethnic entity. At one end of the range, some parties were purely ethnic (e.g., Congo, Ashanti, Baganda); at the other, there were some genuine supra-ethnic organisations (e.g., Tanganyika African National Union [TANU] in Tanganyika, Rassemblement Démocratique Africain [RDA] in the French West African Federation and Partido Africano da Independência da Guiné e Cabo Verde [PAIGC] in Portuguese Guinea). Though expediency most often settled the debate, each party's position on the issue of identity was an indication of the notion of political community being envisaged for the independent nation-state.[36]

It ultimately mattered greatly for the fate of post-colonial countries whether the dominant myth was particularist or universal, however artificial such notions may have been at their inception. How much of a nation an African country is today is often the direct consequence of the position taken by the leading nationalist organisation before independence. That this position was often influenced by colonial ideology (more centralist for the French or more localist for the British) does not detract from the general argument about the relevance of the notion of identity for the complexion of the post-colonial political community.

The issue of modernity turned on the argument of whether the nationalists were modernist or conservative. The conservative discourse was that of 'African authenticity', that is reference to a notion of an idealised African community the values of which were said to need to become the guidelines of the present. Nyerere, Mobutu, Kaunda and many others, in their different ways and at different times, sought in the notional African community of the past the path to progress. The Tanzanian *ujaama* or the Zaïrean *authenticité* were attempts to establish a 'traditional' legitimacy for the modern nation-state.[37] The fact that socialism and capitalism could each be found to have their antecedents in the pre-colonial African community is a commentary on the ideological nature of such etymological exercises.

The modernist, on the other hand, argued that it was the unnecessary weight of the past which hampered the construction of a modern community. To him, what had happened in Africa was not so much the modernisation of tradition as the 'traditionalisation' of modernity.[38] The exploitation by greedy politicians of the symbols of the past led to the degeneration of nationalist parties. The use and abuse of 'Africanness' as the explanation for the peculiar political myth was a smokescreen. Modern politics required the adoption of modern normative values. There was nothing pre-ordained in the African community to make it unsuited to democracy, industry, efficiency or technology. Here again, there were modernists of all political hues, though perhaps the most zealous were socialist.

Not infrequently, of course, those who conceived the African identity in particularistic terms were conservative while the modernists had more universalist notions of individual identity. But there was more. The modernist saw the party as the vehicle for change, the organisation by means of which the independent government would mobilise the resources of the nation for economic and social development. The conservative tended to take the view that the party was merely an organ of representation and unity. The modernist intended the party to reshape existing communities into a single purposeful national community. To him the fate of the independent country depended on the extent to which this self-conscious community had been created. The conservative was more concerned about the role of the party as political machine: an organisation through which the various communities could express themselves and obtain satisfaction.[39]

This was an argument about instrumentality, that is, about the nature of the power relation between party and community, and not simply about political opinion. Nkrumah (modernist) and Senghor (conservative) were both 'socialist', yet they had diametrically opposed views about the role of the party in the national political community.

There were obviously some correlations between the positions assumed on the questions of identity and modernity on the one hand and, on the other, the ideological complexion of the nationalist party. Radical parties were more likely to be modernist, universalist and voluntarist. Yet, the distinction was not always so simple and it is useful analytically to distinguish political ideology from the other two issues.

What was at stake here was the relation between development and community. Radicals were modernist but not all modernists were radical for the radical was, in the African context, usually a socialist and socialists tend to relate community to class. The ideological debate, therefore, was really about class. While the modernist and conservative disagreed on the nature and role of the modern African community, the socialist was concerned about the division of communities into classes.

On this issue, Nkrumah's early position and Senghor's view differed little but they both differed from Sékou Touré who soon conceived the nationalist party largely in class terms. The extent to which Touré's position changed over the years is a good illustration of the difficulty of conceptualising the relationship of community to class in Africa. (It is also a brilliant example of political opportunism.)[40] Ideology was thus one important independent variable in the development of nationalist parties, one more dimension to the invention of the modern political community.

The invention of unity was the necessary final stage in the gestation of the nation-state. Once the nationalist myths and the nationalist party had been created, unity (of community and of purpose) had to be demonstrated. Because colonies were entirely artificial edifices, such unity could be no other than the product of imaginative labour. The boundaries of the colonial territory were accepted by all nationalists and have remained hallowed since independence. Yet, the mere fact that the territorial boundaries had been etched on the map by the colonial powers did not make any less necessary or any less difficult the task of inventing the unity of the political community which was to constitute the nation defined by those boundaries.

For the colonial masters had only paid lip-service to the concept of unity while governing within the framework of existing or newly created (ethnic, regional, racial, religious, or hierarchical) divisions. They demanded of the nationalists a unity which they did not believe existed. Conversely, the nationalists needed to preach a unity the contour of which they had not chosen. The texture of that unity depended on the factors which I have discussed above, but the very success of the enterprise often turned on factors which were beyond the control of the nationalists. In other words, whatever the myths and whatever the organisation, the degree to which unity was achieved was in no small part determined by the nature of the colonial territories which had been marked out by the Europeans.

Unity of political community (whatever its precise meaning) was not equally plausible in all colonial territories.[41] In colonies in which there was a dominant (ethnic, religious, or racial) group (e.g., Senegal, Kenya, Burundi,

Sudan) or the legacy of a dominant political hierarchy (e.g., Uganda, Rwanda, Mauritania), the rest of the community had little chance of escaping a form of unity which favoured the dominant. In colonies where there were several such dominant groups (e.g., Nigeria, Congo, Angola), unity was not likely to be sought at the expense of submission to a rival. The nation-state was likely to be perceived as a competitive political arena rather than an overarching political community.

Only in those countries with no obviously dominant group(s) (e.g., Tanzania, Cameroon, Togo) had the nation the potential of being the aggregate of the many united in the purpose of inventing the single new community. There were, however, very few 'logical' colonies (e.g., Lesotho, Swaziland, Cape Verde), comprising relatively homogeneous populations where the question of the meaning of communal unity did not really arise. In most African colonies the achievement of the unity of the political community was an act of will as much as of imagination.

It was also an act of compromise with the colonial order. Whereas the nationalist myths and the nationalist parties were designed to suit the African community as perceived by the nationalists, the process of unification followed the colonial diktat. Nationalist unity was necessarily constructed as the reverse image of colonial unity. Nationalists and colonialists, while rivals, conspired to invent the unity which the former intended to inherit from the latter.

To be charged by the colonial state with fomenting anti-colonial agitation was often the most efficient and most official means of gaining recognition as nationalist leader. The mark of the nationalist's achievement in the invention of national unity was most compellingly measured by the degree of censure from the colonial government. Her Majesty's most loyal foes (e.g., Nkrumah, Kenyatta, Banda) or the French Republic's most persistent enemies (e.g. Touré, Houphouët-Boigny, Modibo Keita) became the leaders of the newly independent countries which they had helped to fashion.

That sleight of hand, however, also meant that national unity was constructed on the legacy of colonial unity and that, like it, it would have to rely on state coercion to maintain itself. The weaker the foundations of national unity, the more open to challenge and the less legitimate it was, the more the state would have to resort to coercion. In the end, unity came at a much higher price than was realised or admitted by the nationalists. How deeply rooted the new political community was largely determined the viability of the nation-state.[43]

What is clear, in conclusion, is that the process by which the pre-colonial and colonial communities were transformed into the modern political community embodied in the independent nation-state was infinitely more complex than most political analysis of contemporary Africa suggests. The construction of that political community derived from processes which were specific to each colony and we need a precise historical account of what took place in order plausibly to analyse the post-colonial politics of each successor country.

The continuities and ruptures between pre-colonial, colonial and post-colonial communities provide the material from which it is possible to understand the contemporary nation-state. Our failure to make sense of some of the most momentous (if not tragic) events taking place today in Africa can often be traced to our lack of understanding of the notion(s) of communities held by the various actors involved in those events. The Chadian, Sudanese, Nigerian, Zaïrean, Rwandan and Ugandan civil wars, to take only those examples, are better explained by reference to the genesis of their various political communities than merely by the fickleness and viciousness of their leaders. Without an understanding of the meanings of political community there can be no political analysis.

3 Political Accountability

Where there are political communities, there are relations of power. What determines the nature of such relations is political accountability. Like the concept of political community, the notion of political accountability is universal. It is not ideologically, conceptually, historically, or even geographically, specific. It belongs to political analysis, the analysis of power, everywhere and at all times. To understand political accountability is to understand how power becomes power, how it is exercised, how it is constrained and how it dissipates;[1] for power is not an abstract concept or, rather, as abstract concept it is of little interest.

Political accountability is simple to understand but difficult to conceptualise. At its core is the notion of political obligation, the obligation of the members of the community towards each other.[2] A community is defined as a political community by the way in which its members create, re-create and abide by the existing principles of political obligation. Political analysis is essentially concerned with the principles of political obligation between the governors and the governed, for it is those principles and the manner in which they are put into practice which define political accountability in a particular political community.

Political accountability is thus, minimally, the institutional, traditional and symbolic mechanisms by which, on the one hand, the governed call their governors to account for their deeds and, on the other, the governors discharge the responsibilities of political obligation. It is, more broadly, the ensemble of formal and informal factors which impinge on the way in which rulers and ruled relate to each other in a political community. The analysis of political accountability is, in short, the analysis of the constantly changing determinants of the theory and practice of political obligation between those who hold power and those who do not.

Political accountability, therefore, is a relation. As such it does not exist in and of itself, *sui generis*, outside of a particular context. It is the central political axis of the community, the way in which that community is defined politically and the manner in which it operates. It concerns the reciprocal responsibilities of the high and low, the mighty and the meek, those who hold and those who endure power. As I have written elsewhere:

> Political accountability is a relation of reciprocity and inequality between the rulers and the ruled: kings and subjects, chiefs and villagers, colonial administrators and *indigènes*, party leaders and followers, revolutionaries and peasants. It is a relation of collaboration, coercion

and violence. Above all, it is a relation which constantly changes as the external and internal context itself changes.[3]

The notion of political accountability is thus central to the understanding of politics; it is at the heart of any historically grounded political analysis. Whatever the political community and whatever the nature of power relations within it, power only exists as power through political accountability. Where political accountability (whatever its complexion) dissipates, there no longer is a political community, nor is there power. In a state of war, absolute lawlessness or absolute violence, there is no political accountability but only force. But power is a relation of reciprocity between members of a political community. Where there is only force there is no power.

As Lonsdale writes accurately, political accountability is:

> part of the moral calculus of power; it concerns the mutual responsibility of inequality. Because it raises questions about the control of power and its purposes, accountability must also be concerned with political organisation. For if power is not to some extent shared there can be no effective base from which it may be controlled, nor any protected right to discuss its purposes. So political accountability, or public morality, is the chief end of political freedom. Whether it also guarantees social justice and economic development is an altogether thornier question.[4]

Political accountability, then, is about how power is shared. It is a political myth, an enduring cliché, that the sole purpose of politics is the accumulation of power for its own sake. The business of politics is, to use contemporary jargon, to maximise the relation between power and production (a concept which I examine in a later chapter). Power without production is sterile, pointless, unproductive as it were. For power to be productive it has to be shared. How it is shared and how the process of sharing evolves over time depends on the relationship between rulers and ruled.[5]

Political accountability thus defines the political arena within which the rulers seek to maintain, and the ruled seek to combat, the relations of inequality and coercion which all power relations entail. Whether power, always the reflection of a precarious equilibrium between rulers and ruled, is stable or not depends on the degree to which a particular form of political accountability is rooted within a particular political community. Changes in political accountability, therefore, are changes in the nature of power.[6]

Although historically there have been political communities in which the exercise of power was absolute, just as there have been communities in which there were no formal rulers, these were mere exceptions to the general rule. Absolute power, the total absence of accountability, cannot last; it is inherently self-destructive. Absolute equality cannot be productive even if it may have endured in small-scale communities of hunter-gatherers.[7] In most political communities, power is defined by political accountability. The purpose of political analysis must thus be to identify the components of political accountability and its mode of operation within a particular political community.

Power cannot be assessed in and of itself. To understand power is to understand the relations of political obligation which it contains. Only then is it possible to explain why, for example, formal power may or may not be effective; why power may lie where it is not seen, or be seen where it does not exist, or be effective where it is not formal; why, to take another example, governments may appear to rule but not have power where chiefs or religious leaders or military commanders have the power to overrule government.[8] In this respect, Lonsdale's article on political accountability is most useful: not only does it show how the concept is relevant to the study of politics in Africa from the pre- to the post-colonial period but it also makes it possible to analyse relations of power from a much broader and more easily comparative perspective.[9]

The notion of political accountability is often associated, when not confused, with notions of political legitimacy or political representation. But the three represent three different levels of conceptual and historical abstraction. Political accountability is the deeper, more historically grounded, concept. It is one which encompasses political processes from a longer and broader perspective. Crises of accountability are ruptures between political epochs or revolutions.

Political accountability defines the framework within which the political legitimacy of rulers is assessed, the criteria by which they are judged. Political legitimacy is thus the short-term and more contingent perspective of regime and government analysis, for the political legitimacy of a regime fluctuates regularly according to the political life of a community. In pre-colonial Africa, rulers could lose legitimacy if the rains failed.[10] Today, rulers can lose legitimacy if the price of rice doubles.[11] That loss of legitimacy does not necessarily alter the rules of political obligation, the texture of political accountability, which characterise the political community but it impinges directly on the fate of particular rulers. Political legitimacy is, then, more immediately relevant to the visible and perceptible life of a political system. It is the blood of day-to-day politics.

Representation, at once a fundamental concern of liberal political theory and class analysis, is tied to the mechanics of power – the institutional and structural arrangements of power control and power sharing.[12] Representation has to do with the modalities of political obligation, the formulae which govern the reciprocities of power. It can only be the central question in political analysis where there is little dispute about the meaning of political accountability and the nature of political legitimacy within a given political community. The study of forms of representation (e.g., elections, formats of one/multi-party rule), however important it is, has been excessively narrow in much political analysis of Africa and has tended to obscure more important, deeper, prior and more historically significant political processes for which the liberal notion of representation did not provide an adequate conceptual framework.[13]

Political legitimacy and political representation are concepts which are contained in the notion of political accountability and which are essential to political analysis. Both are part of the integument of the relation between power and production. In all political communities, political legitimacy and representation are fundamental. Where political legitimacy disappears, and this may well follow the end of representation, the process of political accountability is altered and relations of power change accordingly. But how they change is far from straightforward or easily understood. All political regimes are based on some notions of legitimacy and representation. The question for political analysis is the quality of this political legitimacy and the texture of representation.

There is, however, a certain logical relation between the three concepts. Within a given order of political accountability, there can be different forms of political legitimacy. Within a given order of political legitimacy there can be different forms of representation. In other words, notions of legitimacy and forms of representation can change within a given political order of accountability.[14]

Perhaps the most acute and clearest such case was the process of dynastic change in China. The overriding principle of political accountability in imperial China was contained in the notion of 'Mandate from Heaven': the divine right of the Emperor to rule.[15] That principle was not seriously contested until the twentieth century. Dynastic changes were (sometimes cataclysmic) ruptures in political legitimacy. That is, a particular dynasty had lost political legitimacy and no longer was endowed with the Mandate from Heaven. But for the new dynasty, the existing notion of political accountability (the principle of the 'Mandate from Heaven') continued to determine the nature of political obligation within a new world in which the old political order had been thoroughly rejected and everything else had changed.

Just as importantly, accountability, legitimacy and representation are affected by external factors. Changes in accountability, that is, political ruptures or revolutions, are often the outcome of external factors (e.g., wars, invasions, conquest, empire-building, capitalist penetration). So, to pursue the example of China, the end of the dynastic order itself, which was largely due to external factors and which led to the 1911, and later the 1949, revolution, constituted a complete rupture in political obligation and led to the establishment of a new principle of political accountability.[16] This new order of political accountability necessarily entailed new forms of political legitimacy and of representation.

In Africa, then, how did political accountability, political legitimacy and political representation change from the pre- to the post-colonial period? And how were those changes conceived in the political analysis of the continent?

There have been two ruptures in political accountability, two political revolutions, during this period: the establishment of the colonial order and independence. To understand these two fractures in the political order of Africa is to understand, simultaneously, the nature of the political continuities and discontinuities between the old and the new. To speak of political revolution or rupture is not to imply, as is sometimes simplistically assumed, that the break between the old and the new is either complete or final. Each revolution builds on the ruins of the previous political order and the way in which it does so largely determines its complexion and its fate. One can easily be misled by the fact that some ruins are more visible than others. The understanding of political revolution depends as much on the analysis of the ruins as on that of the new edifice.[17]

The colonial revolution, that is the imposition of formal colonial rule which followed the Scramble for Africa, appears to have been more ruinous (for African societies) than the revolution of independence.[18] In some sense this is true. Colonial rule, however differently imagined and differently applied, meant in the end the attempt to abolish the old political order. The establishment of discrete colonial territories, achieved through 'pacification', most often entailed the destruction of the existing order of political accountability. The setting up of a colonial administration was at the expense of the continued functioning of pre-colonial African political structures. The success of the colonial age was seen to depend on the construction of a new political community, a new political order which would owe as little as possible to the pre-colonial political order. It depended, in other words, on the creation of new relations of power, a new political accountability.

Yet, for all the efforts at the destruction of the pre-colonial order and for all the changes carried out to create a functional colonial world, the colonial revolution was very much building on the ruins, planting on the humus perhaps, of that unwanted (or at least very much misunderstood) pre-colonial Africa.[19] There were two causally interrelated processes at work here. The first was the adaptation of the pre-colonial order to the colonial world; the second was the adaptation of the colonial order to the African world.

Even when pre-colonial communities were militarily defeated by the colonial conquerors (e.g., Ashanti, Ndebele), they were not destroyed. Nor did the principles which governed their political life simply vanish. They were transmuted into new principles congruent with the colonial diktat. Indeed, what is most remarkable about the colonial revolution is not how much was destroyed but how much remained. Witness how colonial officials were perennially frustrated in their attempt to create not just new formal structures but also new individuals, new mentalities and new communities. To take one example, the repeated colonial attempt to criminalise certain so-called traditional tribal activities (e.g., cattle-raiding in Kenya) gives ample proof of the failure of the new colonial order to abolish or even de-legitimise age-old African communal practices.[20]

Equally revealing of African adaptability is the famous example of migrant cocoa-farmers in southern Ghana before the First World War.[21] The construction of a phenomenally successful African economy within existing socio-economic structures is perhaps the clearest example in colonial Africa of the possible development of capitalist farming within lines of continuity stretching from the pre-colonial period. In Africa, generally, the colonial period saw many examples of the adaptation of pre-colonial 'modes of production' to the modern economy, that is the development of so-called informal economies. Such informal economies could be so successful that, in settler colonies for example, the colonial state had to introduce regulatory measures in order to maintain control over production.[22] Countless other examples could be given of the survival, if not the thriving, of 'traditional' Africa in the new colonial order.

Conversely, the colonial order was having constantly to adapt to the African world. Whereas it is clear that before the Scramble for Africa, the confrontation between Europe and Africa had largely been to the advantage of the latter – of which there is no better example than the history of the *prazos* of the Zambezi valley (the Africanisation of a European institution, as Isaacman calls it) – the colonial period is seen as the reverse.[23] But the contrast can be overdrawn. From the most abstract to the most concrete, the colonial world was deeply 'Africanised'.

For example, Lord Lugard's theory of indirect rule, that pristine revelation about the nature of the British colonial mission in Africa, was based on his experience in Uganda and on the reality of political 'cohabitation' in northern Nigeria;[24] it was a theory derived from the confrontation and accommodation of two political orders with two differing principles of political accountability. Similarly, the administration of the locality by district/circle officers was severely tempered by, and in time came to resemble, 'traditional' chiefly administration.[25]

Equally, the colonial obsession with 'tribalism' issued from the colonial (mis)perception of and adaptation to the so-called traditional African community. Although colonial Africans were meant to become modern citizens, the colonial mind found it necessary (and, of course, expedient) to continue to see them in tribal terms.[26] That it was convenient for colonial rule so to categorise the 'natives' does not detract from the process by which modernisers saw themselves bowing to what they believed to be the realities of African customs. Finally, the creation of so-called customary law and the adaptation of European laws to Africa was based on the colonial interpretation of local 'traditional' customs and practices.[27] All these examples illustrate the point I wish to make about the real (if sometimes perverse) 'Africanised' nature of the colonial order.

The second political revolution, the coming of independence, is now usually conceived (except by orthodox nationalist history) as a process in which the continuities far outweighed the discontinuities with the colonial order. It is often argued, in conservative as well as radical accounts of decolonisation, that the post-colonial political order owes far more to its predecessor than to the political community invented by the nationalists. Independence is often seen as the hoisting of a new flag and the replacement of white by black master, that is merely the Africanisation of the colonial administration and of its principle of political accountability.[28] By this account, independence does not really qualify as a political revolution, but merely as a change of governors.

It is true that often, though not always, decolonisation was a colonially conceived and constructed process of gradual devolution of power which sought to formalise the continuation of the existing political order. The colonial powers enfranchised their African subjects, encouraged or endured the creation of political parties (and organs of popular representation), introduced local and general elections, set up regional and territorial elected assemblies, and eventually devolved power to legally elected local governments.[29]

Nationalists, whoever they were, played the game of decolonisation according to the rules laid down by the colonial masters. At independence, the nationalists simply inherited the colonial state. Yet the manner in which they inherited it and precisely what it is they inherited are (large) political questions which singularly trouble the clarity of the received wisdom on the post-colonial continuity with the colonial order. Equally, they impinge on the nationalist myth of political revolution, that is the claim that independence erected a new African kingdom which broke entirely with its colonial antecedents.[30]

The revolution of independence is a different admixture of continuities and discontinuities from the colonial revolution but, like it, it contains processes of political confrontation and accommodation. Even in cases where independence appeared to be granted to reluctant nationalists through a process of decolonisation in which the former colonial power retained a large degree of control (e.g., Senegal, Côte d'Ivoire), the end of colonial rule marked a historical rupture. Conversely, even in countries where the process of decolonisation involved a war of national liberation and appeared to involve the wholesale overthrow of the colonial order (e.g., Angola, Mozambique, Zimbabwe), the political rupture was not nearly as marked as appeared to be the case. In other words, the experience of what appear to be two extreme cases in a range of possible forms of decolonisation probably turns out to have more in common than in contrast.

Regardless of the apparent differences in the modalities of decolonisation – and wars of national liberation are, in one respect at least, nothing but another form of decolonisation – the political process whereby nationalist parties took over the government of independent African nation-states represents a fundamental change in political accountability. In the end, history will probably record that the colonial period was a mere hiatus in the history of Africa, but a hiatus opened and closed by consequential crises in political accountability. The analysis of these two political revolutions, these two ruptures in political accountability, makes up the rest of this chapter.

Crises in political accountability are what Lonsdale calls 'civilising missions'. Civilising missions are the historical imperatives which drive new rulers, the political revolutionaries, to seek to create new political communities. As Lonsdale writes:

African history is unusually full of cautionary tales for impatient rulers. Visionary in their claims, they have been taken at their word. African kings drummed up support by proclaiming the fertility of their rule. Some of them were killed when they became senile or when the rains next failed. Colonial rulers claimed to be essential to civilising Africa, instilling the rights of property and the property of writing. They were ousted by those Africans who first appropriated both. Kwame Nkrumah, inspiration for all later nationalists, urged Africans to seek first the political kingdom. Some have been tearing it apart almost ever since. Leaders of national liberation movements entrusted their future to their peasantries. Peasants now do not much like paying for the future of socialism.[31]

Crises in political accountability, in other words, are nothing new in Africa. What, then, were the civilising missions of the colonialists and the nationalists? And what is their relevance for the political analysis of post-colonial Africa?

The colonial revolution established, and was perceived by Africans to establish, the pre-eminence of a superarching political power over existing systems of political accountability. Like all conquerers, the colonial powers were only accountable to themselves but like all conquerors they had to devise a new form of political accountability to legitimise their conquest.[32] Their self-proclaimed mission was, literally, to civilise the Africans. Imperial rule was legitimised by the call to civilise. Europe, the pinnacle of man's moral and material achievement, now undertook to bestow its blessings unto Africa – 'instilling the rights of property and the property of writing'[33]

At the level of high discourse, the colonial powers were thus only accountable to God and the Greater Idea of Civilisation. At the lower level of governance, colonial officials were accountable to their employers, the colonial government. The colonial government in turn was accountable to the imperial government. Like all conquerors, however, the colonial powers disregarded the conquered at their peril. Consequently, in the process of 'reading the mind of the native', colonial government had to map out the boundaries of the new political accountability in a way which took some account of the 'native mind'.[34]

In practice, colonial political accountability contained the two distinct, and somewhat contradictory, principles of progress and expediency. Colonial officials were under instructions to uphold and when possible to promote the individual, social, and economic well-being of their colonial subjects within the colony's constraints on resources – determined, of course by colonial or imperial government. The measure of their success was assessed by colonial reports and colonial statistics. Failure, on the other hand, was measured by African non-cooperation, unrest, protest, and violence. This was an exceedingly primitive guide to the functioning of the colonial machinery but in such terms was political accountability conceived.

There were good and bad colonial officials but the extent to which they were good or bad at achieving progress (whatever that meant) tended to be most easily measured by the principle of expediency.[35] Ultimately, colonial political accountability was assessed in terms of 'cost-plus-law-and-order'. Excessive expenditure or unrest were always bad, whatever their causes. In the absence of better mechanisms of political representation than the 'consultative councils', formally the only forums where the colonial subjects could call their colonial rulers to account, unrest and violence were the most readily available options.

The colonial political imperative was that of the conqueror: how best to establish the political legitimacy of conquest and what form of representation to allow the conquered. The legitimacy of colonial rule was constructed on the myth of pre-colonial Africa as a land of tribal division, primitivism and perennial violence and on the claim of the benefits a better, more efficient and more advanced colonial system of governance and administration would bring. Each colonial power claimed for itself a moral ground superior to its African predecessors or its European rivals.[36]

Once 'pacification' was over, once Africans had recognised (even if not accepted) that they could not forcibly remove the conquerors, once the basic colonial infrastructure had been laid down and colonial governments had settled to the task of ruling the empire, the notion of colonial legitimacy changed. It was now perceived to be commensurate with its ability to provide the means to achieve the progress it claimed for its colonial subjects. During this period, the heyday of colonial rule, colonial governors could concentrate on the 'management' of men and resources which best benefited the empire without constantly having to look over their shoulders. The legitimacy of their colonial mission appeared secure.

This period, however, was relatively short (no longer than one generation). Soon after the Second World War, colonial governments had to seek yet again a new form of political legitimacy. Because, for historical reasons, the legitimacy of colonial rule was waning at home and nationalist pressure was mounting in Africa, the colonial rulers invented a new civilising mission: self-government. Now colonial rule was legitimised on the grounds that it sought to prepare the colonial territories for self-government and, ultimately, independence. The wheel had come full circle. The conquerors were legitimising the inevitable demise of their conquest on the grounds that their mission was fulfilled.[37]

The forms of representation offered to the colonial subjects also varied in different colonies and over time, but essentially they fell into two distinct categories: 'traditional' and modern representative bodies. For the colonial government the legitimacy of these 'traditional', meaning 'native', representatives was determined by the degree to which they chose to collaborate rather than by their legitimacy within the African community. In other words, and this is crucial, 'traditional' authorities, whether genuine or spurious, were now essentially accountable to the colonial master.[38]

Representation in the colonial system thus entailed a radical change in the 'traditional' notion of political accountability. As a result of collaboration many 'traditional' authorities' lost legitimacy in the eyes of their communities. Or, to be more specific, those 'traditional' authorities who now had colonial duties to discharge (particularly taxation and forced labour) lost legitimacy whereas those (e.g., spirit mediums) who had little or no contact with the colonial world maintained much greater legitimacy.[39]

Only where colonial rule had (or chose) to tolerate a large degree of political and economic autonomy (as, for example, with the emirates of northern Nigeria or the Muslim brotherhoods in Senegal) did the 'traditional' authorities manage to collaborate *and* retain much of their legitimacy. In those cases, representation, whatever its guise, remained closer to what it had been before colonisation. The colonial order merely added one more layer of administrative bureaucracy to enforce the dominating principle of colonial political accountability.

Modern representative bodies varied enormously between (even within) colonies and over time. For practical purposes, the two issues which mattered were whether these bodies had consultative or executive powers and whether they were elected or appointed. The general trend, in British and French colonies, was for the colonial powers to give these bodies greater executive power, to increase the proportion of those elected and to widen the electoral franchise. The pattern was also to devolve (some) executive power to elected bodies at the local level first.[40]

There were many exceptions. In the Portuguese and Spanish colonies, for example, executive power was never devolved to Africans and meaningful elections never took place. In settler colonies (e.g., Kenya, Rhodesia) as in some French colonies, the process was both slower and more unequal as separate electorates for the different races ensured continued white domination of such representative bodies. The French allowed (limited) elected representation at the imperial centre before they devolved power locally. Nevertheless, where representative bodies became more representative (that is, elected) and acquired more executive power, their legitimacy increased even if ultimate accountability lay elsewhere.

The colonial revolution, as it sought endlessly to maintain its legitimacy, distorted existing forms of representation and introduced new ones. Collaboration and representation became largely synonymous. But what it is important to emphasise is that, however 'representative' colonial governments were (and they were not very representative until the principle of independence had been conceded) they never were, nor could they be, really accountable to those over whom they ruled. They could listen to their subjects, they could allow them some measure of representation, they could give them a larger measure of control over their day-to-day life, they could promote their well-being but they could never alter the principle of colonial political accountability.

As colonial historians never tire of saying, colonial governments ultimately deferred to a colonial secretary who, in turn, usually deferred to an exchequer. Whether independence came as a result of nationalist pressure or not, ultimately it was granted not so much, as colonial ideology had it, because the colonial governments accepted that accountability to their subjects now required it, but rather because the imperial governments were accountable to nations which no longer wanted colonial rule to continue. As the selfsame colonial historians elegantly put it, colonies were now 'too bloody expensive', or, in more elevated language, the colonial mission had been achieved.[41]

The nationalist mission, independence, was not so much the transfer of power (as it is usually called) as the creation of a new principle of political accountability.[42] The nationalist revolution entailed a genuine and radical rupture with the colonial order, even if the modalities of independence seemed to make for a smooth transition and to guarantee continuity. African nationalists argued, of course, that independence was a total break with the past. What they meant was that the Africans were now masters in their own house – they had achieved their political kingdom. The former colonial masters (who saw themselves as the nationalists' tutors) emphasised the degree to which the newly independent countries were building on their colonial foundations.[43]

Both positions, however, are a simplification of what was really at issue in the colonial revolution. The post-colonial order followed the colonial one and naturally built on it, regardless of how violent or destructive the nationalist struggle had been. Equally, independence did entail a fundamental break with the colonial past, regardless of how much the administration of the new nation owed to the colonial administration (and sometimes to its former colonial administrators). What really matters about the transition from the colonial to the post-colonial order is the rupture in political accountability.

Independence meant the sudden and irreversible break in the principle of colonial accountability. After the midnight of independence, a new principle of political accountability had to be created. The ease or difficulty with which it was created and the form that it took owed as much to the process of decolonisation as it owed to the formal political and administrative structures bequeathed by the colonial government. But the interpretative error committed by nationalists and Africanists alike was to have assumed that the forms of political accountability created during the nationalist campaign and the period of formal decolonisation would readily and co-herently be transformed into a general principle of political accountability for the independent nation-state.[44] For historical reasons this could not be so.

The parameters of nationalist agitation and the representativeness of various forms of nationalism were defined by the colonial framework in each particular territory. Whoever nationalists thought they were, what they were doing was to promote nationalism in the concrete and possible ways which colonial rule made possible or necessary. National congresses were formed to agitate and participate in elections; fronts of national liberation undertook to pursue their aims through armed struggle. All sought to establish new principles of accountability in order to inspire and consolidate the legitimacy of nationalism. However accountable they were (or thought they were) to the people who supported their campaign, their ultimate political accountability was to the greater aim of the revolution: independence.

They were accountable to the people insofar as the people supported their struggle for independence. Whether they were conservative or radical nationalists, the people supported them only insofar as they appeared to be the best placed to wrest independence from the colonial masters. That is, their support derived, perhaps primarily, from their chances of success. In some settings (e.g., the British colonies), success depended on the nationalists' legal agility; in others (e.g., the Portuguese colonies), on their ability to mobilise the countryside for a war of national liberation. In all cases, however, the peculiar circumstances of decolonisation enabled the nationalists to operate according to a principle of political accountability, the historical task of ending colonial rule, which would *ipso facto* change at independence. It is in this sense that independence was a political revolution and not in the sense that nationalists were necessarily revolutionaries.

The need to create a new principle of political accountability had important consequences for the realities of post-colonial political legitimacy and representation which have largely been overlooked in the political analysis of contemporary Africa. The legitimacy of the new state derived from its nationalist credentials, and its representativeness either from pre-independence elections or from its victory in the nationalist struggle. But to whom and in which way was it accountable? Whereas the success of nationalism depended on the ability of the nationalists to demonstrate their representativeness to the colonial rulers and, beyond, to the world community, the viability of the post-colonial government depended on the legitimacy of the nation-state it created. The state was now accountable to the nation, or rather to the nation-in-making.[45]

The post-colonial state contained two distinct components, bureaucrats and politicians, with two distinct principles of political accountability. The colonial bureaucracies, with few exceptions (e.g., Angola, Mozambique), simply became the bureaucracies of the independent nation-states, and the victorious nationalist parties, without exception, became their governments. When they were brought together to form the core of the new state, there was no easy synthesis. All bureaucrats became nationalists and all nationalists became bureaucrats, but that was not enough. Bureaucracies had decades of colonial experience in which the routine of hierarchical accountability to the colonial state and the precepts of stability over change had been perfected. The nationalists, on the other hand, had the experience of years of political mobilisation and a rather more millenial outlook. Both represented avenues of advancement for the ambitious. Soon, a third constituent body, the army, would emerge with its own claims for a different principle of political accountability.[46]

The post-colonial principle of accountability thus emerged out of this complex and unstable situation. In theory, the bureaucracy was accountable to the state and the state was accountable to the nation; but the country had yet to be fully consolidated as a nation-state. In the meantime bureaucrats, politicians and the other constituent components of the state continued to operate as before but without the colonial constraints.

Bureaucrats no longer had to defer to the colonial masters and deferred to the new masters as little and as infrequently as possible. The politicians were simply not in a position to enforce the new rules of bureaucratic accountability.[47] They had yet to 'capture' the bureaucrats.[48] Bureaucrats thus became politically powerful within the new state.

The politicians for their part no longer needed to justify the legitimacy of their power. Their tenure of power, the proof of their nationalist success, was their badge of legitimacy. In the post-colonial period, tenure of power would tend to become synonymous with political legitimacy but, in order to retain power, the politicians now had to acquire control of the resources of the state. And in order to do that they had to become bureaucratically powerful within the state. Henceforth, bureaucrats, politicians (and others) would struggle for control of the state.

Therefore, whereas before independence both bureaucrats and politicians had had to operate according to principles of political accountability in which there was an ultimate sanction enforced by the colonial rulers, this was now no longer the case. And because the new political community, the nation-state, was yet to be fully established, it did not possess principles of political accountability to which the new masters, bureaucrats and politicians alike, could readily be made to subscribe.

The principles of political accountability of the newly created African nation-states would thus be invented in the practice of post-colonial politics. In this process of invention, the principles of political accountability from the pre-colonial, the colonial and the nationalist past would come into conflict. Above all, however, the new principles of political accountability would be determined by the nature of the political relation between state and civil society in the years which followed independence.[49]

4 The State

The state is scarcely a new concept in the political analysis of Africa.[1] Almost all accounts of post-colonial African politics take as their starting point an examination of the state. There are now probably more books on the state in Africa than about any other political issue. To talk about politics in Africa is virtually to talk about the state. Yet, there is precious little agreement on its conceptual meaning or the interpretative implication of its analysis. Like all abused notions it has become virtually meaningless. We all agree that it is an indispensable concept of modern political analysis but we do not agree on why it is so important to understand its role in the politics of post-colonial African countries. For this reason, and also because it is the general approach of this book, we need to start again at the very beginning.

It is implicit in what I have said so far that the concepts of political community and political accountability are theoretically prior to that of the state (and to the other concepts I shall discuss). Without some understanding of the meanings of political community and accountability in their particular historical setting it is not possible plausibly to conceptualise the post-colonial state. We need, and this is one of the themes of this book, an understanding of its colonial and even pre-colonial antecedents.[2] It is thus not profitable, and it may be misleading, to discuss the post-colonial state *sui generis*, as though it had issued from some pristine void in a spontaneous process of self-creation. As Lonsdale has written: 'Otherwise than in myths, states do not have origins: they are formed'.[3] The post-colonial state, whatever it is, is the outcome of a protracted historical process by which various political communities and various principles of political accountability have combined to give birth to the independent, and now sacrosanct, nation-state.

What this means is that the post-colonial state, both the symbol and the overarching political structure of the independent African country, derives historically from specific processes of change best approached (in part, at least) through the analysis of the concepts of community and accountability. All post-colonial states look alike but their genesis differs. The political communities which came to form each colonial territory and the principles of accountability which defined the relations between governors and governed within that colony were historically specific. The understanding of the specificity of these processes must come before any general notion of the state is applied to the analysis of the post-colonial politics of any particular country. In other words, the specific/concrete must precede the general/abstract. It is, I believe, the failure to move from the historical to the theoretical which has caused an obsessive, and somewhat sterile, focus on the state as concept.[4]

There were, and still are, good reasons for this obsession. The post-colonial state was at once the most present and most recognisable of all political institutions. At independence, the new African countries were defined by the colonial boundaries which delineated their territories and, especially, by the state which took over their administration.[5] Everything else was unclear. It was the state's business, or rather the business of those who took control of the state at independence, to give life and reality to the newly created nation-state. The very identity of the nation depended on the action of the state.

The state was, or appeared to be, the embodiment of the nation-in-making. States behaved like states; they spoke the language of states to their own citizens and to the rest of the world. States possessed governments, bureaucracies, armed forces, police; they ran schools, hospitals, dispensaries, postal services and airports; they controlled marketing boards and trade licences; they issued communiqués and made political statements; they had representation on international bodies like the United Nations (UN) or the Organisation of African Unity (OAU). In short, states were visible and understandable.

The African state seemed to be like the state everywhere else. But its reality was not so simple. If the African post-colonial state looked like the European state it was because it had been designed thus – the 'official statement' made by the colonial power at the end of decolonisation rather than a reflection of the realities of community and accountability in independent Africa. To focus political analysis on the formal structure and operation of the state was to confine understanding to the world of shadows, to confuse cause and effect. The post-colonial African state may have been decreed a state which *looked* like a European state but to start from the assumption that it *functioned* like one was to take for granted a historical causality which did not exist. What the state in post-colonial Africa was *in reality* ought to have been the object rather than the premise of political analysis.[7] For the notion of the modern state in Europe is a concept derived from the analysis of very specific political developments in the history of modern Europe. The same should apply to the notion of the state in Africa.[8]

There are least three distinct (though partly overlapping) approaches to the concept of the post-colonial state in Africa: the developmental where the state is virtually coterminous with government and is defined by its function in the political system; the Marxist where the state is the arena of the class struggle determined by the country's position in the international capitalist system; and the notion of the overdeveloped state, that Leviathan begat by the colonial state. In each approach, the very definition of the state determines the analysis of its role in African politics. I briefly examine the three in turn.

The developmental notion of the state owes much to functional political analysis and it dominated the work of most political scientists of Africa in the decade which followed the first wave of independence (1957–64).[9] It has now reappeared in different guise with democratic theory. Here the state was defined, when it was defined, as the apex of the political system, that is the government and the other essential executive, coercive and judicial bodies. The state was conceived, therefore, as it is in Western political theory, as a democratically elected representative government accountable to parliament, implementing policies defined or approved by the legislative bodies and defending the integrity of the nation.

It was assumed, rather than demonstrated, not just that the political system functioned as it was believed to function in Western democracies but that the ambit of the politic was functionally distinct, as it is conceived to be in Western political theory, from that of the economic or the social. As a result, the analysis of African politics consisted most often either of an examination of the various functional spheres of the state (e.g., leadership, government secretariats, ideology, bureaucracy) or of the relationship between the various components of the state and other politically relevant institutions (e.g., party, armed forces, police, trade unions).[10]

This model of the African post-colonial state rested on three basic assumptions. The first was that the state could be conceived ahistorically, that it was possible to conceptualise it regardless of the specific history which informed its genesis. The second was that there existed a recognisable and universally agreed notion of political community as well as a recognisable notion of the body politic which defined the nation-state. The third was that there was in independent African countries an established and operational principle of political accountability.

These assumptions were unwarranted. The post-colonial state in Africa is the product of very specific historical circumstances, circumstances which differ radically from those of the emergence of the modern European state and make it imperative to conceptualise it differently. Furthermore, it is precisely because, in the independent nation-states of Africa, the notions of political community and accountability were so vague, unformed and malleable that (in the post-colonial context) it was difficult to define the boundaries of the body politic. The state was not easily definable in functional terms when the political system remained so poorly understood.[11]

At best and when used comparatively, the developmental approach could give some indication of the formal evolution of the post-colonial state in different countries. Yet it focused too narrowly on the explicitly institutional and structural dimensions of politics to enable us to understand African politics in depth. It eventually foundered on the inescapable realisation that the gap between what the African post-colonial states were supposed to be and what they actually were was too wide to be explained in terms of the notion of the political system as conceived by functional analysis.[12]

The Marxist notion of the state is straightforward if somewhat difficult to apply analytically. It is concerned less with what states are than with what states do. The state, or rather the various state apparatuses which compose it, is deemed to be the political instrument of the economically dominant classes. The nature of the state is the outcome of existing class struggles. Class struggles are determined by the evolution of the economic structure, that is its mode(s) of production. The economic structure of the nation-state is itself determined by the country's position in the international capitalist order.[13]

From the Marxist perspective there were two important aspects to the economies of independent countries: internally, they contained capitalist and non-capitalist modes of production; externally, they were dependent, that is their development was conditioned by the country's position in the world economy. In order to conceptualise the state is was thus necessary to understand the class implications of the articulation of various modes of production within dependent capitalism. This entailed defining classes and explaining the relations between classes and the state apparatuses in each particular country.[14]

There were two difficulties with the Marxist approach to the state. In the first instance, the post-colonial state was primarily determined by the colonial state, that is by the outcome of the process of decolonisation, rather than merely by class struggle. Marxists themselves conceded that nationalism, and hence decolonisation, could not simply be conceived in class terms. The state was thus overdetermined: a political superstructure was well and truly installed by fiat over an existing economic structure.[15]

The second was that classes in Africa were not so easily identified. It was unclear what the class nature of pre-colonial mode(s) of production was and how it was articulated with the capitalist mode of production. More problematically, it was not clear either how dependent capitalist classes were determined. Since there was a state and since that state *de facto* controlled much of the economy, it became the primary task of Marxists to attempt to identify which classes (or fractions of classes) controlled what part of the state apparatus.[16]

Although some progress was made on the analysis of rural class development, less was achieved in the identification of class fractions within the state. Everyone agreed that the post-colonial state was in the hands of the *petite bourgeoisie* but there was no consensus on the nature of this *petite bourgeoisie*.[17] Nor was there agreement on the notion or even existence of a 'bureaucratic bourgeoisie'. Marxist analysis thus largely failed to illuminate the African post-colonial state beyond a high level of generality simply because it could not convincingly account for the relation between class and state. It, like the developmental approach, was too ahistorical.

Perhaps this is not surprising. Gramsci, rightly regarded as one of the most perceptive of the European Marxists, had clearly shown that the understanding of the modern state required a far more precise and deeper analysis of the historical and cultural context of class development than could ever be provided by Marxist analysts of Africa.[18] The lively debate on the class basis of Ugandan and Kenyan politics reveals in stark terms the limitations of the Marxist political analysis of the state.[19]

The notion of the overdeveloped state was conceived partly in reaction to the shortcomings of the other two approaches and partly out of the recognition that, since the post-colonial state was historically specific, it might also be conceptually specific.[20]

The starting point for the notion of the overdeveloped state was the historically accurate observation that the post-colonial state essentially derived from the colonial state. Its size, structure, organisation and its political role had largely been determined by the operational requirements of the colonial state. After independence, the state did not seem to be congruent either with the needs or the resources of the new nation. For example, it was obvious that post-colonial states were overmanned, overbureaucratised and overpampered. These were the conditions most congenial to the operation of the colonial state but they were hardly the most auspicious for the effectiveness or financial viability of the newly independent nation-state.

Furthermore, the power of the post-colonial state appeared awesome, almost limitless. It seemed that at independence it had suddenly and artificially been endowed with an inordinate degree of power, given the means to control the fate and the resources of the independent country effectively unhindered and unaccountable. It was not just that the post-colonial state possessed all the formal powers and attributes of the colonial state, it was also that it was not subject to the constraints of colonial political accountability. Until new principles of political accountability were established, the post-colonial state was in effect largely unrestrained.

In short, then, the post-colonial state (in all its manifold ramifications) in Africa was overwhelmingly the dominant actor in the new political community and the holders of state power were overwhelmingly the most powerful and privileged members of that community. As a consequence, politics in post-colonial Africa rapidly began to turn on the control and composition of the state. Political success and failure were now necessarily determined by one's position in relation to the state.[21]

The notion of the overdeveloped state provided one important insight into the nature of the post-colonial state in that it highlighted the peculiarly perverse reality of an apparently top-heavy, lopsided, political system. It also provided a plausible account of why, very soon after independence, African politics seemed to become a naked competition for control of the state. Coups, assassinations, violence, ethnic strife, all appeared to be single-mindedly geared to the seizure of state power. It was thus an interpretative advance over the two previous concepts.

Nevertheless, it rested on two important assumptions which subsequent events invalidated. First, it assumed that, in and of itself, the analysis of the state politics of a particular African country made possible an understanding of its contemporary politics. Second, it assumed that the power of the state was proportional to its (over)development, in other words that the post-colonial state was indeed truly a political Leviathan.[22]

The analytical process by which it became apparent that African politics could not be explained simply in terms of the politics of the state was the starting point for the realisation that the state was not as powerful as it had been conceived to be. The conceptual limitations of the notion of the overdeveloped state were exposed not so much because its analysis was inaccurate but because its importance within the body politic had been misconceived. The state was indeed overdeveloped and, indeed, it was the central actor in the political arena. But it was neither as central nor were the boundaries of the political arena as clear-cut as they had been conceived to be.

I do not want here to engage in further theoretical debate about the notion of the post-colonial state. Rather I should like to draw from recent work on the African state to show the usefulness, and by implication the limitations, of all three conceptualisations. This work illuminates a number of political processes at work in contemporary Africa and, in particular, highlights two aspects of the state which are essential to its political analysis.

First, as Bayart writes, the state is an excrescence in that it did not, as in Europe or Asia, grow organically from and against civil society.[23] Because of this it is both soft and overdeveloped. By this I mean that, although it is overdeveloped in the sense discussed above, the post-colonial state is not as solidly anchored to African political communities as the European modern state was to European societies.[24] In this respect, therefore, it is soft: weak in foundations, structurally deficient, without deep legitimacy and generally lacking the political means of its putative power over civil society.

As a consequence, second, the state, or rather the holders of state power, are seeking constantly to achieve and maintain (economic and political) hegemony. State power is a necessary but not always a sufficient condition for (economic and political) hegemony.[25] This is because, despite the received wisdom, the post-colonial state in Africa is neither as powerful nor as monolithic as has often been assumed. And it is precisely the understanding of how powerful and how monolithic it is which can provide insights into its actual, rather than imagined, role in contemporary Africa.

To understand the post-colonial state in Africa, whatever its complexion and however it was born, it is necessary to start from the colonial state. The colonial state, whatever the colonial power, had certain important characteristics which distinguish it from others, notably the early and modern European states.[26] This is not to say that there are no connections between these different historical types but simply that it is imperative to understand the differences before making any assumptions about their commonality as states.

The colonial state was the creature of very specific historical circumstances. Broadly, it was the legal and political superstructure invented to control and manage the colonial territories acquired in Africa through conquest. What sort of state was constructed derived essentially from the nature of the imperial state and from the nature of its objectives in Africa. There were in this respect some important differences between the colonial powers, differences which have a bearing on the analysis of particular colonial and post-colonial states. But I am concerned here to paint a broad canvas.

All colonial states issued from conquest.[27] All meant to establish imperial sovereignty on the conquered territories. All sought to legitimate their rule and to ensure their subjects' allegiance. All set up the administration and infrastructure needed to rule the colonies at minimal (financial and coercive) cost to the empire. All were charged with exploiting the resources of the colonies. Finally, all attempted (in their very different ways) to 'civilise' their colonial subjects in their own image.

The colonial state was thus a conquest state. Like all conquest states, it embodied the tensions of being both an outpost of the empire and an autonomous state. Like all conquest states, it needed local collaborators in order to rule – collaboration is always cheaper and infinitely preferable to force.[28] Like all conquest states, it attempted to invent a new political community to suit its imperial designs. The fact that the colonial state was a conquest state had important consequences.

First, the colonial state rested on force, however much it appeared to rule by consent.[29] Colonial rule was not old or deep enough for colonial legitimacy to be more than superficial. Challenges to colonial rule were necessarily challenges to the state and, ultimately, they were always met by force. Second, the colonial state was the architect of the political community. It defined the boundaries of the community, created its political infrastructure and invented the rules of the game, rules which could always arbitrarily be changed to suit the situation at hand.

Third, the colonial state was the dominant economic actor. It created a currency; it levied taxes; it developed markets; it codified the uses of labour; it introduced new crops; it controlled production, internal trade and export; it brought in foreign labourers or encouraged settlers, etc. Above all, the colonial state sought to integrate the economies of the colonies into the imperial economy and in so doing it was at once the arbiter and the main agent of economic activity.[30]

The colonial state was also a bureaucratic state, in the sense defined by Weber, a state the *modus operandi* of which was essentially new in Africa.[31] But whereas bureaucratic states elsewhere (e.g., Europe, China) had developed internally in symbiotic relation with civil society, the colonial state was imposed from above. This meant that the political community and civil society were made to adapt to the bureaucratic state rather than, as historically had been the case, the reverse. The creation of a bureaucratic state in such conditions had important consequences for the development of civil society which I discuss in the next chapter. Suffice it to say here that it imprinted an indelibly powerful bureaucratic mould on colonial politics.

The boundaries of the political sphere, the rules of political activity, the identity of political actors, the very language of politics, were all the product of a bureaucratic interpretation of politics. The establishment of a bureaucracy, at once the symbol and the structure of the colonial state, largely defined the relationship between the individual and the state. To the individual, the bureaucracy in effect *was* the state. To be a colonial subject meant to enter into a relationship with the colonial bureaucracy.

The colonial state made the law, its bureaucracy implemented it, adjudicated, passed judgement and carried out sentences. The bureaucracy defined the identities and occupations of the Africans and determined what their lawful activities were or could be. In short, for all practical purposes, it was the bureaucracy which ruled over the colonial subjects. But access to the bureaucracy was also one of the chief means of personal advancement for the African. Admission to the bureaucracy, by means of an education provided or regulated by the colonial state, was not just a badge of civilisation but also one of the most secure and rewarding investment of one's labour. The colonial state, therefore, not only created a bureaucracy, it also created an indigenous bureaucratic class and with it a bureaucratic mentality.[32]

Finally, the colonial state was centralised and coercive.[33] It was centralised because its legitimacy ultimately depended on its ability to control and manage the political community it had created rather than on enabling representation of its constituent parts. A centralised state is not a state where there are no local structures of government but one in which local government is accountable to central government rather than to the citizens of the locality. The colonial state was never defined in relation to its constituent, parts; rather the constituent parts were defined in relation to the state. Local government was the transmission belt of central government, however sophisticated consultative or 'representative' councils appeared to be or however 'indirect' colonial rule was claimed to be.[34]

The colonial state was coercive not simply because it had the monopoly of legally sanctioned force – all states possess such monopoly – but because colonial coercion was ultimately sanctioned by colonial political accountability, that is, by political power external to the (colonial and African) political community. The use of coercion was not simply determined by the political calculus of state power but by reference to the ultimate sanction of the colonial secretary, himself only accountable to the imperial government. The colonial state thus derived its power from legally sanctioned coercion unaccountable to the subjects of the state.

The rule of law and the use of force were, in the end, legitimated only by the colonial 'civilising' mission.[35] The colonial judges upheld the law and the colonial police maintained the peace, but the content of the law and the nature of the peace derived from colonial policies reflecting imperial imperatives.[36] Even decolonisation, for example, was not so much the process by which *colonial* states were becoming less coercive because they were becoming more accountable to their colonial subjects, as the process by which *imperial* states responded to the effects of colonial and international pressure on their own domestic constituencies. Thus could nationalist leaders be thrown into jail only to be released later to head the post-colonial governments.[37]

It was precisely because of the overwhelmingly dominant position of the state in the colonial order that the primary purpose of independence was accurately perceived by the nationalists to be the conquest of the colonial state. Witness Nkrumah's famous 'Seek Ye the Political Kingdom'. Whether they were radical or not, the nationalists had no doubt that the capture of state power would *ipso facto* give them the means of their political ambitions. To capture the state was to acquire the means of creating a nation-state, that is to fashion a modern African political community according to new principles of political accountability.

Conceptually, therefore, the nationalists made a distinction between the ideological basis of the state and its instrumentality. What was wrong with the colonial state was that it fulfilled the colonial mission, not that it was bureaucratic. Change the mission and its machinery could be used for nationalist, meaning African, purposes.[38] With hindsight it has been argued that the nationalists were misled in such beliefs and that, in fact, the reverse happened: the nature of the colonial state overdetermined the nature of the post-colonial state.

Whether this is right or not is now a moot point. The nature of the colonial state was such that it was historically correct to assume that the takeover of state power was a necessary condition for the creation of the independent nation-state. In the African colonial context there never was the remotest possibility that the nationalists, whatever their political inclinations, would ever be in the position to dispense with the machinery of the colonial state and to create a new state *ab initio*.

The governments of the independent African nations thus inherited the colonial state, even if what they inherited differed greatly in different colonies.[39] The characteristics of the post-colonial state were therefore indeed overdetermined in that the very existence of the nation-state depended on a political superstructure elaborated by the colonial power.[40] To have contested the legitimacy of the state would have meant contesting the legitimacy of the nation. Where (e.g., Sudan, Uganda, Chad, Nigeria) the legitimacy of the state has been contested, the nation has risked disintegrating as nation.

The legitimacy of the post-colonial state *qua* state was largely tied to the very machinery which had been installed by the colonial masters for their own purposes. It would thus necessarily be the machinery which the masters of the independent governments would have to use. For, even if there were good political reasons for wanting to change or overhaul the structure of the inherited state, there were often compelling practical reasons why it was not possible or advisable to do so.

More often than not nationalist unity had been achieved as the lowest common political denominator. If all (or at least most) agreed on the necessity to oust the colonial masters and take over the state, that is where agreement stopped. To tamper with the received structure was almost necessarily perceived as an attempt to gain unfair political advantage and almost always led to a loss of political legitimacy. At a very fundamental level, therefore, it was the structure of the inherited colonial state which held the nationalist state together – at least in the early years of independence.[41]

Although the structure and organisation of the post-colonial state usually replicated that of the colonial state, the end of colonial rule created a void at the core of the political order which had to be filled by the nationalists. How they filled it determined how the post-colonial state was transformed.[42] The post-colonial state had to invent new principles of political accountability.

Where there was constitutional decolonisation, the colonial powers sought to establish a framework for 'democratic' political accountability replicating that of the metropolis. Where the colonial powers were ousted by force of arms, the nationalists were in a position to introduce their own principles of political accountability. Whatever the case, however, the new principles had to be adapted to the inherited colonial state. The fact that political legitimacy was so intimately bound up with control of the state in a context where principles of political accountability were still shifting created special political problems.

In Nigeria, for instance, the constitutional democratic framework devised by the British proved to be a less than ideal principle of political accountability. The new independent nation-state of Nigeria was inherently unstable, as all colonial officials well knew. In the event, the operation of the post-colonial state came into conflict with 'democratic' politics and the political system collapsed with the 1966 coups and the ensuing civil war.[43]

Equally, in Guinea-Bissau, where independence was achieved through armed struggle, the nationalists found that they lacked the means of capturing the inherited colonial bureaucracy, Maintaining control of the post-colonial state quickly took precedence over establishing the new principles of 'revolutionary democracy'. By the time of the 1980 coup, the PAIGC's nationalist legitimacy had largely dissipated.[44]

Furthermore, at independence, the nature of state power changed in three crucial respects: in the notion of state legitimacy; in the relationship between the individual and the state; and in the relationship between state resources and state action.

Independence changed the notion of state legitimacy. Whether decolonisation was the outcome of gradual and legal devolution of power or the outcome of an armed struggle, it created new principles of political accountability which affected the legitimacy of the state. Whereas the legitimacy of the colonial state had rested on its ability to maintain the colonial order, the legitimacy of its successor lay in the extent to which the nationalists were seen both to embody the African political community and to represent its aspirations.[45]

Since the legitimacy of the post-colonial state issued from its (real or perceived) nationalist success, consequently, the notion of state legitimacy became inextricably linked to that of the successful capture of power. What this meant was that the legitimacy of the post-colonial state derived more from it having power than from the legitimacy of its role within the political community. It was legitimate that the 'right' nationalists should capture state power but the way in which power was captured and exercised would inevitably affect the very legitimacy of the state itself. The notion of the legitimacy of the post-colonial state as it evolved historically implied a conceptual equation between the legitimacy of power and the legitimacy of the state *qua* state.

Second, independence changed the relation between the individual and the state. On the one hand, it abolished all legal, economic, racial and political restrictions on those who hitherto had been colonial subjects. Overnight the state lost the official means arbitrarily to discriminate against certain individuals or groups of individuals. The post-colonial state was self-evidently the state of all citizens, regardless of their previous position in the colonial order. On the other hand, it acquired new obligations *vis-à-vis* its citizens. The universal ideologies (whether radical or conservative), to which all nationalists subscribed, committed the state to provide the same range of services which modern post-war European states provided.

Much was expected of post-colonial states partly because, in time, much came to be expected of colonial states and partly because the nationalists believed, or convinced their followers that they believed, in the creative, productive and munificent potential of independence. Independence erased much of the distance which had existed between rulers and ruled in the colonial order. While the post-colonial state started life with infinitely more popular support than the colonial state ever could have mustered, it also started life with infinitely more commitments. The new masters found themselves with new obligations and less space for tergiversating.[46]

Finally, independence changed the nature of the relation between state resources and state action. Partly because of the expectations generated by the nationalist campaign, independence brought greater and more pressing demands than were ever made on the colonial state. The colonial state, however, had had access to extra-colonial (financial, political, symbolic or coercive) resources with which to discharge its duties. The post-colonial state did not. This is important. The state is defined, perceived, understood, largely through what it does and how it does it. Colonial states could deploy resources from the metropolis or the empire to meet new demands and challenges. From the very beginning it was clear that the post-colonial states would not be in the position to deploy resources on the colonial scale.[47]

It is true that independent African countries could call on the former colonial powers or other nations to provide aid and assistance;[48] but such external resources could never match, in scale or timing, those available to the colonial states. Above all, the independent countries had no immediate control over such extra-national resources. The post-colonial state thus found itself called upon to match or exceed the achievements of the colonial state with a fraction of the resources available. Though it started life with an immense capital of symbolic resources (e.g., nationalist fervour) which greatly added to its political capital, its financial and economic resources could not possibly match its stated ambition. Disappointment engendered discontent. Consequently, and for reasons of expediency, the post-colonial state became increasingly coercive.

At this stage of the discussion it might well be asked why so far I have eschewed any discussion of the relation between state and class. The reason is simple. The class composition of the post-colonial state was not nearly as important as has generally been claimed.

In the first place, the new holders of state power hailed broadly from similar backgrounds: with some exceptions, new rather than old, modern rather than 'traditional', colonial rather than pre-colonial élites.[49] Second, the 'class position' of these new élites derived largely from their place in the colonial order rather than from their position in the 'capitalist' economy. Their place in the 'capitalist' economy was thus largely a product of colonial politics. In other words, their élite status did not necessarily come from their economic position; their economic or 'class' position was frequently a product of their status in the colonial order. It is in this sense, and this sense only, that they can legitimately be qualified as *petits bourgeois*.

It is true that 'class' gain could be achieved under colonialism, that there were many successful 'capitalists' and entrepreneurs. Yet, it was more often the case that economic success came to those who were well placed in the colonial order, whether they had been economically successful in the pre-colonial period or not. Notwithstanding the extraordinary case of the migrant cocoa-farmers of Southern Ghana, successful 'capitalist' entrepreneurship in colonial Africa was almost always the consequence (rather than the cause) of colonial privilege.[50]

Under colonial rule, the achievement and maintenance of economic power was inextricably linked with the politics of power. The colonial period clearly showed how control of the state meant control of the economy. An essential aspect of the whole process of nationalism was, consequently, the determination of the nationalists and of those who supported them to gain access to the economic leverage which control of the state would provide.

In this sense, state power determined class position rather than the reverse. Political hegemony determined economic hegemony. What this implies is that the colonial economic élites needed to gain access to the state if they were not to lose economic hegemony to those who captured the state at independence. The post-colonial state in Africa was thus not so much the political superstructure of a given economic order as the political infrastructure for economic hegemony. It was not so much the reflection of class dominance as the locus of class formation, not so much the politico-legal protector of class appropriation as the battlefield for economic hegemony. To understand hegemony in contemporary Africa, therefore, it is more fruitful to look at the multiple and complex ways in which power has determined class than merely at class formation *per se*.

To conclude, then, the concept of the post-colonial state which I propose, a notion now amply confirmed by monographic research, is at heart relational rather than structural. It contains the notion of the new dialectical relationship between state and civil society which was brought about by the rupture in political accountability caused by independence. In other words, I argue that the state cannot simply be understood as a political 'entity', however sophisticated our analysis of the many components of its structure, but rather that it must be seen as the focal point of the drive for hegemony.[51] It is the drive for hegemony, the political contest for supremacy between state and civil society, which is the hallmark of contemporary African politics.

In this respect, then, independence was a transformation of the political order which was sudden and the consequences of which were determinant for the political causalities at work in the new political community. It has now become clearer that the effects of these changed causalities led to the development of a state, the chief characteristic of which was its drive for political and economic hegemony. Thus the key question in the political analysis of post-colonial Africa is the extent to which the state has managed to fulfil its hegemonic ambitions.[52] And that has largely been determined by the politics of civil society – a concept to which I now turn.

5 Civil Society[1]

The notion of civil society, like that of the state, is not new to political theory.[2] It is now being introduced into the political analysis of Africa largely because the (over)emphasis on the role of the state has led to a definition of the political sphere as being virtually coterminous with the politics of the state. As the interpretative capacity of state-centred conceptual frameworks has decreased over time, it has become quite evident that political scientists have been led astray by the mirage of high politics: constitutions, parties, governments, parliaments, ideology, etc.

Not only is the state being revealed as much less powerful than it was conceived to be, but in some cases it can be seen to have lost political control altogether (e.g., Chad after the fall of Tombalbaye, Liberia in 1990/91, Uganda under Amin, Zaïre for most of Mobutu's reign, Mozambique since 1980). Generally, recent research has shown that the state is neither all-encompassing nor all-signifiying; that the essence of politics does not just lie in the format, structural, institutional or mobilisational, of the state, but in the interaction between state and civil society. It is now clearer that the examination of the politics of civil society, low politics (or *la politique par le bas*), is central to political analysis. It is also a key to understanding the state itself.[3]

The significance and character of the African post-colonial state, therefore, derive in large measure from the nature of civil society and its mode of coexistence with it. For states do not operate in a vacuum and, ultimately, it is their relation to civil society which determines their complexion and the fate of their policies. Successful states (e.g., Senegal, Côte d'Ivoire, Cameroon, Tanzania) devise *modi operandi* which adapt and respond to civil society and in so doing they construct workable principles of political accountability. Unsuccessful states either dissolve (e.g., Chad, Sudan, Uganda), absorbed piecemeal by civil society, or they turn to absolutism, tyranny, in opposition to civil society (e.g., Guinea under Sékou Touré, Uganda under Amin, Equatorial Guinea under Macias Nguema).[4]

So what is civil society? Although there are countless possible and plausible definitions of civil society, the genesis of the notion matters less than its conceptualisation for African politics. In the African post-colonial context, where the state preceded the nation, civil society is necessarily determined first and foremost in its relation to the construction of the state.

Here I take my cue from Bayart:

Though it is arguable that the concept of civil society is not applicable outside European history I shall define it provisionally as 'society in its relation with the state . . . in so far as it is in confrontation with the state' or, more precisely, as the process by which society seeks to 'breach' and counteract the simultaneous 'totalisation' unleashed by the state . . . The notion of civil society is thus an ambivalent (and not just conflictive), complex and dynamic relation between state and society. [Civil society] is not necessarily a discrete entity completely external to an equally discrete source of power. That much is obvious in the case of institutions or organisations which represent civil society within political society, such as parliaments, parties or trade unions. But it is equally true of the power structures themselves, these are by no means immune to the particularistic pulls of civil society . . . Moreover, civil society is not necessarily embodied in a single, identifiable structure. It is by its very nature plural and covers all sorts of different practices; any unity there is requires human creativity. Finally, civil society is not merely the expression of dominated social groups. It encompasses not only popular modes of political action but also the claims of those socially dominant groups which are no less excluded from direct participation in political power.[5]

As Bayart rightly emphasises, in the African context, civil society, in so far as it can be formally defined, consists not just of what is obviously not part of the state but also of all who may have become powerless or disenfranchised: not just villagers, fishermen, nomads, members of different age groups, village councillors, or slum dwellers, but also professionals, politicians, priests and mullahs, intellectuals, military officers and all others who are, or feel they are, without due access to the state.

Civil society is thus a vast ensemble of constantly changing groups and individuals whose only common ground is their exclusion from the state, their consciousness of their externality and their potential opposition to the state.[6] Those very few members of the *polis* who have no such consciousness (for the state in contemporary Africa is overwhelmingly the central political referent) are politically amorphous, though not necessarily politically insignificant, members of civil society.

A useful distinction, therefore, lies in the notion of power. At independence, civil society in Africa possessed formal power through the system of representation established by decolonisation. Soon, however, formal representation lost its substance almost everywhere in Africa and civil society became devoid of formal power.[7] Thereafter, its force lay in its capacity to resist, penetrate or neutralise the state, and thereby to re-appropriate some (informal) power. Civil society in contemporary Africa is thus often without formal powers but it is not, and therein lies the importance of its study, without power. However, the informal power of civil society is most often obscured by the apparent hegemony of the state.[8]

The state aims at political and economic hegemony. Civil society is the object of this hegemonic appropriation. The African post-colonial state has sought since independence to capture as much of civil society as it can manage. Civil society, for its part, seeks to evade or undermine such capture and it is essentially this process of reaction to the state which defines it as civil society.[9] In other words, civil society is transformed from the object of the state's hegemonic drive into the self-conscious subject of its own politics in the process of responding (actively or, more frequently, passively) to the state project of domination. Its politics, therefore, are the politics of counter-hegemony.[10]

This is not to say that civil society speaks with one voice for it is divided into a myriad of individuals or ensembles of individuals, each with its own voice. Nor is it to say that the politics of the many constituent parts of civil society are homogeneous, coherent, logical, purposeful, even less mutually supportive. It is precisely the multi-layered complexity of the politics of civil society which makes it so difficult to understand and so easy to discount. The politics of civil society do not readily fit into our standard categories of political analysis.[11] Nevertheless, it is important to attempt to provide some conceptualisation of the counter-hegemonic politics of civil society.

Individually, collectively, by avoidance, stealth or confrontation, civil society in post-colonial Africa has been responding to the state. Its action becomes political when it is counter-hegemonic, that is when it is intended to impinge on state politics, as opposed to being merely anomic. The form which this action takes may or may not be definable as political in the conventional sense. Often it is only noticeable in the failure of a given course of state action or even the absence of action – as void is only conceivable as the absence of matter. For example, the strength of the politics of rural civil society is rarely apparent.[12] Rural dwellers, atomised and seemingly passive, do not overtly challenge the state. Yet, their decision to increase or reduce production, surely one of the central economic factors in the life of African countries today, is very largely the consequence of their response to state politics.[13]

It will be objected that the notion of civil society is a concept specifically derived from a particular European intellectual and historical context. This is true, and yet it seems to me that the concept is eminently appropriate to the political analysis of contemporary Africa, even if it needs to be rethought.

At this stage the notion of civil society in Africa remains conceptually somewhat loose and difficult to turn operational. It does not lend itself neatly to definition. I hope that, in the process of enunciating what I take to be the specifically African aspects of the concept and furnishing examples of what I mean, it will become clearer why the notion of civil society is central to an understanding of power in Africa.[14]

What is specific about post-colonial Africa, then, is not that state and civil society confront each other in the political arena but (especially in contrast to Europe) the position from which they do so. In Europe, the modern state is the outcome of struggles within civil society. In contemporary Africa it is the reverse. Because the African post-colonial state is historically prior to the nation and because it is necessarily hegemonic, it is the state which determines the texture of the politics of civil society. This means that the nature of the relationship (its language, form and content) between state and civil society is, or at least appears to be, dictated by the state, that is by the discourse of high politics.[15]

The politics of civil society are often not registered or not understood simply because they are not intelligible to the political language of the state. Similarly, the state defines the boundaries of political legitimacy, so that the political action(s) of civil society are almost inevitably confined to the realm of political illegitimacy.[16] When the legitimacy of the state itself is reduced or disintegrates, the realm of legitimate political action narrows and, eventually, withers. The voice of civil society is then often officially silenced even if it continues to be heard.

It is important to understand the place of the notion of civil society within the conceptual framework offered in this book. Civil society is not synonymous with political community. The community is the ensemble of the citizens, regardless of who they are and what political power they possess. It is an objectively given whole. There may be questions as to whether some individuals (e.g., Asians in Uganda, Lebanese and Syrians in Senegal) should be part of that community but, at any given time in history, they objectively are or are not part of the community.

Civil society, on the other hand, is defined *in relation to* the state or rather the politics of civil society are defined *in relation to* the politics of the state. Civil society is, therefore, subjective, unstable, discontinuous and unquantifiable.[17] It can only be identified by approximation, *ex post facto*, in the effects which its politics have – somewhat in the manner in which the uncertainty principle applies in physics.

The nature of the relationship between state and civil society is governed by the principle of political accountability extant. At its most general level, political accountability defines the rules of conduct within a political community.[18] In its specifics it determines the relationship between the rulers and the ruled.

Where accountability has depth, where power is legitimate and representation effective, the politics of civil society will be accommodated within the political system. Where accountability is shallow, power challenged and representation feeble, the politics of civil society will tend to operate outside the political pale. In other words, the principle of political accountability, the extent of state legitimacy, and the nature of political representation determine whether the politics of civil society is 'legal' or 'illegal'. The greater the political accountability, the more extensive the realm of legal politics will be. Protests, debates, strikes, etc., are legal within political systems where political accountability has some depth. They are not immediately deemed banditry or hooliganism.

But where the politics of civil society is *ipso facto* illegal, where the realm of legal politics is virtually nil, the confrontation between state and civil society becomes sharper, more extreme and more final.[19] The space for accommodation narrows. The state is quick to reject the legitimacy of any civil society politics and to repress it. By extension, it brands any (overt or covert) action from any section of civil society as illegal. For example, young delinquents, beggars or street-traders are often seen as political trouble-makers and dealt with as such. Whether delinquents really are political opponents is almost a moot question. By treating them as such, they are given a political quality which they might not otherwise have had.[20]

Looked at historically, the relationship in post-colonial Africa between the state and civil society derives in part from that between state and civil society in the colonial period. The politics of colonial civil society contained three distinct (though overlapping) components: the politics of so-called 'traditional' society; the politics of modern civil society and nationalist politics.[21]

To begin with the last, from the perspective of the colonial state, nationalist politics was usually conceived as the politics of civil society. Insofar as the colonial state did not usually give voice (and when it did, nationalism had won) to those who agitated for the end of colonial rule, nationalism operated largely through the politics of civil society. Because independence became a political goal shared by the immense majority of Africans, nationalist politics tended to dominate the politics of civil society and obscure all else. Although nationalist politics was by far the most visible and the most successfully articulated aspect of the politics of late colonial civil society, it was not the only, or even necessarily the most significant, aspect of the politics of civil society under colonial rule. In the long term, the politics of 'traditional' and modern civil society perhaps mattered more.

The distinction between 'traditional' and modern (colonial) civil society is not neat, nor is it easy to make in practice, such is the interpenetration of the two. Conceptually, however, it is useful to try to understand the difference. By 'traditional' – a most unsatisfactory but inevitable formulation – I mean deriving directly and organically from pre-colonial civil society. By modern I mean civil society as it was created under colonial rule.[22]

Of course, in the real world individuals belonged, and continue to belong, both to 'traditional' and modern society. In colonial Africa there were very few (if any) who were simply 'traditional' or modern creatures. In some real and important sense, we are all hybrid creatures. And it is precisely this mix of 'traditional' and modern which needs to be understood in order to understand the politics of post-colonial civil society.[23]

Pre-colonial African societies operated according to certain sets of moral, religious and philosophical principles which guided everyday life and marked the boundaries of social, economic and political activities. In such societies – as in all societies – there were rights, duties and obligations, there were important social, kin and family ties, and there were (religious, medical, political, social or economic) élites. One of the hallmarks of pre-colonial society was that the boundaries between the social, religious, political and economic were porous and fluid. Nor was there a notion of the individual distinct from that of the community – as there was to be in the colonial world.[24]

The pre-colonial social order was thus organised according to principles of social existence which favoured the community over the individual and conceived of the world as an interconnected whole rather than as the sum total of discrete components. There was, consequently, no clear division between civil society and the political sphere except, perhaps, in those African societies (e.g., West African states) where the state was highly developed. But even there, there was a far greater degree of interpenetration between the social and the politic realms than was to be found in colonial societies. Pre-colonial civil society was, to simplify a highly complex historical process, largely covalent with political society.[25]

The colonial process – that form of civilisation which befell African societies – set out to modernise 'traditional' society. This meant, *inter alia*, to separate political from civil society along European lines. The colonial order thus decreed, or at least attempted to decree, distinctions between the individual and the community, the religious and the temporal, the civic and the political, the state and civil society. It abolished, or sought to abolish, those 'traditional' attributes of individuals and communities which were in conflict with the theory or practice of the modern colonial order. It integrated, or at least attempted to integrate, those characteristics of the pre-colonial socio-political order which were compatible, useful or expedient for the 'modernity' of colonial rule.[26]

Although colonial rule created a modern state, on the model of the European state, the civil society which developed in relation, in reaction, to that state, was inevitably a combination of modern and 'traditional'. The colonial order defined the area of legitimate political activity. Civil society, as conceived in colonial terms, was given legal means of representation in the various modern and 'traditional' representative bodies which were established within the colony. Nevertheless, because of the nature of the colonial state, the scope for legal action was narrow. The colonial state had space for only a few collaborators and many of its policies, particularly in settler colonies, were not congenial to the majority of colonial subjects.[27] Civil society grew in size and in strength, eventually becoming a self-conscious opposition to the colonial state.

Whilst nationalist opposition was the overarching modern voice of civil society, the unifying *idéo-logique*, it was neither homogeneous nor was it consistent. Nor, and this is more important, did it necessarily successfully integrate the modern and 'traditional' in colonial civil society. What nationalism did was to articulate the 'traditional' in the modern idiom: it articulated the voice of colonial civil society in the language of the colonial state. Although the nationalists, and even some of the colonialists, knew that this was a very partial translation of the language of colonial civil society, decolonisation was carried out and the post-colonial order was constructed as if nationalism was civil society's single unifying voice.[28]

Whereas the colonial state had attempted to re-create African society into its image of European society, the nationalist state-to-be meant successfully to integrate the 'traditional' and modern. However, because the African nationalist parties were (with few exceptions) in the hands of modern rather than 'traditional' élites, the nationalist (like the colonial) state only recognised those 'traditional' voices which it wanted or needed to recognise. The process of decolonisation thus disenfranchised some 'traditional' voices (e.g., chiefs, spirit mediums), even if (or because) it still acknowledged their power (witness the perennial importance – and today the so called rebirth – of 'witchcraft').[29] In so doing, it added to the potential opposition of 'traditional' civil society to the post-colonial state.

This, of course, is nothing new in the evolution of human societies. As societies move (in complex and rarely linear ways) towards more modern social and political order (whatever the precise meaning of modernity), new voices become dominant and old ones are extinguished. This happened in Europe as it happened in Africa. But the historical circumstances which characterised the rise and fall of the colonial order in Africa made for a much less coherent, continuous and consistent transition. The old did not inform the new nor did the new derive from the old as organically as it had in Europe. In Africa, the European modern colonial social and political order co-existed with a 'traditional' which it neither fully comprehended nor completely dominated.[30]

It is less important here to define precisely what 'traditional' means than to understand that the process of decolonisation did not, as nationalists and Africanists rashly claimed, erase the dualities between 'traditional' and modern found in colonial civil society. Quite the reverse. Decolonisation constructed a social and political order, which the nationalists inherited, with a modern façade but largely 'traditional' foundations. This is evidently not because African society is inherently more 'traditional' than any other society in the world. It is rather because the colonial process of change, a process largely extraneous to the organic development of African societies, was neither deep nor protracted enough to allow for a coherent transition from pre-colonial to post-colonial civil society.

The error made by many nationalists and Africanists alike was to have assumed that there was a directly causal and unilinear link between the processes of colonisation and of 'modernisation'.[31] There was not. And just as it was important to understand how the 'traditional' had been modernised, it would have been important to understand how the modern had been 'traditionalised'.[32] The process of change went both ways, for the process of historical change is always one in which the modern is nourished by the 'traditional'. Modernisation is the transformation rather than the replacement of the 'traditional'.

Colonial civil society was conceptualised the wrong way around. While it was believed that modern civil society had superseded 'traditional' civil society, it had merely been absorbed by it. Although this was not obvious, because the voices of 'traditional' civil society had to be interpreted by the spokesmen of modern civil society (the nationalists), it was nevertheless crucial. In terms of understanding post-colonial civil society, decolonisation was largely a trick of the light. 'Traditional' civil society was obscured by the glitter of modern colonial civil society. Our understanding of the politics of post-colonial civil society has suffered accordingly.[33]

Independence was a rupture, a political revolution, in the relationship between state and civil society. On the surface, the post-colonial state continued where the colonial state had left off, whether the transition of decolonisation had been smooth or not. The post-colonial state appeared to be a modern state, just as its counterpart, civil society, appeared to be modern. The real situation was much more complex. In the first instance, the post-colonial state was, as I have argued, overdeveloped, soft and hegemonic.[34] Furthermore, the very fact that the nationalists were now in power changed the configuration of civil society and the nature of the relationship between state and civil society.

The post-colonial state was confronted by both 'traditional' and modern civil society which it had neither the incentive nor the resources to reform. The new relationship between state and civil society was one in which, on the one hand, the state sought to achieve political and economic hegemony over – to capture – civil society and where, on the other, civil society (in its individual and collective guises) sought to penetrate the state. It became a straightforward competition for power and, in the process of vying for supremacy, the division between 'traditional' and modern civil society (always a tenuous one at best) vanished. Power lay with those who could control, influence or obstruct the state, regardless of whether they were 'traditional' or modern élites.[35]

For example, the question of ethnicity – perhaps the issue which has most divided political analysts of post-colonial Africa – can only be profitably understood if one takes into account its role within civil society. Ethnicity is not, as is now abundantly clear, an attribute of 'traditional' Africa. Nor is it bound to be erased by 'modernisation'. Rather, it is as good an instance as can be found of what I call the 'traditionalisation' of colonial civil society. For ethnicity, as we understand it today, was the colonial (modern) interpretation of one of the many aspects of what was a complex 'traditional' civil society. Ethnicity thus straddles 'traditional' and modern civil society. The apparent flaring up of ethnic politics in post-colonial Africa is, therefore, better understood as part of the contest between state and civil society than as evidence of the resurfacing of the 'dark side of traditional Africa'.[36]

At independence, the state seemed in a position to dictate the rules of the game. As most political observers of contemporary Africa have noted, the post-colonial state was both modern and powerful. It appeared to be in a commanding position 'to capture' most 'traditional' sectors of civil society and continue the modernisation of society begun by the colonial state.[37] It was a question of political development, of the institutionalisation of modern political practices and the routinisation of political accountability. In that view, it seemed clear that it was the modern elements of civil society (e.g., the Western educated, the economically successful, the armed forces) which had the greatest chance of penetrating the state or exercising decisive influence over it.

This interpretation was strengthened by the events which followed independence. As its political grip tightened, the state looked more and more able to control the pressure of civil society. The narrowing of representation, the increase in coercion and the greater bureaucratisation of society all buttressed the position of the power-holders and reduced the (overt) means by which large sections of civil society could exercise influence over the state. The state grew larger, more all-encompassing, economically more dominant and politically more powerful. It seemed well advanced in what Bayart calls the 'totalisation' of society.[38] Civil society appeared increasingly weak and bereft of resources.

Yet the process was not nearly as smooth as it seemed in the heyday of state power which followed the first few years of independence. The rulers (by now as often as not military men) and those who observed them were easily misled by the apparent strength of the state and the apparent weakness of civil society. Force was mistaken for power. Because states were coercive, repressive, easily violent against their citizens, they were thought to be strong. The reverse was the case. The greater need for the use of force was, in fact, an indication of the (real or putative) strength of civil society. It was not, for example, simply a question of Africa not needing multi-party competition, fair elections, civilian governments, or even the rule of law because 'Africa had its own traditions'. It was a question of rulers seeking ways of holding on to power – of successfully resisting the challenges of civil society.[39]

As the arena of legitimate political action shrank (and in some cases disappeared altogether), larger and larger sections of civil society were disenfranchised, that is given less and less legal political space. The politics of civil society were increasingly being deemed illegal. The voice of civil society was muffled, when not silenced altogether. Silence was easily perceived as acquiescence or meekness, at any rate powerlessness. However, the greater the formal powers of the state and the greater the silence, the larger and more threatening civil society loomed.[40]

Where access to the state was increasingly shut out and where civil society was silenced (e.g, Chad, Uganda, Guinea) opposition to the state grew. The legitimacy of state power, and by implication the very legitimacy of the state, were eroded. In countries where state legitimacy disappeared altogether (e.g., Equatorial Guinea, Central African Republic, Uganda), absolute rule was instituted. Absolute rule depends for its survival on naked coercion and cannot be productive.

In most African countries, where the state was concerned to maintain some legitimacy, it had no alternative but to coopt and coerce different sections of civil society judiciously. Cooptation comes at a price and, the more limited the legal space allowed civil society, the greater that price is. Coercion also comes at a price. The balance between cooptation and coercion is difficult to maintain where there is limited accountability and legitimacy. To maintain it means restoring some power to (some sections) of civil society. In practice, it is the measure in which states succeed in this difficult balancing act which determines the nature of the state, its power, and the complexion of its relation with civil society.

Post-colonial civil society thus reacted to the politics of the state. The extent of its strength or weakness was not easily judged by the legal space it occupied or the vigour of its voice. Rather, it is better assessed in the success or failure of the state's political and economic hegemonic drive. Looked at in this way it becomes immediately obvious that the apparent power of the post-colonial state is often illusory.[41] It has certainly not been a one-way contest. Many of the state's victories over civil society have been Pyrrhic. It is true that holding state power remains the most decisive asset for individual and collective accumulation. Powerful men are rich men in Africa, as they are in many parts of the world. However, there are also countervailing pressures from civil society which limit the extent to which power and accumulation go hand in hand. There are also rich and powerful men within civil society.

Several processes are at work. First, power comes at a cost: cooptation, clientelism, patrimonialism, prebendalism and corruption are expensive. In other words, individuals or groups within civil society must be appeased, rewarded, bought off or maintained in order for rulers to stay in power. Second, coercion itself is expensive: the armed forces, the police, the paramilitary, the presidential guard, etc., must all be satisfied if they are not to take power themselves.

Third, production (which I discuss in the next chapter) depends largely on the political balance between state and civil society. Where the state appropriates in excess of what is tolerable to the directly productive arm of civil society (e.g., farmers, peasants, workers, tradesmen) production declines and/or is diverted away from the official economy. The state may continue to appropriate a larger proportion of production but production can be made to decline to such a degree that appropriation also declines in absolute terms. The search for absolute hegemony is inimical to production.[42]

There can be no clearer example of the vacuousness of state power and of the power of a seemingly shattered civil society than that provided by the cases of African countries where, because of the politics of the relationship between the state and civil society, the state loses control over production. Uganda under Idi Amin illustrates the consequences of the unbridled exercise of state power.[43] Production escaped the state and the so-called parallel economy far outstripped the official economy. The same is true today in Mobutu's Zaïre.[44] In Ghana and Guinea (Conakry), for example, a very significant proportion of production was at times diverted illegally across the border.[45] In Guinea-Bissau, Mozambique and Angola, attempts at state hegemonic economic control (whether because of war or ideology) led to a collapse in production, a flourishing parallel economy and a return to economic autarchy in some regions.[46]

Thus even, or perhaps particularly, in countries where the state appears all-encompassing and politically all-powerful, civil society can respond by reducing and/or diverting production from the state. Given the hegemonic ambitions of post-colonial African states, to be able to undermine the productive basis of the state, even if it is at some economic cost to oneself, is to have considerable power indeed. The present struggle in South Africa illustrates the general principle I am putting forward here: it is the putative power of economically necessary but otherwise disenfranchised black workers to undermine the productive capacity of the South African economy which has been the most serious long-term threat to Apartheid.[47]

There are countless other (if less spectacular) ways in which a largely disenfranchised civil society 'chips at the state from below' and, sometimes, even from above.[48] Religious leaders, particularly Muslim, often give political leadership to the believers and the state must listen. 'Traditional' élites also can represent groups of citizens which are, or perceive themselves to be, disenfranchised. Similarly, university staff and students, businessmen, market-women, miners, plantation-workers, war veterans, writers and artists, etc., can give voice to the voiceless and powerless. Even the refugee, the destitute, the ill, the starving and the dying can reduce the power of those who control the state and influence policy decisions, for it is now often a constituency with powerful international representation.

As these examples make clear, it is indispensable to conceptualise politics in Africa more in terms of the ever-fluctuating power relations between constantly changing state and civil society than in terms of the logistics and topography of formal power.[49] Consequently, it is important to understand the multiple ways in which the politics of civil society impinge on the day-to-day politics of post-colonial African countries. This demands that we shift the focus of our analysis away from the state and rethink our notion of the politic in post-colonial Africa. At the very least it means giving equal attention to high and low politics.[50] Given the bias so far in favour of high politics it is particularly urgent to begin to devise ways of analysing low politics. This entails not just identifying those groups within civil society which are seemingly of greatest political relevance but also devising methods to decode their language and make sense of their action.[51]

While it is relatively simple, for example, to analyse the politics of the armed forces or of significant religious groups, it is far more difficult to interpret the contemporary relevance of ethnic politics, and even more the

politics of those who are by definition atomised and voiceless (e.g., peasants, refugees, nomads).[52] When this is accepted, it becomes immediately
apparent that it is not possible to understand the politics of civil society
without a sharper and historically deeper notion of the evolution of the
politics of so-called 'traditional' (civil) society. The relentless focus on the
colonial notion of civil society and the post-colonial state perspective on
civil society have left us with far too little understanding of the evolution of
the 'underbelly' of African society.

Trying to understand better the 'underbelly' of African society does not
mean following the lead, as some Africanists have done, of those African
politicians who, tautologically, explain African politics by means of their
'Africanness'. Quite the reverse. It means following the lead of scholars
like Iliffe or Polly Hill who bring a historically comparative perspective to
the examination of certain sections of civil society.[53] African rulers today
may be cheered by Iliffe's revelation that poverty in Africa is not a recent
phenomenon but they are less likely to be cheered by his conclusion that
many African states today are worse at alleviating poverty than colonial
states were, and that the failure to alleviate poverty is politically consequential. Equally, they may not be cheered much by the (re)discovery that
when the rains fail the rulers must pay – indeed, many African rulers have
already paid dearly for drought.

Polly Hill's examination of rural indebtedness and rural inequality, to
give other examples, are far more relevant to the understanding of the
politics of rural civil society than most discussions on the African peasantry.[54]
There can be few more revealing insights of the mentality of rural producers
than that provided by the preamble, 'How the farmers outwitted the bureaucrats', to her latest book. She writes:

> One of the underlying themes of this book is that farmers in the rural
> tropical world are commonly not the docile, subservient or angry
> 'peasants' portrayed in many textbooks and official publications, but
> rather men and women with a proper and controlled contempt for external
> authority – a contempt which they often delight in concealing under a
> veneer of acquiescence.[55]

David Lan's study of the role of spirit mediums in the politics of
Zimbabwe's nationalist war is equally revealing.[56] It illuminates the nature
of the relationship between, on the one had, the 'traditional' and the modern
and, on the other, civil society and the party (state-to-be) in political conflicts of this nature. What the book demonstrates is how relevant the so-
called 'traditional' (symbolic, religious and political) African social order is

to the construction of the post-colonial political order. Terence Ranger's study of the nationalist struggle in Zimbabwe also adds another comparative dimension to the understanding of rural civil society and provides an instructive contrast to the analysis of the high politics of wars of national liberation.[57]

Bayart himself has convincingly shown how the study of high politics in Cameroon could be sharpened by a more sophisticated understanding of its low politics. As he points out, the notion of delinquency is highly political. Delinquency may or may not be the political expression of a gagged underclass but the state's reaction to it is undoubtedly an indication of its perception of the potential political nature of apparently anomic behaviour.[58] The study of delinquency in independent Africa echoes the study of banditry in the colonial period.[59] Both merit examination as possible forms of low politics. Both need to be studied in the appropriate historical context if their political significance is to be properly assessed.

Of course, not all banditry or delinquency have deep political relevance, and it would be otiose to read political statements in every utterance and action of the disenfranchised. Whether such utterances and actions are politically meaningful depends in part on the self-consciousness of those who profess and perform them and in part on the perception of those in high politics. Only a better and more refined understanding of the politics of civil society can gauge their relevance.

It may be thought that the notion of civil society merely serves to obscure that of class in that, in the absence of sharper class definitions, the concept of civil society remains eminently vague. Not all groups and individuals within civil society matter equally for politics. How can one meaningfully compare Islamic brotherhoods and armed forces to market-women and nomads? In which ways are their politics relevant to the politics of the country in which they live? The answer turns in part on the use of the notion of production, a concept prior to that of class,[60] for class divisions issue out of the development of modes of production over time. Until we have some understanding of the historical context of the meaning of production in post-colonial Africa, it is not very profitable to use class as one of our basic concepts.

It is, however, also important to emphasise that the notion of civil society is relevant to the political analysis of post-colonial Africa above and beyond the possible uses (and abuses) of class analysis. However well defined and politically consequential classes are in Africa, and there is some debate as to how well defined they can be, the analysis of civil society makes it possible to examine the relevance of low politics in both its organised and non-organised manifestations. In other words, the analysis of civil society need not be at the expense of class analysis. The two ought to be complementary.[61]

The advantage of the notion of civil society is that, unlike that of class, it does not start from limiting conceptual categories. Where classes cannot be identified, it is difficult to analyse class politics. Civil society, on the other hand, is defined in relation to the state, whatever the genesis and complexion of the state. Since the most characteristic feature of post-colonial African countries is the space occupied by the state and the consistency of its hegemonic mission, it stands to reason that the notion of civil society is eminently appropriate.

Furthermore, class analysis can easily be incorporated in the conceptual scheme which I offer. Dominant classes, where they can plausibly be identified in relation to the process of production, belong to the state. Other classes, in Marxist terms self-conscious and politically organised ensembles of working people (workers, peasants, etc.), are organised groups within civil society. The degree of their organisation, their place in the production process, and their representation within the state, determine the success of their politics.

Miners, as a self-conscious and organised working class, have more clout than atomised and unorganised groundnut-producers but the political action of the latter, whether organised or not, can affect the productive basis of the state equally dramatically. Groundnut-producers may not be a class of peasants but the basis on which they make economic decisions is as politically relevant to the understanding of the country's politics as the action of any trade union.

Another benefit of the analysis of the politics of civil society is, it seems to me, that it is likely to shed light on the politics of the state. The nature of civil society and the complexion of its politics are reflected within the structure and politics of the state. What Bayart calls 'the revenge of civil society' is not just the manner in which civil society impinges on the state but also, and perhaps more importantly, the manner in which low politics transforms high politics.[62] It is analytically fruitless to bemoan the fact that the post-colonial state in Africa is patrimonial, prebendal, clientelist, corrupt, etc. What matters for analysis is to understand how these characteristics of the contemporary African state are the results of the reciprocal influence of high and low politics.

For the state, in the African context, is continuously adapting to civil society in ways, however, which are not always discernible to the outside observer. Few problems, for example, are as analytically intractable as those of ethnic politics. Yet, it seems clear that the only way to make sense of what is usually called ethnic politics is to conceptualise it as one of the many political idioms by means of which state and civil society joust with each other. The same applies, to give another example, to the deployment of new or re-invented local 'indigenous' religions which the state, unsurprisingly, perceives as a direct political challenge.[63] Similarly, what is called corruption is also better analysed as the process of reciprocity between high and low politics, or what is sometimes called patron–client relations.[64]

All these examples, and many others which could be given, illustrate the complexities of the principles of political accountability between state and civil society in post-colonial African countries. In each country, particular aspects of the politics of civil society will be more salient during particular periods. It should be the object of political analysis to identify which they are and why they are politically salient at that particular time. Only thus will we be able to understand the real as opposed to the imagined role of the state.

6 Production

Power and production are the two coordinates of society.[1] They determine the parameters of the relations between the economic and political spheres. Within any conceptual framework, production is the economic axis between the individual and society. The modes of production, the forms of production, the means of production, the relations of production and the appropriation of production are at the heart of the political dialectics between state and civil society, in Africa as elsewhere.[2] For this reason, an analysis of the concept of production is essential to the understanding of the political history and current politics of any African country. What is at issue here is not just what production is, but how production is political and how best to conceptualise its politics. After a brief discussion of the notion of production, I examine in some detail the productive basis of pre-colonial and colonial economies. I leave until Chapter 9 the discussion of production in the post-colonial context.

Production, like power, cannot be discussed in the abstract, for all human activity is production of some sort. Any notion of production must thus contain a notion of the purpose of production. Why are people producing, above and beyond survival and reproduction? What are they producing for? What is the meaning of production within the existing socio-political structure of the community? How does the purpose of production change over time? And why?[3]

Any discussion of the reality of production must start with a consideration of the objective (e.g., geographical, climatic, ecological) and historical context of production, for its is undoubtedly true that, in the first place, production is determined and constrained by such a context. Historically, it is the way in which individual countries have managed to utilise a given combination of resources and technology in order to overcome the fundamental constraints of production imposed on them by fate and history which has determined their economic success.[4]

To ask about production is also to ask about the movement of production, (trade), for very little production (if any) takes place within a vacuum, in autarchy. Indeed, one of the fundamental purposes of production is exchange, and where there is exchange there is an economic relation based on some notion of exchange value. The distinction between use and exchange value is thus useful whatever the economic system and whatever the relations of exchange.[5] But, here again, notions of value entail notions of power, for exchange values are conditioned by the domestic and international determinants of market factors (e.g., terms of trade, tariffs, taxes, market prices).[6] Production, therefore, can only be conceptualised within the framework of given relation of power. This is why power and production are indissoluble.

The question of which, power or production, is historically prior to the other, that most intractable of all issues of political economy, need not detain us here as we are not concerned about determining primal causality. What we need to examine carefully is the historical context of the dialectical relationship between power and production. At certain times in the history of political communities power may have decisive purchase on production. At other times it is the reverse. The relation between power and production is necessarily unstable and fragile.

Political revolutions, of which colonial conquest and decolonisation were two instances, often have a determinant effect on production. New political kingdoms, new relations of power, alter the political and sometimes the physical framework within which production takes place. Alternatively, economic revolutions (of which the integration into the world capitalist economy is certainly one) usually have a profound effect on politics. Where the productive basis of power is seriously altered the political realm is transformed. The introduction of new crops, new technology, new systems of exchange; the onset of drought, disease, etc., all affect production and, thereby, power.[7] The key question for political analysis is thus to understand the relation between the productive basis of power and the politics of production within a given historical setting.

In order to do so, we need first to have some sense of the general characteristics of the pre-colonial productive basis of power or, as Marxists would put it, to understand its modes and relations of production.[8] This means, firstly and most importantly, to refer specifically to the physical (geographical, climatic, topographic, demographic) setting of production. For example, agriculture – production from the soil – is in the first instance specific to the area in which it takes place, even if areas can be usefully compared at greater levels of generalisation. For this reason, discussions about pre-colonial modes of production can obscure more than they reveal if and when the data are made to fit into preconceived conceptual categories.

What matters most about rural production is not its general quality but the particulars of its practice within specific ecological and historical settings. Thus, many of the discussions about pre-colonial modes of production fail to come to terms with the specific productive practices and class formation of different, though neighbouring, areas.[9] For instance, class analysis has sometimes failed to account meaningfully for the differences *and* interconnections between nomadic, pastoralist and agriculturalist 'modes' of production in areas like East Africa simply because of an excessive emphasis of concept over context.[10] Generally, it seems to me that too little attention has been paid to what I call the physical context of production.

It is, second, to understand the commerce of production in its proper historical context. At times, excessive attention has been given to the search for specific modes of production, in the form of detailed accounts about the technological, social and economic basis of production, without a sufficient understanding of the relevance of exchange to production. Here again, it is important to point our that, other than in the European fantasy of the 'Dark Continent', there never was in pre-colonial Africa production without exchange. Even Pygmy and Bushmen communities (the most isolated of all African communities), for instance, traded with their neighbours. Trade was widespread in all parts of Africa and extra-African trade (with, for example, north Africa, the Middle East and even Asia) existed long before the Portuguese 'discoveries', let alone the Scramble for Africa.

The productive systems of African state or stateless societies, were integrated within (sometimes) vast systems of exchange, of which the most notorious (though not the only one) was the slave trade.[11] As Wallerstein has argued at some considerable length, the integration of African economies into the developing world capitalist system was consequential both for the developing 'centre' and for the African 'periphery'.[12] Any understanding, therefore, of colonial and post-colonial Africa must be informed by the context of productive exchange within which pre-colonial economies developed or failed to develop. It would certainly be useful if historical details were available for Africa similar in quality to those provided by Braudel for the Mediterranean world.[13]

We need, third, to be more sensitive to the concepts of accumulation and appropriation in their pre-colonial setting. Inherent in any discussion of modes of production, there are assumptions about the nature and purpose of accumulation and about the relationship between accumulation and power. In all societies some production is accumulated and in all societies accumulation is related to power. It serves little purpose to establish artificially rigid dichotomies between pre-colonial and colonial modes of production in this respect.[14]

The chief distinction between pre-capitalist and capitalist modes of production is not so much the extent but the purpose of accumulation. It is common to argue that in pre-capitalist systems accumulation is primarily intended for consumption and displays of social status while in capitalist societies it is used productively, that is reinvested. But that is a crude distinction, forced on analysis by excessive deference to Marxist theory. We know, even if only partially, that pre-capitalist states (e.g. the Ashanti is perhaps the best documented of the West African states)[15] could invest productively just as we know that there is enormous consumption and display of status in the most resolutely capitalist societies in Africa today. In this respect, analytical confusion only serves to highlight the need to discuss power and production together.

The key historical question is that of the causal relation between accumulation and technological innovation. This is what marks capitalism from other modes of production. But here the issue is complex. Beyond platitudes about the relationship between the rise of capitalism and the industrial revolution, the causalities between accumulation and technological innovation are not always well understood.[16] Witness the debate on the causes of the Chinese technological advance – but more importantly its subsequent decline – in relation to Europe.[17] Certainly, the assumptions made about the economically static nature of pre-colonial Africa will have to be revised if we are to understand some of the economic changes which took place during and even after the colonial period. Was there, for instance, no precolonial basis to the success of the migrant cocoa-farmers in Ghana?[18]

Finally, there are questions about the scale of production. Here also, dichotomies are usually taken for granted. Pre-colonial production was on a small scale, with very definite limits on the possibility of increasing scale within the existing means of production. Capitalist production, on the other hand, provided the means to expand efficiency and scale. This, of course, is true as far as it goes. But it does not necessarily enlighten us about the purpose of production in relation to power.

The productive capacities of some pre-colonial states were considerable even if there were definite (physical, ecological and technological) limits to production.[19] How efficient production was depends on one's assessment of the economic values of the various factors of production extant at a given period of time. Where land is plentiful, fertilisation may not be 'efficient'. Where labour is cheap and, periodically at least, abundant, technical innovation may not be 'efficient'. Similarly, economies of scale may not be 'efficient' or even productive in certain given economic contexts – for example, where the cost of transport is high. The question of whether economies of scale are always 'efficient' is one which is still debated today.

If anything, the latest evidence about agriculture and agro-industry in Africa would suggest that concentration for the purpose of economies of scale is economically undesirable. Recent research on agricultural production has established that 'traditional' production could in fact be both more efficient and innovative than was hitherto believed by, among others, the gurus of the green revolution.[20] It has almost become a cliché of current aid ideology that innovation must arise out of 'traditional' production rather than the reverse. Whether this is always the case or not, what I wish to emphasise here is that an understanding of pre-colonial production is essential to an understanding of production in post-colonial Africa.

From the point of view of production, the colonial revolution, that is the partition of Africa and its transformation into colonial territories, was an economic revolution as well. This was not only, as is usually remarked, because it implied the integration of Africa into the capitalist world economy – which was already taking place before the Scramble and would no doubt have continued to take place without it – but because it artificially created colonial economic enclaves.[21]

The colonial powers set up, even if not always very successfully, economic entities within each of the territories they administered. The identification (in part through taxation) of Africans as economic subjects belonging to specific territories, their integration into a money economy, and the delineation of an economic space intimately linked to that controlled by the colonial state, all contributed to the erection of an economic superstructure above and upon the existing systems of production, exchange and accumulation. It may be as misleading to speak of a colonial mode of production as it is to speak about a pre-colonial mode of production, but it is certainly true that the organisation of the colonies into discrete economic entities radically redefined the parameters of production in Africa.[22]

The creation of 'economic' colonies was, naturally, slow, erratic and incomplete. The two French zones of Occidental and Equatorial Africa had far more porous territorial boundaries than, for example, the British colonies. There was widespread movement of people across colonial boundaries throughout the colonial period. Certain regions attracted labourers in search of employment (e.g., in mines, plantations, services). Conversely, Africans fled from regions where the pressures of taxation, forced labour or forced cultivation were adjudged excessive.[23] Nevertheless, in the longer term the establishment of colonies, and by implication, of territorial economic zones, had the most profound impact on production in Africa.[24]

It has often been pointed out that colonies, carved for reasons having to do with the logic of conquest, artificially separated peoples who lived within a single political community. But it is equally the case, and it may even be more consequential, that the division of Africa into colonies was done with no serious consideration for economic, particularly capitalist, economic logic. Now, it is true that, historically, nations have seldom evolved into nation-states for economic reasons,[25] but there can be few examples of greater systematic economic arbitrariness than the division of Africa into colonies.

What matters for political analysis, however, is to understand the political implications of the creation of colonies for production – the political implications of what Marxists call the articulation of pre-colonial and colonial modes of production. There are here three areas which it is important to discuss: the nature of pre-colonial production; the consequences for production of the integration of the colonies into the metropolitan and world markets; and, finally, the characteristics of the economies which developed during the colonial period.

There has at times been much debate about the notion of pre-colonial African mode of production and it is appropriate to ask, in the first place, whether it is plausible to speak of a single pre-colonial mode of production.[26] Marxists have sometimes sought to identify a pre-colonial African mode of production somewhat along the model of the Asiatic mode of production,[27] but the problems here are two-fold. First, it is not entirely clear what, in specific historical terms, the Asiatic mode of production is. Second, it has become apparent that it is not possible to conceive of a recognisable African pre-colonial mode of production other than at a level of generality which pre-empts meaningful historical analysis.

Nineteenth-century Africa contained vastly different economic areas with vastly different modes of production, from the gatherers of the Kalahari desert and the Pygmies of Central Africa to the Ashanti state and the emirates of West Africa. The colonial powers thus conquered areas with different local economies, from the most undeveloped to the relatively sophisticated. The question of whether there is a specifically linear development in African modes of production to account for the vast differences evident in the nineteenth century is one which concerns those seeking to find linearity in the development of economies the world over.[28] For our purposes, what matters more is the distinction between pre-capitalist and capitalist economies.

Pre-colonial production, however sophisticated it was, was not capitalist, even if pre-colonial Africa already had links with the world capitalist economy. The transformation of the economic relations between Europe and Africa in the nineteenth century was largely the result of the expansion of capitalism rather than simply, as is often assumed, that of the (later) actual physical conquest of the continent.[29] Or rather the conquest of Africa was part of a strong rivalry between the main European powers to which capitalist expansion was central.

The fundamental difference between pre-capitalist and capitalist modes of production is not exchange but accumulation. In Africa there were, and long had been, economies which traded over large areas of the continent or beyond. We know of commerce between Africa, the Arab world, India, and even East Asia. The Europeans were at first no more than another group of traders in an economic system in which there were, in fact, very few areas uninvolved in some form of local or long-distance trade. Pre-colonial production thus involved exchange at its very economic core.[30] Where it differed from capitalist production was in the nature and purpose of accumulation.

It is a cliché, but (to use another cliché) broadly true, to say that accumulation in pre-colonial societies was, both in theory and in practice, different from what it was in European capitalist economies. The politics of production gave entitlements to accumulation at different levels in the political community. Family heads, community elders, chiefs, emirs, state officials and kings were all entitled to accumulate. It is generally recognised that the chief purpose of accumulation was two-fold. The first was to establish rank and status; the second was to ensure the means of redistribution which sustained rank and maintained the cohesion and survival of the community.[31]

The varying relations between power and production were governed by principles of political accountability (sometimes erroneously called relations of clientelism) which were at the heart of the existing political community. This relation between power and production could be ruthlessly exploitative but it operated within the reasonably well-defined limits of a recognisable and legitimate moral political economy. Where the notion of the individual was subsumed under that of the community and where the purpose of accumulation was not primarily further accumulation, these limits were well understood by rulers and ruled alike. Rulers ignored them at their peril. Even conquered peoples and slaves were given a 'rightful' place within this political economy for, ultimately, power mattered more than accumulation or, rather, accumulation was only the instrument of power.

Pre-colonial production was, as it had been in most of the world for most of human history, one of the means by which the rulers buttressed their power and maintained order within the political community.[32] This is not to say, as is sometimes claimed, that there was in pre-colonial Africa neither inequality nor poverty. There was as much inequality and poverty as in any other group of political communities.[33] It is to say, however, that in African pre-colonial modes of production, accumulation was the foundation of power rather than the means to further accumulation. For in a context where accumulation is not primarily due to technological innovation, there are objective limits to how much accumulation can take place.

The colonial revolution changed the political economy of African political communities. Indeed, the most consequential economic consequence of colonial conquest was the rupture in the political economy of pre-colonial production. It is often argued that the most serious effect of colonial rule was the introduction of an economy sustained by taxation and forced labour of some description. It is true that this was the most blatant indication of colonial subjection, but it was not always the most significant. Africans in pre-colonial Africa had almost always been subject to some taxation and to some form of forced labour, and they had almost always had the use of a currency for exchange – whether cowrie shells or cloth. The colonial rulers were just the latest in a long line of more or less exploitative rulers. However, the development of a capitalist economy, or rather the integration of the colonial economies into the metropolitan and world markets, was a fundamental rupture in the political and moral economy of Africans.[34]

The most basic aspect of this break between power and production was the change in the relationship between the individual and the community.[35] The colonial political economy redefined the economic identity of the individual. The individual was no longer simply a constituent member of the community but he became primarily an individual economic agent. Whatever his place, his rights and obligations within the existing political economy of his community, he was now considered by the colonial masters to be a discrete economic unit. Taxation, labour and production were all conceived in terms of the economic production, value and cost of the individual colonial subjects. It was thus not so much the introduction of monetary taxation but that of tax *per caput*, not so much the obligation to labour but forced individual labour, not so much the requirements of colonial production but the necessity to produce as single units, which undermined the existing political economy.[36]

The colonial system of taxation, labour and production conspired to alter, irrevocably, the pre-colonial modes of production. The colonial subject was now part of two economic worlds, two economic logics of production and accumulation. Whether the African was a willing or unwilling participant in this new economic logic, he soon found that the foundations of the pre-colonial political economy had been subverted. His position in relation to production and his ability to accumulate were now determined by the interplay between the two (new and old) economic logics. Of course, some (e.g., nomads) could resist the new longer and some (e.g., chiefs) could benefit more rapidly from the straddling between the new and the old.[37] Indeed, not a few thrived in the colonial economy. My point is not to pass moral judgement but to stress the importance of the process by which the transition from one political economy to the other occurred.

Perhaps nothing better illustrates the import of this process than the evolution of the nature of bride-price in colonial Africa.[38] Where once the man's obligation had been regulated by his position in relation to the community as a whole, it was now more often determined by the new logic of accumulation introduced by the colonial economy. Whereas before, men had been asked to contribute to the loss of a female worker within the family- and kin-productive unit, they were now asked to pay in cash or in labour according to a new moral economy in which the bride's father (rather than mother) sought to maximise his return on the production of a daughter. Hence, the inflation in bride-price.

The second change inherent in the colonial economic logic was the transformation of the economic value of labour and land. Whatever the nature of the relationship between the individual, the community, labour and land in pre-colonial Africa (and there were very wide differences between different parts of the continent), colonial rule introduced a capitalist logic.[39] Both labour and land became commodities. Of course, this process was neither smooth nor consistent in that the colonial rulers recognised the impossibility and indeed the undesirability of 'abolishing' existing modes and relations of production. Nevertheless, it was an irreversible process in the gradual move towards a political economy in which individuals became producers or labourers and in which they could buy and sell land at a price now broadly determined by the laws of supply and demand.

To be sure, much labour and production were still outside the colonial economic logic and much land was still in 'communal trusteeship', but the value of labour, the value of production and the value of land, insofar as they were defined economically, were eventually defined according to a capitalist logic.[40] Men and women laboured for wages whatever their position in the 'traditional' economic community. Agricultural producers produced for the colonial market, whatever the (legal and economic) constraints on that market, even if the bulk of food production was outside the market. Where land was short, or where it demonstrably became a means to accumulation, it was sold and bought according to the laws of the colonial economy – and in settler colonies, land alienation led to shortages of land and landlessness, an economic condition more serious in the colonial than in the pre-colonial economy.

The consequences of such profound changes have sometimes been conceptualised in terms of the notion of dual economy.[41] This argument, favoured by some Marxists and many underdevelopment theorists, is that the integration of pre-colonial modes of production into the capitalist world market led to the creation of an economy in which the modern, capitalist, sector could achieve unparalleled levels of exploitation because it could 'buy' labour from the non-capitalist sector below its reproductive costs. What this means is that, because African labourers (whether seasonal or not) remained part of a 'traditional' economy which could ensure their survival and reproduction (i.e. they were not fully proletarianised), they could be paid below subsistence wages. The development of a capitalist economy was thus made possible by the maintenance of pre-colonial modes and relations of production – hence the notion of the colonial economy as dual economy.[42]

There is some considerable force in this argument as it demonstrably applies to forced labour or to those many African workers who were employed on cleverly devised seasonal contracts and paid below subsistence wages. Even Africans working in the cities on annual contracts not infrequently were paid below the costs of their reproduction as labour and survived because of their links with the rural areas. It is also the case that in many colonial economies many Africans were made to produce agricultural goods at prices which did not compensate for the cost of labour and other inputs required for production – i.e., they were paid a price below production costs. Equally, in settler colonies, Africans were sometimes made to work on white farms on terms which, *stricto sensu*, did not guarantee their reproduction as labour.[43]

There were, however, enormous variations between, and sometimes even within, colonies, so that no simple generalisation about the notion of a dual economy will do justice to the complexities of specific colonial economies. It seems more profitable to contrast, on the one hand, the East and Southern African settler colonies with the West African 'peasant' economies and, on the other, those countries possessing mineral resources with those without.

In settler colonies, the concept of dual economy has greater validity. Where the whites settled in significant numbers, a substantial proportion of cultivable African land was alienated, the productive capacity of Africans was substantially reduced and both landlessness and proletarianisation were considerably greater than in other colonies. In addition, the protection of settler economic interests led colonial governments to impose greater control and constraints on what Africans could produce and sell.[44] To generalise, therefore, African producers in settler communities suffered more from unfavourable economic conditions than those in non-settler colonies. By confining Africans to land reserves and/or by depriving them of the means of unfettered agricultural production and trade, settler colonies created hybrid economies in which (with, as always, some notable exceptions, as for example in Kenya) capitalist development, insofar as it occurred, was largely at expense of the African population.[45]

In the colonies of West and Central Africa, where white settlement was not possible, the impact of the colonial economy was different. Here, the colonial governments controlled exchange rather than production.[46] The newly introduced colonial market economy was used to increase the production of export crops, the (internal and external) trade of which could be profitably taxed. In this part of Africa, large-scale plantation production was rarely profitable and it was more expedient for the colonial masters to convince or coerce Africans to produce those crops most profitably exported (e.g., groundnuts, palm kernels, coffee, cocoa, fruits).[47]

Here the notion of dual economy (at least in its classical formulation) is less relevant, though it could still be argued that such tight colonial control of exchange was only possible because of the continued existence of a local 'non-capitalist' economy, in particular for food production. Nevertheless, it is generally true that, in West Africa, producers, middlemen, tradesmen and businessmen penetrated (and hence benefited from) the developing capitalist economy to a degree which was not possible for their Eastern and Southern African counterparts. The development of cocoa and, to a lesser extent, coffee production in West Africa also illustrates the ways in which the precolonial mode of production could successfully be transmuted into capitalist agriculture.[48] In West Africa, it is at least possible to see, concretely and historically, what the integration of pre-capitalist and capitalist modes of production could mean.

Such general discussions about the impact of capitalism on pre-colonial African economies can all too easily obscure a prior, and even more fundamental, discussion about the productive resources of individual territories. The arbitrary division of Africa into colonial territories largely determined what the human, ecological, agricultural and mineral resources of these colonies would be. No single argument about 'modes of production' can possibly provide meaningful insights into the economies of countries as different in size as, for example, The Gambia and Zaïre; as different in population as, for example, Guinea-Bissau and Nigeria; and as different in resources as, for example, Burkina Faso and Zimbabwe. Plausible comparison depends on commensurate scales.

In this perspective, Africa can be divided into at least three types of economies: those which were not productively viable, those which possessed mineral resources, and those which had good potential for agricultural exports.

It is too readily forgotten by analysts of contemporary African politics that a number of colonies were economically not viable and had no conceivable means of becoming viable independent countries. Many of them, particularly in French Occidental Africa and French Equatorial Africa, were integrated within the economies of vast regions and did not possess sufficient resources to sustain economic development after independence.[49] Colonial territories such as Upper Volta, Mali, Chad, Oubangui-Chari (now the Central African Republic) etc., often with large nomadic populations and devoid of agricultural potential because of their ecology, had little productive potential for development. Some (e.g., Upper Volta) became labour reserves for richer neighbours (e.g., Côte d'Ivoire). Others, like Mauritania, discovered exportable mineral resources with which to fill their exchequer. But many (e.g., Mali, Chad) had little prospect of developing their economies.[50]

Those colonies with mineral resources were immediately integrated into the metropolitan and world economies. The exploitation of mineral resources requires capital, know-how and labour. During the colonial period, the metropolis provided the capital and the know-how and repatriated what proportion of the profits it chose. The colonial governments were in a position to determine the conditions under which they would employ local unskilled and, sometimes, skilled labour. The question of whether mining economies spurred or hindered the development of capitalism locally is difficult to answer in the abstract.[51]

What it is possible to say is that, under colonial conditions, full-scale proletarianisation was rare (owing to the 'dual economy') and that, since in most instances the transformation industries were located in Europe, the scope for local industrial development was limited. Only in South Africa can one speak of the development of an industrial productive base in parallel with the exploitation of mineral resources. The cases of Mozambique and Lesotho (admittedly both unusual in their own way) would seem to indicate that labour migration to the mines contributed decisively to the gradual erosion of the productive capacity of the areas of emigration, even when the mining wages were re-invested in agriculture back home.[52]

The exploitation of the mineral resources of the colonies may have boosted government revenues but it did not necessarily contribute to the development of the productive capacity of the territory. The independent countries which inherited those mineral resources or discovered new ones found that their bargaining position on the world market depended, on the one hand, on their need for outside capital and know-how and, on the other, on the vagaries of total world production. It was certainly better to have mineral resources than not to have them. Yet, the extent to which the possession of mineral resources led to the development of the productive capacity of a country depended in large measure on the prior productive capacity of that country.[53] Botswana (and perhaps Gabon), with exceptionally vast deposits of valuable mineral resources (diamonds, oil and uranium) and exceedingly small populations, may be some of the few African countries in a position to construct development on the revenues of their mineral exports.

Where (as, for example, in Zambia, Zimbabwe, Zaïre, Angola before independence) there was an industrial infrastructure and where some of the transformation of the mineral resources could take place in the country, there was greater scope for the further development of that country's productive capacity after independence. Where, on the other hand, mineral resources were extracted in a country with minimal or no industrial capacity, the effects of that extractive industry on the productive capacity of the country were likely to be minimal.

Whatever the case, the revenues from mineral exploitation have not infrequently been disbursed on the tertiary sector, a sector which often adds little to the productive capacity of African countries and which becomes very expensive to sustain if the marketable value of the mineral resources wanes.[54] The lesson from those African (and other) countries with mineral resources is that, unless the revenues from those resources are reinvested productively, the value of these resources may turn out to be eminently evanescent.

The majority of African countries which had potential for agricultural exports were divided into two groups: those countries with a sufficient agricultural capacity to provide for the bulk of their food needs and those without. There is little question that, in general terms, colonial economies favoured the production of exportable rather than food crops and that, as a result, the production of food in Africa declined. In any event, it often became cheaper to import than to produce food. In some areas, the (forced) production of export crops (e.g., groundnuts, cotton) led to a serious reduction both in the fertility of the soils and in the production of food. Whether it is true that the production of export crops necessarily always led to a fall in the production of food and thus increased the probability of famine is not so simply proved or disproved. What we can say is that the likelihood that it did so is by no means negligible. More precise answers can only be given through specific case studies.[55]

Here, again, the major distinction is between settler colonies and 'peasant' economies. In the former, land alienation, settler-production of food and exportable crops together with the constraints imposed on African agricultural production, all led to serious distortions in the agriculture of the colonies. There, the pace of the development of a capitalist African agriculture was largely dictated by settler interests. The heavy dependence of the colonies on the export of some crops and the reduced capacity to produce food had serious consequences for the development of the productive capacity of the independent countries which inherited such economies.

In the other African countries, where export crops were produced by Africans, the colonial economy controlled agricultural production through trade duties and, above all, marketing boards.[56] Whether a capitalist agriculture developed and whether the cultivation of export crops was at the expense of food depended on the productive capacity of the colony and on the rigours of the colonial economic climate. Cocoa production in the Gold Coast, São Tomé and Príncipe, and Côte d'Ivoire provides interesting contrasts on the very different conditions under which the same crop could be produced and exported.[57] Similarly, the production of groundnuts in Senegal, The Gambia, Portuguese Guinea and French Guinea offer interesting contrasts and defy overly simple generalisations.

Whatever the extent to which African capitalist agriculture developed, the primary consequence of the colonial reliance on export crops for revenues was an increased dependence for African economies on these crops after independence.[58] Since in virtually all cases, save for settler plantations, an increase in production was most usually achieved by means of an increase in land cultivated or labour input rather than modernisation, the productive foundations of agriculture remained fragile. There were real limits on how much increase in production could be achieved without modernisation. When those limits were reached, increased production was at the expense of soil fertility and/or food production.

Given the ecological constraints on agriculture in most countries and given the uncertainly of food production, increased production of export crops could only be achieved through a mix of coercion or incentives. The balance between coercion and incentives could be maintained only so long as prices were relatively attractive and there was sufficient food – which was generally the case before, but often not after, independence.

For all that, the colonial legacy was heavy. True, there was in many colonies a modicum of capitalist farming, but the bulk of food and export crops was still produced by Africans as it had always been produced. Transport and trade had been improved but the structures, methods, and means of agricultural production remained essentially what they had been at the beginning of the colonial period. Yet the dependence of African colonies on the export of very few crops and, often, the inability to maintain self-sufficiency in food, left their economies in an excessively vulnerable position at independence. The fact that international market prices for agricultural exports are notoriously volatile and that the value of agricultural goods has, historically, tended to fall relative to that of manufactured goods, meant that the economic position of most newly independent African countries was weak.[59]

Those nation-states without either mineral or industrial resources were thus left at independence with minimal productive capacity – other than 'primitive state accumulation' – to finance growth. But 'primitive state accumulation' requires a state infinitely stronger than the African post-colonial state could ever be. Without such power, the only means of increasing agricultural production is to provide better economic incentives to producers. There can be no incentives for increased production, however, unless the terms of trade between agricultural and manufactured goods are fair (that is, when there are manufactured goods available) and these terms cannot be fair if (hegemonic) states require a surplus from agriculture to finance manufacturing industry.[60]

The other option was a green revolution on the Asian model. But the ecological and climatic conditions for green revolution were not propitious in most parts of Africa.[61] Moreover, green revolutions in Africa have almost invariably failed because they were not easily compatible with existing production methods and techniques – that is modernisation has usually been conceived and implemented from above with scant regard for the existing socio-economic parameters of production. Agricultural production (by itself) was thus not, at independence, a strong enough economic base on which to develop an industrial economy, though it need not have been the terminal handicap which greedy states have claimed it was.

It could (and no doubt will) be noted that my discussion of production so far has eschewed any reference to class. It could (and no doubt will) be further argued that the most meaningful causal relation between production and power is bound with class formation and class struggle. This is not untrue, or at least it is not untrue of capitalist societies at particular stages in their historical development. It is, however, much less concretely true of pre-capitalist societies. Marx himself, and Marxists generally, have always found it considerably more difficult concretely (if not conceptually) to identify classes, delineate class formation, and explicate class struggles in non-feudal pre-capitalist societies than in feudal and capitalist societies.

Furthermore, the notion of the African mode of production has not been as historically illuminating as that of the feudal or capitalist modes of production. Given that the concepts of the Asiatic and feudal modes of production are on the whole not relevant to the historical development of African societies, it remains difficult to devise meaningful and operational notions of class formation for pre-capitalist Africa. For instance, Cabral's scheme of a three-stage historical development of African societies, to take one of many possible examples, is over-simplistic, historically inaccurate, from a Marxist perspective conceptually dubious and of very little practical analytical use.[62]

Finally, it has not been possible so far to account plausibly for the development, or absence of development, of African pre-colonial societies in class terms. Class analysis has been more (even if still partially) useful in the analysis of colonial or post-colonial societies, that is for the period in African history which follows, rather than precedes, capitalist development.

Since it is my argument that the analysis of post-colonial politics in Africa requires an equally clear understanding of the productive basis of pre-colonial and colonial societies and since class analysis is least efficient in this area, it seems more profitable to proceed from the concept of production rather than from that of class. This is not to say that production and class are not related, as they demonstrably are in feudal and capitalist societies, but simply that the development of a meaningful class analysis must start from an understanding of production.

Since it is also my argument that colonial conquest and decolonisation were political as well as economic revolutions, it follows that we must be prepared to consider the possible consequences for production of, in Marxist terms, changes in the political superstructure. In other words, any preconceived notion on the nature of the causal relation between power and production is likely to make it more, rather then less, difficult to understand the changes in the productive basis of African societies. In short, then, production is the analytical category through which it may become possible better to define and use class analysis.

Part III
The Construction of the African Post-Colonial Political Order

Introduction

In the remainder of the book I attempt to use the concepts outlined above to reinterpret the politics of contemporary African countries. In Part III, the emphasis is on understanding how the governments of the newly independent nation-states attempted to construct political order, how they analysed and responded to the most significant political crises which confronted them after independence and how these crises were or were not overcome. I believe the five crises which I have chosen to examine form the five central axes of, though they obviously do not exhaust, the politics of post-colonial Africa. They are, respectively, the crisis of nationality and sovereignty, legitimacy and representation, accumulation and inequality, good government and political morality and, finally, violence and survival.

Although the notion of crisis is not new either to the political analysis of 'developing' countries or to African studies, it is here used differently. First, unlike teleological theories of political development, I do not look at these crises as obstacles on the road to political 'maturity'. Rather, I relate them to the multifarious ways in which Africans have organised politically to meet the domestic and external challenges of colonisation and decolonisation.

Second, I have chosen which crises to examine with regard to their relevance to the universal historical process by which nation-states were created and survived, thus allowing a comparative rather than strictly 'African' political perspective. In other words, I seek to understand how crises which are, broadly, common to the creation of all modern nation-states worked themselves out concretely in the African context. In particular, I assess the relevance for the 'overcoming' of these crises of decolonisation – that specific historical process by which colonies were transformed into independent nation-states.

Third, the purpose of these five chapters is to stress the lines of continuity, as well as the ruptures, between the pre-colonial and colonial context of these crises and the construction of the post-colonial political order. For this reason, I attempt to understand the African responses to these crises specifically from the perspective of their historical antecedents. In order to do so, I construct an analysis which is historically grounded rather than simply driven by our interpretation of current domestic or international political events. Only thus, it seems to me, can we begin to evolve plausible explanations for events which we Africanists have all too often artificially divorced from their historical sediments.

What is at issue in this part of the book is an understanding of the political revolution triggered by decolonisation. What did independence mean? What were the political consequences of decolonisation? How did the transformation of colonial territories into independent nation-states work itself out in political terms? What were African expectations about independence and how were these expectations changed in the post-colonial experience? Finally, and perhaps most importantly, how was the colonial political legacy assimilated and transformed in the unfolding of these five crises?

The consolidation of historically determined geographical and cultural areas into nation-states is the hallmark of the political world system as it evolved in the nineteenth and twentieth centuries. All nation-states are thus modern and all nation-states share broadly similar political characteristics – even if their shape, size, composition, resources, cultural homogeneity, political complexion, etc., can be (and indeed often are) completely different. Some nation-states are more plausible and have greater historical depth than others. Nevertheless, the construction of a nation-state, however implausible and shallow, establishes a corporate and political entity with recognisable characteristics which is likely to survive as nation-state in the foreseeable future. Indeed, the remarkable feature of the modern age is the durability, rather than the expected demise, of the nation-state.

But if all nation-states share many structural and political characteristics, the process by which they were invented and constructed differs widely. African countries belong to that group of countries which issued from colonial territories, that is nation-states in which the creation of the state was prior to that of the nation. This had important consequences for their genesis and for the resolution of the five crises inherent in the creation of the post-colonial order. I propose, in the chapters that follow, to show in which ways the historical specifities of the birth of African countries impinged on the construction of the modern nation-state in Africa.

Nevertheless, it is my argument here that, however singular the genesis of African nation-states was, their construction is best understood through the analysis of crises which are common to the establishment of all modern nation-states. For it seems clear that the viability and quality of life of contemporary nation-states is, in large part at least, determined by the manner in which these crises have been perceived, addressed and resolved – or not resolved, as may be the case. And although I do not claim that the five crises I have chosen to discuss cover all aspects of the process by which nation-states are consolidated, I think they cover adequately the essential ones.

In particular, I think they focus attention on those aspects of the creation of African nation-states which relate to their colonial genesis – aspects which are central to their history even if they ought not to be exaggerated. At the same time, however, they relate closely enough to the historical crises which attended the creation of, say, European nation-states, to make it possible to see what the contrasts are and how meaningful these contrasts might be. This is important because my argument is that it will only be possible to understand what is specific about Africa *after* we understand how what is happening to Africa today is part of the universal process of the formation of modern nation-states.

Of the five crises discussed below, the first three (nationality and sovereignty, legitimacy and representation, accumulation and inequality) are universally at the core of the formation of any modern nation-states. Without some satisfactory resolution of these issues, there can be little chance of a nation-state becoming or remaining viable. The other two crises (good government and political morality, violence and survival) are equally central to the viability of nation-states but they are probably more relevant to the early years of their consolidation. For it must be the case that it is during that time that nation-states are most likely to grapple with problems which may still threaten the survival of the country, heighten violence and diminish the odds for good government.

Nevertheless, the fact that some of these crises may appear to be specific to contemporary Africa, where nation-states are still very young, should not induce us to make any assumptions about a putative linear process in the political 'development' of modern nation-states. It is enough to look at the impact on the nation-state which the collapse of communism is having in eastern Europe and the Soviet Union to realise that it would be historically vain to search for permanent solutions to the crises of nationhood. Equally important, it is likely (if not inevitable) that the nation-state as we now know it in its classical nineteenth-century European variant will change in the future. As it does, new crises will emerge – some with strong historical resonance (ethnicity or religion?) – which will also require resolution.

The sense in which I use the notion of crisis should not, therefore, be taken to mean that, having resolved some of these crises, European states are necessarily more politically 'advanced' than African ones. Nor should it be interpreted as implying that, should African countries successfully overcome these five crises, their future as modern nation-states is *ipso facto* assured. Whether some European nations may be more assured in their nationhood than others and whether the future of some African nation-states is more secure than that of others are practical questions which can only be answered historically.

7 The Crisis of Nationality and Sovereignty[1]

I discussed earlier the notion of political community and showed why and how it was appropriate to think of the African nation-state as an imagined community. This is important. For however we may regret the salience of the nation-state, it is, as Benedict Anderson shows, the key contextual determinant of national and international politics today.[2] Without an adequate understanding of the African post-colonial nation-state there can be no understanding of contemporary African politics.[3]

The central feature of African nationalism was its attempt to invent a nation with which to justify its capture of the colonial state. It is easy to understand why the nationalists should have wanted to establish nation-states on the basis of existing twentieth-century models. The emergence of modern nationalism in nineteenth- and twentieth-century Europe gave shape to the countries which colonised Africa. The colonial state was both the embodiment and the extension of the metropolitan modern nation-state. Quite simply, to be a country in the second half of the twentieth century was to be a nation-state on the European model.[4]

It is less easy, however, to understand the process by which the colonial state was transformed into a nation-state. Nationalism demanded the invention of a plausible political community, the creation of an effective nationalist party and the cementing of nationalist unity. The ultimate aim of nationalism was independence, whatever the nationalist party's political project. Yet, the speed with which independence was achieved depended only partly on the perception by the colonial powers of the validity of the case made (peacefully or violently) by particular nationalists. Many other (domestic and international) political factors extraneous to African colonies impinged on the metropolitan approach to decolonisation.

The timing of independence was a reflection of colonial (metropolitan and African) politics rather than simply an indication of the success with which the nationalists had invented a nationalist myth.[5] In this respect then, independence, however crucially important it was historically, was more of a symbolic than substantive contribution to the *actual* construction of a modern nation-state. The land had been staked, planning permission had been won and the foundations had been laid. But the building remained to be done.

Once the nationalists had gained independence and captured the state, they faced the difficult prospect of building on foundations which were rarely as solid as they would have wished them to be. Few African countries were 'natural' nation-states, that is geographically, ecologically, ethnically, culturally, economically, socially or politically homogeneous, cohesive or even coherent. Most were amalgams and patchworks, with predictable consequences for the nation-builders. Some were hardly plausible candidates for nationhood. In almost all cases, therefore, the task of constructing an African nation-state was difficult, on balance more difficult (though in different ways) than it had been in Europe, Asia or Latin America.[6]

In Europe nationalism had bound together language and class. Nationalism had made it possible for would-be dominant classes to garner the support of linguistically cognate labouring masses in order to challenge the hegemony of linguistically alien political masters. In Latin America, nationalism had enabled linguistically homogeneous 'creole' élites to secure the (active or passive) support of racially different 'natives' in order to cast off the colonial yoke.[7]

The situation in Africa was wholly different. The nationalists were bound together only as Africans, a category clear enough in racial terms but in every other respect extremely loose and vague. Except in those cases where the colonial boundaries had some historical logic (e.g., Lesotho, Swaziland), the identity of African nationalism was a reflection of the identity of the colony. At independence, the nationalist state did not just have to construct the nation-state; it also had to invent the categories with which to construct it.

For this reason, the post-colonial state was immediately confronted with the twin crisis of nationality and sovereignty. The crisis was as inevitable as it was necessary, for only its successful resolution would enable the nationalist state to overcome its limitations as a *neo*-colonial state. The colonial state was, as I argued earlier, a coercive state.[8] Consequently, the *neo*-colonial state was also born a coercive state. In order to govern by consent, that is to establish post-colonial political accountability, the new rulers thus had to seek to resolve the crisis of nationality and sovereignty. The measure of their success in so doing would determine their success in constructing a plausible post-colonial nation-state.

Nationality and sovereignty are the two principal attributes of the modern nation-state, in Europe as in Africa.[9] Historically, the two are inextricably linked but, for the purpose of political analysis, it is helpful to conceptualise them separately.

By nationality I mean the cluster of historical and cultural characteristics which are (implicitly or explicitly) recognised by the national subjects as defining a particular country, if only in relation to other countries. Each country would probably provide a different definition of nationality and within each country the definition of nationality changes over time. It is, therefore, less important to give an objective and 'final' definition of any given nationality than to understand that, whatever it means in specific historical settings, it always is the self-perceived expression of a particular people at a particular moment in its (invented) national history. Whatever nationality means, its meaning is shared by the immense majority (though rarely the totality) of the population of a particular nation-state.[10]

By sovereignty I mean the international recognition and legal acceptance of the legitimacy of the assertion of nationality and of its statehood.[11] Recognition and legitimacy are dialectically related because any change in the one directly affects the other. The legitimacy of a particular nationality at a particular moment in history depends both on the extent to which it is shared by the population at large and on the extent to which it is recognised outside. Conversely, the recognition of a particular nationality depends on its domestic and international legitimacy. Where there is no outside recognition of a legitimate nationality (e.g. Kurdish or Palestinian) there is no sovereignty for that nationality.[12] Where there is no domestic recognition of an internationally accepted nationality (e.g., the South African or Lebanese), that nationality loses legitimacy.[13]

With few exceptions, African nation-states belonged to that category of modern countries where there was little or no congruence between nation and nationality.[14] The definition, viability and legitimacy of the nation derived from the wholesale invention of a nationality. In most European, Asian and Latin American countries, there were at least some common cultural, racial or linguistic foundations on which to construct a nationality. In many instances, there already was a historically recognisable nationality upon which to build a nation. But in Africa, as in some other colonies, the historical process was inverted. The construction of the post-colonial nationality started from colonial premises. Colonial premises, however, had largely been erected on the ruins of pre-colonial African nationalities.[15]

In practice, this meant that the post-colonial state was forced to build a nation on the foundations laid down by the colonial state. For any attempt to challenge the colonial invention (which in most cases had provided the territory not only with its boundaries but with its name) would have been to challenge the very concept of the nation-state.[16] Few such challenges on colonial boundaries have ever been attempted and where they have been, the only conceivable way of resolving them has been by reference to the colonial order. Attempts at secession (e.g. in Nigeria, Zaïre),[17] that is challenges to the colonial legacy, have failed largely because they have had virtually no support from other African countries. Nevertheless, some of the most bitter conflicts today in Africa concern cases where there is a contested interpretation of the colonial legacy (e.g., the former Spanish Sahara, Ethiopia, Somalia, Chad).[18]

To invent a nationality from above, which is what the nationalist state was condemned to do, is both difficult and politically sensitive. The educated and Westernised nationalist élites derived their notion of the nation-state from modern European models which had few historical connections with pre-colonial African political communities. The nationality which they required was not to be found in the African past.[19] Although nationalists justified their enterprise by reference to glorious episodes in African history when Africans had resisted foreign encroachment (perhaps none more famous than that of Samory Touré) and although they often constructed visions of the future based on the myth of an edifying past, they never seriously doubted that an African nation-state ought to be like its modern European counterpart.[20] Thus, nationalism had to invent a sovereign nationality.

The first obstacle they often faced was that a section of their population either was not part of, or had disassociated itself from, the nationalist project. This was not so much because those groups rejected the notion of independence *per se* (though they sometimes did) but rather because they did not recognise the legitimacy of the nationalists. For example, (established or appointed) chiefs and the leaders of some religious brotherhoods, who had collaborated profitably with the colonial masters, were less than keen to submit to the diktat of the 'new boys' of nationalism. Where they were strong enough (as in Senegal) they could ensure that the nationalists enlisted them as collaborators.[21] Where they were not they formed as an opposition to the nationalist state (e.g., the Ashantis in Ghana) or they were crushed (e.g., the chiefs in the Fouta Djallon of Guinea).[22]

It is too readily forgotten (no doubt because they were on the wrong side of history) that there were in almost all African colonies substantial groups of people who, for their own varied and different reasons, rejected the independence they were being offered by the nationalists. This naturally had consequences both for the formation and for the viability of the newly independent African countries. Much instability in Africa today is the outcome of such fundamental disagreements over the nation-state which the nationalist myth obscured but which have resurfaced since.

Uganda is perhaps an extreme case in that the Baganda were both the most powerful group in the country and the one most favoured by colonialism.[23] Their opposition to an independence which they would not dominate was to be expected. But it is not difficult to find examples of similar problems in many other African countries. The diffidence of southerners in

Mauritania and Sudan, Mandinkas in Senegal, Kimbundus in Angola, northerners in Chad, Makua in Mozambique, Somalis in Kenya, etc., towards the creation of a nationality they disliked is well known. The political weight of these individual groups, whose commitment to the independence offered was weak and whose acceptance of the new nation-state was feeble, has on occasion considerably reduced the legitimacy of the post-colonial nation-state as it was created.

The opposition of these groups to independence on the nationalists' terms was always perceived by them as a threat to national integrity and as an impediment to the formation of a nationality. Yet they often had to find ways of accommodating such opponents, if not necessarily their demands, for the one characteristic that many of these groups had in common was continuity with the past. Where they had historical weight (as the marabouts in Senegal or the Baganda in Uganda) ignoring them was impossible and crushing them too costly. Thus the original, pre-colonial, importance of these groups, buttressed by their special status under colonial rule, could make them formidable opponents to the nationalists.

Where they could not be defeated they had to be accommodated. But whether they were defeated or accommodated, their quiescence came at a price. In exchange for their acceptance of the modern nation-state these groups sought some special recognition within the official definition of the new nationality. But official recognition of a particular group, particularly one with strong historical roots, can easily cause resentment among other groups in the country and, in turn, weaken their commitment to the nationalist state. To this date, for example, it has not been possible to conduct a proper census of Nigeria, such is the fear of what the results would imply politically in terms of the balance between North and South.[24]

It is not that many of these groups have seriously considered seceding from the established country but that their rejection of the legitimacy of the nationality on which the new nation-state is built has made them reluctant partners in the construction of the post-colonial political order. These groups, which are often homogeneous in ethnic, linguistic and racial terms, can form a self-conscious and recognisable unit within civil society and are potentially strong politically. Where the construction of a nationality was relatively successful (e.g. Kenya, Cameroon), it diminished the potential threat of homogeneous sub-groups by eating slowly into their body politic – i.e., individual members of these groups could be successfully 'coopted' into the nationality. Where it was not (e.g., Sudan, Chad), the very concept of nationality remained at risk.

The second obstacle to the creation of a nationality in post-colonial Africa was the absence of a common language and culture. With the rare exception of those culturally homogeneous African countries with a historical logic (e.g. Swaziland, Lesotho, Cape Verde), all other colonies were patchworks of ethnicity, language and culture.[25] Given how central language had historically been for the construction of nation-state in Europe, the absence of a common (African) language was a grave handicap. There, again, the construction of a nationality had to be from the top down, by means of the colonial language. As Cabral, the Cape Verdean nationalist leader, repeatedly told his followers in Portuguese Guinea, their most important colonial legacy was the colonial language, Portuguese (even if they could converse satisfactorily in *crioulo*, the age-old *lingua franca*).[26]

Where there was no pre-colonial language to bind the colonial subjects together, the adoption and active promotion of the colonial language was thus essential to the invention of the nation-state. However desirable it might be in the long term to codify and teach the various regional languages, there has been unanimity in post-colonial Africa about the necessity to cement the nation together with the colonial language.[27] This is why the efforts made by most African countries to strive for universal literacy in the official language have been colossal – as a rule far in excess of what the country could realistically afford to spend on education.[28]

By all accounts, progress has been impressive. It is almost universally true that a majority of Africans under twenty years of age understand and speak (though they may not read and write) the official European language. Even in countries which are economically destitute, education has received a high priority and its achievements in terms of literacy have been commendable. Indeed, it is scarcely an exaggeration to say that it has been the one undoubted success story of independent Africa. Even countries like Angola and Mozambique, where illiteracy at independence was over ninety-five per cent, have pursued vigorous and, within the constraints of civil war, relatively successful literacy campaigns.[29]

It is with some confidence that we can expect Africa to remain a continent of English, French, Portuguese and Spanish speakers though, clearly, the French, English, Portuguese and Spanish languages which will be spoken there a few decades hence will have evolved their own cultural dynamics (on the pattern of the languages spoken in the Americas). Africa is and will remain a continent of multi-lingual speakers. Some regional languages and creoles/*linguae francae* either have been or will probably be given a written form and be taught in schools but they are not likely to displace the official national languages of European origin.[30]

A national language is necessary though not sufficient to the creation of a national culture. It is through the national language that the cultural histories of the peoples of each African country can be fashioned into a national culture. For this reason, it cannot be emphasised enough how essential the national language is to the construction of a nationality. In those countries where there is still disagreement about the national language, usually because the political supremacy of the speakers of that particular language (e.g. Arabic, Somali, Amharic, Afrikaans) is contested, there is little possibility of a national culture developing. The quicker and more complete literacy in the national language is, the easier it becomes for the national culture to develop and the more effective the national culture becomes in sustaining the nationality. This is a process, however, which is likely to take generations – as it did in Asia and Latin America – and for which there are no short cuts. Cultures grow at their own pace, not at the behest of politicians.

The creation of a national culture, however essential it is to the survival of the African nation-state, is not necessarily at the expense of pre-existing local cultures. Nor are national and local cultures mutually exclusive. What ensures that a culture is national is its use of the national language. But what ensures the viability of a national culture is its capacity to bind the cultural past of the peoples of that nation-state with the new nationality.[31] Not all national cultures are equally successful at contributing to the creation of a nationality. The present debate about the use of national as against regional languages is, in this respect, instructive.

In Angola and in Mozambique where, because of the history of decolonisation and of the post-colonial civil wars, the very survival of the nation-state is at stake, the government is making colossal efforts to increase literacy in Portuguese and to use Portuguese to create a national culture. The writing of an Angolan or Mozambican literature in Portuguese is considered to be of the utmost importance, both as a contribution to the identity of the new nation-state and as a foundation for a national culture. Because there is so little to bind the different peoples of the national territory together above and beyond the party's national political project, itself severely contested, the invention of a nationality is very largely dependent on the creation of a national culture. In countries such as Angola and Mozambique, it may be appropriate to debate the putative importance of regional languages and cultures but it is politically much more imperative to contribute to the success of the literacy campaign and to the development of a national culture.[32]

By contrast in Kenya, Ngugi wa Thiong'o, one of Africa's foremost English-language writers, is leading a campaign for the use of regional languages.[33] Ngugi now no longer writes fiction in English but in Kikuyu. He argues with great rigour and vigour that the use of a European language continues a pattern of cultural imperialism and prevents the development of a genuine African culture. His argument, which will be familiar to the student of European literature, rests on the simple, but overwhelmingly convincing, premise that culture, language and literature cannot be separated.

Why has Ngugi taken this position and why is he so fiercely contested in his country? Ngugi is threatening to the English-speaking Kenyan élite for three reasons. First, as an eminently successful (and famous) African English-language writer, his argument for a switch to regional languages cannot be dismissed as that of a second-rate artist seeking fame in a smaller pond. Second, and very much more importantly, Ngugi conceives of his use of Kikuyu as a means of giving a voice to grassroots culture, the culture of the exploited and the voiceless – civil society. He argues that English is the language of the establishment and ruling élite.[34] Third, Ngugi is a radical opponent of the regime in Kenya and considers the writing of a regional-language culture a potent political weapon against the regime. It is easy to understand why Ngugi should be perceived as such a threat to the ruling classes of Kenya though it is less easy to understand why they should think that incarcerating him would reduce the threat.

What is more pertinent to the discussion about nationality and national culture is the timing of Ngugi's decision to stop writing in English and to start writing in Kikuyu. From the point of view of the political analyst, two factors are immediately relevant here: the strength of the national culture and the viability of the nationality. Both have to do with historical context. Kenya today is, and has been for some time, secure in its national identity. Neither its nationality nor its sovereignty are seriously in doubt either domestically or internationally.

There is in Swahili a national *lingua franca* and English, as a national language, is widely understood and spoken (if not always written). English in Kenya has acquired enough depth and reflects enough local culture to have become Kenyan English (as there is Indian English). An assault on Kenyan English as the sole language of Kenyan culture is no longer an attack on Kenyan nationality. Conversely, a desire to write in Kikuyu is no longer the divisive and potentially secessionist cultural statement that it might have been at independence.[35]

In contrast, the use of regional languages in South Africa is rightly seen by Africans as the chief means by which the ruling élite seeks to keep its African population divided and uncultured.[36] Both sides understand that the creation of an English-language South African nationality, which is what the opponents of Apartheid want, would be an exceedingly powerful weapon against the regime. For when such an English-language-based national culture is created, as it will be one day, Afrikaner culture will cease to be the foundation of the country's nationality and will revert to what it really is, a regional (or minority) culture, on a par with Xhosa, Zulu, Sotho, and Tswana.

It is, therefore, evident that the choice of a national language, the creation of a national culture and the development of a nationality are all interconnected and historically specific. The salience of the issues of language, culture and nationality is determined by the extent to which the former African colonies succeed in transforming themselves into viable modern nation-states. It is well to remember, however, that success in this respect is a relative affair, even in European nation-states.[37] Language, culture and politics still combine to threaten the integrity of some European countries.[38] Nor is it at all clear that these issues can ever be settled 'for good', as it were.

The creation of nation-states and the evolution of nationalisms are not unilinear or teleologically determined. Ngugi's stance is in this respect akin to that of some European writers. There are more writers writing in Provençal, Catalan, or Galician today than there were fifty years ago, just as there will probably be more Kenyans writing in Kikuyu, Luo or Somali fifty years after, rather than at the time of, Mau Mau.

The third obstacle standing in the way of the construction of the modern African nation-state was the national integration of the various ethnic, racial, religious, regional and cultural groups which formed the population of the country.[39] I prefer a formulation which brings together these five characteristics (or a combination of some of them) rather than the near-universal focus on ethnicity found in the political analysis of Africa. Ethnicity is very often an important (sometimes dominant) factor but whether it is or not, it is essential to keep a sense of the interrelation of the many factors which combine to constitute an individual's identity, both self-perceived and as perceived by others. It seems to me beyond dispute that, with the benefit of the historical and cultural knowledge we now have of Africa, any attempt to understand the political relevance of ethnicity in specific countries must start from precisely such a broad and catholic definition of identity.[40]

The task of national integration was different in each country and so, consequently, was the nature of the problems, or potential problems, as perceived by the post-colonial governments. Whatever the differences, however, the process of integration was broadly similar. With the exception of those few countries (e.g., Cape Verde, Lesotho, Swaziland) which were linguistically and culturally, if not socially, homogeneous, all other post-colonial nation-states needed to integrate various ethnic, racial, cultural, religious or regional groups. Even in those countries with a degree of ethnic, social and cultural homogeneity rarely found in Africa, there were problems of integration. To give but one example, after independence (1975), Cape Verde had to confront real problems of geographical, racial and social integration.[41]

In this respect, there were two broad categories of nation-states: those where there was a dominant (ethnic, racial or religious) group and those where there was not.[42] The question of whether a group was politically dominant and whether that political dominance was problematic are neither simple to understand nor easy to settle.[43] Dominance takes many forms and size is not always the most relevant factor. Each case was different. There are, however, a number of considerations which are relevant to the analysis of the crisis of nationality in post-colonial Africa. They come under the three rubrics of contextual, historical and structural factors.

Contextual factors refer to the geographical, physical, ecological and natural coordinates of any given African country. The location of each country, its geography, the size, distribution and density of its population, as well as its climatic, ecological condition and natural resources, are self-evidently of determinant prior importance. It is in this respect a paradox that monographs on individual African countries often include such contextual introductory chapters but that comparative political analysis of African countries almost always neglects to do the same.[44] Even assumed 'natural' geographical regions as, for example, West Africa or southern Africa contain countries which are so different that it is difficult meaningfully to compare their political evolution.

Consider, for instance, the contextual constraints which bear on a political comparison of, say, The Gambia and Nigeria.[45] Both are West African countries, both are former British colonies, both became independent at roughly the same time, both inherited broadly similar colonial structures and institutions. On the surface, then, a comparative political analysis of the two appears, and has appeared to many, as plausible. Indeed, a superficial examination of some political structures (e.g., parliament, parties), some institutions (e.g., civil service, judiciary, the armed forces) and some processes (e.g., multi-party elections, the threat of coups) would confirm some (very) broad political similarities.

No doubt, such comparative analysis, however superficial, would point out the notable differences in the political evolution of the two countries – Nigeria's violence and The Gambia's relatively stable 'democracy'. But it might well be argued, and argued plausibly, that such an exercise distorts far more than it reveals. Nigeria and The Gambia are so immensely different in so many crucial respects that to compare the process of national integration between the two requires first a convincing account of the political significance of context. Can the process of the construction of a nationality substantively be the same in two countries so profoundly dissimilar? Or, even more importantly, in which ways do the differences make this process different?

Earlier historians of Europe may have exaggerated the importance of context over process in that they blithely saw the size of national territory and population as the *ultima ratio* of domestic and international politics. Although these factors were and remain important, there were, of course, many other considerations impinging on the importance of the crisis of nationality and sovereignty in the creation of modern nation-states.[46] But at least these historians were mindful of the weight of contextual factors in historical development. Some of their concerns might be relevant to present-day political analysts of Africa. A country with a population of half a million or a territory the size of Belgium cannot seriously be compared to a country with a population of over a hundred millions or a territory the size of Western Europe, even if population densities are not so dissimilar. The construction of a nationality in The Gambia would thus have been nothing remotely as complex as that of Nigeria – regardless of some of the apparent similarities.

Historical factors are the second set of factors which I want to discuss here. The ease or difficulty with which the African nation-state was constructed after independence depended significantly on such historical factors – to which, in fairness, political analysts have paid greater attention.[47] What I mean by historical factors is the combination of pre-colonial and colonial historical processes which, together with the contingencies of decolonisation, provided the framework within which post-colonial African governments sought to resolve the crisis of nationality and sovereignty.

The geographical boundaries of colonial territories almost never took into account the realities of pre-colonial Africa and thus neglected to consider whether these boundaries would make it more or less likely for the peoples of that territory to live together. During the colonial period it was often possible to suppress discontent on such issues but after independence they came back to the fore. Where there was long-standing (i.e. pre-colonial) friction between groups (as, for example, between coastal and interior peoples in West Africa), the construction of a nationality was very much more difficult.[48] Even where there was no overt antagonism, the end of the colonial order and the coming of independence released political and psychological forces with roots in the pre-colonial past. It was as though the resolution of the crisis of nationality demanded that the post-colonial political order be reconnected to its pre-colonial past, above and through the colonial period.[49]

Colonial policies were of course crucial to the forging of a 'territorial' consciousness. All colonial states explicitly wished the subjects of the territory to start thinking of themselves as citizens.[50] This was seen as desirable both because such self-consciousness – as opposed to 'particularistic' allegiance – was taken to be a sign of 'civilisation' and because it made it easier to administer the colonial territories. Despite the moral imperative of 'civilisation'. however, colonial states were essentially concerned with political order, the requirements of which not infrequently conflicted in practice with those of the integration of the peoples of the territory.

One need not believe in a conspiracy theory of 'divide and rule' to see that the outcome of colonial rule was, more often than not, the establishment and/or consolidation of the colonial peoples into discrete, distinct and explicitly defined ascriptive groups.[51] Whether these groups had any pre-colonial or even colonial logic is less important than the fact that they became politically significant. In each colony it is not difficult to point to some groups which were privileged and others which were discriminated against. This was politically consequential for the post-colonial order.

The process of decolonisation itself was crucial to the historical context within which the construction of the nationality took place. If, again, the avowed aim of the colonial powers (those, that is, which agreed to decolonise) was to contribute to the establishment of a united political entity, the reality was different. Equally, although the nationalists sought to unite the peoples of the country in order to press for self-government, the practice of nationalist mobilisation often revived old divisions or created new ones.[52]

The colonial state wanted above all to minimise disruption to the process of preparing the territory for independence even if it meant changing political tack and dumping old political allies. Thus, the reality of 'divide and rule' often changed during decolonisation.[53] On the other hand, the nationalists' priority was to create the united front which would convince the colonial state that it deserved to form the first independent government. Here again, the urgency of the task and the necessity to achieve a broad nationalist alliance did not always coincide with the most politic approach to national integration. Where, for example, nationalist success demanded the political 'elimination' of one (ethnic, religious, racial, regional or even social) group, trouble was being stored for the post-colonial order.

Third, structural factors also affected the resolution of the crisis of nationality and sovereignty. By structural factors, I mean the factors impinging on the structural relationship between state and society at independence.[54] On the formal side, this included the political institutions set up for the government of the country – political parties as well as all the constitutional and other functional devices established to promote the construction, stability and good management of the nation-state.

Attempts made to give structural reality to some form of isomorphism between society and state (for example to maintain regional, religious and ethnic balances in state institutions) would obviously be relevant here. More importantly perhaps would be the form and texture of political accountability built into the post-colonial political system. For, as I have repeatedly argued, the nature of political accountability and the way in which it operates in practice are probably the single most important indicators of the relations between state and civil society.[55]

It is important to note here that the action of post-colonial governments, like that of colonial governments had unintended effects on the process of national integration. At the simplest level, the decision to recognise discrete social, religious, racial or any other category and to give it (formal or informal) political representation as a means of cementing unity and exorcising fissiparous tendencies was as likely as not to reinforce or even create a politically consequential sense of 'otherness'. If being 'other' matters politically, differences become more pronounced.[56]

There is thus a sensitive dialectical relationship between the construction of a nationality and the appeasement of the politically self-conscious constituent elements of civil society. It is in this respect eminently instructive to remember that in the sixties and early seventies some political analysts of 'developing countries' held Lebanon and Sri Lanka to be the most successful cases of the creation of political structures capable of maintaining national integration.[57] By the same token, it would be most unwise to make predictions about which African countries are more likely to have successfully constructed a viable nationality.

What emerges from this discussion is not that political analysts of Africa have been wrong to emphasise the crucial importance of national integration. Indeed, the process of the construction of a nationality is central to the politics of all modern countries, as recent events in the Soviet Union, China and many (Eastern or Western) European countries have shown. What has often been missing is a sense that the question of nationality and sovereignty is not peculiar to contemporary African politics but central to the politics of the nation-state *qua* nation-state.[58] Understanding the specific nature of the crisis of nationality and sovereignty in the African post-colonial context requires an analysis which sets the process in its world historical, and not just African, setting. The emergence of nationalism as a powerful political force which led to the creation of nation-states is a modern historical phenomenon of which Africa, by way of the colonial process, became a part.

The very creation of a nation-state, in Africa as elsewhere, reveals new political motives and brings together new political interests which tend to work for the preservation of the nation-state.[59] On balance, it is in the interest of more people to maintain than to destroy the nation-state. Even those who are, or consider themselves to be, disenfranchised politically from the nation-states rarely consider seceding or constructing a new one. Their aim is usually to take over control of the state so as to create a political balance more favourable to them (as was the case, for example, of the Eritrean People's Liberation Front [EPLF]).[60] Thus, once created, the nation-state is more likely to survive as a nation-state than not. Furthermore, the international community acts as a guarantor of existing nation-states and a deterrent to their dismantlement.

There are, of course, significant exceptions and these exceptions matter. In Africa, as elsewhere, there are a number of countries where groups of people do not accept the legitimacy of the existing nation-state and would wish to join or create another nation-state.[61] Not surprisingly, however, there has hitherto been in Africa an impressive consensus not to admit changes in the boundaries inherited at independence. The key question is whether this consensus will survive the post-colonial period during which nation-states are still unsure of their nationality and mindful of the fragility of their national integration. The history of Europe would suggest that fissiparous tendencies sometimes re-emerge with greater vigour once the nation-state *qua* nation-state is considered strong and mature. The same could easily happen in Africa.

It may be, therefore, that in Africa, as elsewhere, the nature of the crisis of nationality and sovereignty will change over time, as the nation-state itself changes both domestically and in relation to others. The process by which nationalist governments undertook at independence to create a nationality and uphold sovereignty was not in and of itself different from that which attended earlier national constructions in Europe and elsewhere. By this I mean not that the problems were the same but that the construction was.

It is apparent that there is significant continuity in the development of nationalism worldwide and that post-colonial Africa is but the final episode in the process of the construction of the modern nation-state. There is little prospect that many new nation-states will now be created (Palestine probably but Kurdistan probably not). If that is so, the management of the crisis of nationality and sovereignty and the evolution of the nation-state in Africa are likely to bear some considerable resemblance to that of the evolution of the nation-state everywhere. The likelihood of African countries surviving intact into the twenty-first century is likely to be determined by the same factors which affect the viability of nationhood elsewhere. The plausibility of Zaïre as a nation-state is no better and no worse than the plausibility of the Soviet Union. Now that the two have been constructed, the probability that they will survive as nation-states is similarly dependent on a number of domestic factors which, however different, do have some common implications.

Because the nation-state is often a more recent construction in Africa than it is elsewhere, one would expect African governments to move swiftly against any challenge to their national integrity. For this reason, one can be confident that no African nation-state will be readily dismembered from within.[62] Beyond that, however, it is as likely in Africa as anywhere else, that political discontent will manifest itself in challenges to the very notion of nation-state. What would then be at issue, as it already is in some parts of the world (witness the problems in the Soviet Union), is not so much the existence of an independent country *per se* but the rigidities in the political system which its construction as a nation-state implies.[63]

Historically, the construction of nation-states has required linguistic and cultural homogenisation (what B. Anderson calls *russification*), strong administrative centralisation and a form of political representation which favours the centre at the expense of the locality. There is now growing opposition to these characteristics of the modern nation-state in many parts of the world. It is reasonable to expect that similar opposition will in due course arise in Africa.[64] It is equally reasonable to assume that in Africa such opposition will be resisted on the grounds that, as newly created nation-states, African countries cannot afford to give in to demands which would threaten the very existence of the nation. It is on those grounds that most African governments argue that multi-party systems are not appropriate to Africa. But these claims ring increasingly hollow.

Although superficially it may appear as if the original crisis of nationality and sovereignty in post-colonial Africa continues unabated, in most instances this is not the case. There are, it is a true, a number of countries (e.g., Sudan, Ethiopia, Chad), all countries in some crucial respect different from the mass of Black African states, where the *Ur*-crisis of nationality and sovereignty is still unresolved. Nevertheless, the immense majority of African countries, even those which became independent more recently (e.g., Angola, Mozambique, Zimbabwe) are no longer threatened by secession – Biafra was the turning point in this respect – even if their governments are engulfed in civil war. Neither the União Nacional de Independência Total de Angola (UNITA) nor the Resistência Nacional Moçambicana (RENAMO) are seeking to break up Angola and Mozambique as nation-states and to establish new, separate, nation-states. What is at stake now is no longer the national integrity of the post-colonial African countries but their political complexion, that which I have called the relationship between state and civil society.

The politics of civil society take many forms, including ethnicity, regionalism, religious revival, racial tension, etc. The state typically interprets, or pretends to interpret, such opposition in terms of challenges to the integrity of the nation and harks back to the original crisis of nationality and sovereignty which followed independence. This is not surprising. Nor is it new. Many non-African states still resort to the same arguments. What is at issue, however, is not the survival of the nation-state, perhaps the strongest political unit in the world today. What is at issue is the politics of the state.

The strong, centralising, homogenising, coercive and politically supreme state is today under attack throughout the world. Civil society is fighting back against the state-centred model of society, which is the legacy of nineteenth-century nation-building. In many European countries, the new political agenda stresses a move away from that model and calls for decentralisation, regionalisation, individualisation, etc. The same is likely to happen in Africa, regardless of the state's integrative discourse. For in Africa too there are now strong indications that civil society is becoming both more active and more successful in its resistance to the 'totalising' state and its concomitant statist politics.

8   The Crisis of Legitimacy and Representation

Once the legitimacy of colonial rule began to dissolve, colonial power was fatally undermined, for power without legitimacy can only be sustained by force and the use of force is costly. Colonial political accountability gradually became meaningless. The demise of colonial legitimacy was paralleled by the near-universal recognition of the historical legitimacy of the demands for self-government and independence. Nationalism was now legitimate for all. Thus, the legitimacy of nationalism legitimised nationalist politics, even when the colonial state objected to the identities and tactics of the nationalists. The colonial powers (except Portugal) came to realise, even if they loathed to admit it, that ultimately nothing could prevent the transfer of power to the Africans.[1]

During that historically crucial period of decolonisation, power was conceived largely in instrumental terms. The paramount question was that of the political significance of the evolving balance of power between individual nationalist organisations and the colonial state – that is, who would eventually be entrusted with the government of the new country. After independence, after the establishment of universally recognised nation-states, however, the issue of the legitimacy of power re-emerged with greater urgency than ever.[2]

The connection between legitimacy and representation during the period of decolonisation was straightforward.[3] Competing nationalist organisations attempted to demonstrate their legitimacy as nationalist spokesmen by claiming to represent the colonial subjects. This was tested by the colonial state through elections (when free and fair elections were allowed) before independence. Where there were no elections, the nationalists sought to prove before the UN and other international forums their claim to represent the colony's population by (peaceful or violent) political mobilisation.[4] Whatever the means by which a particular nationalist party established its credentials, the proof of its claim ultimately rested upon its success. Whichever party was recognised by the colonial state as its official interlocutor *ipso facto* became the legitimate representative of the inhabitants of the nation-to-be.[5]

What this meant was that during decolonisation not only were the notions of legitimacy and representation virtually coterminous but they were also overdetermined by the colonial political context. Within that context, legitimacy and representation had a fairly narrow definition. The scope of legitimate nationalist political action, although it expanded as independence drew near, was tightly circumscribed by the colonial state.[6]

From a broad perspective, the overall legitimacy of the nationalist claim, whatever its political persuasion, was a result of the (domestic and international) erosion in the legitimacy of colonialism rather than of the representativeness of specific nationalist parties *per se*. In other words, the legitimacy of nationalist parties derived rather more from their nationalist quality than from their representativeness as organisation.[7]

Nevertheless, one of the most effective means of containing nationalist pressure was to insist that nationalist organisations should be representative of the African population on whose behalf they claimed to speak. So long as the colonial state could find sufficient division of support within the nationalist movement, it could question the legitimacy of its claim – even if officially it recognised the legitimacy of the transfer of power.[8]

This instrumental quality of both legitimacy and representation did not provide secure foundations for the post-colonial political order. The legitimacy of power and the nature of representation in the newly created nation-state were now largely determined by the greater goal of constructing its nationality and guaranteeing its sovereignty. Because the legitimacy and representativeness of the nationalist party which had taken power at independence derived primarily from its political success, the notion of power which guided the early years of its rulership followed the same pattern.

Success in achieving national unity, creating a nationality and managing national integration, was often taken to be sufficient proof of the continued legitimacy of the regime. Conversely, any opposition to the regime was usually construed as a challenge to the national integrity of the nation-state.[9] There is nothing new in this. All post-revolutionary regimes (and independence was a political revolution) legitimise their existence and justify their deeds by reference to a greater god.[10]

It is important, therefore, to analyse the post-colonial crisis in legitimacy and representation in its appropriate historical context. This means that any attempt to define these notions and examine their relevance to the understanding of the politics of contemporary Africa must also clarify the relation between the conceptual and the historically specific. Analysts of African politics ought not to discuss the issues of legitimacy and representation in modern Africa as though there were nothing problematic in the use of these concepts in the post-colonial period. The question of whether a particular post-colonial regime is legitimate and/or representative cannot meaningfully be answered unless we have some notion of what the construction of the independent nation-state implies for the concept of power.[11]

Power entails a notion of political reciprocity. But there can only be political reciprocity when power is legitimate. And power can only be legitimate when it is organised on a (recognisable and mutually acceptable) principle of political accountability.[12] In practice political accountability must ultimately be sustained by some form of representation, however unlike it may be from that offered in liberal political theory. Thus, legitimacy and representation are interrelated and it is the task of political analysis to determine the patterns of causalities which link them within a particular historical context.[13]

The origin of the crisis of legitimacy and representation in (independent) Africa derived from two sets of contradictions: first, the contradiction between the colonial and post-colonial meanings of power; second, the contradiction between the *pays légal*, that is the constitutional order of the new nation, and the *pays réel*, that is the realities of post-independence Africa.

Colonial power issued from the fiat of conquest. Its limits were not marked out by the legitimacy of colonial rule in the eyes of the colonial subjects but by the twin constraints of consent and collaboration. Post-colonial power issued from the conquest of the colonial state which, although it inherited the colonial instruments of power, derived its legitimacy essentially from its nationalist success. However, the principle of colonial political accountability which determined the context within which nationalist legitimacy and representation were defined was not easily compatible with the constitutional foundations on which the new nation-state was to be erected.[14]

Regardless of the mechanisms of decolonisation, all African countries set down constitutional limits on power within the *pays légal*. These rested on concepts of legitimacy and representation which had no precedents in the *pays réel*, for at no point during the colonial period and during decolonisation had the limits of power been defined in terms of the notions of legitimacy and representation eventually written into the new constitutional order. In other words, the *pays légal* had no deep historical roots in the *pays réel*.[15] It should thus have come as no surprise that the political practices of post-colonial states were at some considerable variance with the constitutional order in place. Political analysis is more fruitfully employed in attempting to understand the specific historical nature of the gap between *pays légal* and *pays réel* than in berating the existence of such a gap.

The history of political legitimacy in the post-colonial order went through at least three phases. The first was the post-nationalist period, during which the legitimacy of the African regimes stemmed from their nationalist antecedents. The second was the period during which the holders of state power sought to fend off demands for greater representation by invoking a doctrine of legitimacy derived from the historical tasks of nation-building and economic development, that is the period of the construction of the patrimonial/prebendal state.[16] The third (and, for most African countries, the current) period appears to be that of the 'popular' challenge – the claim for greater representation, leading often to the call for multi-party democracy. The evolution (by no means immutable or linear) through these phases reflects the increasing distance between the present political order and that which emerged at independence.

During the first phase, the length of which differed for each country, the rulers of the newly independent countries were able to stretch the limits of power (as defined in their constitutions) because the legitimacy of their political action derived almost wholly from their nationalist credentials. Governments faced no politically credible opposition simply because they possessed a monopoly of nationalist legitimacy. All opposition to the regime was construed to be, and often was, opposition from those who had not acquitted themselves well in the Manichean nationalist struggle. Although such opposition frequently did represent genuine and substantial political opinion, it could be dismissed as being 'counter-revolutionary'.[17]

For the most part, even those who opposed the regimes in place accepted the legitimacy of their 'civilising mission' (nation-building and economic development) just as, on the whole, they accepted the continued need for national unity.[18] During this first period, the more severe the threats to national integrity were (as they are still today in the more recently independent countries of Angola and Mozambique), the more compellingly powerful was this notion of legitimacy and the more determined governments were to resist calls for greater representation.[19]

Eager post-colonial regimes engaged in the task of (political and economic) nation-building easily overstretched themselves. Where legitimacy was unchallenged and where representation was weak, political accountability was unsubstantial. Constitutions were revised or, more often, ignored and the limits of power stretched even further. Where that happened (e.g., Guinea, Ghana), legitimacy declined and resistance grew. In some countries (Côte d'Ivoire, Senegal), where the perceived threats to national integrity were minimal or where there was an exceptional degree of political unity or, even, where the rulers understood early the dangers of limited accountability, efforts were made to restore some balance between legitimacy and representation. In the majority of cases, however, the decline of legitimacy was compensated by an increase in coercion.[20]

Looking at political events in those countries which became independent around 1960, it is quite clear that the first period, during which regime legitimacy was unquestioned, lasted only about five years. For it was approximately around 1965/6 that there occurred a rupture distinctly marked by political convulsions in many African countries. There was at around that time a wave of sharp political reorientations such as the 'turn to the left' in countries like Guinea, Ghana, Uganda, Congo, Tanzania, Mali, etc.[21] More ominously, it was at that stage that many African governments were overthrown by their armed forces.

This was not coincidental. With very few exceptions, African armies either did not exist prior to independence or had not participated in the nationalist struggle. As African regimes expanded their armed forces and deployed them against their internal foes, they undermined their own legitimacy and made it possible for the men in uniform to claim to represent the voice of the silenced civil society.[22] Even in those countries where coups did not take place, the role of the coercive arm of the state was considerably strengthened – frequently leading to coups at a later stage. Whether civilian regimes were overthrown or not, the spate of 'unconstitutional' challenges to post-nationalist regimes which occurred at that time demonstrated the extent to which the limits of power had been (over)stretched and representation stifled.[23]

The second period witnessed the attempt by (civilian and military) regimes to construct a new principle of post-nationalist political accountability. In the face of disintegrating political unity and growing opposition, rulers now sought to transform nationalist legitimacy into the new legitimacy of a more realistic political order. This involved a dual process. On the one hand, the state acknowledged that the myth of political unanimity could no longer be sustained. There were genuine differences of political opinion and not every dissenting voice aimed to destroy the newly created nation-state. On the other hand, it claimed that the constitutions inherited at independence were unworkable because they were inappropriate to Africa. It argued that local political conditions should determine the framework of political action.[24]

What this meant in simple terms was that the rulers of post-colonial African states were willing to recognise some of the paramount political interests in the country, and to some extent share power with them, in exchange for an acceptance of a new and more tightly regulated political order. The notions of legitimacy and representation were redefined accordingly.

Whereas in the first period Africans accepted the post-colonial political order in Africa, universally the one-party state, because they recognised the legitimacy of the party as the bearer of national aspirations, they now questioned the claim of the party-state to speak on their collective behalf. Elections for single candidates were only acceptable when it was believed that the post-nationalist state worked for the commonweal. Once that illusion had been banished, the ruled began to clamour for proper representation. Rulers were no longer given a blank cheque; they were called to account for their action. A new principle of political accountability was developing.

This period, which lasted roughly until the late seventies/early eighties, saw the development of what is usually taken to be the 'African' model of politics, that is what is often called patrimonialism and/or prebendalism.[25] The political system remained unitary (i.e., one-party state) but it allowed increased 'representation' by means of widespread networks of patron–client relationships.[26] Such networks, which essentially provided vertical lines of patronage between the centre and the localities, legitimised the political regime, at least in the eyes of those who benefited from patrimonial largesse.[27]

Political bosses were 'legitimate' because they could provide for their clients access to state resources. Their 'representativeness' as political bosses issued from their ability to deliver. Inevitably, there were many without bosses and hence without access to the state. There continued to be opposition to the regimes whose survival depended on their ability successfully to manage the patrimonial state. Though military regimes had the added advantage of controlling the state's means of coercion, they, as regimes, were subject to the same political pressures. When they did not deliver, they lost legitimacy.[28]

The third period began when, from about the mid-seventies onwards, African regimes began seriously to run out of resources. The 1973 oil crisis ushered in an era of economic degradation in Africa from which (with the exception of states like Botswana and Gabon) it has not recovered. The crisis of indebtedness which followed further weakened African economies. The eighties witnessed catastrophic economic failures and exposed the insatiable greed of state rulers and African élites. This continuing economic crisis has revealed the excesses of state appropriation, the weaknesses of state economic structures (e.g., parastatals) and the inability of political bosses to satisfy their clients. It has also revealed the limits of existing principles of accountability as well as the growing strength of civil society.[29]

As a result there has been yet another shift in the notions of legitimacy and representation. Even in those countries which only became independent in the seventies, nationalism has long ceased to be the legitimising factor. No regime in Africa today can plausibly claim greater legitimacy on account of its nationalist ancestry – as even Mugabe is finding out today. Nationalism is now part of the deep political history of the country. In those countries where the original nationalist party is still in power it derives even less legitimacy from its nationalist origin than from its ability to have survived in power.

The decline in resources available in African states is also very largely the result of the greater assertiveness of civil society against a generally weakened state.[30] The unitary political state has broken down even if the shell subsists. The politics of civil society have undermined the state where it matters most: in the economic sphere. In response to the state's attempt at economic hegemony, civil society has diverted production away from the state. Consequently, almost everywhere the state has lost legitimacy and, with it, power. Even where the state continues to appropriate prodigious amounts (as in Zaïre) it is losing untold revenues to the parallel economy (in effect the exchequer of civil society).[31]

As the structure of political power between rulers and ruled has changed, the crisis of legitimacy and representation has taken on a new form. There has been a greater recognition on the part of rulers and ruled alike that there is a closer link between legitimacy and representation than post-colonial African political systems had allowed for. Where there is no effective representation there is little legitimacy. Where regime legitimacy dissolves, parallel channels of representation are created outside the direct control of the state.[32]

If patrons can no longer provide for clients, the meaning of patrimonial representation changes. Unprovided clients become disenfranchised citizens and swell the ranks of civil society. They in turn seek other 'representatives', other means of being represented. They bypass the state. In the end, patrons without clients are equally, if not more, vulnerable than clients without patrons, for rulers without revenues are also without power. Producers can always find other patrons, other markets. The state, it is true, remains the great enabler. It is still the dominant economic actor. But where the representation and legitimacy of patrimonialism breaks down, the state inevitably loses ground to civil society.

The present political crisis in contemporary Africa is thus also a crisis of legitimacy and representation. The state in Africa today is searching for a response to the 'revenge' of civil society.[33] In a condition of greater penury, the state must be more sensitive to its constituents – allow more substantive representation – or it loses even more legitimacy. In political systems such as one-party states, where elections rarely provide sufficient depth of representation, other avenues have to be found. The weakness of so many African states, and the concomitant relative strength of civil society, has placed the question of representation squarely back at the centre of politics. In many African countries there is at the moment an attempt to devise new forms of representation with which to strengthen the badly eroded legitimacy of the state – hence the vigour of the calls for greater democracy in Africa.[34]

The post-nationalist state also sought legitimation in the need for 'development' – what came to be called later the model of 'development dictatorship', that is sacrificing 'formal' democratic representation in order to spur economic development.[35] Now that the legitimacy of the state has been gravely weakened, not least because its hegemonic interpretation of representation has failed to achieve substantial economic development, there are strong demands for what Sklar has called a 'developmental democracy'.[36]

The advantages of democracy in respect of representation are obvious: a democratic state would introduce more substantial representation and achieve greater legitimacy. These calls for greater democracy parallel demands by international and national aid donors for a move towards the liberalisation of the economy. For it is now believed in aid circles that free (or at least freer) market conditions would be infinitely more beneficial to Africans than state-led development.[37]

Whatever the merits of the economic arguments, there is no denying the present mood in Africa for greater democracy. There have recently been moves in several countries to hold much freer elections, for some of the military regimes in power to seek either electoral legitimacy or to relinquish power, and for some civilian regimes to allow or to announce some form of multi-party competition. It remains to be seen, however, whether these calls for greater democracy will lead to any recognisable abatement in the state's hegemonic drive.[38]

Of course, a general desire for more democracy and limited moves by some governments to introduce formally more representative forms of governance are no indications that democracy has broken out in Africa. But it is, and this is my point, evidence of the retreat of the state and of its consequent attempt to regain new legitimacy through greater representation.

Perhaps the most ample, and best documented, account of the evolution of the legitimacy of the state in Africa is to be found in literature. Certainly, literature is one of the most useful and consistently solid (though greatly neglected) sources of information about African politics. Writers of fiction have been among the most lucid and critical analysts of the African political order. While in the first period, they broadly went along with the state's ideology of legitimation, they were among the first to reveal the erosion in state legitimacy and to expose its hegemonic drive. The fact that many writers advocated radical or populist solutions is less important here than the fact that they denounced the vacuousness of the post-nationalist ideology.[39]

Rather more important for political analysis is their changed perception of the masses, that is civil society. Their earlier despair at the failure of the ruled to hold their governments to account has been qualified, if not replaced, by their recognition of the power of the politics of civil society. Ngugi's decision to write 'popular' theatre in Kikuyu, for example, is not just the invention of another means of fighting the regime; it is also partly (or perhaps primarily) a reflection of his perception of the strength of popular culture.[40] Reading African literature confirms that the present crisis is not just a crisis about the African state but a crisis about the political order in Africa.

I have so far insisted on the historical context of legitimacy simply because the period associated with decolonisation and independence was so momentous for the African political order. Nevertheless, political legitimacy contains a historical dimension which is not exhausted by the events of that period. The legitimacy of rulers in African countries today is also a product of the historical evolution of the legitimacy of rulership in Africa from pre-colonial times. As time elapses, the nationalist revolution becomes less relevant to present-day politics and the lines of continuity with the pre-nationalist political order re-emerge.

The failures of the post-nationalist period have reduced the legitimacy of that political order itself and contributed to a revival of interest in pre-nationalist as well as pre-colonial forms of political legitimacy. Above and beyond the nostalgia for 'traditional' politics which are harboured by a few in Africa (as anywhere else in the world), there is the much more persistent and pertinent issue of the relation between present and past notions of legitimacy.

The recent argument that democracy is indigenous to Africa, like the earlier argument that socialism was indigenous to Africa, is an argument about the quest for a modern political order based on 'traditional' African virtue.[42] In the face of the evident failure of the 'democracies' instituted at independence, there is some merit in asking whether the failure is due to Africa's inherently different political ways or to the unworkability of the political systems which independent Africa inherited.

At its most illuminating this line of enquiry focuses attention on the eminently relevant question of the contextual determinants of legitimacy. Here, paradoxically (or not), the ideas of Macchiavelli, Locke and Burke may turn out to be more relevant to the quest for the understanding of the legitimacy of rulership in Africa, even pre-colonial Africa, than the gyrations of some historians or political scientists.[43] To give one example, from a perspective different from that of liberal democracy, it becomes possible to understand why the private wealth (however gained) of African politicians may be a positive, not negative, contribution to their political legitimacy.[44]

What I want to emphasise here is the importance of the historical aspect of the very concept of legitimacy itself. To take another example, it is easy enough to understand, in terms which are familiar to the political experience of modern Western countries, why the post-colonial state has lost so much legitimacy in the recent past. It is less easy to see, in the selfsame modern liberal European terms, why individual members of discredited regimes do not always lose their own political legitimacy.

The apparent paradox may be linked to a notion of legitimacy which pays too little attention to the depth of the historical continuity between present and past political concepts. For this reason it might well be more appropriate to seek to understand these concepts, which quite obviously have modern political resonance, (at least partly) in terms of the analysis of pre-modern rather than modern European politics.[45] In other words, it is necessary to find a mode of analysis which does not fall prey either to the tautologies of cultural relativism or to the simplifying instrumentalities of functional or structural analysis.[46]

The legitimacy of political systems, of political action, of individual political actors, thus derive in part from factors which are not contained in the formal structures of the post-colonial political order. Consequently, it is limiting to seek to interpret changes in legitimacy in structural rather than in societal terms. Just as the state has lost ground to civil society, even if it has increased its means of coercion, so the concept of legitimacy derived from state-centred politics has lost ground to a notion of legitimacy sanctioned by civil society.[47] There is today in Africa increasing resistance to the forms of legitimacy peddled by the hegemonic state (particularly where patrimonialism cannot be sustained) and widespread disaffection with state politics, now largely bereft of legitimacy. And it is this lack of legitimacy which induces so many individuals, or groups, to undermine, abuse or even ignore the state.

In a situation where the legitimacy of 'modern politics' is in doubt, it is natural that the legitimacy of counter-élites, the 'representatives' of civil society as it were, should be strengthened. Not surprisingly, given the dominance of modern élites since independence, many of the counter-élites are 'traditional' politicians or political brokers.[48] It is therefore understandable, if not necessarily cheering, that thirty years after the end of colonial rule, so called 'traditional' politics should be more alive than it was in the decade which followed independence.

Modern and 'traditional', in the sense in which I have been using them, are of course not mutually exclusive. Nor are they the preserve of Africa. They are present in all polities. The important question for political analysis is the nature of the balance between the two. To some extent the re-emergence of apparently superseded 'traditional' politics is easily explained by the natural process of political adjustment which was bound to follow independence. However, it is also undoubtedly an indication of the lack of legitimacy of 'modern' politics and of the growing assertiveness of the politics of civil society.

The relationship between power and legitimacy, however, cannot be properly understood without reference to the notion and practice of representation.[49] The simple and straightforward relationship between the two contained in the liberal and socialist constitutions of the new African nations was never very convincing, or rather its relevance to the African political order was never very clear. It is even less clear now. Representation and legitimacy are causally very closely linked. Since there have been in Africa considerable shifts in the meanings and practicalities of political legitimacy, it stands to reason that the same has happened to the meanings and practicalities of representation.[50]

Without rehearsing the arguments to be found in the most illuminating studies on representation, it may be useful simply to list the different meanings which may be contained in the notion.[51] To represent means, in the first instance, to be like, in descriptive terms, to be objectively and subjectively similar, as a human being, to those who are being represented. Second, it means to stand for, that is to be perceived as a representative, the legitimate spokesman for or interpreter of the objective, subjective and symbolic characteristics which define those who are being represented.

It means, third, to act for – to be mandated to take specific action on behalf of – the represented. Fourth, it means to represent the general but unspecified interests of a political constituency: to look after what the represented consider to be their legitimate interests but in relation to the general national interest. Finally, it means to represent the interests, that is to look after and defend the narrowly defined sectional interests, of the members of the represented political community (on the assumption that it is possible for these interests to be clearly defined and clearly perceived as sectional interests by others).

It will be self-evident, even without providing specific examples for each of the meanings of representation above, that the liberal and Marxist concepts of representation (the two prevalent constitutional models in Africa today) are narrowly defined and contain only some of those meanings.[52] This is because their system of formal representation and their definition of the representative presuppose a (freely evolved or class) consensus on the appropriate meanings of representation.

Liberal and Marxist analyses start from the premise that political representation means the representation of specific, objectively defined and universally recognised interests. They also agree on the genealogy of such operational definitions: the concept of representation has evolved into its present, formal, structural form (elections) because of the historical evolution of the body politic within modern society. Where they differ is in their analysis of the causalities. Marxist theory posits that class defines interests. Liberal theory assumes that individual interests issue out of the ever-changing conditions of the citizenry and can meaningfully be aggregated across socio-economic lines.[53]

The establishment in post-colonial Africa of political systems based on liberal or Marxist premises led to a theory and practice of representation which emphasised specific, limited and limiting, instrumental meanings. The assumption that the primary purpose of political representation was to give voice to the 'interests' of individual citizens or members of particular classes rested on a prior assumption about the relationship between the socio-economic and political spheres. This had important implications.

In a situation in which the creation of the state had preceded the construction of the nation-state, such assumptions narrowly constrained representation to what was never likely to be, and patently was not, a sufficiently meaningful and plausible political process for large numbers of people. Though the notion of self-interest contained in liberal and Marxist theory has universal application, it was not in and of itself sufficient to account for the various levels of representation relevant to the citizens of the new African countries.[54] Insofar as the constitutionally defined forms of representation failed (in practice at least) satisfactorily to include the levels of representation which were meaningful to the majority of the population, they lost legitimacy.

The post-colonial African political system thus evolved in two different ways. On the one hand, the formal political processes were altered by political practices moulded and modified by differing (often dubbed 'traditional') meanings of representation. On the other hand, other political processes were invented (chiefly within civil society) to give substance to the meanings of representation which were not contained in the formal political system.

The structures of political representation extant at independence derived partly from colonial practice and partly from the theories of the modern European state. Whereas colonial rule had allowed, and often encouraged, a corrupted continuation of the representative structures derived from the 'traditional' African communities which came under its jurisdiction, nationalism sought to bring together all structures of representation in the one nationalist moment. In the process, the nationalists frequently attempted to extinguish, or at least to reduce the political force of, many of the 'traditional' forms of representation.[55] For obvious reasons, they wanted to achieve a modern political consensus in which nationalist legitimacy would be transformed into representativeness.

The nationalist party, however, never represented more than an overarching nationalist *general will* for independence and the creation of a modern nation-state. This level of representation was superimposed upon, and did not necessarily contain, the other meanings which had been present in colonial and pre-colonial times. In one-party states, the only effective means for the party to represent local constituencies lay in its role as political machine. When it failed, its representative function ceased.

The functioning political machine could act as a funnel for the informal representation of ethnic, regional, religious, racial, professional, social, economic and other interests. These individual and collective interests, however, were not easily aggregated nor were they easily satisfied within a unitary (one-party state) political structure. Party representation, in the modern European form to be found in Africa, is a political structure best suited to the fourth meaning of representation discussed above (i.e. the representation of the general interest of a political constituency). It is not a particularly appropriate or effective political mechanism for the other four levels of representation. For this reason, the presently much heralded multi-party political system would not in and of itself address the fundamental cause of the present crisis of representation in Africa – although plainly it would go a long way towards reducing political abuse and enhancing the legitimacy of state politics.

Formal structures of representation (as in western Europe) work because there is an historically logical fit between the consciousness and formulation of political interests and the existing party channels, not because the multi-party political system is *ipso facto* better. When this fit disappears, as it has done on occasion in the not-too-distant past of those selfsame European countries, the effectiveness and legitimacy of the representative system dissolves. There is a crisis of legitimacy and representation. The same applies to Africa. In the world of the modern nation-state, this crisis works itself out, domestically, in the conflict between state and civil society – the ultimate stage of which is civil war. It is for this reason that I lay such emphasis on the need to understand the politics of civil society in contemporary Africa.

As concerns representation this means starting at the very beginning. We need to understand the various meanings of representation present in civil society. We need to understand the political relevance for representation of the relationship between forms of individual self-identity and allegiance to the community. We need to examine the different political functions which individual Africans and Africans collectively expect their representatives to perform and to understand how these expectations impinge on the body politic.

This means, *inter alia,* that we need to analyse how apparently non-political activities fulfil eminently political roles. We need to know how religion, both as a system of belief and as an organisation principle, affects the meanings and functions of representation. We need to take into account kinship, family and other forms of interpersonal relations. We need to pay particular attention to the political functions of the so-called informal (social, cultural and economic) structures which abound in Africa. We need, finally, to work towards an analysis capable of accounting for the horizontal links between such informal structures and the vertical links between the localities and the centre.

9 The Crisis of Accumulation and Inequality

Although I have so far concentrated on more overtly political issues, many would argue that the root cause of the political crisis in contemporary Africa lies in its economic failure, that is in the widespread crisis of production.[1] There is no doubt that the present economic condition of Africa taken as a whole is not cheering. There seem to be today more frequent cases of more severe famines than there were ten or thirty years ago. All the economic indicators, from debt to growth, are poor, if not downright alarming.

Food production appears to be increasingly insufficient to feed Africa's population. Population growth rates are among the highest in the world. Prospects for self-sustained economic growth are, in most countries, exceedingly slim. Africa's industrial development is lagging behind that of other so-called 'Third World' countries, particularly in Asia. External dependency on aid is growing. Social and economic inequalities appear to be sharpening over time.[2] The political implications of the economic crisis are clear, even if its precise nature is not necessarily as clear, for, as I argue above, power and production are linked. Where production is deficient, whatever the reason, power is diminished. Where power is diminished, the political crisis deepens.

There are, of course, severe objective constraints to the potential for economic growth in many African countries, although it must be recognised that several African countries (e.g., Nigeria, Zaïre, Angola, Cameroon) do have enormous economic resources.[3] Many of these constraints are beyond the control of the governors of these countries. Plainly, there is little that human agency can do about the abysmally low productive capacity of many countries or about the brutalising effects of an unpropitious ecology and an unpredictable climate.

All this is true but I want here to focus my attention on the economic consequences of political action. However severe the constraints on African economies, it can scarcely be denied that the present crisis of production is largely man-made.[4] While there can be no satisfactory generalisation about the causal relationship between political mismanagement and economic crisis – each case must be studied on its own merit – it is not difficult to show that the economy is better managed in some African countries than in others.

Among the poorly endowed countries, Malawi and Cape Verde, for instance, are more successful economically than Mali or Guinea-Bissau. Among the generously endowed countries, Botswana and Côte d'Ivoire have been relatively well managed while others, like Nigeria, Guinea, Zaïre and Angola, have sunk deeper and deeper into economic crisis.[5] Whatever the immediate reasons for the economic success or failure of these countries (and all have been affected by the current debt crisis), such diversity of political cause and economic effect points to the decisive political relevance of human agency on the economic condition of individual African countries.

I have chosen specifically to examine the crisis of accumulation and inequality – rather than the more general crisis of production – because it seems to me clear that these are the two aspects of production which are most directly amenable to human agency.[6] Both are central to economic practice. Theories of economic development, whatever their perspective, emphasise the relationship between accumulation, growth and development. Accumulation enables individual and collective actors, above all the state, to invest and spend productively. The capacity of the state to accumulate is a fairly precise indication of its power and of its ability to act productively upon the economy. Without accumulation, however, there is little scope for productive investment. The same is true of producers and entrepreneurs. Without a surplus, some form of accumulation, there can be no individual economic progress. Whether state accumulation or individual economic progress are *ipso facto* productive for the community are separate questions.

If accumulation is a raw economic indicator, inequality is a raw social indicator. All social theories, whatever their perspective, propose accounts of inequality derived from specific assumptions about the link (causal or not) between the economic and social realms. In all human societies there is, patently, economic and social inequality. The question for political analysis is whether such inequality is, or can be, productive.[7]

Liberal and Marxist theories both argue that inequality is the primary motor of economic development though, of course, they disagree about the causes, political implications and possible remedies of economic inequality.[8] The notion of inequality is thus not, in and of itself, sufficient to determine the nature and depth of an economic crisis. However, the politics of inequality, of which famine is one extreme, are indicative of the relationship between power and production. In this sense, understanding inequality is supremely relevant to an understanding of politics in contemporary Africa.

An analysis of the crisis of accumulation and inequality means, there-fore, an analysis of the various way in which post-colonial governments have proposed to manage their economies and of the various means which they have employed to do so. It is not my intention here to review the economic policies of African states, and even less to provide a balance sheet of economic success and failure. Others have done this.[9] I want instead to analyse comparatively, and in the appropriate historical context, the political implications of the processes of accumulation and inequality at work in Africa since independence. I want above all to examine some of the as-sumptions made about the relationship between political action and the crisis of accumulation and inequality.

The political analysis of post-colonial Africa has tended to focus atten-tion on two sets of factors: on the one hand, the weakness and extroverted nature of African economies and, on the other, the largely unproductive quality of state accumulation.[10] Both are broadly relevant.

There is no denying the consequences for Africa of its integration into the world economy during the colonial period.[11] Whatever the complexion of the colonial economy, its central feature was the exploitation (*stricto sensu*) of the colonies to further colonial economic development. Whether this meant that the management of such exploitation had economically productive effects for the colonial subjects is a separate question which can only fruitfully be answered by historical research on different colonies.[12]

The immediate consequences of the integration of Africa into the world economy were, first, to make African producers, and by implication African economies, dependent on markets outside their control and, second, to transfer decision-making about the colonies' economic development away from Africa.[13] Since the vagaries of the colonial economy largely determined the parameters of post-colonial production, it is beyond doubt that, at independence, the governments of the new African nation-states found that their options were limited.[14]

It can, of course, be argued that the exploitation of Africa's resources was in the long-term interest of Africa. At independence, African countries would in any event have wanted to exploit the resources they possessed and, to the extent that the colonial economy had successfully initiated and properly managed such exploitation, it would have helped develop the productive capacity of the new nation-state. The profitable exploitation of agricultural and mineral resources necessarily implies trade on the world market. Hence, in this view, the extroversion of African economies is the result of the resources they possess rather than of colonial policy.[15]

This is a plausible but rather mischievous argument precisely because power and production are always causally related. During the colonial period, power lay in the hands of the colonial state and it was for the interests which the colonial state represented that accumulation and inequality were productive. Its economic policies derived primarily from colonial political accountability even if at times they were productive for some colonial subjects. However productive these policies might have been, there can be no gainsaying the determining importance for African economies of their colonial experience.[16]

There is, however, no necessary causal link between the nature of the colonial legacy and the management of that legacy by the post-colonial state. Even given the extroversion of African economies, their reliance on a limited range of agricultural and/or mineral resources and their relatively unfavourable comparative advantage, it can be argued that the post-colonial state wasted much of its colonial legacy.

If, to follow a well-worn argument, it is true both that the colonial state was efficient in the management of the exploitation of African economies and that it siphoned off most of the profit, then it must also be true that the colonial state stood to gain much from the acquisition of such means of exploitation. Some analysts thus conclude that the primary cause of the present economic crisis in Africa is not so much the position of weakness from which the new nation-states started as the consequence of the colossal incompetence and insatiable greed of those who have been in control of the post-colonial state.[17]

Much recent analysis of Africa's economic crisis thus focuses attention on the unproductive nature of state accumulation.[18] The argument here is twofold. First, the state is overdeveloped and consumes a disproportionate share of the country's revenues. This is partly a consequence of the colonial legacy and partly because the state is the main locus for individual (social and economic) advancement. The colonial state was relatively unproductive because it was more concerned with the exploitation of the colony than with its development (but at least was relatively well managed). The post-colonial state became even less productive and it was poorly managed.

The post-colonial state became hegemonic and patrimonial, that is it served the individual and class accumulation of those who had access to its revenues. It grew in size, personnel and greed out of all proportion to the resources of the country. In time the state came to need greater and greater revenues simply to satisfy its priority constituencies (e.g., some ethnic groups, armed forces).[19] The consequence of such excessive appropriation of the country's resources were profound. Potential resources were diverted away from the official economy in order to avoid the clutches of the state. This, in turn, led to a decline in the state's revenue and thus to even greater efforts at state appropriation.

Second, far too small a proportion of the state's accumulation was being invested productively.[20] Post-colonial African states, the argument goes, have often tended to spend money where it was least likely to generate economic growth. Admittedly, at independence, African governments incurred necessary expenditures on education, the infrastructure and social services simply to redeem some of the pledges made during the nationalist campaign. Education is probably Africa's success story. Beyond this, however, African governments have frequently spent large amounts on parastatals and/or prestige industrial or agro-industrial projects which simply could never be productive. The systematic attempt to develop import-substitution industries or to set up large agro-transformation industries for which neither supply nor market existed are examples of what many analysts consider to be counter-productive policies.[21]

Furthermore, critics argue that there has generally been in Africa a bias towards urban and/or industrial projects which is also economically counter-productive. Few African countries have the financial or natural resources, or indeed the market, to sustain a profitable industrial development in that area. Even where foreign aid is instrumental in setting up industry, the projects still divert considerable resources, provide few local jobs and are almost never profitable. Investment is wasted twice over because it is not used productively in other sectors of the economy. The bias towards urban development, understandable as it is given the political weight of urban areas, is diverting resources away from agriculture, still the major productive sector in most African countries.[22]

The argument against what Sklar calls 'developmental dictatorship' is not just that it serves as justification for widespread abuse of power but that, from the economic point of view, it fails to bring about economic growth.[23] African governments have had ambitions to pursue policies of 'primitive accumulation' (i.e. the exploitation of rural production) to achieve industrialisation. Although they have often constructed authoritarian political structures, they have not achieved either the degree of accumulation that is necessary or the degree of investment that is wanted for successful industrialisation.

African states may be authoritarian but they are weak. Despite formidable coercive powers, African rulers are rarely in a position to enforce 'primitive accumulation' and rarely able to resist the demands of political clientelism. As a result, they lose both the control of the productive economy and the support of those producers who suffer from the state's relentless hegemonic drive.[24]

The history of the relationship between the state and agricultural marketing boards is, in this respect, highly instructive.[25] On the whole, the colonial state was coherent in its use of these marketing boards for the exploitation of agricultural resources. Since it wanted them to maximise both production and revenues, it maintained a relatively careful balance between what went out and what came in. Price stabilisation could profitably be used to help maximise production. Exploitation was made possible by monopoly control of exchange within artificially defined trade zones. The colonial rulers knew that excessive appropriation would result in reduced or diverted production.

Their post-colonial successors were less careful. They saw rightly that marketing boards could be used to maximise revenues for the state but they failed to see with the same clarity that, for the system to work, a delicate balance had to be maintained between state appropriation and producer income.[26] The marketing boards had originally been set up to protect producers from fluctuations in world market prices. This they had done, with relative success, under colonial rule. But the hegemonic post-colonial state often ignored this essential function.

The relentless and systematic attempt by the state to use the marketing boards simply as a means of 'primitive accumulation' could not be sustained.[27] Where producers considered that the boards had ceased to serve them usefully they bypassed them. State coercion simply led to a reduction in the production of export crops and to a shift into food production (usually profitable since food has often been in short supply in Africa since independence). Where possible, there has also been smuggling (sometimes on a gigantic scale) across borders. The end result has been decreased production of export crops and, reduced revenues and, consequently, diminished foreign exchange for the state.[28]

The paradoxical outcome of the exactions of the African state is that excessive appropriation, whatever form it takes, reduces the state's capacity to accumulate. This has most obviously been true in respect of agriculture but it is also true of areas of economic activity which the state controls far more directly, such as nationalised industries and parastatals.

The argument in favour of nationalisation was that it would be the most effective means of spurring economic development. Private enterprise could not be expected to provide the investment needed nor could it be trusted to work in the best, and most efficient, interest of the country as a whole. Leaving aside at this stage the theoretical and ideological arguments about the economic desirability of nationalised enterprises, it is instructive to ask why such policies did not have the desired effects.[29]

Where nationalised industries and parastatals failed, it was often because of, rather than despite, state policy. In the first instance, economic decisions about the need for state industries or parastatals were often taken on non-economic grounds such as national prestige (e.g., car-assembly in Guinea-Bissau) or ideology (e.g., parastatals in Tanzania).[30] Second, even where there was a justifiable economic ground for the setting up of such enterprises, they were often run as mere extensions of clientelist politics. (See, for example, the record of nationalised industries in Sékou Touré's Guinea or Nkrumah's Ghana.)[31] In other words, they were assessed more in terms of what they achieved politically than economically.

Third, even where (as in Tanzania) they were run according to economic logic, they often became instruments of individual appropriation instead of state accumulation.[32] Finally, even (or perhaps, particularly) when they performed relatively successfully, state enterprises (such as marketing boards) were often abused by the state, leading to a decline in productivity and profitability.

The widespread failure of African governments to run nationalised enterprises successfully has been very costly. Enormous resources have been wasted unproductively in a context where there was very little available for investment in the first place. This failure would be less economically and politically consequential if African governments actually did have a choice about whether or not to have national enterprises. But this is not really the case. All African governments, whatever their political complexion and whatever their managerial capability, require a certain number of national enterprises, if only because there are areas of vital economic activities for which no private (domestic or foreign) interest would ever be forthcoming.[33]

Thus, the central issue about national enterprises is not whether they are necessary but why they so consistently fail to perform as effectively as they ought to. To say that nationalised industries always perform badly is evidently nonsense – as is well demonstrated by the success of, for example, many French nationalised industries. There is no doubt a good case to be made for reducing the number of nationalised industries and parastatals in many African countries. Too many were set up for the wrong reasons. In the ultimate analysis, however, there will always be national enterprises in Africa, even in the most radical IMF blueprint.[34] The state will not simply go away. It is therefore essential properly to understand, in more general terms, the economic and political implications of the state's failure to use accumulation productively.

There are two possible lines of argument here. The first is that the present economic crisis in Africa is essentially the consequence of the state's incapacity to manage the economy productively.[35] The second is that, since it is not the business of the state to manage the economy, it should cease to interfere with the productive interplay of market forces.[36] The two arguments start from different theoretical and historical premises but they do agree on the centrality of the state. The one advocates a better and more efficient state, the other argues for a slimmed-down, less interventionist state.

The first line of argument is very much a child of the political and ideological climate of the post-war era in which there seemed to be an unbounded belief in the productive role of the state. European countries had largely been rebuilt by the state. In some countries (e.g., France and Italy) nationalised industries had blazed the trail of economic recovery. In Japan, the state closely supervised industrial policies. Indicative planning – consultation between the state and industry on the broad indicators of economic production – had proved to be both effective and rational. Furthermore, there had been the establishment of the welfare state, universally recognised as a major advance against inequality.

It thus stood to reason that the newly independent African countries, born (in the 1960s) during the European economic 'miracle', should consider the economic role of the state crucial. Where the colonial state had demonstrated the effectiveness of central economic control, the post-war European state was a lesson in the productive management of the economy. There was in the sixties near unanimity about the central economic function of the African state. Even the American experience, in which recovery from the deepest economic crisis of the twentieth century had been achieved by state-led action, pointed in the same direction.

The second line of argument is more recent, although there were, in the sixties, voices (most notably that of Milton Freedman) which spoke against any economic role for the state. On the whole, however, the reinterpretation of classical political economy into the notion that the state ought not to seek to manage the economy is recent.[37] It has its roots in the widespread disillusionment with the economic failure of African states and with the gradual realisation that, in Africa, state economic hegemony appears incompatible with the rational, let alone productive, use of accumulation.[38]

This view was sharply reinforced by the backlash against the welfare state and the revival of the doctrine of the free market economy which have swept Europe and America since the late seventies. This change in attitude is itself connected with the consequences of the economic crisis which started in the mid-seventies with the rise in oil prices. The remark by a British politician that in future British aid should be conditional on 'Third World' countries adopting British-style privatisation is typical of the present passion for market-led solutions.[39]

European and American economists, aid experts and international civil servants have always interpreted events in Africa (at least partly) in response to the political *desiderata* of their domestic constituencies. It is thus less important to trace the genealogy of these debates than to understand their relevance to Africa. The policies of the IMF/World Bank and of the many national and international organisations which are active in Africa are all determined by the donor governments.[40] The politics of aid are not primarily about listening to the inhabitants of Africa, even if the current fashion is for donors and lenders to claim to speak on behalf of 'the small guy' against the state.

In conceptual terms, however, there has always been too little connection between theories of economic development and an understanding of the role of the state in Africa. Just as the notion in the sixties of state-led development was based on a naïve reading of the possible economic role of the state in Africa, the present imperative of taking the state out of the economy is based on an illusion which is not likely to survive the next serious economic crisis in the West.[41]

The present economic crisis in Africa is essentially a crisis of production. The single most important constraint on state action is the context within which the country's economy operates.[42] It is worth repeating yet again that a number of African countries are probably not economically viable, at least not in the sense in which it is usually understood. This crisis in production works itself out in the crisis of accumulation and inequality, in which the state is the central but not the only economic actor.

Historically, economic development (as opposed to survival) has been the successful resolution of crises in production, or rather the productive resolution of crises of accumulation and inequality.[44] Development depends on technological innovation, accumulation and investment. African countries potentially have access to the technology they need. Their development thus rests on the productive resolution of the crisis of accumulation and inequality. I have hitherto only discussed accumulation. Let me now turn to the question of inequality.

I refer to a crisis of inequality rather than distribution precisely because I want to avoid making assumptions about the historically specific role of the modern state. The concept of inequality is one which is applicable to political communities across time and space, ancient, pre-modern or modern, African or European, whereas that of distribution derives from more specific historical settings in which there is a central political authority (e.g., the state) with responsibilities for distribution.[45]

The relation between inequality and accumulation may not be immediately apparent and yet it is fundamental to the process of economic development. At its simplest, in an economic zero-sum game, accumulation is proportional to inequality, that is accumulation by some is only possible at the expense of others. Where rich get richer, poor get poorer. All theories of economic development, however, are premised on the assumption that the economic system is not a zero-sum game. Again, in simple terms, this means that productive investment will produce more wealth than it started with, thus spurring economic growth.[46]

In the long term, therefore, the historical justification for the inequality which fuels development is that growth will create additional wealth for the community as a whole. Whether as a result, inequalities (that is the disparities between rich and poor) increase or decrease depends on the balance of power between rich and poor, rulers and ruled. All theories of economic development, whether liberal or Marxist, claim that inequalities are eventually offset by a general rise in living standards.[47]

What this means, then, is that inequality is inherent in economic development. The central issue is thus not whether there is inequality but how productive inequality is for economic development. The charge that the African state has presided over unacceptable levels of inequality is made not because there are firm moral principles with which to measure inequality but because inequalities in Africa have been so unproductive.[48]

It is true that where there is famine, a government has little moral legitimacy.[49] Yet even in cases of extreme inequalities, the historical assessment of regimes (like Stalin's) which achieve high levels of economic growth while starving their populations depends very much on the perception of the achievements rather than simply on the morality of the policy. In other words, the charge against African states is one of failure to achieve economic development rather than simply of exacerbating inequality.

Why is it that inequality in post-colonial Africa has not been as productive as it might have been? There are, it seems to me, at least three sets of reasons: historical, structural and political. The first refers to the conditions under which African countries became independent. The second has to do with the structural constraints on production found in most African countries. The third concerns the political overdetermination of the economic system in post-colonial Africa.

The historical conditions under which Africa became independent were not propitious for productive inequality.[50] For a revolution to be productive it needs to unleash the accumulated force of the inequalities of the previous regime for productive purposes. It is not difficult to see how the 'great' revolutions (e.g., French, Russian, Chinese) led to a mutation in the economic system which made it possible to increase production vastly.[51] But the colonial situation was different. Colonialism itself had led to a revolution in African production. Even where capitalism had not penetrated deeply, either geographically or economically, the creation of colonies linked their economies to the world economy. African production became part of a global economic system. It was that (economic) revolution which laid down the foundations for the economic development of the new independent African nation-states.[52]

Colonial rule thus exploited productively the inequalities created by the changing economy. While it is customary to think that, in doing so, colonial rule created a large class of exploited, disaffected and alienated Africans who were to become the bulwark of the nationalist movement, the reality was rather different. It is certainly true that the colonial economy created new, sharply felt, economic inequalities and that those who had clearly lost out were eager for the nationalists to triumph. However, and this is the key, colonialism also created a substantial class of Africans who benefited directly from the development of the new, modern, colonial economy. Africans, that is, who benefited from the inequalities created by the colonial revolution.[53]

With very few exceptions, it was those new African élites who constructed, financed, and often led the nationalist parties.[54] That they did so for honourable nationalist reasons does not detract from the fact that they believed independence would make it possible for them to benefit even more from the productive inequalities which the colonial economic revolution had brought about. Their intention was never to subvert the existing economic system, even less to construct an entirely new one. In that sense, the new African élites were not, and could not be, revolutionaries.

As concerns production, then, nationalism was based on a monumental misunderstanding – one which Fanon well understood and against which he warned.[55] The masses who supported nationalism expected or were led to expect that independence would bring an end to colonial inequalities. But the new African élites, who largely ran the nationalist parties, expected for their part that independence would permit the unfettered development of the pattern of productive inequalities which had served them well. Where (as, for example, in Côte d'Ivoire, Cameroon or Kenya) these new African élites (or their representatives) gained power at independence, they opted for what is usually labelled a capitalist road to development, that is, in effect state capitalism.[56] Where (as in Ghana, Guinea, Tanzania, Mozambique) they failed to take power, they were generally thwarted by politicians who favoured a non-capitalist road to development, that is, in effect, state socialism.[57]

The similarities between state capitalism and state socialism, however, were greater than the differences. Both systems allowed rulers to control the economy. Both systems enabled the state to continue to use the mechanisms of accumulation and appropriation which the colonial state had introduced. In both systems the state became a channel for individual economic advancement on a scale unparalleled in colonial history. As a result, the gap between state and civil society grew larger and sharper.[58] Most importantly, in both systems, economic and political power came to rest in the same hands. In such circumstances, inequalities became less productive, for it became easier for the state simply to appropriate rather than to reinvest accumulation productively.

The second set of reasons has to do with the structural constraints on production found in post-colonial Africa. For inequalities to be productive there must exist some form of economic structures in which accumulation can be invested productively. The colonial economy had not achieved this. To be sure, it had laid the foundations of a modern economy and it had created mechanisms for economic appropriation, but what it had rarely done, because that was not its task, was to create an infrastructure (e.g., investment banks) geared to national development. The economic development of individual African colonies was not considered from the perspective of future independent countries but rather from the more general perspective of the imperial economy. This is not surprising but it is crucial.[59]

Two consequences ensued from this structural deficiency. The first was that, while the legacy of the colonial order contained well-organised and highly efficient structures of appropriation, the post-colonial state inherited few structures of productive investment. To put it another way, most colonies simply did not possess the mechanisms by which accumulation and investment could profitably be linked.[60] Colonial decisions about appropriation had largely been structurally disconnected from decisions made about investment.

For all the emphasis on the need for colonies to be financially self-sufficient, little was done by the colonial powers to relate the balancing of colonial budgets with economic development.[61] The perspective of the colonial state was that of the intendant not of the entrepreneur. The perspective of the imperial captains of industry was different but whether or not they reinvested their colonial profits to benefit the future development of the local economy was determined by considerations which had little to do with the future health of the independent African nation. Generally, there were better and quicker profits to be made in commerce than in manufacturing industry.[62]

The second consequence was that imperial decisions about investment were not necessarily logically related to decisions about accumulation. The major period of investment in the African colonies occurred during the fifties and sixties for reasons which had less to do with economic rationality than with political expediency.[63] For it was after the Second World War that the major colonial powers decided to invest in the colonies so as to give substance to their colonial claim.

Given the context of world politics after the Second World War, the independence of India and Pakistan, the Chinese revolution and the fiascos of the Indonesian and Indo-China conflicts, colonial legitimacy demanded a new commitment to the social, economic and political welfare of the colonial subjects. Such investment could not easily be made out of colonial revenues and was therefore often financed by the metropolis. In the post-war historical context which gave rise to the welfare state in Europe, the imperial powers now accepted that they had direct responsibilities for the welfare of their colonial subjects and were thus willing to invest.

Since the impetus for such investment was extraneous to the colonies, there was a dichotomy between accumulation and productive investment which had serious effects. This belated imperial munificence for the welfare of their colonial subjects, largely financed from the metropolis rather than local accumulation, created the illusion of a state possessed of the means to take responsibility for the welfare of the people.[64] This was a myth so strong that it generated expectations which the post-colonial state could never fulfil, for such levels of state provisions could not be financed from the resources of the local economy.

These expectations were enflamed further by the implicit promise of nationalism to do even more for the welfare of Africans. Indeed, post-colonial states invested heavily in social and educational facilities after independence. Unfortunately, these investments were not made on the basis of any coherent economic logic. Above all, they were made with only a fraction of the resources which had been made available to the colonial state by the metropolitan exchequer. They could not be sustained and they sometimes bankrupted the state, further diminishing its capacity for pro-ductive investment.[65] The dramatically disastrous financial consequences of the Congo's commitment to free universal education are in this respect most revealing.[66]

The third set of factors is related to what I call the post-colonial political overdetermination of the economy, by which I mean that, since independence was a political revolution, political logic determined economic practice. The post-war era of decolonisation was a period when political considerations were pre-eminent, both for the colonial power and for the nationalists. While it was during that period that African colonies developed most economically, the decisions which most affected Africa's immediate and future life were political.

While it is true that, in theory, the colonial order favoured the development of indigenous capitalism, in reality capitalist development was curtailed whenever it was politically expedient or necessary to do so. Because of the delicate political situation in the African colonies from the fifties onwards, the colonial state was concerned above all to maximise political, rather than economic, returns – first to forestall, then to manage decolonisation.[67]

Similarly, the nationalists favoured political over economic considerations, or rather they had every reason to believe that political control would make economic success a reality. The nationalists were often supported by the new African economic (rural or urban) élites who, not surprisingly, considered support of the nationalist cause the most profitable purchase on their economic future they could make. But even when the nationalist party was in the hands of counter- (*socialisant*) élites, political considerations came first. Whatever the relationship between African economic interests and African nationalist parties, the colonial legacy and the experience of decolonisation dictated that it was those who held political power who would control the economy after independence. The post-colonial state was thus *de facto* the economic master of the new nation-state.

The political momentum for the post-colonial state's economic hegemony was thus well-nigh unstoppable. In a situation where the development of state capitalism or state socialism was conditioned by political interests, there were no structural or institutional safeguards against unproductive appropriation. Where (as, for example, in Kenya and Côte d'Ivoire) there was a substantial capitalist sector with direct access to the state, it was nevertheless constrained by political factors. Given the fragile and evanescent nature of power in post-colonial Africa, capitalists sought to maximise immediate profits (and store them in foreign banks) rather than reinvest in the economic future of the country. Where (as, for example, in Tanzania, Nigeria, Cameroon and all the 'socialist' states) the capitalists were rarely in power, their ability to continue to function successfully, or sometimes to function at all, depended on the nature of their political relation with the (civilian or military) holders of state power. Here again, then, political factors determined economic practice.

If the quest for power is the highest economic objective and if the degree of control of state power is the most accurate indicator of economic success, it is not to be expected that accumulation and inequality will necessarily be productive.[68] This is the nub of the crisis of accumulation and inequality in contemporary Africa.

In African countries (such as Côte d'Ivoire), where there are sufficient (agricultural or natural) resources and where the management of the economy is relatively sound (the latter does not necessarily follow from the former), there can be a certain balance between accumulation and inequality. The patrimonial state can continue to nourish sufficient networks of patron–client relationship to legitimate existing (and even growing) inequality. There is a relatively productive stalemate between state and civil society.

In the other countries, (e.g. Mali or Zaïre), where resources are insufficient and/or management is deficient, there can be no such equilibrium. Accumulation results, and is perceived to result, in growing inequality. Appropriation merely feeds the state's hegemonic drive. The gap between state and civil society grows. The state, and by implication, the political system lose legitimacy.

10 The Crisis of Good Government and Political Morality

I have so far deliberately eschewed normative and ethical questions because I believe it is important to distinguish, even if the distinction is somewhat vague and arbitrary, between the normative and the analytical. Or rather, it is important to make it clear when normative analysis is of relevance to political analysis. Nevertheless, like all political analysts, I have approached my task with a certain set of preconceived ideas and a certain notion of what political good and bad are. This chapter is an attempt to make these ideas explicit.[1]

The issues of accumulation and inequalities discussed in the previous chapter inevitably raise the question of political morality. They also raise the normative question of the competence and probity of government. It seems, therefore, appropriate at this point to consider some of the ethical issues which are at the heart of politics. If politics is about power, power is morally justified only insofar as it is legitimate. If the legitimacy of power diminishes, it carries less moral authority.

In order to assess the legitimacy of power, we need to have some notion of the nature of political right and wrong. This is not easy, or rather it is not easily anything other than arbitrary. The analysis of post-colonial African politics, as of the politics of 'Third World' countries, generally, is replete with value judgements. If the early Africanists often justified the misdeeds of African rulers on the ground that the demands placed on governments were excessive, present observers often blame the failings of African governments on the unjustifiable excesses of their rulers.[2] It is simple to be certain of one's high moral ground, although it is more difficult to accept that one's high moral ground is largely historically determined. It is less simple, however, to devise categories of political analysis which make it as possible to illuminate political processes as to pass moral judgement.

The notions of good government and legality are, it seems to me, useful in giving substance to the concept of political morality, for political morality is very much a matter of degree, of shades of grey.[3] Notions of good and evil, right and wrong, are relevant to the definition of the context within which political morality evolves, but they are too stark and absolute to be of much practical help in determining the concrete boundaries of political morality. Without a notion of the boundaries of political morality, however, it is tempting either to ignore the question altogether or simply to view it through the caustic clarity of cynicism.

There are two commonly accepted points of reference in the definition of (practical) political morality: the constitution and the judiciary. All African countries possess constitutions and, nominally, a constitutionally separate judicial system. Examining these constitutions and assessing the degree to which the judiciary is structurally independent from the executive are a necessary part of the assessment of the context of political morality in African countries today.[4]

The constitutions of African countries fall into two readily identifiable categories: the liberal and the socialist. The former are usually derived, with some minor differences, from the constitutions of the former colonial powers. The latter issue from the constitutions in vigour in (hitherto) socialist states, that is constitutions which legitimise the political dominance of the ruling 'revolutionary' party. Similarly, the judicial systems in force in Africa are consistent with the constitutional order: the rule of law for liberal regimes; the revolutionary code of justice for the others.

An important first step in the analysis of political morality is thus the assessment of the degree to which rulers in Africa respect the constitutional and judicial order by which they are supposed to be bound. Amnesty International, for example, examines records of human rights within the context of the existing legal order in each country – other than the death penalty which it opposes on principle. Amnesty International carries strong moral authority precisely because it forces governments to account for their deeds on the basis of their own judicial systems. This is a useful and workable means of assessing the morality of a given political order.[5]

Amnesty International is an effective pressure group because it dissociates its call for justice from any judgement on the political morality of particular regimes. It has thus achieved results which undifferentiated moral outrage or pressure would not have achieved. It has also highlighted the degree to which judicial systems, even those least concerned with individual human rights, provide (when they are allowed to function) strong individual protection against state abuse. Curbing human rights abuses often depends less on the invention of better laws than on the unimpeded functioning of the judiciary. The reason why the law is so frequently broken is precisely because it universally affords some considerable individual protection against state exactions.

Political analysts of contemporary Africa gain much by using Amnesty International's reports. Political analysis, however, cannot limit itself to such a narrowly defined assessment of political morality if it is at all to understand the processes underlying changes in political practice. In post-colonial Africa as elsewhere, the constitution and the law are often ignored, or at best they are irrelevant to political practice.

Almost all governments in Africa rule (at least partly) through executive decrees. Even where parliament has some independence and can call the government to account, the one-party state system makes it spectacularly easy to garner the (two-thirds or three-quarters) majority required to amend the constitution. The same applies to the law, which can readily be changed by decree or legislation. In any event, whatever the law, the rule of law is only as good as the independence of the judiciary. What appeal is there against politically-minded judges bending the law – in any country? This is why it is useful to set the assessment of the constitutional and judicial practice of any government within a larger framework of political morality.[6]

I enter one important caveat here. Below a certain threshold of political morality, almost universally recognised by ordinary human beings (if not always by their rulers), it is imperative to sweep away any justification and to condemn abuse on strictly moral grounds. It is convenient, though not convincing, to imagine that different peoples have different ethics and that what is morally wrong in one place is morally acceptable in another.[7] Whatever differences there may be between the morality of distinct political communities, they are no greater or no smaller than the differences in political morality between the members of any political community (including our own). The Universal Declaration of Human Rights must apply to all.

There is nothing more demeaning than the tortuous attempts to provide historical justifications for the deeds of those (like the Khmer Rouge) whose political morality is utterly inhuman.[8] Whatever one's political opinion and whatever one's notion of morality, there can be no justification for the abuses committed by some African rulers (e.g., in Uganda, Equatorial Guinea, the Central African Republic, South Africa, Rwanda) against their own or neighbouring populations. In cases of such stark brutality, understanding must not obscure condemnation.[9] Equally, however, it would be as otiose to charge Africa as a whole for the crime of some of its contemporary (black or white) tyrants as it would be to charge Europe as a whole for the crimes of its twentieth-century tyrants.

The notion of good government is a useful and workable criterion of political morality.[10] Good government is an ancient political category but strangely it is one which has not often been used in respect of Africa. Admittedly, it is a concept more easily understood in theory than it is adjudged in practice. For when is a government good? Good in comparison to what? Good for what? Good for whom? Yet it is a fundamental concept, for what is the justification for politics, if not good government?

The notion of good government is less imprecise than might at first appear, as it lies at the heart of the exercise of power and is central to political accountability. Both liberal and socialist political theories have concepts of good government. So do the ordinary members of any polity. It is also a concept particularly relevant to the political analysis of Africa because Africanists have often exhibited an almost pathological passion for ideologies and political discourses, at the expense of the more hard-headed examination of the effects of political rule.

It remains, however, difficult to define explicitly. John Dunn writes:

> As a concept good government is holistic and consequentialist rather than specific and procedural. It implies, *ceteris paribus*, and in relation to the policies that it actually pursues, a high level of organisational effectiveness; but it certainly does not imply the choice of a particular ideological model of state organisation: a government of laws but not of men, a minimal state, or dictatorship of the proletariat. Good government is best defined ostensively rather than by semantic prescription. It is what Sweden and Singapore enjoy, and what Zaire and Ethiopia distressingly lack. In principle, heavily repressive regimes may on occasion exemplify good government. But they can do so only where there is a direct and palpable link between the effective contributions of their rulers to popular welfare and the modes of repression which they employ – good government is not to be equated, for example, with ingratiating or virtuous government. Since any repressive regime in any public forum, national or international, is likely to justify its coercive activities by their putative contribution to popular welfare, the concept of good government is necessarily anti-ideological in intention. Its analytical purpose is precisely to distinguish the professed or actual self-understanding of ruling groups from their real causal contribution to the prosperity or misery of their subjects. The presence or absence of effectively guaranteed civil and political liberties does not in itself ensure the prevalence of good or bad government. But any set of repressive practices, as Jeremy Bentham salutarily noted, is in itself a direct contribution to human suffering.[11]

Dunn's essay stresses two points which seem to me important. The first is that the notion of good government is consequentialist rather than procedural. The second is that good government is very largely about what he calls 'effective state power', that is the ability to govern effectively. How good a government is has very little to do with its ideological complexion. Good government cannot be prescribed or decreed; it is achieved.[12]

Good government depends largely on the effective management of the economy, for, in contemporary Africa, as elsewhere, it is economic management which determines most directly the well-being of the immense majority of the population. The ruling élites always do well however good government is. But for the rest of the population, bad government has untold consequences on everyday life. This is why it is a myth to believe that the ordinary African cannot tell the difference between bad and good government.[13]

As Dunn says, the concept of good government is anti-ideological. It will no doubt be argued by some that the notion of state effectiveness is not ideologically neutral but in the present age of *glasnost*, this is a resoundingly unconvincing argument. Nor should it be forgotten that socialism was originally meant to provide a more efficient management of the economy than the capitalism it was to replace.[14] It is, in addition, a concept with which African governments would agree. All African states, whatever their ideological complexion, profess to aim at effective government.

The notion of good government also meets the objection of the presently vocal born-again libertarians who advocate *laissez-faire* as the morally superior form of political economy. For if the ideal libertarian polity is one without a state, the best they can expect on this earth is a state doing well whatever it has to do. Even they can readily agree with a notion of good government which emphasises effective state management. Since no one believes that the state in Africa either is about to wither or that, if it were to wither, its functions could easily be performed by the market, it seems safe to assume that the notion of good government is as relevant to them as it is to the rest of us. Whether privatisation assists good government is a practical and not a theoretical question.[15]

The notion of good government, especially when it is redefined as effective state management, it also amenable to comparative political analysis. And it is more important to be able to compare African countries with others than to be able to provide a watertight definition. The notion of good government makes it more practicable to compare regime performance independently of political orientation, of the precise meaning of development or of our particular view on the political morality of states in Africa.[16] Again, as Dunn writes:

> Effective state powers in African territories are unlikely to charm well-informed liberal observers by the manner in which they govern. But, other things being equal, they may at least succeed in furnishing reasonably good government, and in doing so they will be able to spare their subjects the miseries of anarchy and civil war from which the peoples of Africa have suffered so desperately in recent years.[17]

Whatever the criteria used to define good government, its meaning is relatively clear. Most analysts would agree that there has been in post-colonial Africa an unequal distribution of nation-states with good government. There have been a small group of relatively effectively governed countries (e.g., Senegal, Tanzania, Botswana), a majority of countries (e.g., Nigeria, Cameroon, Gabon, Kenya) where government has been, alternately, good and bad, and a small group of countries (e.g., Zaïre, Chad, Uganda) where government has been positively bad.[18] The question for analysis is whether it is possible to come to some conclusion about the causes of the relative absence of good government in post-colonial Africa.

It is well to keep reminding ourselves that good government is a rare commodity in the history of the world. Although Europe and North America usually consider themselves particularly well endowed in this respect, the most cursory examination of their twentieth-century history reveals otherwise. It is also well to remind ourselves that, for obvious reasons, good government is even rarer in the 'Third World' than in the developed world.[19] Here again, an examination of the history of the governments of the countries which started developing before Africa shows that, on balance, there were more bad than good governments. Thus our quest for the understanding of the relative absence of good government in Africa must always be kept within the appropriate historical context.

African countries also belong to that group of modern nation-states which were first created as political communities by colonialism. It is appropriate, therefore, to seek to understand the degree to which that genealogy is relevant to the presence or absence of good government in Africa today.[20] The first point to be noted is that the arbitrariness of the colonial boundaries could not have been propitious to either colonial or post-colonial good government. The absence of any historical, cultural or geographical logic in the delineation of national boundaries was undoubtedly an impediment to effective government, at least in the early years of independence.

To assess how good government has been in post-colonial Africa, it is necessary to assess how good government was in colonial Africa. Although colonial governments had broadly similar ambitions, there were important differences in the practices of the different imperial powers in their respective colonies. While it is true that the significance of the differences between forms of colonialism can easily be exaggerated, it is clear that, as concerns good government at least, these differences were relevant.[21]

Given the quality of government in Portugal, Spain and Italy, it takes no special insight to infer that the colonial governments of the Portuguese, Spanish and Italian colonies stood very little chance of being effective. The quality of government in the Portuguese colonies, to take one example, is a monument to some of the most backward practices of arbitrariness, bureaucracy and incompetence ever displayed by a European country.[22] Thus, it was the fate of those Africans who now speak Portuguese to inherit the remnants of a colonial state unsuited to good government.

The picture in the British and French colonies is more complex.[23] It is usually said, at least in Britain and France, that colonial government in 'their' African colonies was relatively good. Indeed, some historians of Africa have shown how excellent colonial government was and, by contrast, how dreadful post-colonial government has been – arguing that if the post-colonial states had only managed the colonial legacy a little more effectively their countries would not be in the sad state in which they are today.[24] That the animus for such arguments often lies in a sharp reaction to nationalist, radical and much Africanist discourse does not invalidate the point. But how accurate is the argument?

There is no doubt that the major British and French colonies benefited from a quality of government that was inconceivable in the Portuguese, Spanish and Italian (and perhaps even Belgian) colonies.[25] Senegal, Guinea, Côte d'Ivoire, Ghana, Nigeria, Cameroon, Kenya and Rhodesia, for example, were privileged colonies in almost every respect. They received substantial resources from the metropolis, they attracted investment from the private sector, they possessed the cream of the colonial service and they benefited disproportionately from the transfer of skills, knowledge and technology. They were in every sense Britain's and France's showcase colonies and, for this reason, were managed as effectively as was possible and expedient. Nevertheless, there were differences between settler colonies (e.g., Kenya, Rhodesia), where the presence of a relatively large white population forced the colonial state to pay special attention to the question of good government, and the other colonies (e.g., Guinea, Nigeria) where dedication to good government was tempered by cruder cost–benefit considerations.[26]

Furthermore, the argument that, where colonial government was good, post-colonial government ought also to have been good is highly reductive.[27] There is no reason to believe *a priori* that what was good for colonial rule would *ipso facto* be good for the post-colonial order. There are important nuances here which the present revival in imperial pride conveniently obscures.[28] Only the most fanatical colonialist would want to argue that every colonial act was good for post-colonial government.

For example, education is usually taken to be desirable for good government and, in this respect, the subjects of the privileged colonies benefited from better education than those of the other colonies.[29] But even here the type of education mattered. Good colonial government might have required a small number of educated collaborators but financial and political considerations made it undesirable that too many Africans should be educated. Yet it was precisely this lack of middle-ranking educated manpower which was so highly inimical to effective government after independence.[30]

In other colonies, the quality of colonial government was not nearly as good. In the French Occidental African Federation and the Equatorial African Federation, much of the important work of government was carried out in the two Federal centres (Dakar and Brazzaville) and not in the outposts of the Federations. Countries like Mauritania, Mali, Soudan, Niger, Togo, Dahomey, Chad and Gabon were very much at the periphery of the French colonial world and thus did not profit nearly as much from the benefits of efficient, colonial government. Similarly, The Gambia, Sierra Leone, Lesotho, Swaziland and Malawi were hardly at the centre of British colonial concerns.[21]

These were colonies where either climate or ecology was less favourable, where there were fewer agricultural or natural resources, hence little private investment – colonies often considered backwaters to which the best of the colonial élite declined to go. The argument that the British and French colonies were the beneficiaries of good colonial government must therefore be tempered by the realisation that a significant proportion of colonial Africa was from the beginning and remained throughout, very much at the margin of the French and British empires.

This matters because, plainly, there is some correlation between the absence of good colonial government and the absence of good post-colonial government.[32] On balance, it is among the group of more privileged former colonies that one finds a greater proportion of relatively good governments. In other words, the inequality at birth between African colonies, that is the arbitrariness which delineated settler, well-endowed and ecologically favourable colonies on the one hand and non-settler, poorly endowed and ecologically weak colonies on the other, was compounded by the fact that the former enjoyed relatively good colonial government. Looking at Africa as a whole, however, it is clear that a majority of colonies did not enjoy particularly good colonial government.

Whether colonial government was efficient or not – and my argument so far stresses how crucial good colonial government was – there were certain characteristics of colonial government *per se* which undermined the possibility that its successor would benefit fully from the relative merits of the administration it inherited. The colonial state was, as I argued earlier, centralist, interventionist and coercive. Above all, colonial government was bureaucratic.[33]

Leaving aside the question of whether these were positive attributes of the colonial state or not, what is clear is that they were not inherently propitious to good post-colonial government. This is because good government derives essentially from the ability successfully and efficiently to manage the tasks at hand. The more centralised, interventionist, coercive and bureaucratic government is, the more complex and demanding the tasks of management are likely to be.[34] Since very few post-colonial governments had either the financial resources or the personnel for such tasks, the colonial bureaucratic inheritance made it in fact less likely that these governments would operate efficiently.

Colonial government was a government in which the bureaucrat was king. In the absence of meaningful distinctions between the legislative, executive and judiciary, virtually all aspects of policy-making, policy-implementation, administration and adjudication were in the hands of bureaucrats. Furthermore, the majority of those civil servants (especially at the higher echelons) were European and not African. Their allegiance was to the imperial ethos and the colonial state, not to the colonial subjects from whom, as the arm of government, they maintained some considerable distance. Since these bureaucrats served a state with such extensive powers and so little political accountability, it was inevitable that their governance would turn into a supremely bureaucratic government.[35]

While bureaucratic governments have many undoubted qualities, including order and procedure, they are only effective when they operate properly. A poorly run bureaucracy is calamitous. More ominously for the fate of post-colonial government, the efficiency of a bureaucracy with such wide powers of intervention depended entirely on its individual and collective quality. In the best of circumstances this quality is difficult to maintain. In the circumstances of the immediate post-independence period, when European bureaucrats had to be replaced in large numbers and at short notice by largely untrained Africans and when the tasks of government were extended even further, the likelihood of good government was slim.[36] It is here that the privileged colonies fared better. They had many more and better-qualified African civil servants and they were able to retain the services of a larger number of European civil servants on secondment than could second-rank colonies.

Second, colonial government was a government of patronage. Whatever the differences between various forms of 'direct' and 'indirect' rule (differences which are often vastly exaggerated), the practice of colonial rule rested on the successful maintenance of a delicate balance between patronage and coercion.[37] By patronage, I mean that the exercise of good government depended on the purchase of collaboration, good will, consent and aquiescence which would make the need for coercion redundant or, at least, merely implicit.[38] Colonial political accountability, of which popular mandate formed such an insignificant part, was based on a system of governance in which patronage was absolutely central to the functioning of the colonial government.

The forms taken by patronage were infinitely varied but the consequences of government by patronage were fairly uniform. At the heart of government by patronage is the primacy of multiple networks of patron–client relationships which are mutually (if unequally) beneficial to all parties. There is, of course, nothing very remarkable in the observation that all government works (partly at least) through patronage. Colonial government, however, was singularly dependent on patronage. Its efficiency was therefore inextricably linked with the success of its system of patronage. But the right balance between patronage and efficiency is not easily maintained, as the post-colonial state was to discover. Where government is nothing but patronage, it cannot function effectively as government.[39]

Third, colonial government was a government of expediency, of means rather than ends; it was a *policeystaat*, by which I mean that its highest objective was good policing rather than good policy.[40] It is of course true that good policy can make good policing easier and more plausible. However, the two are not necessarily always causally connected since good policy must needs consider the intrinsic and ultimate desirability of its aim whereas good policing need not do so. Whenever a choice had to be made between the two, colonial government was likely to favour good policing. Now, good policing is often a hallmark of good government, especially if it can be achieved by consent rather than coercion, but the systematic pursuit of good policing may not be in the long-term interest of good policy.

Here again, the nature of colonial political accountability was such that it was possible for good government to be achieved in the *policeystaat*. Colonial government could ignore long-term (i.e. post-colonial) policy. The inheritance of a 'well-policed' state was obviously better than the inheritance of a 'poorly policed' state but the inheritance of the colonial government's primacy of policing over policy was a mixed blessing.[41] Where post-colonial government pushed the logic of the *policeystaat* to its extreme, it undermined the very possibility of good government.

Finally, colonial government was a government of the arbitrary. All governments can at times be, or be perceived to be, wholly arbitrary but because colonial government was not accountable to the people it governed, the scope for arbitrariness was large. This is not to say that the colonial subjects had no means of signifying their disapproval of colonial government. Nor does it mean that colonial government was any more arbitrary than was strictly necessary for good policing. It does mean, however, that there were few constraints, other than (financial or coercive) costs, to the arbitrariness of government.[42]

It can readily be seen how colonial government could easily justify arbitrary administrative measures for the greater objective of efficient government. Where administrative resources are limited, good policing must depend on carefully crafted arbitrariness. But here again, it is clear that the excess of arbitrariness which quickly marked many post-colonial regimes could easily defeat the purpose of good government.[43]

I am concerned here not with a judgement of the political morality of colonial government but with an assessment of the meaning of good government in the colonial period. For it seems to me clear that an understanding of the quality of post-colonial government requires both an understanding of colonial government and a means of being able fruitfully to compare colonial and post-colonial government. Post-colonial government started where colonial government left off, however radical the political changes induced by the struggle for independence appeared to be. Not only did most post-colonial governments preserve the administrative and bureaucratic structures they had inherited, they also largely entrusted the new administration to former colonial bureaucrats.

Nevertheless, and this is crucial, independence radically altered the state.[44] The new political masters had other ambitions, other responsibilities, other priorities, other methods and other constituencies. The machinery of the inherited bureaucracy of government was now put to radically different use. New principles of political accountability were established. New policies were formulated. In short, the nature of power was changed. Yet, the new rulers swiftly realised that many of the qualities of colonial government were useful to their ambitions or, rather, that the structures of colonial government were readily adaptable to the politics of the new age.[45]

Independence brought a number of important changes in the nature of the relation between policy-makers and administration which were not propitious to good government. First, most African rulers chose a statist (whether 'socialist' or 'capitalist') path to development. As a result, the new rulers entrusted the bureaucracy with massively expanded administrative tasks. Second, the state sought further to centralise power. Third, the state's role of patronage increased. The state became patrimonial and prebendal in a way which had been neither possible nor desirable under colonial rule.[46]

These changes had profound consequences for the conduct and quality of government. The state, now fully politicised at every level, thus placed enormous administrative demands on post-colonial governance. It required a government capable of intervening effectively in virtually every sphere of the citizens' life and a government capable of maintaining a system of individual and collective patronage to placate its many constituencies.

The immediate result of such changes was to expand the scope of governmental responsibilities beyond the administrative capacities of most post-colonial governments. Paradoxically, it was often in those countries (like Guinea-Bissau, Mali or Chad) where colonial government had been least efficient that the post-colonial state expected the most of its bureaucracy.[47] In the privileged colonies, the new rulers were more familiar with the machinery of the colonial government, the bureaucracy was more efficient and the nationalist state was more assiduous in its continuation of colonial practice. In Kenya, Senegal and the Côte d'Ivoire, for example, independence brought far fewer radical changes in governance or administrative practices than in most of the other, less privileged, colonies.[48]

The post-colonial age was one in which most governments were faced with duties they found difficult or impossible to discharge satisfactorily. They simply did not have the technical, administrative and financial resources or the personnel required for the responsibilities entrusted to them by the new rulers. Thus, a fundamental reason for the absence of good government in post-colonial Africa had to do with the sheer incapacity of the bureaucracy to discharge its (admittedly vastly increased) duties. It was not so much a matter of ill-will or deviousness on the part of the administration as a matter of incompetence. It is too readily forgotten that in most colonies the colonial administrators had not trained Africans to succeed them after independence. The case of the Belgian Congo, where virtually no African was allowed to rise in the colonial bureaucracy, may be extreme but it is revealing of the colonial mentality.

Africanisation *à tout prix*, although immensely popular because it suddenly provided so many Africans with secure jobs to which they could not normally have aspired, was nevertheless not propitious for the quality of government. Again, the case of the Belgian Congo, where the Belgians left overnight after proclaiming they would never leave, may not be typical but it does illustrate the sheer magnitude of the problems faced by the successor African government.[50] The poor quality of government in the post-colonial Belgian Congo is at least partly the consequence of its decolonisation. There is in post-colonial Africa a very significant correlation between the quality of government (whatever the political complexion of the state) at independence and the presence of qualified (European or African) personnel.

Furthermore, the state-led form of economic development pursued (perhaps inevitably) by the immense majority of African states made ever-increasing demands on government and administration.[51] As party and administration became one, the boundaries between the political and the administrative became more and more blurred. The requirements of political expediency and governmental efficiency inevitably clashed. In the highly charged political climate of state voluntarism, particularly (but not exclusively) in socialist states, the red usually triumphed over the expert – that is, political logic prevailed over the logic of good government.

State-led economic development, if it is to function at all effectively, requires an extremely high degree of administrative competence, probity and dedication. For, in this respect, the advantages of capitalist market economies is that they make fewer demands on state administrations. The fact that a large number of African rulers (for historically understandable reasons) opted for 'socialism' meant they placed such burdens on their administration as virtually to rule out the possibility of good government.[52]

It may be thought that, because socialism and good government are necessarily incompatible, it was unwise for African rulers to hanker after socialism in the first place. This is a reassuringly simple thought. However, the record of 'non-socialist' government in Africa is not such as to produce an easy correlation between political ideology and governmental effectiveness. Most of the unspeakably bad post-colonial African governments (e.g., Uganda, Chad, Central African Republic, Equatorial Guinea) were also supremely anti-socialist. Moreover, even non-'socialist' African rulers readily opted for state-led economic development.

It is now argued more plausibly that the real choice is not between 'socialist' and 'capitalist' development but between state-led and market-led development.[53] Admittedly, since independence, relatively good government (as, for example, in Senegal, Côte d'Ivoire, Kenya, Cameroon) has more often been found in countries where market forces operate relatively freely than in others.[54] It is also true that market-led development would reduce the burden of the administration and limit the scope for bad government. The problem is, however, that since it is in the most privileged former colonies that market-led development has flourished most, it is not easy to determine cause and effect.

Leaving aside the intrinsic merit or viability of socialism, what I think it is useful to say is that the choice of state-led ('socialist' or 'capitalist') development, whether that choice was made out of necessity or conviction, was very largely inimical to the possibility of good government. Consequently, it is not surprising that those countries (e.g. Ghana, Guinea, Mali, Guinea-Bissau, Angola, Mozambique) which attempted to move more radically towards 'socialism' failed most in their ambition to generate economic development. This failure is in large part due to the absence of good government.

Finally, the growth of a thriving patrimonial state further reduced the putative viability of good government. Since the legitimacy of the post-colonial state tended to depend on its capacity for patronage, it was inevitable that patrimonial criteria should prevail over criteria of effectiveness. This in itself may be acceptable insofar as there is a societal consensus on the need for states to be patrimonial. But where patronage becomes a political end, political expediency tends to prevail over good government.[55]

Patronage furnished the most convenient and most effective means of governance. As patronage became institutionalised, however, it greatly reduced the scope for effective administration. Since administrative resources are scarce in Africa, patronage becomes essential to the survival of patrons as well as clients. If civil servants do not earn enough to eat, their most effective means of survival is to find clients – in other words, to be 'corrupt'. A vicious cycle is engendered. The fewer the resources of the state available for patronage, the more vigorously its administration markets its power. The more the administration markets its goods in this fashion, the less government is able to govern effectively.[56]

The process by which state legitimacy becomes dependent on patronage militates against the possibility that rulers will be prepared to pay the political costs of good government. Or rather, it means that rulers will demand of its bureaucracy that it performs incompatible functions. This is only a paradox if it is assumed that the colonial antecedents of the post-colonial state made it more rather than less likely that good government would be achieved. However, colonial government itself was only good insofar as it had the means of its political expediency. Where colonial government was starved of the required financial resources (as it was in much of Portuguese Africa, for example), political expediency became incompatible with good government and corruption thrived.[57] When considering the quality of government in post-colonial Africa it is well to remember the cost of good government.

Another consequence of the development of the patrimonial state is that the exchequer is starved of a (sometimes staggeringly high) proportion of state revenues which is diverted by patrons towards their clients. Such appropriation breeds corruption at all levels of government. It is not only, therefore, the fact that large revenues are withdrawn from the state coffers but also that the institutionalised practice of graft seriously reduces the amount which reaches the coffers in the first place. There may be sound reasons why rulers in contemporary Africa feel justified in their exploitation of the patrimonial state and there may also be sound reasons for thinking that corruption is an effective redistribution of scarce resources but such reasons do not include a concern for good government.[58]

Good government has been rare in post-colonial Africa because of a combination of historical, economic, political and institutional reasons. The widespread absence of good government has undermined the legitimacy of post-colonial states as well as their capacity for purposeful action. It has consequently weakened the state and contributed significantly to political instability. It has brought about a crisis in political morality. Whether that crisis can contribute to the construction of a political order in which good government is at a greater premium remains to be seen. It seems sensible to remind ourselves that good government is historically rare and that the conditions for its existence are rarely as simple as some of edifying accounts of the glories of colonial rule would have us believe. As Dunn writes pithily:

A very large proportion of the worst that has happened to Africa has happened as a result of foolish or vicious political choice. Many of these crimes and follies are very likely to be repeated in the future. But not a single one of them *has* to be repeated. Africans, like the rest of us, are free agents judging on the basis of imperfect understanding and choosing under constraints. They are as well placed as any other segment of the human race to learn politically from their own history. By now, a good quarter of a century after independence in many countries, there is a good deal for them to learn.[59]

11 The Crisis of Violence and Survival

Perhaps the most enduring, even if not the most accurate, image of Africa in the seventies and eighties has been that of a continent of violence perennially on the edge of survival. Africa appears to be, at least in the popular imagination of the West, a land of hunger, famine, flood, civil wars and above all a land of refugees – millions of refugees fleeing areas of natural or made-man disasters and congregating in camps where their chances of survival are sometimes only marginally better.[1]

There is in the West a belief that Africa is possessed of a concentration of violence and a need to struggle for survival which are unique. Asia (despite Kampuchea and Sri Lanka) has often given an impression of a more peaceful and more dignified existence though natural disasters and famine are endemic.[2] Africa thus stands singled out as a continent of uniquely violent politics, a continent where force makes the everyday life of the people even more demeaning and demanding than in other poorer parts of the world.[3]

It is instructive to ask ourselves why it is that we have such a perception of Africa and whether in fact our perception is shared by others. Do Africans, for example, also perceive their continent in terms of violence and survival? The answer is that they do, or at least that some of them have the courage to say that they do.[4] Not surprisingly, however, they do not believe that Africa is unique in this respect. Their willingness to confront the continent's violence is not fed by naïvety about other parts of the world but by a desire to see Africa treat its people better.

On the other hand, it seems to me clear that this near-apocalyptic image of Africa which the West often holds is derived in the first place from a misunderstanding of the crises I have discussed above. Where we fail to understand the politics of the transition from colonial to post-colonial era, we tend to resort to clichés.[5] It has been my purpose to show that a more precise historical and conceptual analysis helps to place understanding in a more appropriate context and, in so doing, to make clear that contemporary African politics are not just a cauldron of primeval and unmediated conflicts but, more plausibly, the outcome of specific processes in specific settings.

The notion of violence and the meaning of survival are thus much more historically contextual than we like to imagine when we pass judgement on other peoples and other countries. I say contextual and not relative precisely because I believe that our understanding of so-called 'Third World' politics has not been helped by a readiness on the part of some, outsiders as well as insiders, to dismiss the notion of the crisis of violence and survival on grounds of cultural relativism.[6] Violence and starvation are violence and starvation anywhere. What I want to emphasise here is that understanding depends on the analysis of a context which goes beyond the immediate circumstances of the crisis of violence and survival. Explanations based on cultural relativism are the opposite of understanding because they are tautological.

Our notion of contemporary Africa as a continent where the crisis of violence and survival is particularly acute stems, it seems to me, as much from our perception of what we think should have happened in Africa as from what has actually happened there. The colonial view of Africa, the last bit of empire which Europe relinquished, was of a continent of many problems but great potential. The fifties and sixties had seen massive investment in the colonies and there were great plans for development afoot almost everywhere.[7] Because it was a period of relatively successful economic development, there were high expectations for the future. When it became clear that Europe would have to decolonise, these great expectations were transferred onto the independent states. The gains of colonial prosperity, it was believed, would provide solid foundations for the development of independent Africa.[8]

These expectations generated a climate of optimism fuelled by the 'benevolent paternalism' of a Europe which had just seen its African progeny come of age.[9] They were also shared by nationalists and Africanists who sometimes made even more optimistic assumptions about the economic potential of the continent. To question those assumptions at the time was to lend voice to those (conservatives and anti-nationalists) who argued that Africa was not mature enough to benefit from its colonial inheritance or even to become independent.

Thus it was inevitable that the colonial ideals, myths and illusions should be disappointed just as it was inevitable that the nationalist millenium never materialised. Perhaps it takes a generation to be able to accept newly independent countries for what they really are instead of what it was thought they could become if only they managed their colonial inheritance wisely. The consummation of disappointment, however, often leads to excessive despair.[10] It is no coincidence that, a generation after independence, Western perception of Africa seems to have swung to such extremes of gloom. The long-held perception of India as a more 'civilised' continent than Africa is, in this respect, instructive.[11]

Beyond this (important) issue of perception, the apparent lack of political order in Africa strengthens the notion that it is a continent in severe crisis. Again, lack of political order is by no means specific to Africa nor is the connection between disorder and violence.[12] Although it is true that the conditions for political order do not seem to be propitious in post-colonial Africa, there are few parts of the world which have been spared political disorder. Whatever the causes for disorder, they often breed violence. What it is important here is to ask why it is, beyond the reasons that I have discussed so far, that political order has apparently been so fragile in post-colonial Africa.

There are at least four sets of factors which are generally adduced to have contributed to the sharpening of the crisis of violence and survival. The first derives from Africa's economic situation within the world economy. The second is a result of Africa's precarious ecological balance. The third stems from the peculiarly vicious internal and regional conflicts which have afflicted large parts of Africa. The fourth has to do with the apparent readiness of contemporary African rulers to commit violence on their own people. I examine each in turn.

Africa's international economic situation, however it is interpreted, is not favourable.[13] Because it is not favourable, the governments of independent Africa have often been deprived of the economic assets which could have helped them to generate and make prosper the resources their populations so urgently need. Whatever its political complexion and however good a government is, a government without sufficient resources is less likely to address the causes of violence and survival than one with resources. The converse, as we well know, is not necessarily true. There are many relatively rich African countries (Zaïre, to give only one example) which preside over political systems in which violence is commonplace and in which the survival of the many is sacrificed to the greed of the few.[14]

Africa is not a continent without resources but it is one made up of countries of which only a few are in a position to maximise revenues from the resources they have. All countries which trade are dependent on the world market but not all are dependent in the same way. Africa's dependence is particularly unproductive for its population, if not for its rulers.[15] First, dependence on the export of agricultural or mineral resources is a serious constraint on economic choice. Second, dependence on foreign technology and know-how often limits the scope for the development of a more diversified economy.[16]

African countries are divided between those which have mineral resources and those which haven't. The former can earn substantial revenues but these revenues are subject to constant (sometimes wild) fluctuations which are out of their control and therefore make planning difficult. In addition, there are a few African countries (such as Botswana and Gabon) with the favourable ratio of wealth to population which makes it possible both productively to invest the revenues earned and to provide the exchequer with the cash to underpin development. Those countries without mineral resources are almost entirely dependent on agricultural exports for which the terms of trade have tended to decline over the years. Those countries without either mineral or agricultural exports are very heavily dependent on outside financial aid.

All African countries, even those which produce oil, buy the bulk of their manufactured/semi-manufactured products and, crucially, an increasingly large proportion of their food on the world market. Most do not earn enough to purchase what they need. Consequently, they have to borrow and thus become dependent on outside aid. Having to borrow more and more to meet a smaller and smaller proportion of debt repayment, a large number of African countries default. When they do, they become additionally dependent on the willingness of the world financial institutions to reschedule and/or write off their debt. The price of such dependence is that they must implement structural adjustment economic programmes which have far-reaching social and political consequences.[17] Some countries become increasingly dependent on world charity for the survival of their population. All dependence, even dependence on charity, has a cost.[18]

Whatever the orientation, competence and probity of African governments, the costs of dependence are largely inimical to good government. Dependence constrains government, changes its outlook, affects its policies, and introduces a political dimension which distorts both political accountability and the relation between state and civil society. In some African countries, a point has been reached where government is primarily devoted to the management of dependence rather than to the business of running the country in the interest of its citizens. Even where such is not the case, dependence necessarily alters the complexion of government and impinges on its policies. The post-colonial history of Guinea-Bissau is a case in point. The Luiz Cabral regime (1974–80) seemed overwhelmed by the need to manage its dependence. The successor Vieira regime has, since 1980, been adjusting its policies according to the *desiderata* of outside donors.[19]

It may well be that in many instances the degree of dependence is directly the result of bad government but, whatever the reason for dependence in the first place, reducing dependence seems beyond the capacity of most African countries, even those rich in mineral resources. From the point of view of those on whom violence is visited and who must daily struggle for survival, what matters is that dependence tends to deepen the crisis in which they find themselves. For the greatest violence committed by governments on their subjects is to deprive them of the means of survival. Famine is the ultimate proof of the failure of the government to govern.[20] Whether dependence works in the interests of rulers is a question which I discuss in Chapter 14.[21]

I do not argue here that there is a direct correlation between dependence and the crisis of violence and survival, even less that dependence *ipso facto* explains, let alone excuses, the intensity of that crisis. I merely point out that dependence, which (whatever its cause) is endemic in Africa, reduces the potential for good government. When rulers are more concerned about the economics of dependence than they are about the welfare of their subjects, they become even less accountable to those over whom they rule. As a result, the level of violence they commit on their populations may well increase.

This is perhaps best illustrated by the effects of the economic adjustment programmes which African governments must implement in order to qualify for IMF/World Bank financial support.[22] Leaving aside the debate about the theoretical or practical economic logic of structural adjustment, its most immediate consequences are to reduce the level of state subsidies on basic necessities, devalue the currency, reduce government expenditures and liberalise the economy. In the immense majority of cases, this combination of measures adversely affects a significant proportion of the population. In the short term, structural adjustment is painful. Whether in the long term it stimulates economic growth and whether growth benefits the population at large remain unanswered questions at this stage.[23]

Governments, whatever their political intentions, are thus continually placed in the situation of having to choose between bankruptcy or policies which would not readily be acceptable to a large proportion of those to whom they ought to be accountable. Indeed, whether African governments would get an electoral mandate to pursue structural adjustment if elections were held truly to test popular feeling on the issue is a question which (particularly Western) analysts ought not to neglect so thoroughly.[24] The vice is not in the admittedly good (theoretical) intentions of the lending institutions but in the inevitable consequences for Africans of the condition of dependence induced or suffered by their governments.

The erosion of political accountability which dependence entails has a direct bearing on the relationship between state and civil society. Reduced political accountability often brings about a reduction in the productive contribution of civil society to the economy.[25] As the state needs more revenues to reduce dependence, it necessarily seeks to appropriate more from civil society. The increasing spiral of coercion which follows can sometimes lead to the breakdown of the social and political order.

Admittedly, the danger is less in those countries with a less 'statist' political order, for the larger and more brutally hegemonic the state, the greater the violence it can commit on civil society. Nevertheless, the condition of dependence which exists in Africa is a contributory factor to the violence visited on its people. Given the nature of the post-colonial state in Africa, it is thus not altogether surprising that the level of violence is high.[26] Violence is of course politically counter-productive in the long run, even if it benefits rulers in the short term, but in the meantime it does make it more difficult for those without power to survive in their daily struggle with poverty, inequality, bureaucracy, arbitrariness and exploitation.

Africa's precarious ecological balance has also been a factor in the deepening of the crisis of violence and survival though here it is important to separate myth from reality. It is commonplace to argue that the continent's ecology is such as to make famine and disease inevitable.[27] This is not the case. The ecology of Africa is fragile in places but in most of the continent the potential for agricultural production is good, even if health hazards are many.[28] Other than in the Sahelian zone, an area which is sparsely populated though it does encroach on many countries from West to East Africa, African countries do not suffer from ecological or climatic constraints notably worse than other tropical parts of the world. Natural (as opposed to man-made) disasters – droughts, floods, illness and disease – are no more frequent in Africa than they are in many other tropical countries.[29]

There are many other parts of the world with similarly precarious ecological balances but even greater constraints on survival. Large parts of Asia, and not just China and India, have to sustain populations which are infinitely larger in absolute and relative terms than they are anywhere on the African continent. Despite a widespread belief to the contrary, Africa is not overpopulated in the sense in which these Asian countries are.[30] Population densities and the ratios of population to cultivable land in Africa are not anywhere near as dramatic as they are in Asia.

Nor is the endemic level of malnutrition as high, at least in areas (free of war) where normal agricultural production is possible. In comparative terms, then, Africa is relatively fertile and is relatively underpopulated. Overpopulation, however it is defined, is not the primary cause of malnutrition, famine or disease in Africa. Nor are the health hazards greater in Africa than they are in other tropical areas. Nor, finally, and it is crucial, is poverty in Africa new, as some seem to believe. Africa has always been a land of poverty and inequality.[31]

Given Africa's relatively favourable ecological conditions and given its relatively low population, the question that must be asked is why African countries have failed to maintain food-production and combat malnutrition. Is the colonial legacy at fault? Most African colonies benefited from health provisions which enhanced the quality of life and increased the life expectancy of the Africans. Despite the population increases which followed such improvement in health care, most African colonies could feed their population. Famine and even malnutrition were relatively rare,[32] and although some colonies had to import food, many others were able to export it.

The same cannot be said of Asian colonies. India, for example, suffered several catastrophic famines in the first half of the twentieth century which, although not caused, were certainly aggravated, by 'overpopulation'.[33] However, differently from India which, since independence, has made (slow) progress towards self-sufficiency in food, African countries appear to find it increasingly difficult to feed their populations. Since Africa does not remotely suffer from population pressure on the Indian scale, a more elaborate explanation is required for the food crisis.

Other than in those few (mostly Sahelian) countries where severe ecological constraints militate against self-sufficiency in food, Africa's hunger and famines have been caused by man. In many cases, (mis)management of the ecology has directly contributed to the decline in the potential for agricultural production – this is particularly true in those areas bordering the Sahel where desertification has increased.[34] In other instances, over-intensive use of the land has reduced land fertility – this is the case, for example, in countries where a system of land reserves has forced too high a concentration of population onto too limited an area.[35]

In other cases, excessive production of export crops has adversely affected the production of food – as has happened in several groundnut-producing West African countries.[36] In yet other cases labour migration to the mines has led to labour shortages which have drastically reduced food-production – this is the case of many of the countries bordering South Africa.[37] Finally, in most of Africa, economic conditions are such that it has become cheaper to import food than to support domestic food-production.

In the case of each country it is of course possible to provide an historical account for the decline in food-production. It is possible to understand, and thus to explain, why it has happened. Whatever the explanation, however, I am here merely concerned to make it clear that what has happened is a consequence of human action rather than ecological fate. Hunger, malnutrition and famine have almost invariably been the outcome of human agency. Natural disasters (drought, flooding, locust invasions, etc.), where they have occurred, have been considerably aggravated by man. The most devastating famines suffered this century in Africa have occurred in the Cape Verde Islands, Ethiopa, Sudan, Somalia, Chad, Mozambique and Angola. All of these were considerably aggravated by man's action (or inaction), even if they were often triggered by a breakdown in the ecological balance.

Cape Verde, where up to twenty per cent of the population died in the famines of the 1940s, was the victim of an ecological system where self-sufficiency in food is impossible.[38] But, famine came as a result of colonial callousness in that the Portuguese were unwilling to commit resources to the improvement of agriculture. When drought struck, they failed either to undertake the measures necessary to provide water or to supply the food required by the colony. Since independence in 1975, a different system of ecological management has prevented any recurrence of hunger, even if there still is malnutrition. Cape Verde will never be self-sufficient in food but it need not suffer famine.

The 1974 famine in Ethiopia was caused by the failures of a moribund feudal system, a system of government which considered famine to be an act of God. The repeated famines since 1984 are the consequence of the policies of a 'revolutionary' regime at war with its own population and using hunger as an instrument of state policy.[39] Almost all cases of famine in post-colonial Africa are the direct consequence of civil war. In Sudan and Somalia, the government is also using hunger as a weapon of war.[40] In Mozambique, famine is the result of the government's failure to support rural producers and of a singularly nasty civil war against an opposition (RENAMO) for whom violence is an end in itself.[41] In Angola, the civil war (aided and abetted by outside powers) has reduced the country to one huge battlefield and provoked massive shortages of food.[42] Similarly, the civil war in Chad has precluded serious food production in one of the Sahelian countries where ecological conditions are truly not favourable.[43]

Of course, the conclusion that man's action rather than ecological fate brings about famine is unremarkable – as Amyarta Sen has shown.[44] It only bears repeating so that we can finally escape from the tyranny of the tautological causalities which are so single-mindedly applied to Africa. Africa is not starving *because* it is Africa. Africa is not violent *because* it is Africa. Starvation and violence in Africa, as anywhere else in the world, are primarily the consequences of the politics of man. We thus need to understand the relationship between power and poverty, a relationship as ancient as the organisation of men and women into political communities, for if it were not the case, as I argue in Part IV, that hunger and violence were productive for some, violence and hunger would not be as widespread as they are today.

The third set of factors which contributes to violence and makes survival difficult in Africa is (domestic or international) armed conflict. If military coups in Africa have, on the whole, been relatively bloodless, other forms of armed conflict have been particularly vicious. The immediate victims of military coups are soldiers and sometimes the deposed rulers – on occasion shot in public. The new military rulers are usually keen to minimise violence against the 'ordinary' man and woman for only at this price can they hope to establish some form of political legitimacy. Coups, therefore, have not contributed significantly to the violence which marks many African countries. Military regimes, however, have not been slower than their civilian counterparts in launching armed attacks on civilians.

It is, indeed, civil wars and regional conflicts which have inflicted the greatest violence on 'ordinary' African men and women. There are in Africa clusters of festering conflicts which have devastated vast regions and jeopardised the survival of the local population. The civil wars in Chad, Sudan, Nigeria, Zaïre, Uganda, Equatorial Guinea, Rwanda, Burundi and now Liberia have been particularly nasty and have resulted in hundreds of thousands of casualties. Many other clashes between neighbouring countries (e.g., Mauritania–Senegal, Chad–Libya, Western Sahara–Mauritania, Tanzania–Uganda, Angola–Zaïre, Ethiopia–Somalia) have seen the killing of thousands and have laid vast border regions to waste.

But undoubtedly, the most vicious conflicts of all have been the two regional battlefields of the Horn of Africa and Southern Africa. There, the wars between one dominant power (respectively, Ethiopia and South Africa) and its neighbours have been on a massive scale and have caused the gravest injury to millions of Africans. The intensity of these wars has been enormous and the level of foreign (extra-African) involvement has been significant.[47]

The immediate causes of these many conflicts are many but they all ultimately stem either from the violent sedimentation of the post-colonial political order or from the adjustment of a regional 'superpower' to that post-colonial order.

The wars in the Horn of Africa and in Southern Africa were originally the consequence of the refusal of the internal populations of the two regional 'superpowers' (Ethiopia and South Africa) to accept the consequences of the colonial legacy – though now the conflicts have degenerated far beyond their borders. In the Horn of Africa, European fickleness split the Amharic, Tigre, Wollo, Somali, Eritrean and other peoples largely in favour of Ethiopia. That division was never accepted by the non-Amharic population, particularly the Eritreans and Somalis, and there have been wars ever since. In South Africa, white rulers have refused to end Apartheid and have gone to war against their black population and many of their independent African neighbours in defence of their prejudice.

Of the two, the conflict in the Horn of Africa is the more intractable since there is little prospect of the OAU agreeing to the redrawing of colonial boundaries. Nevertheless, the precedent of the inevitable settlement of the conflict in Western Sahara and the possibility of a break-up of the Ethiopian 'empire' may lead to a solution which will entail either boundary changes or the creation of an 'Ethiopian federation' composed of autonomous nationalities.[48] It seems less likely that a Greater Somalia will ever be conceded.[49] In Southern Africa, the end of the regional conflicts will come with the abolition of Apartheid and a political settlement in South Africa which is acceptable to its African population. The prospect for such a settlement, although not assured, is infinitely better today than it has been for the past forty years.

Most other regional conflicts between African countries have been the consequence of civil wars. Civil wars which degenerate frequently spill onto neighbouring countries, if only because of the ethnic connections between peoples across borders. Regional conflict is more often the unintended consequence of civil war rather than the deliberate attempt by one African country to gain regional prominence.[50] This is important, for it points to the depth of the commitment of African countries to the colonial borders inherited at independence. Not even Nigeria, the giant of West Africa, has made any attempt to use (as it might well have done) the Biafra conflict or its military involvement in other countries (e.g. Chad, Liberia) to redraw the colonial boundaries. Similarly, Tanzania's invasion of Uganda (to oust Idi Amin) never threatened to turn into territorial conquest and, because of this, it received the support of most other African countries.

The single most important cause of violence in Africa, therefore, has been civil war. Although civil wars are of course not unknown in other parts of the world, their frequency in Africa needs explaining. Because civil wars in Africa have most often pitted ethnic groups against each other, such conflicts have usually been attributed to tribalism – perceived as a singularly African condition. The recent experience of the Liberian conflict will have done nothing to change that view since newspaper coverage universally explained the conflict in tribal terms.

Yet, the most cursory examination of twentieth-century civil wars throughout the world would reveal that most civil wars have involved conflicts between different national, regional, linguistic, religious or ethnic groups.[51] Ethnic strife is decidedly not a peculiarly African characteristic, as, to take only one example, the present violence in Yugoslavia demonstrates clearly. Where there are different ethnic groups there is always potential for conflict, in Africa as elsewhere. Serious political analysis must seek to uncover what lies beneath the 'tribalism' of civil wars.

It is true that some of the most severe civil wars in Africa have occurred in countries where vastly different populations do not accept that they are part of the same nation. The conflicts in Mauritania, Chad, Sudan and Ethiopia (as well as that within South Africa) have been aggravated by the hostility between peoples separated by race and culture as well as religion. The 'Arab/Berber' populations of Northern Mauritania, Chad and Sudan are light-skinned and Muslim whereas their Southern compatriots are dark-skinned and Christian (or non-Muslim). Conversely, most of the Eritreans and the Somalis are Muslim whereas their Amharic counterparts are Christian. These are deep and significant differences with a potential for divisive politics which is amply demonstrated outside Africa (e.g. the Armenians in the Soviet Union, the Muslims in India). Yet the ultimate reason for civil war in these countries has more to do with the flaws in the construction of the post-colonial political order than with the inevitability of atavistic hostility.[52]

In this they rejoin the other, equally severe and perhaps even more dreadful, civil wars (e.g. Uganda, Rwanda, Burundi, Equatorial Guinea, Nigeria, Zaïre, Angola, Mozambique) which have so demeaned Africa in the eyes of the world. Each civil war is the outcome of very specific political processes which are only meaningfully understood in their appropriate geographical and historical context. I do not propose here to 'explain' Africa's civil wars. What I want to do, however, is to reflect on what they have in common, namely the incomplete or unsatisfactory sedimentation of the colonially induced nation-state.[53]

I speak of sedimentation because it seems plain to me that the construction of the post-colonial order is a process which is only achieved in that incremental fashion which the geological analogy implies. The frequency of civil wars in Africa is, in part at least, to be explained by the convulsions which accompany such a process of sedimentation.[54] Virtually all Black African countries contain deep ethnic, religious, racial or other societal faults which can easily result in political fractures, unrest and violence. At independence, there was a potential for civil war in nearly all African countries.

Where (e.g., Chad, Zaïre, Sudan, Angola, Mozambique) the political legitimacy of the new nation-state was not universally accepted, civil war was almost inevitable. Many of these wars are still going on and they may yet continue for a long time. Where (e.g. Mauritania, Rwanda, Burundi, Chad, Sudan, Ethiopia) the lines of cleavage combined racial, religious, social and political divisions, the potential for civil war was high – as the

potential for earthquakes is always high in areas with deep faults. Where
(e.g. Uganda, Cameroon, Zaïre, Nigeria, Angola, Mozambique) the lines of
cleavages are predominantly social and political – even if they are played
out along ethnic lines – the outlook is slightly less bleak, for social or
political differences are more amenable to being solved than ascriptive
ones.[55] But even there, the likelihood of renewed civil war must remain high
until sedimentation is deeper.

How well and how rapidly sedimentation occurred in Africa was influenced by a variety of factors. Not all colonies were equally divided by the
Europeans; some were more fortunate than others. Equally, African rulers
influenced the process of sedimentation. Not all nationalists built on the
precarious foundations of ascriptive (ethnic, racial, religious, etc.) politics;
some were wiser than others. Finally, not all independent countries were, or
indeed are, equally viable.[56]

Although the immutability of the present nation-states is taken for granted
worldwide, it is clear that not all present nation-states, in Africa or elsewhere,
will survive unchanged into the future. Predictions about the break-up of the
Soviet Union or other countries may be premature but it would be naïve to
discount them altogether. There are a number of countries in Africa (e.g.
Zaïre, Sudan, Ethiopia, Chad, Mozambique, Nigeria, Angola) where the
potential for division is immense. In those countries, sedimentation may
never be deep enough to preclude secession, even if today the only political
principle which unites all African countries is the rejection of secession.

What this means is that in Africa, as elsewhere, the potential for civil war
is greater in some countries than in others, even if it cannot ever be ruled out
in any country. There is nothing startling in this conclusion except for those
who persist in looking at Africa through an exclusively 'African' looking-
glass. The main reason for the frequency of civil wars in contemporary
Africa is not that African countries are any less viable or any more vulnerable
than countries elsewhere but simply that the process of political sedimentation is still in its early stages. The conflicts in Northern Ireland, Spain,
Lebanon, India, Sri Lanka and other countries should remind us that that
process is never complete.[57] We are all ruled by the principle of instability.

The fourth set of factors, the apparent willingness of African rulers to
inflict violence on their subjects, is even less specific to Africa than the
previous three. Just as European explorers were fond of thrilling their
audiences back home with tales of horror – *inter alia*, cannibalism and the
slaughter of slaves – today's tabloids feast on the black despot, the Idi
Amins, Nguemas and Bokassas of the continent. There is no need to pursue
that line of argument. The cruelty and viciousness of rulers towards their

subjects is one of the most consistent themes in human history, as is the perception that the cruelty of 'the other' is infinitely worse than our own. The important issue for political analysis is the understanding of the genesis and implications of that violence.[58]

Here it is well to distinguish between what we usually consider to be violence: active violence by rulers against their citizens, and violence by neglect, or passive violence – the violence which derives from the unwillingness or incapacity of the governors to carry out the policies which would remove the causes of suffering, violence and oppression. While it is true that active state repression, the killing of unarmed civilians, is utterly repellent, the passivity of rulers who allow their citizens to starve in their thousands is perhaps even more appalling.[59]

The scope for violent state repression in contemporary Africa is, contrary to popular prejudice, often more limited than in other parts of the world. The reason for this is simple. The African state is not strong enough to establish, let alone maintain, a true totalitarian political system. While there are undoubtedly many instances of totalitarian 'tendencies' in Africa, there has not been (even in the case of Ethiopia) any example of successful totalitarian rule on the Soviet, Chinese or east European model. The relation between state and civil society in Africa simply does not make totalitarianism viable – despite the wishes of some of Africa's more sinister rulers.[60]

Many more have suffered and died in Africa because of violence by neglect than because of overt repression. Indeed, the scale of suffering endured by Sudanese, Angolans, Mozambicans, Ethiopians and all the others who are made refugees through war or famine is infinitely larger than that caused by political repression in all African countries put together. For all the publicity surrounding the arbitrary violence of an Idi Amin, a Bokassa and the Nguemas, the vicious follies of those tyrants is, relatively, as nothing compared to the violence visited on the anonymous millions who are caught in the midst of war or famine. And while it is otiose to establish scales of suffering it would be odious to focus on the relatively few cases of systematic state killings at the expense of the millions who suffer and die because of neglect.[61]

Looking at Black Africa as a whole, therefore, what marks the post-colonial period is not so much the violence of repression – of which there was an equal amount in many other parts of the world – but the violence of neglect and of unintended consequences. If we exclude the unspeakable violence wrought (even if indirectly) by Ethiopia on its population and by South Africa in Angola and, particularly, Mozambique, most of the violence extant in post-colonial Africa issues from bad government.

While this may seem a peculiarly unspectacular conclusion, it is in fact ominous. For civil wars, drought and famines do end, even if they recur, whereas bad government may endure over generations. And the consequences of bad government, though not as spectacular, are ultimately more far-reaching.[62] Even if we accept that in most societies throughout history the majority of mankind has battled merely to survive, we cannot contemplate with equanimity the prospect that in Africa, where there is potential for living well rather than merely surviving, bad government will continue to cause such needless suffering.

The reality of contemporary Africa, however, is that political change is rapid and continuous. It is a mistake to think of the last thirty years as a homogeneous period characterised by continuous violence. Our perception of the violence of Africa derives from a few (in)famous cases and has been constantly reinforced by the series of wars and catastrophic events which have befallen large (but often different) parts of Africa. The sedimentation of the various nation-states of Africa started at different times and is progressing at a variable pace but on the whole it is progressing.[63]

Many of the fires of conflict which triggered violent events (e.g. Nigeria, Zaïre, Cameroon) have now been extinguished, although the possibility of further ignition can never be entirely ruled out. Countries have learnt how to survive as nation-states, even if their governors have not always been up to the task. But above all, the political system with which African countries started their independent lives has been changed, adapted, rehauled or reconstructed in the endless fluidity of the contest which binds together the rulers and the ruled.

Whereas most rulers started their reign presiding over a state which was both potentially strong and at the same time only thinly rooted in the existing political community, post-colonial politics rapidly reshaped the relation between rulers and ruled, state and civil society. This process was not equally smooth or equally successful in all parts of Africa. There were many incidents along the way, incidents which almost invariably resulted in violence. The case of Nigeria is perhaps the most instructive in this respect.[64] There, the most serious and violent attempt at secession in post-colonial Africa, triggered rather than provoked by political instability, has caused the country's governors to construct a multi-state federal political edifice that will withstand more easily Nigeria's strong centrifugal forces and will thus help to buttress the nation-state.[65]

Generally, therefore, except in those polities where bad government has reduced the whole political edifice to rubble, progress has been made towards the creation of a new African political order, or rather the creation of a political order to suit a new Africa. Where this has occurred, new forms of political accountability have evolved. In Africa, as anywhere else in the world, the ruled judge political progress by the degree of political accountability which they can enforce. What these forms of political accountability are and whether we recognise them as such from our vantage point is less important than the fact that they are being constructed. Ultimately, there is no better safeguard against violence than political accountability.

Part IV
Political Change and Continuity in Contemporary Africa

Introduction

Part IV brings together the different arguments developed so far. It seeks to overcome the somewhat artificial distinctions made (for the sake of analytical clarity) in Parts II and III between various concepts and different crises. Here, I focus on the dynamics of political change in contemporary Africa. I try to provide an explanation for what happens in the real, as opposed to the theoretically imagined, world: I use the arguments presented earlier in the book to test some ideas about what best characterises the practices of politics in Africa today.

I do not aim to furnish a 'comprehensive' picture of political change and continuity in contemporary Africa, for that could only fruitfully be understood within the context of each country's specific history. Nor can there be any such thing as a 'comprehensive' picture, even less a simplifyingly singular or unilinear political cause for change. I am not looking for a single explanation, a causality or *ultima ratio*.

Rather, I attempt to give a sense of some of the most significant political processes at work in contemporary Africa by concentrating on a few key aspects of political change which are relevant to all African countries. Above all, I try to reflect upon the deeper, less visible and more subterranean movements of African politics, for it is surely in the examination of the complexities of such processes that we can begin to make sense of what has happened in post-colonial Africa.

What has guided me in this section of the book is the very persistent question of why it is that so many accounts of African politics, with the exception of Bayart's recent book, do not seem to give a realistic explanation for what is happening in Africa. Although there are now a fair number of fine monographs on the very concrete political realities of individual countries, political scientists of Africa (and other observers) often fail to provide plausible interpretations of Africa's contemporary politics.

As I indicated earlier, the weight of paradigms has often been the cause of such failure. Ideological preconceptions have also hindered serious analysis of African politics. Equally, considerations of international politics (e.g., Cold War, 'Third Worldism', ethnocentricity) have induced political observers to follow the shadows of their own obsessions instead of opening their eyes to the everyday realities of African countries.

Finally, and perhaps most importantly, many have felt that, in the aftermath of independence, it was not appropriate for outsiders to be overly critical of what was happening in Africa. There were good reasons for this. The most violent denunciations of African political practices have often come from those (e.g., unreconstructed colonialists, racists, conservatives) who never accepted that Africa was ready for independence or felt that Africans were congenitally incapable of ruling themselves.

But these are now historically spurious arguments which no scholar ought to take seriously. They need no longer detain us. Africans themselves have called for a realistically critical analysis of post-colonial politics and it is time that we outsiders felt secure enough to answer that call. To avoid looking squarely at what is happening in Africa is not to do Africans a favour (whatever that would mean) but to patronise them. It is also to avoid our responsibility as political analysts and, consequently, to forfeit our credibility.

Part IV is thus a contribution to that task of looking squarely, dispassionately, and without any hidden moral superiority, at what is happening politically in post-colonial Africa. It is more properly an attempt at initiating a debate than an attempt to come to any firm conclusions. For it seems to me that politics in Africa, as elsewhere, is often better understood in the search for a language which adequately reflects what is observed than in the setting out of neat analytical conclusions. Enunciation is, or ought to be, a significant part of analysis.

Four chapters make up this section of the book. They are, respectively: 'The Dynamics of Political Africanisation', 'The Dialectics of the Hegemonic Drive', 'The Politics of Dependence' and 'The Reproduction of Power'. Although these titles may at first sight appear unnecessarily obscure, they in fact encapsulate a discussion of processes which are easily understandable.

'The Dynamics of Political Africanisation' refers to the all-important process whereby the political legacy – the ideas, practices and institutions – of colonial rule and decolonisation was assimilated, transformed and re-appropriated by Africa. By focusing on a notion of Africanisation which eschews facile cultural relativism, I propose a reinterpretation from an African perspective of changes which have often been summarily dismissed as the corruption of political order. Africa, far from being a continent of incomprehensible political convulsions, must be seen as a continent creating its own political order.

Chapter 13, on the dialectics of the hegemonic drive is a discussion of the multiple ways in which the search for political and economic power impinges on the relation between state and civil society. I argue that in order fully to understand the complexities of that relation, it is important to see how state and civil society are accomplices as well as adversaries in the struggle for power. In a situation where it is difficult to relate causally 'class formation' with hegemony and where the boundaries between state and civil society are both ill-defined and ever changing, the relations between political and economic power fit no neat structural scheme.

'The Politics of Dependence' is perhaps a slightly misleading title as the purpose of Chapter 14 is not to show how or why African countries are dependent but to understand the political causalities engendered by dependence. It is illusory to search for the simple, univocal consequence of dependence – and even more to construct an interpretation of African politics on a theory of dependence. The meanings and implications of dependence are multiple. For example, dependence may be seen as a liability for the country but it may be translated into (political or economic) resources for many individuals or groups within civil society. What matters for political analysis is the way dependence works itself out in practice within the body politic.

The final Chapter, 'The Reproduction of Power', is concerned with the most central question in the study of political change, namely how power passes from one generation to the next. Here, I try to see whether there are any discernible patterns to be found in the political practices of post-colonial Africa which would help to explain how power is reproduced. I discuss why power in contemporary Africa is eminently fluid and evanescent and why it is that the reality of power is not easily exhausted within the realm of state, or even formal, politics. I argue that in order to understand the processes by which power is reproduced we need a fairly catholic approach, combining political, social and cultural analysis.

Taken together these four chapters ought to give an indication of what I believe to be some of the most profitable lines of enquiry into the politics of post-colonial Africa. Although they do no more than touch the surface of what are undoubtedly complex political issues, they illustrate one possible approach to the political analysis of contemporary Africa, one possible interpretation of its politics. At the very least, Part IV of this book should provide the framework for further debate.

12 The Dynamics of Political Africanisation

The assumption most widely shared by Africanists in the past thirty years has been that of 'development', a movement forward, progress, between a notional 'traditional' and 'modern' Africa.[1] To be sure, there have been many different, and often contradictory, views on the causalities between economic and political development. Whatever those differences, however, the political analysis of contemporary Africa has, with few exceptions, been constructed upon an (implicit or explicit) teleology. The interpretation of what has happened in contemporary Africa has thus rested on a prior assumption about what ought to have happened there after independence. Even, for example, a concept as useful as that of the 'shrinking political arena' – which actually does illuminate what seems to be a general rather than aberrant process in much of Africa – rests on a notion of what the development of a 'political arena' ought to be.[2]

A concern about the movement of politics is of course legitimate insofar as political analysis seeks above all to understand how and why politics change in changing circumstances. The concept of 'political development', however, is misleading. The very idea of development (like the mathematical notion of vector, of which it is a derivative) presupposes a starting point and a direction.

The starting point is, broadly, the colonial period. The direction is, with variations, the march from 'tradition' to 'modernity'.[3] Of the two, it is the assumed starting point which is the more misleading. It is patently absurd to assume that the antecedents to contemporary African politics are wholly contained and wholly revealed within the colonial period.[4] It is rather the colonial period which is contained within African history. The notion of a movement from 'tradition' towards 'modernity' is of very little use in that it makes assumptions about the transformation of the one into the other which are not warranted and which historical research has revealed to be either hopelessly vague or vacuous. Only when modernisation is conceived in more narrow technological (or scientific) terms is it possible to point to an incontrovertible movement from 'tradition' to 'modernity'.

Without a proper starting point and a definable direction, the notion of political development is meaningless. It is more useful to consider the movement of politics in non-teleological terms and thus to abandon the fruitless quest for the notion of development most 'appropriate' to Africa.[5]

Once this is conceded, it becomes easier to reconsider the political processes for which our well-ordered developmental analysis fails to account. Most crucially, perhaps, it enables us to look for the internal dynamics of politics as they are revealed to us rather than simply in their relationship to an assumed process of change.

It is within this context that I want to consider the concept of political Africanisation. The notion of Africanisation is not new, but it is usually taken to mean the replacement, by Africans, of white (colonial, expatriate) personnel – in the bureaucracy, the services, the police, the armed forces, business, etc. Here I use the notion of Africanisation in a much broader connotation. I am interested in the process by which colonial politics was Africanised after independence, that is, how it was re-appropriated by Africans (rulers and ruled) in the context of a (historically) modern world of nation-states. In other words, I am interested in the process by which post-colonial Africans 'digested' the political legacy left by their European conquerors.[6]

To speak of Africanisation is immediately to raise the spectre of cultural relativism – the argument about the specificity of African politics. Contemporary African politics, it is sometimes argued, can only be profitably understood within the context of the political 'traditions' of Africa. This is misleading. Most attempts to explain today's African politics by reference to the 'traditions' of Africa have been reductionist and/or circular, when not downright patronising. The politics of contemporary Africa are no more and no less rooted in the 'traditions' of Africa than the politics of Europe are in the 'traditions' of Europe. What is of interest here – and this is what I mean by Africanisation – is how these 'traditions' have evolved and how they have been incorporated into a modern post-colonial Africa.[7]

It is, perhaps, easiest to understand the notion of political Africanisation by analogy with social and religious Africanisation. A few examples should help to explain what I mean. The development of the Zambezi *prazos* in the centuries which followed the early Portuguese penetration of the area is the foremost, though by no means the only, example of the 'Africanisation of a European institution'.[8] The *prazos* were landed estates in the Zambezi valley to which Portuguese citizens (often Indians from Goa) were granted hereditary titles by the Portuguese Crown in an attempt to claim and maintain control over this strategic area of Eastern Africa.

While on paper the *prazos* seemed to be a case of the successful implantation of a European ('feudal') institution in Africa, the reality was the reverse. The European structure had been assimilated, 'digested' and adapted to the existing African socio-economic development. The Portuguese title-holders had become African chiefs who eventually had to be dislodged by force of arms when, after the Berlin Conference, the Portuguese sought to enforce effective occupation in Mozambique. Similarly, the apparent Europeanisation of the Kongo kingdom in the sixteenth century turned out to be a case of the Africanisation of Portuguese religious and political structures.[9]

It is, however, the history of the independent African churches which best illustrates the notion of Africanisation.[10] For it is here, perhaps, that the dynamics of the African appropriation of foreign beliefs and institutions are most clearly revealed. Independent churches were breakaway churches often founded and run by African converts to Christianity who felt the need for an 'African' – as opposed to European – church. They rejected the claim that European Christian churches were based on universal principles shared by all.

The process by which independent churches appropriated the message of a universal church and readapted it to local conditions was threatening not just to the official church but also to the colonial order. This is easily understandable. Independent churches claimed an African universal God, reinterpreted the dogma in African terms and adapted the practices of the universal church to the needs of Africans in their specific historical settings. A religion relevant to colonised Africans thus provided an explanation for the colonial conquest and a vision of its finality. It was *stricto sensu* anti-colonial.

Independent churches were independent because they exposed the parochialisms of the so-called universal churches.[11] The gap between in-dependent and orthodox churches indicated the degree to which the latter resisted Africanisation. But today the universal Christian churches have been Africanised, even if they still pay their dues to Rome or Lambeth Palace. Being outside official religious or political control, however, inde-pendent churches remain very strong in some parts of Africa where, un-derstandably, they are a threat to unpopular political regimes. Today, the appeal of both independent and official Christian churches, their success as religion, is tied to their success in meeting the spiritual and (frequently) concrete needs of their parishioners.

But perhaps what I mean by Africanisation will become even clearer if we think in terms of an analogy with Japan.[12] For in the case of Japan, it does seem universally accepted that the process by which Japanese society assimilated, appropriated, redefined and set about utilising the Western experience was intimately connected with its own cultural, social and political identity. It would not occur to any serious analyst of modern Japan to neglect to take into account this process – 'Nipponification'? – when attempting to explain contemporary Japanese politics. If this is true of

Japan, how can it fail to be true of Africa? The fact that Africa was not as developed as Japan was in the nineteenth century or that its economic growth since independence bears no resemblance to that of Japan are analytically irrelevant. This process – Africanisation in the case of Africa – is universal. Each civilisation is thus constructed.[13]

I do not pretend here that I can singlehandedly define and enunciate 'the' process of political Africanisation. This can only be done by many and in stages. Here I merely want to illustrate what I mean and to show why it is that an understanding of political Africanisation will make it easier for us to understand what is happening in contemporary Africa. I examine four key elements of post-colonial African politics, respectively: the notion of the individual and the relation between individual and community; the notion of representation and the role of elections; the notion of leadership and the relation of ruler to ruled; and, finally, the notion of corruption and the relation between wealth and power.

1. The individual and the community

The political order bequeathed by the colonial powers to the newly independent nations was one based on the historically specific notion of the individual as conceived in post-revolutionary Europe and America. It issued from a conception of the autonomous human being willingly contracting him/herself to the community according to specific forms of reciprocal obligations between individual and political community. The notion of the polity as an aggregate of the political will of individuals and the concept of political accountability contained therein defined the body politic and drew the boundaries of the political sphere.[14]

Constitutions, bills of right, declarations of human rights, all enshrined the rights of the individual and devised political mechanisms by which the individual would both be represented in and protected from the state. The modern European political order thus reflected the supremacy of the individual, as political actor, over the community. The English, American and French revolutions provided a model for the role of the individual in politics which was not challenged until the great socialist revolutions of the twentieth century when the supremacy of the individual was replaced by the new dominating principle of class supremacy. The fact that socialist revolutions – in which the new community (class) overrides the individual – took place in countries in which the old communities had not yet been broken and atomised by the development of capitalism is surely not a coincidence.

Although colonial rulers readily gave attention to the existence and organisation of African communities, they did so from the individual perspective with which they were familiar. Their obsession with African communal identities (pushed to its absurd logical conclusion in South Africa) originated in their need to define the individual rather than under-stand the community. It is because they were so concerned with the identity of the individual that the colonial rulers needed to establish the communal/ ethnic characteristics of each colonial subject. Thus, while the Europeans claimed that their identification of African communities explained the 'African-way-of-being-in-the-world', the definition of African communities provided by the colonial order was in fact based on the very European notion of the central role of the individual within the political sphere.[16]

The European understood that the African was 'tribal' in that he defined himself in communal terms but the European mind needed to define 'trib-alism' in individualist terms. The African, who did not need to ponder about his sense of self-identity, sensibly obliged the European by reducing his notion of self to that of the 'tribal'. The result was a double misunderstanding. The European believed that he had cracked the African mind and thus understood how Africans individuals deferred to the communal. The African for his part, believed that the colonial order was organised according to peculiarly colonial communal criteria which he was happy to adopt so long as it was profitable to do so.

Once the European colonial powers realised that they had to decolonise, they naturally set about doing so in their own image. When it came to demonstrating nationalist strength and organising the transition to self-government, they insisted that the Africans display their political credentials according to the rules of the metropolitan political game, that is individual representation, party politics and parliamentary regime. Consequently, the political order instituted at independence bore little relationship to the preceding colonial, even less pre-colonial, political order. There was a real gap between the political superstructure thus established and the communal infrastructure on which it had been erected.

What has happened since independence is that the relationship between individual and community has been Africanised. This is not to say that there is 'one' African notion of the individual and the community, even less that such notion corresponds to timeless and 'traditional' static realities. The process of Africanisation means not the 'return' to a specifically given 'African' relation but the adaptation of the formally defined relation in response to the changing circumstances of modern post-colonial Africa. Thus, the reality of African politics today is often far removed from the constitutional notion of the relation of individual to community.[17]

The Africanisation of that relation has entailed a move towards a notion of communal (rather than politically single and autonomous) individual. By this I do not mean to subscribe to the view, again fashionable today, that Africans are 'tribal' after all. Rather I mean that the individual African's relation to the existing political system is one which involves communal considerations which are not contained in the notional constitutional political order which officially governs his life. Africans do not generally accept an individualist political theory. They consider the position of all politicians, bureaucrats, soldiers, etc., in the context of their relation to their communities. Political Africanisation thus entails a process whereby the African notion of the individual has been incorporated within and in turn has reconstructed the post-colonial political order.

As a result, to give one example, the complexion of government in Africa must necessarily reflect the communal (e.g., regional, racial, religious and ethnic) complexion of the country as a whole. This is not simply because this is the only way to safeguard the interests of the various communities (although it often is) but because the very validity of a government *qua* government depends on such communal representation. Whereas few African constitutions make reference to this need for communal representativeness, African rulers and ruled alike are quite clear that this is one of the foremost requirements of regime legitimacy.[18]

Similarly, it is well understood by rulers and ruled that the notion of individual *ipso facto* contains the communal. It is self-evident to all that politicians conceive of their own interests in communal terms. Their success and failure is the success and failure of their families, their villages, their communities, etc. No one disputes the connection between individual and communal self-interest. Houphouët-Boigny's fantastic extravagance in the development of his 'village', Yamassoukro, is objectionable not because the President is lavishing millions on *his* 'village' but because he is lavishing too many millions. The same applies to Mobutu's 'village', which includes a private runway to accommodate the Concorde hired for his foreign travels.[19]

On a different register, the widespread use of the metaphor of the family in the political discourse of African rulers is another indication of one of the meanings of the process of political Africanisation. Most observers view such displays of paternal rhetoric merely as a smokescreen. Yet, in part at least, they are better conceived as the expression of an implicit relation between ruler and political community which arises from an Africanised perception of the relation of the individual to his community. To recognise the validity of this dimension is not to argue that it alone explains African politics but merely to point out that an understanding of contemporary politics in Africa demands an appreciation of this discourse. Analysis ought to ask whether such paternalist language is not in some sense a modern post-colonial adaptation of the communal pre-colonial language which obviously finds an echo in today's African countries.[20]

The point to emphasise, therefore, is that the common belief in a dichotomy between the 'traditional' notion of the individual as communal and the 'modern' notion of the discrete individual is misleading. The reality of the notion of the individual in Africa today is neither the one nor the other. It is rather a synthesis, which I call Africanisation, of the colonial (European) concept of the individual and the African notion of the individual as transformed by the colonial and post-colonial experience. Some would argue that the same process is at work in Europe, where the supposed dichotomy between individual (modern) and community (traditional) has been overdrawn, if present evidence of 'communal' politics is anything to go by.

Thus, the relations between individual and community in contemporary Africa should not be taken for granted, nor should assumptions be made about their 'modernity' or 'traditionalism'. The nature of those realities can only be deduced from the examination of concrete case studies in their proper historical context. This means, *inter alia,* studying the movement of the *politique par le bas* – the way in which the politics of civil society affect the politics of the state.[21] For, even if the study of the degree to which state politics deviates from the constitutional order gives us some information about African politics, it is ultimately the understanding of the perception of the object of politics by ordinary men and women which provides the best guide to that aspect of the meaning of political Africanisation.

2.   The meaning of representation

The relationship between the individual and the community which developed after independence had a direct impact on the process of political representation and on the role of elections in Africa. It has often been pointed out that African polities soon became one-party states and that, as a result, elections became perfunctory. This is true as far as it goes but the deeper question is what this evolution means for the understanding of African politics.

There are many historical and contingent reasons why post-colonial African polities could not operate viable multi-party systems. Yet, today, when context and contingencies have changed, it remains as true as it was thirty years ago that most African countries are one-party states, even if 1990 has seen a strong movement for multi-party democracy in Africa. It seems to me that, if we are to understand why this is so, we need to understand the relevance of the process of Africanisation to party politics and elections. Again, I do not claim that 'African ways' are inherently inimical to multi-party systems nor that democracy is not suited to Africa.[22] I merely want to show that the processes of representation in post-colonial Africa are not explained by or even contained within the formal representative structures set up at independence.

If the notion of the individual in Africa today is, in part at least, 'communal' in the sense discussed above, it follows that representation cannot simply be conceived, as it is in Western political theory, in terms of the political representation of individuals. This has a bearing on the role of parties and the place of elections in the polity. What does representation mean in contemporary Africa? How have parties and elections been Africanised?

Zolberg, in *Creating Political Order*, gave a perceptive account of the evolution of party politics in the early post-colonial period.[23] He explained why it was that the move towards one-party states took place. However, he restricted his analysis to high politics (the politics of the state) which explains why he was unable to connect the process he observed with the perception of representation found in low politics (the politics of civil society).[24] This is crucial.

The move to one-party states, the narrowing of democracy and the use of elections as rubber stamps, are usually all attributed to the machinations of the rulers. They are perceived as the process by which the political arena is deliberately shrunk by those in power. But this is only half the picture, for what is at issue is not a straightforward reduction in representation but the development of parallel systems of representation which are not contained within the party structure of the existing political order.[25]

The importance of the relationship between the individual and the community means, first, that the identity of the representative overdetermines the nature of representation. To represent an individual is to represent his/her community. To represent that community is to be representative of that community. This may or may not mean to be a recognisable 'leader' of that community but it almost always means to be a representative in which the community recognises itself. It usually implies an ethnic congruence between representative and community but it means very much more besides: not just that only a member of the community can represent the community but also that only a member of the community can be expected not to be accountable to that community. Hence, the need for that person to be elected is seen as less significant than the need for that person to be representative in the sense defined above.[26]

Representation is seen within a context of communal rather than individual competition. Or rather, individual competition is contained within communal competition. Within that framework, therefore, the notion of multi-partyism *per se* is of limited relevance. For what the individuals and communities need is access to the party in power, not to any 'loyal' party of opposition. Elections are not conceived as a means by which to choose between competing representatives but as a demonstration of support for the representative chosen by the community. This does not mean that elections are meaningless. When the choice of the representative has been made from above, without consultation and/or approval from below, electors will often vote against the candidate. What it does mean is that, whether there is a single- or multi-party system, the candidate's legitimacy often derives from the representative legitimacy of his/her selection prior to the elections.[27]

At a second level, representation means representing the interests of the community – looking after its specific material needs. The notion that the representative is elected to look after national rather than constituency interests has very little currency in contemporary Africa. Elections are not perceived as a means of choosing the rulers most able to rule the nation as a whole but of choosing those who will best promote and protect the interests of the community.[28]

As it is not expected that the representatives of other communities will look after the interests of one's community, it is seen as necessary to safeguard the interests of one's community with the selection of a representative who will have productive access to power. Local and national responsibilities need not be in conflict but where representatives fail to look after the interests of their community they cease to meet the local criteria of representation, whatever their prominence as national rulers.[29] Thus it is that, when free elections are held, many ministers are voted out – even within a one-party system.

Once this Africanised notion of representation is understood, it becomes easier to see why in Africa there is, in Western eyes, such a 'mercenary' quality to the politics of representation. To cast it merely as corruption is to miss the very important mechanisms by which civil society holds state rulers to account.[30] If access to the state is the most productive way of promoting the interests of the community, then it follows that the process of representation (including elections) must provide the community with that access. We may frown on the minister who favours the economic development of his region (necessarily at the expense of other regions) but those who have chosen him as a representative have every cause to rejoice at his representativeness. Nor should we pretend that Africa is unique in this respect.

Third, representation means to make manifest the virtues of the community. To be representative is to display the self-perceived qualities of that community. This is important because the position of any community within the polity is identified by reference to its specificities – in contrast to the specificities of other communities.[31] Where a community ceases to be identifiable, the defence and promotion of the interests of its individual members becomes well-nigh impossible.

Because of this, the individual merits of the representative, his personal qualities (e.g., intelligence, probity, stamina, honesty, industry) may well matter less than his embodiment of the (real or sometimes imagined) communal virtues (e.g., prosperity, piety, business acumen, diplomacy, nobility, racial purity). In some cases this may mean that the representative should be a member of a royal or chiefly family. In other cases, it may be the reverse. In yet other cases, the community will look to someone with a higher education or to a religious scholar. Often, wealth (however gained) will be the single most important criterion.[32]

An understanding of the complexities of the Africanised notion of representation helps to comprehend processes which, from a narrow Western perspective, make little sense. In particular, it makes clear why elections *per se* are only a limited (though vital) part of the process by which communities select representatives and by which they seek to hold these representatives to account. It also sheds light on the relation between rulers and ruled.

3. *Political leadership and rulership*

The concept of political leadership in contemporary Africa has often been dissociated from its relevant historical context.[33] Without an understanding of that context, in which the relation of individual to community and the notion of representation are central, it is difficult profitably to analyse the relation between ruler and ruled. Most discussions of political leadership focus either on the individual qualities/defects or on the political discourse of African leaders. These tend to be the characteristics of leadership which matter most in Western polities and which are most easily identifiable by the foreign observer. Also, because African leaders abroad are very often consummate practitioners of the Western art of leadership (e.g., deportment, media presence, diplomacy, pageantry), they invite observers to consider them from that angle.

The art of rulership in Africa, however, is far more complex than these edifying pictures suggest. It is not easily understood simply in terms of personality and ideology. While it is true that a successful leader anywhere in the world needs very special skills, the range of skills needed is determined above all by the texture of the existing relation between ruler and ruled. Other than in dictatorships and tyrannies, found in Africa no more frequently than elsewhere, leadership must rest on legitimacy.[34] Legitimacy derives from factors which change over time but which can usefully be gauged by the nature of the political relation between state and civil society. What reduces or enhances the legitimacy of any particular African ruler is often misperceived by foreign observers. For example, whether a leader has been freely and fairly elected may well be less important than whether, in given historical circumstances, he is seen to embody the required national virtues.

The story of post-colonial rulership in Africa was at first largely the story of the historic nationalist leaders – those who were the undisputed symbols of the new nation-states at independence. Whether issued from old or new élites, these nationalist leaders were legitimate not so much because they had been freely chosen by the populace but because their nationalist success endowed them with the qualities which the citizens of the newly independent countries expected of their leader. The colonial rulers themselves had accepted the nationalist leaders as the 'natural' leaders of their communities. This gave the new rulers an overwhelming advantage over all putative competitors.[35]

It was, however, but an evanescent advantage. As time passed, nationalism mattered less and less. The qualities and defects of nationalist leaders were revealed for what they were. It is for this reason, and not only for reasons having to do with the dereliction of the 'democratic' political process set up by the departing colonial power, that there was disillusionment with many of those historic nationalist leaders. Quite simply, Africans often realised after some time that their leader was not what a leader ought to be.[36]

It was the process of political Africanisation which shaped the relationship between ruler and ruled and marked out success from failure. What I mean here is that the assessment made by Africans of their rulers and the criteria which marked out good leadership now issued from their Africanised notion of rulership rather than from the colonial legacy. The legitimacy of African rulers was determined by local expectations and perceptions rather than by the constitutional legitimacy of the office they held. Or rather, the legitimacy of the office they held depended on factors not simply or directly related to the formal political structure which guided rulership. African civil society judged their rulers according to a much wider range of criteria than in Western polities – and this was not always clear to foreign observers.

It is, I believe, easier to understand what I mean by the Africanisation of rulership if we examine the case of Houphouët-Boigny, by any standards one of the most successful African leaders since independence (1960).[37] Urbane, francophile, sophisticated, clever and Westernised abroad, he is often seen by the foreign press as being pompous, paternalistic and repressive at home. His opponents readily allege that he is a dictator. Re-elected with metronomic regularity (even in the 1990 elections), presiding firmly over a one-party state, neither charismatic nor ideologically inclined, he is nevertheless one of the foremost instances of the nationalist leader who has most successfully adapted to the process of political Africanisation as I conceive it.

Houphouët-Boigny's success stems above all from his ability to reconcile his role as the head of state of a modern nation-state with an Africanised notion of rulership. His achievements as a nationalist leader, like those of all successful nationalist leaders, derived from the strength of his legitimacy among his African constituency as well as from his skills as a negotiator *vis-à-vis* the French. Though not of chiefly lineage, he cultivated his links with the chiefs and established himself as their representative (in the sense discussed above). He acquired the accoutrements and substance (e.g., wealth, status, pomp) that befit a worthy chiefly representative. At the same time, he likes to be seen as a 'man of the people'. Generous with those who support him, he has sought to coopt, entice or coerce those who do not by means which, though maybe not readily acceptable in Western Europe, have hitherto not been excessively repressive by world standards. He has wooed rather than bullied, and scolded rather than eliminated.

The metaphor of his rulership has always been that of the *pater-familias*, firm but just.[38] He has used the constitutional framework inherited at independence where it has suited his style of politics and he has discarded it where it has not. He has sought to enhance the well-being of the population at large while making sure that his ruling élite reaped the largest profits. He has allowed dissent and political challenges only insofar as they could be accommodated within the extended family – the one-party state. The success of his rulership has necessarily been at the expense of those who believed they should replace him. Like all paramount chiefs he must resist challenges to his rule but, equally, he must be magnanimous towards those whose challenge has failed. There have been no political executions in Côte d'Ivoire.

Whatever outsiders may think of him, and few have seen him as a 'democratic' leader, the success of his rulership is not easily explained simply by reference to his dictatorial powers. Houphouët-Boigny is undoubtedly a dictator but he is also, by any standards, an accomplished politician. We may regret that he is dictator, and he may soon be overthrown because of this. Nevertheless we have to recognise that in many ways he has been the epitome of the successful modern African leader, by which I mean that the quality of his rulership has been most compatible with the relation between the state and civil society which has characterised post-colonial Africa.

Such rulership must, at a minimum, accommodate the notions of representation discussed above.[39] It must also be consistent with the perception of the political community which ordinary Africans have and with the tasks which they expect their rulers to perform. The success of any ruler derives from the legitimacy of his rule. In contemporary Africa, the legitimacy of rulership is based above all on its congruence with certain assumptions concerning the conduct of politics rather than constitutional or ideological considerations. The most rewarding way to comprehend what I call the Africanised concept of rulership is comparatively to examine the causes of the success and failure of post-colonial African leaders. This in itself requires some understanding of the ruled's perception of what success and failure are.

Above and beyond the universally recognised notion that staying in power is *ipso facto* a sign of success (if not necessarily of legitimacy), there are, it seems to me, some important differences between the contemporary Western and African concepts of rulership. While the former is above all concerned with policy, the latter combines a much wider range of pragmatic and symbolic qualities. An African leader will be judged both on his ability 'to deliver' as well as on his qualities as a representative of the community of which he is the titular head. Because these two functions, which have been dissociated in the modern Western world, are not always compatible, the relation between ruler and ruled is much more complex than is usually conceived in standard comparative theory.

I would suggest, at a fairly elementary level, that the legitimacy of post-colonial African rulers has had relatively little to do with the method of their selection.[40] Some unelected leaders (e.g., leaders of *coups d'état* like Rawlings or Babangida) have had greater legitimacy than the elected rulers they displaced. Conversely, some regularly elected leaders (eg., Moi, Banda) have very little legitimacy.

The very notion of legitimacy, the importance given to the quality of leadership and the texture of the relationship between ruler and ruled are constantly shifting in Africa. The relation between state and civil society is too fluid and unstable to make it possible to define 'a' single notion of rulership. Rulers are both more and less powerful than they are in Western countries where constitutional practices and precedent have narrowed the practical scope of rulership. It is for this reason that the present call for multi-party politics and democratisation in Africa is not likely fundamentally to change the practices of its rulership.

4. *Power and wealth*

One aspect of African rulership – indeed of African politics – which has most consistently intrigued Western observers is the relationship between wealth and power – or what is more often called corruption. A discussion of this issue will illuminate some of the questions I raised above about the multi-faceted nature of the Africanised concept of leadership. It will also show why understanding African politics is more prosaically a matter of examining what Bayart calls *la politique du ventre* than of inventing new concepts and typologies to try to accommodate 'the' African reality.[41]

The analysis of corruption in Africa is usually based on the assumption that in Western nations there is a 'deontology' of politics by which rulers and ruled alike abide. Democratic theory, whatever its variants, rests on the wholly admirable principle of the separation of power from wealth. Indeed, the historical evolution of existing democracies in seen to be the story of the long march from the diktat of ascribed and/or hereditary entitlement to power towards the freedom of electoral political accountability. No one would deny that, even in today's Western democracies, wealth and, indeed, ascribed privileges, can and do make it easier to exercise political influence or even to attain elected office. But, and this is important, they are not central to the quality of legitimacy with which elected politicians are endowed.[42]

It is well to remember, however, that such a concept of democratic leadership evolved over a long period in circumstances which were historically very specific. It is not entirely rewarding to assume that the concept of the separation of wealth from power is equally relevant to the understanding of contemporary African politics. Nor is it useful to assume at this juncture that it is a necessary outcome of 'political development'.[43]

If we are interested in understanding what is really happening in post-colonial Africa, it is important to recognise that, at this stage at least, the legitimacy of power derives in some significant part from the acquisition, possession and display of wealth. Indeed, there is overwhelming evidence to suggest that, in the minds of rulers and ruled alike, wealth is a *sine qua non* to power, just as it is well understood that power brings wealth. Whether this is attributed to the 'traditional' African notion of power, whether it is explained as a characteristic of an 'underdeveloped' polity or whether it is seen as evidence that African politics are 'pre-modern', is ultimately less important than it is to recognise that, in practice, political Africanisation implies such a link between power and wealth.[44]

To recognise this political fact is not to say that it is desirable; nor is it to deny that there are many in Africa, among rulers and ruled, who do not accept the immutability or even the legitimacy of such a relationship. Some African rulers (of whom Julius Nyerere perhaps was the epitome) have elected not to use power to amass personal wealth and have sought to divorce wealth from power. Others (e.g., Senghor, Aristides Pereira, Ahidjo, Neto, Machel) have exercised considerable personal restraint in this respect even if their subordinates have not. Many military leaders (Rawlings, Sankara, Babangida, Nino Vieira), justifying their seizure of power on account of the corruption of civilian leaders, have themselves never been accused of corruption – of using power to acquire (excessive) wealth. The fact that a proportion of top African leaders have eschewed the opportunity of amassing personal fortunes does not, however, invalidate the general observation that in Africa power and wealth go together. They are, as it were, the exceptions which confirm the rule.

It is precisely because power and wealth are so intimately connected that the personal 'integrity' of those political leaders is revealed as different, exceptional, odd even. Equally, their 'integrity' is relative. None of the rulers mentioned above have failed to enrich themselves through the exercise of power. They are remarkable only insofar as they have enriched themselves considerably less than they might have. Finally, and despite a common Western assumption to the contrary, their 'integrity' is rarely the determining factor of their political legitimacy. Some of them have presided over good governments; others have not. Good government is not a function of personal 'integrity' in this sense, although it is fair to say that good government is probably incompatible with excessive greed.

The question of the morality of the relation between power and wealth and the issue of corruption with which it is usually linked are thus best approached from the norms of contemporary African politics.[45] Africans, like the rest of us, can tell the difference between corrupt and non-corrupt rulers. We need to understand how they tell the difference rather than stand on a self-important morally superior pedestal or construct yet more categories of 'African' political morality and corruption. This is more fruitfully done by properly describing and enunciating the politics of everyday life as perceived by Africans. If it is true that the political legitimacy of African rulers implies a certain relation between power and wealth, then it is this relation which must be the starting point of our analysis.

Again, the case of Houphouët-Boigny is particularly instructive because it seems to me that, in this respect as in most others, he is the classic example of the post-colonial African ruler. The extraordinary length of his tenure of power also makes it easier to see, in historical and comparative perspective, his practice of rulership as the 'standard' of political Africanisation. Here is what he said in 1983 in a speech referring to 'his billions' [of CFA francs]:

> C'est le fruit de mon travail. Une des banques gère mes bénéfices sur la culture de l'ananas. J'ai quatre milliards de chiffre d'affaires dans la culture d'ananas . . . J'ai eu deux chutes brutales il y a deux ans alors que

j'avais atteint jusqu'à 3000 tonnes d'ananas par mois, produisant ainsi le tiers de la production nationale. . . . J'ai cessé de faire du café. Autrefois on recevait très peu, peut-être cent millions de francs, mais ces cent millions valent aujourd'hui des milliards. Et j'ai viré tout cet argent dans mes comptes en banque, en Suisse, et cela a produit des intérêts importants. L'une des banques d'Abidjan possède de moi le quart de ses dépôts. Si je n'avais pas confiance en mon pays garderais-je tout cet argent ici? J'ai confiance en la Côte d'Ivoire. Il y a même une banque qui gère mes bénéfices sur l'avocat dont, je crois, je suis le premier producteur en Côte d'Ivoire. Il y a une autre banque qui gère modestement les bénéfices de mon élevage de poulets. Mais ces milliards, parce que tout cela se chiffre en milliards, se trouvent dans le pays.[46]

What is revealing about this statement is not, as many Western observers would emphasise, that Houphouët-Boigny should admit to the enormous wealth which his hold on power has enabled him to amass. It is, rather, his (obviously vindicated) belief that speaking publicly and in such detail about his personal wealth strengthens his political legitimacy. For this is no off-the-cuff remark but a speech duly reproduced in the official national newspaper. As such it is no petty braggadocio but must be read as a carefully crafted piece of political propaganda.

Houphouët-Boigny sets himself as a model of the successful entrepreneur, extolling the virtue of hard work, brandishing the monetary rewards of success and justifying foreign bank accounts by claiming that the high interests earned can profitably be re-invested locally. More importantly, he makes a public display of his wealth to his constituents. Like a great paramount chief, he ensures that the citizens of Côte d'Ivoire know that their ruler is worthy of their trust. Like a chief he claims not to be personally greedy. He sees his personal wealth as a mark of his own substance and, paradoxically, of his probity. For, as he makes clear in the same speech, it is precisely because he is wealthy that he can be trusted to be honest and magnanimous: 'Le budget de la Présidence de la République est de deux milliards de francs [CFA] . . . Je ne suis pas égoïste. Pour moi, l'argent ne compte que par le bon usage qu'on en fait. C'est le bon usage qui donne de la valeur à l'argent'.[47]

Houphouët-Boigny thus makes explicit the significance of the relationship between wealth and power in post-colonial African politics. He also makes plain the degree to which, for African rulers, private wealth and public resources mix. This, again, does not seem to be cause for alarm in Côte d'Ivoire, though it may well be that the construction of Yamassoukro's cathedral (the largest in the world), formally inaugurated by the Pope, is the proof that Houphouët-Boigny has finally overstepped the mark. This may be the symbolic excess which breaks his subjects' forbearance with his chiefly megalomania.

If (or rather when) this happens, it will show that Africans can indeed decide on the proper limits of rulership. For the extent to which rulers are entitled to mix public resources and private wealth is clear to Africans even if they have silently to endure appalling excesses. In many countries, that balance has clearly dissipated. It is alleged, and it is an allegation that many (particularly the Zairean opposition) are inclined to believe, that Mobutu controls for his personal use a significant proportion of Zaïre's national budget. True or not, the allegations have reduced both his political legitimacy and the ability of his government to govern. Zaïre is a country where it is said that politics and greed are synonymous.[48] Nevertheless, Mobutu is by no means unique. His alleged wealth is the product of the enormous wealth of his country. Other leaders (e.g., Sékou Touré, Acheampong, Siaka Stevens, Bokassa, Nguema) are also alleged to have helped themselves liberally from the state coffers.[49]

The point is clear. It is not that African rulers are necessarily more greedy or dishonest than rulers elsewhere – although the vagaries of decolonisation were responsible for the emergence of rulers who in normal circumstances might not have been chosen. It is rather that in contemporary Africa, as in many other parts of the world, the legitimacy of power derives in part from personal wealth and that, conversely, it is legitimate to use power as a means of amassing wealth. Political Africanisation implies here that there is an inescapable dialectical relationship between power and wealth. The search for power goes hand in hand with the will to be rich.

This is not a particularly startling conclusion. Many, particularly Marxists, would argue that political power is always the product of economic power. The difference is that whereas they view the contest in terms of classes, the process of political Africanisation which I have discussed here focuses much more on the relations between individuals and communities. The Marxist analysis of the relation between power and class has often obscured a complex political process which escapes simple dichotomies. For this reason, I find the notion of hegemonic drive more useful than class analysis.

13 The Dialectics of the Hegemonic Drive

The concept of hegemony is central to the notion of power. It illuminates the nature of the link between economic and political power, between culture, social formation and political institutions, between individuals and corporate bodies. It helps the understanding of the dynamics between state and civil society, between élites and counter-élites, between the 'haves' and the 'have nots'. Most importantly, it makes it possible to take a long-term view of the movement of politics in Africa. For if the post-colonial state's hegemonic drive is the most consistently conspicuous characteristic of contemporary African politics, its understanding can only derive from a prior analysis of the meanings and practices of hegemony over time.[1]

The notions of hegemony and hegemonic drive are not the preserve of class analysis even if they are most often associated with it. All political analysis contains an explanation for the genesis and dynamics of political dominance – whatever the name given to the relation between power and production. Class analysis, it is true, is built on univocal causalities between economic power (structure) and political power (super-structure) which make it easy to understand the meaning of hegemony.[2] Hegemony is, *ipso facto*, the control of political power by the economically dominant class(es) or, more accurately, their representatives. Class analysis also possesses a key to the dynamics of hegemony in the postulate that class struggle is the motor of history.

Gramsci's analysis of Italy, an underdeveloped and heterogeneous European (partly) capitalist society of more than passing resemblance to contemporary African countries, exposed the inadequacies of a rigidly orthodox Marxist view.[3] It revealed that both class causalities and the reality of hegemony were considerably more complex than orthodox Marxist theory had anticipated. Gramsci saw clearly that class analysis in its classical form could not easily account for the political development of nineteenth- and early twentieth-century Italy: a country which was the product of a recent nationalist (political) revolution, where capitalist and pre-capitalist modes of production combined, where North and South were fundamentally at odds, where religion continued to play a dominant role and where cultural differences were fundamental.

For this reason, Gramsci's use of the notion of hegemony is of some considerable relevance to the analysis of post-colonial Africa, even if it is pointless to seek to find in it an operational definition.[4] What is important for Africanists is Gramsci's emphasis on the notion of hegemonic *drive* as the attempt by élites and counter-élites to link economic and political power. Whether there can ever be complete hegemony by a definable class is a question best left to class analysts. What concerned Gramsci and what must concern political analysts of Africa is the complex and continuous processes by which competing élites define, organise and implement various strategies of hegemonic drive over time.[5] For those are the realities of day-to-day politics.

Bayart, who has considered carefully Gramsci's notion, proposes the concept of 'the search for hegemony'. His definition is:

> Une telle 'recherche hégémonique' vise à la création et à la cristallisation d'un rapport de forces relativement stable entre les différents groupes dominants, anciens et nouveaux, et entre les segments régionaux ou ethniques de ceux-ci, dans le cadre national fixé par le colonisateur; à l'aménagement des rapports entre cette classe dominante en voie de formation et la masse de la population; à l'agencement des rapports entre cette classe dominante et le pôle de pouvoir politique et économique occidental; à l'élaboration d'une éthique ou d'un sens commun qui donne sa cohérence à l'ensemble et qui cimente le nouveau système d'inégalité et de domination, tout en le camouflant . . . [L]a recherche hégémonique, au Cameroun, paraît reposer sur un processus d'assimilation réciproque et de fusion des groupes dominants anciens et des nouvelles élites nées de la colonisation et de la décolonisation. Les lignes contemporaines d'inégalité et de domination semblent ainsi s'inscrire dans le prolongement direct des structures sociales pré-coloniales, les dominés d'hier constituer la masse des dominés d'aujourd'hui.[6]

In a later book, he qualifies his view thus:

> Définition par trop mécaniste que celle-ci. Elle a pour seul mérite de désigner le triple enjeu auquel se réfère le processus de la recherche hégémonique. Il s'agit tout d'abord de circonscrire, idéologiquement aussi bien que territorialement, l'espace neuf de la domination qu'impose le changement d'échelle colonial, et d'y consigner les dominés. Nous retrouvons là, sous un autre angle, la dynamique centrale de l'ethnicité; celle de la structure du champ de l'État en tant que double champ de l'identité et de l'inégalité . . .
>
> La reconstruction de l'espace social apparaît donc indissociable d'un deuxième enjeu: celui que représente l'opportunité, non pas simplement de l'enrichissement mais d'une vraie accumulation primitive, consistant en la monopolisation des moyens de production par les groupes domi-

nants. Le rapport intime de l'État à cette évolution indique le troisième terme de la recherche hégémonique, le plus manifeste: la détention du pouvoir politique, c'est-à-dire de l'usage de la force légitime qui commande la 'mise au travail' des groupes subordonnés et la maîtrise de l'économie. A cet égard également, le moment colonial a innové. Il a éloigné les acteurs de représentations symboliques ancestrales qui contribuaient à limiter la polarisation sociale; il a introduit la technologie de l'État bureaucratique centralisé qui donne aux dominants les moyens de leurs fins, de l'écriture aux communications modernes en passant par l'armement massif.[7]

Bayart's definition is, quite rightly, centred on the role of the state. Nevertheless, Bayart's enunciation (not amenable to paraphrase!) of that notion is illuminating and it must be our starting point. It contains important elements which do account for the changing complexion of power induced by the rise of the colonial state and amplified after independence by the post-colonial state. I am, however, concerned more generally with the meanings and practices of power in Africa – rather than simply with the state – and for this reason I prefer to extend somewhat the realm of the notion of hegemonic drive.[8]

I now myself qualify what I said in the earlier chapter on the state.[9] What is important is not just the centrality of the state but its consistency. Whereas the colonial state recognisably was a state in the modern European sense, the post-colonial state is more difficult to comprehend.[10] Or rather to comprehend it demands that we suspend judgement on the notion of the state as *a single* entity and, instead, attempt to analyse it more in terms of the central *locus* of the hegemonic drive which it is. The transformation of the post-colonial state is thus most profitably examined as the outcome of the dialectics of the hegemonic drive which governs politics in contemporary Africa.[11]

It is at this juncture that I must temper the sharp conceptual dichotomies implied in the separate chapters (4 and 5) on the state and civil society.[12] Although the organising principle of the struggle between state and civil society is precisely the hegemonic drive, understanding the real (as opposed to conceptual) world means understanding how the two impinge on each other.

Here again, Bayart's qualification of his earlier dichotomies between state and civil society are apposite. He writes:

Une autre analyse de type binaire qu'il convient de récuser consisterait à figer les pratiques de réappropriation historique de l'État sous la forme d'une dichotomie entre le 'haut' et le 'bas' de la société, ou entre la société civile et l'État. A cet égard, l'expression imagée de la 'revanche des sociétés africanes' que nous avons utilisée à certains moments de notre démonstration, ou encore l'hypothèse d'un État taraudé par 'l'économie d'affection', lancée par G. Hyden, ne doivent pas être comprises au pied de la lettre, sous peine d'induire en erreur. *Il ne s'agit pas, en un balancement académique et artificiel, d'opposer au travail de 'totalisation' étatique celui de tactiques divergentes de 'détotalisation', même si la contestation de l'État, son érosion et sa dilution procèdent effectivement avant tout de ces dernières.* En réalité, les logiques de déconstruction du champ étatique ne se départagent pas aussi aisément de celles de sa cristallisation. Les matrices du désordre sont souvent les mêmes que celles de l'ordre . . . [13]

What is most illuminating in Bayart's remarks, above and beyond the attempt to eschew simplistic contrasts, is the search for the formulation which most accurately accounts for what is actually taking place in contemporary Africa. He is right to reject the edifying notion of a struggle between a well-defined and coherent civil society and a separate but equally well-defined and coherent state. The metaphor of the dichotomy can be, and usually is, misleading.[14] The notions of the state and civil society are useful and the dichotomies between them real, but concepts are merely the instruments and not the ends of political analysis. Having outlined the concepts, we need to see how they help us to understand post-colonial politics.

The hegemonic drive has been the guiding principle of political action in contemporary Africa for specific historical reasons having to do with the formation of the post-colonial state and the response which it induced in civil society.[15] The hegemonic drive, however, has taken many forms which are not revealed in the simple notion of a Manichean struggle between state and civil society. Nor does the concept make clear in which ways the hegemonic drive is individual or collective. State and civil society are composed of individuals but these individuals also matter politically as parts of the communities to which they belong. Hence, the discussion of the hegemonic drive must incorporate an analysis of its micro- (individual) and macro- (community) components.[16]

Broadly, the strategies for hegemonic drive take two forms: the one consists in capturing, or, more accurately, penetrating, the state; the other aims at establishing a counter or a parallel hegemonic project to rival and challenge the state.

The strategies for penetrating the state are many but the most effective and successful of them all was decolonisation. The transfer of power resulted ultimately in the wholesale takeover of the colonial state by the nationalist counter-élites. In the course of a few years, Africans gained access to the (vastly overdeveloped) state and ensconced themselves at the centre of a political and bureaucratic machine with a long and successful hegemonic experience.[17] The Africanisation of the colonial state was rightly perceived by Africans to be the most expedient route to hegemony.[18] Because the individual was so intimately connected with the community, the success of one individual in penetrating the state enabled many in the community to benefit. Patron–client relationships developed. Networks of patronage grew.[19] Prebendalism flourished. So, Africanisation had wide ranging effects which reached far into the most remote communities.

Decolonisation was, however, a one-off affair. After Africanisation was complete, penetrating the state became infinitely more difficult. To delay the time when access to the state would become a zero-sum game[20] and because it was in the 'general interest' (of both of state and civil society), the state was allowed to swell.[21] Accommodating more people satisfied the insatiable demand for state employment even if it placed greater and greater financial burdens on an already hypertrophic state. A growing proportion of younger people and an explosion in access to education exacerbated the number of such claimants and their expectations.[22] Not to give them the opportunity to penetrate the state was politically dangerous.[23] Nevertheless, eventually the state could simply no longer assimilate more individuals.

Once this stage was reached, strategies of state penetration changed. The very meaning of 'penetration' changed. On the one hand, state activities were extended further into the economic realm. On the other, the relationship between those within the state and those outside was transformed.

The widespread state-led model of economic development (statism), which was not confined to so-called socialist countries, increased the scope of state activity. Nationalisations and the establishment of parastatals enabled a whole new 'class' of claimants to penetrate the state and in this way successfully to advance their hegemony.[24] It is partly for this reason, and not simply for reasons having to do with the inherently unworkable economic logic of nationalised industries, that nationalisations and the creation of parastatals in Africa were almost universally an unmitigated economic disaster. Disaster, that is, for the national economy but not for the individuals/ communities who profited massively from their involvement in those industries.[25]

While it is easy to show how leftwing economic policies made possible an extension of the state which benefited a large number of people, it is no more difficult to see how other regimes achieved similar ends with different means.[26] In many countries, the party (formally or informally) controlled the economy. Access to the party was thus equivalent to access to the state. In other countries, semi-official ethnic, cultural or religious organisations had an important role to play in the national economy. Islamic brotherhoods, trade associations, ethnic 'aid-groups', etc., not infrequently controlled part of the economy with the tacit agreement of the state.[27] The distinction between regimes of the left and of the right is, in this respect, one of degree rather than kind. Whether officially or not, openly or by stealth, there is no denying the general advance of state involvement in the economy in the majority of African countries.

At the same time, the relationship between state and civil society changed. If direct access to the state was impossible, access to state resources by way of patronage remained feasible. As patron–client relations expanded, the state (in its multiplying ramifications) became evermore a patrimonial state. The need to penetrate the state was transmuted into the ability to tap its resources at distance. The more difficult the penetration of the state, the thicker and more extensive the patrimonial links became.[28.]

For reasons having to do with the relations between the individual and the community in Africa, few of those within the state refused to become patrons, for if their position within the state facilitated hegemony, the consummation of that hegemony was only possible within the community. Ostentatious individual displays of wealth become instrumental in furthering hegemony only when they are acted out through the community. Even presidents need to reveal their power by means of their munificence to their 'villages'.[29]

This process had two consequences for politics. The first was that the bureaucratic or political career ('service to the state') of state personnel was never an end in itself but essentially a means to other ends. Much as a businessman sees his activity as a means to amass wealth in order to re-invest in other activities, those in state employ see their occupation as a means to further political and economic hegemony. For this reason, the notion of the modern bureaucratic state (in the Weberian sense) as instilled by the colonial order could not survive decolonisation.[30]

The second is that the notion of the state became more and more blurred over time. The expansion of the already overdeveloped post-colonial state in numbers and in realms of activity inflated its many constituent parts to such a degree that it became difficult to gauge its limits. The post-colonial state swelled and became involved in all spheres of public life. As it did so, it vastly overextended itself in financial, political and even symbolic terms. The state was everywhere but it did not have the means to fulfil its hegemonic ambitions. Consequently, civil society penetrated the state in its million different interstices. The state began to thin out and be re-appropriated by civil society.[31]

While in contemporary Africa it is possible to identify the core of the state apparatus, it has become much more difficult to outline the boundaries of the state.[32] It is difficult, too, to define the nature of the relationship between the core and the periphery of the state. It is this dilution of the state which puts its relationship with civil society into perspective. The state's hegemonic drive, therefore, is the multiplication of power and wealth not simply by the mighty at the top but also by the vast multitudes who, at the core or at the periphery, directly or indirectly, thrive or merely survive at the expense of the state. In this way the state was indeed re-appropriated by civil society – in a process which Bayart once termed *la revanche des sociétés africaines*.[33]

The strategies of state penetration were considerably reduced, as was state hegemony, by the inexorable reduction of resources and revenues which eventually afflicted all African countries when, a decade or so after independence, at about the time when the oil crisis erupted, they began to pay the price for the profligacy of their governments. Not only had government policies seldom achieved economic growth but the state's hegemonic drive had often resulted in the wholesale plunder of existing resources and in a consequent reduction in state revenues.[34]

This undesirable state of affairs prompted rulers to reconsider their policy of state expansion *à outrance* and thereby to tighten access to the state. Without adequate resources the outer layers of the state began to peel off. Impecunious and overcommitted (state) patrons began to neglect and then to drop clients at the periphery of their network. The effect of structural adjustment programmes is, in this respect, to enable rulers to blame the contraction of the patrimonial state on the IMF, the latest outside *deus ex machina*.[35]

So long as the strategy of state penetration looked remotely feasible it was pursued with the utmost assiduousness. It took political instability (sometimes on a massive scale), violence, arbitrary coercion and, above all, a recognition that the state's resources were finite, when not decreasing fast, to force a reconsideration of the role of civil society *vis-à-vis* the state.[36] Once the limits of the state hegemonic drive had been exposed, counter-hegemonic strategies became more attractive.

Education provides a good example of this process. All African states invested heavily in education after independence both because there was an acute need for qualified manpower and because of the nationalist pledge to better the condition of the younger generation.[37] In the first few years, graduates almost always found state employment. The Africanisation of personnel and the massive expansion of the state apparatus provided them with jobs. As the proportion of those receiving secondary and higher education increased, however, the state reached the limits of its inflation, resources became scarce and the likelihood of graduates gaining state employment was drastically reduced.

Since education had often been conceived (implicitly or explicitly) in terms of training for state employment, it appeared to the age-groups concerned that they were now 'denied' employment. Graduate unemployment became a serious problem. Young people turned more and more readily towards strategies of counter-hegemony, initiating or supporting political action which sometimes led to the overthrow of governments. In the eyes of the ruling classes, they became 'delinquents' or 'subversives'.[38]

In chronological terms, then, counter-hegemonic projects, the politics of civil society, began seriously to impinge on post-colonial African politics after states were perceived to have reached their hegemonic limits. In reality, there had always been counter-hegemonic movements but, in the decade after independence, they were easily dismissed. Nationalism still conferred legitimacy on the state, if not always on some of its rulers. By contrast, political opposition had little legitimacy. Opponents to the regime in place were cast either as enemies of the people or, more prosaically, as power-seekers. The increasing frequency of military coups and the myriad of political plots lent credence to that view of political opposition. In truth, overt opposition was merely the visible part of the politics of civil society. The more significant counter-hegemonic processes were often hidden deeper in the recesses of civil society where the arm of the state did not easily reach.[39]

Nationalist euphoria and a decidedly statist vision of post-colonial African politics often misled participants and observers alike on the actual power of the state. While the post-colonial state readily occupied the vacuum created by decolonisation and while it did seem to embody the reality of the new nation-state, it was not nearly as powerful as it appeared. Or rather, its power, like the power of all post-revolutionary states, derived from the absence of organised counter-hegemonic power. The post-colonial state was in fact a precarious construction and its capacity to resist counter-hegemonic politics was limited.[40]

At independence, there were, of course, important differences between different countries in terms of the balance of power between nationalist and other élites. In some instances (e.g., Guinea, Cameroon, Kenya), decolonisation had involved the elimination of the most potentially troublesome 'traditional' counter-élites and there the power of the state seemed assured. In others (e.g., Senegal, Nigeria, Uganda), the nationalist revolution had hardly touched the power of those 'traditional' counter-élites who, whether in or out of government, continued to play an important role in politics. In yet other cases (e.g., Swaziland, Malawi, Burundi, Lesotho, Botswana), the nationalists were themselves the traditional élites and independence marked remarkably little break with colonial or even pre-colonial politics.[41]

Where the dependence of the post-colonial state on 'traditional' élites was more visible, it was easier to see that state power was neither monolithic nor without limits. Where there was no visible potential political opposition, it was plausible to imagine that the state reigned supreme. Nevertheless, it is now clear that the power of the post-colonial state was overstated.

In the first instance, except in very few cases (e.g., Guinea), the power of the 'traditional' élites did not simply disappear at independence.[42] However impaired and distorted their explicit function may have become, they continued to play an important role in the life of African communities. Second, there were in many countries parallel systems of political/economic/spiritual/ religious power which survived virtually unscathed into the post-colonial era. Muslim brotherhoods, sultanates, kingdoms, ethnic institutions, pre-colonial states, independent churches, trade-associations, age-groups, etc., were all-important components of the new post-colonial Africa, even when they had no specifically recognised power within the state. As during the colonial period, after independence they could readily be used as conduits for the formation of counter-hegemonic projects within civil society.[43]

Third, there were a number of bodies and institutions established under colonial rule which were not always readily incorporated into the new state and represented potential channels for counter-hegemonic politics. Colonial councils, colonial 'chiefdoms', representative and consultative organs, cultural and sports associations, trade-unions and other professional bodies, the official churches and mission societies, ethnic advisory councils, associations of graduates or war veterans, armed forces and police, etc., represented a large number of the citizens of the newly independent countries.[44] The organisations of which they already were a part were readily available for counter-hegemonic politics.

Fourth, many of the groups and associations formed after independence (e.g., students' organisations, press councils, professional bodies, intellectual or political groups, new ethnic institutions, religious revival groups or independent churches) could, and often were, used for counter-hegemonic purposes. There was in fact a proliferation of informal and, sometimes, formal groups in the post-colonial period which ruling élites and Africanists alike failed either to identify or to take seriously. Perhaps the most revealing example here is the revival in many African countries of 'witchcraft' or of some form of 'traditional' religion.[45]

Finally, but ultimately most significantly, there was the mass of the population which was at most only loosely connected with any identifiable structure or institution. Mobilised by nationalism during decolonisation,[46] they were then 'organised' by the new principles of post-colonial political accountability (e.g., one-party state) by which the new rulers sought to legitimise their rulership. The last to benefit from patrimonialism, they were the first to be disenfranchised and to suffer from the state's hegemonic drive.

Whether as a result they supported organised counter-hegemonic politics, whether they retreated altogether from the political arena or whether they created their own counter-hegemonic organisations, they represented potentially the most powerful component of civil society. Because they usually were unorganised, atomised, disaggregated, their power was not easily recognisable. In the final analysis, however, it was their (passive) resistance which most weakened the post-colonial state.[47]

Thus the success of the state's hegemonic drive in post-colonial Africa depended not so much on the exercise of what appeared to be its power as a state but rather on its ability to minimise the threat of counter-hegemonic politics.[48] Insofar as diminishing economic resources made the state less able to incorporate civil society within its various networks, its ability to coopt potential opponents and undermine counter-hegemonic politics was diminished. In countries (like Côte d'Ivoire, Kenya, Cameroon, Gabon) where the state possessed relatively sufficient resources, the danger was limited, if still present.[49] In most other countries, however, the state's economic weakness seriously eroded its capacity for hegemony.

The dialectics of the hegemonic drive led inexorably to a process whereby the state's inability to fulfil its patrimonial function resulted in the growing strength of counter-hegemonic politics. This in turn reduced the economic strength of the state and further eroded its ability to provide, thus inducing more of its clients to turn to counter-hegemonic patrons. There is no clearer example of this process than the development of (sometimes large-scale) parallel economies in most African countries. In some countries (e.g., Zaïre), it is estimated that the parallel economy is substantially larger than the official one.[50]

The strength of the (multifarious) counter-hegemonic drive is not best measured by the ease with which regimes are toppled (although that is evidence enough) but rather by the diminishing power of the state in Africa. Because power and production are inextricably linked, the true test of strength lies in the balance of economic power between the state and civil society.[51] In this respect, the most salient feature of contemporary African states is undoubtedly their diminishing economic power – as evidenced by increased foreign borrowing, reduced agricultural production or even famine.[52]

Since when power is eroded it either dissipates altogether or turns to force, it is not altogether surprising that the level of coercion and violence should have increased over time in post-colonial Africa. This is proof, if proof were needed, that state power has been in decline ever since independence. An increase in state coercion and violence may, of course, deter overt counter-hegemonic politics but it will do nothing to restore state power or regime legitimacy.[53]

The reality of contemporary African politics is that the state is merely shadow-boxing with its declared challengers in a 'shrunken official political arena' while, in a more important 'hidden political arena', élites and counter-élites battle to acquire and sustain the economic means of political power.

The discussion so far has set the stage but it has not given much sense of what the hegemonic drive means for the individual. State and civil society are abstract general concepts which, though useful analytically, tend to give the notion that contemporary African countries are in the grip of Manichean struggles in which there are set-piece battles between the armies of the state and those of civil society. This may be an accurate macro-picture but it fails to reveal the complexities and the fluidities of the day-to-day micro-situation which, for its part, suggests a picture of chaos rather than of ordered hegemonic contest. An understanding of the dialectics of the hegemonic drive must seek to make some sense of this chaos.[54]

The general pattern of political instability and regime changes in Africa, which reflects the force of the battle for hegemonic supremacy, means that the turnover at the apex of the state structure is high.[55] Tenure of state power is unstable and unpredictable. The rise and fall of ruling élites are swift. The position of those below the apex, that is the rulers' immediate collaborators, is yet more precarious, even if it is less frequently exposed to the extreme wrath of counter-élites or the populace. The higher servants of the state are above all the servants of the rulers in place and as such cannot expect to survive their demise. At once 'gatekeepers' and court advisers, they must please but not threaten. Their tenure of power is insecure and arbitrary. The same applies down the line, at all levels of the state administration. Insecurity and arbitrariness are the rules rather than the exception.

This lack of state bureaucratic (in the Weberian sense) order, from top to bottom, implies great fluidity in state employment.[56] While the hegemonic drive of the state remains, the individuals who are in its employ may change rapidly. Each regime change, each coup, each purge, leads to a substantial change in state personnel. There are constant changes in the 'membership' of the state and, hence, of the various counter-hegemonic components of civil society.

Individuals may move from one to the other at a moment's notice and several times in a relatively short period of time (as Zaïre's Karl-i-Bond could readily testify, having several times been dismissed and/or sentenced to death and then returned to ministerial duty by an apparently fickle

Mobutu).[57] For this reason, hegemony and counter-hegemony are inextricably intertwined. At the individual level, the dividing line between the two is very thin. Given the high rate of circulation of the élites, there is always hope for individuals to be able to (re)penetrate the state. Involvement in counter-hegemonic politics is more often a campaign to return to power than a serious attempt to overturn the existing political order.[58]

Consequently, the macro-picture I painted above about the 'shrinkage' of the state which resulted from the diminution of its resources must be qualified by the micro-analysis of the behaviour of individuals. Appurtenance to the state remains a desirable individual option, regardless of the risks, insecurity and arbitrariness involved. The individual's strategy is thus largely conditioned by his relation to the state. Supporting counter-hegemonic politics is often merely the most effective way of being co-opted into the state.

For example, students may be against a particular regime because they have little prospect of state employment rather than because they necessarily support the political opposition.[59] Should the regime in question restructure the administration and make room for them, their opposition would dissolve. The same goes for the armed forces who invariably cloak corporate grievances with high-minded declarations against the corruption of civilians.[60] Equally, ethnic grievances appear and disappear according to the fate of the individuals whose interest it is to voice them.

Thus for the individual, at the micro-level, access to the state (and hence, its resources) remains an eminently reasonable strategy, however economically weak the state may be. For access to the state is usually the key to the operation of economic networks on which most Africans depend. The state may be (relatively) poor but it is still, in most instances, the great enabler. From the appropriation of millions by African rulers to the lowliest constable's ability to generate revenues through 'bribes', access to the state is always productive for the *individual*. To take just one example, the authority to deliver (trading) licences enables the 'licence-giver' to negotiate a financial reward for his authority with producers who are busy smuggling their goods across the borders, beyond the reach of the state.[61]

Attention to the micro-level thus reveals that, for individuals, there is no sharp dichotomy or incompatibility between the two strategies for hegemonic drive drawn above. Penetrating the state is a favoured option but it is not the only option nor is it pursued to the exclusion of the other options. Conversely, counter-hegemonic activities are often nothing but attempts to find the most effective entry point for penetrating the state. The centrality of the state in contemporary Africa is thus not simply the result of the economic benefits which access to it confers but also derives from the fact that all counter-hegemonic projects are defined and organised in relation to it.[62]

In large part, the politics of civil society are aimed not at undermining the state *qua* state but at devising ways of penetrating it. The more fluid and ill-defined the boundaries between state and civil society, the more multiple and complex are these strategies of penetration.[63] Thus, whereas at the macro-level it is possible to point to the struggle between the state and civil society, at the micro-level it is virtually impossible to disentangle the dialectics of the hegemonic drive.

The argument, consequently, that the state is all-powerful, or its converse, that the state has been so undermined by civil society that it has lost all real power, are both equally reductive when examined at the micro-level, for state and civil society are inextricably intertwined. There are indeed rulers and ruled, a distinction between those within and outside the state. However, the rate at which individuals move from the one to the other and the absence of firm boundaries on the ground between the one and the other, necessarily undermine the validity of any generalised macro-analysis.

It is the extent to which state and civil society interpenetrate each other over time and the fluidity of their boundaries which make the relation between the two so productive for *individuals*. However, the factors which are most conducive to the success of the individual may not be those which are most conducive to the economic health of the nation as a whole.[64] In the long run, the maximisation of individual hegemony may well be at the expense of the country's economy.

What this implies, of course, is that there are losers as well as winners in the dialectics of the hegemonic drive. I have so far concentrated on the strategy of the winners – those who successfully negotiate their access to the state and operate successfully within civil society. I have emphasised that the viability of what appears to outsiders as an exceedingly chaotic and unequal political system is partly explained by the belief of the majority in the myth that, for them too, the state can be the great enabler. This myth, which has no more but no less foundation than any other 'original' myth (such as the greatest of them all, the 'American Dream'), sustains a system which appears inherently unstable.[65]

Nevertheless, there are limits to what myths can do and in Africa, as elsewhere, the system is likely to collapse once the proportion of losers becomes, or at least is perceived to have become excessive. Indeed, political order has collapsed in a number of African countries since independence and the analysis of those cases should help us to sharpen our understanding of the dialectics of the hegemonic drive,[66] for, ultimately, the dissolution of a given political order means the victory of a counter-hegemonic project.

Chief among the losers were those disenfranchised on ascriptive grounds. In almost all post-colonial societies there were cleavages along ethnic, regional, racial, religious or cultural lines which could be used by the rulers to disenfranchise some of their subjects. Whether they did so or not depended on a whole host of political reasons, some with deep historical roots. The point is that, in many African countries, individuals and communities have been systematically disenfranchised for ascriptive rather than political reasons.[67]

The disenfranchised groups, for whom the strategy of state penetration was necessarily closed, not unnaturally organised counter-hegemonic projects. Countries with disenfranchised 'minorities' always have had strong, coherent and consistent counter-hegemonic movements. It is in those countries that the state has most comprehensively failed to maintain a balance between consent and coercion or to sustain the legitimacy of its power, for those who are disenfranchised on ascriptive grounds cannot believe in the myth of the permeability of the state. They must either withdraw or seek to overthrow that state.[68]

The cases of Mauritania, Chad, Sudan, Uganda, Rwanda, Burundi, Ethiopia, etc., all furnish us with examples of societies where a (sometimes significant) proportion of the population was/is so disenfranchised. For instance, the recent events in Mauritania, in which Black Africans were the butt of attacks by the 'Moorish' ruling classes, is symptomatic of what is not an isolated type of conflict in Africa.[69] In those countries, there is indeed a battle between the state and its rivals; individuals are often compelled to take sides. For the disenfranchised, the necessity to operate according to the rules of a counter-hegemonic drive is imperative. They must organise to survive. Whether they withdraw or attempt to create a parallel 'state' (either through secession or within a federation) is usually a practical question.

In the rest of Africa, however, the conflict between the state and its counter-hegemonic rivals is less stark and much more murky. Where the disenfranchised are less identifiable and less able to perceive themselves as a group, their counter-hegemonic strategies are likely to be multiple, diverse and discrete. They will range from the organised to the spontaneous, from the collective to the individual, from the violent to the passive, from the religious to the secular, from the orderly to the disorderly, from the general to the local, and from the political to the economic.[70]

Where, as in some West African countries, there are already well-organised Muslim societies, most of the counter-hegemonic projects are likely to be channelled through those societies and their élites are likely to command attention from the state rulers.[71] Where, as in some Eastern and Central African countries, there are readily identifiable dynastic communities with roots in long-established kingdoms, the same is likely to be the case. Conversely, so-called slave or plebeian rival communities will also have a 'natural' channel for organising themselves against such dynastic communities.[72]

Ethnic groups can also organise in similarly purposeful fashion though here the very definition of ethnicity is likely to be singularly contingent. Indeed, despite popular Western prejudice to the contrary, ethnicity is not often a straightforward foundation on which to organise politically, let alone construct a coherent and sustainable counter-hegemonic project. There are few examples in post-colonial Africa of successful ethnic challenges against the state.[73] Ethnicity lends itself far more to the strategy of state penetration for it is ideally suited to patrimonialism and prebendalism.

On the other hand, armed forces and their paramilitary complements are more likely to succeed in their challenge against the regime even if their counter-hegemonic project has little political or ideological substance. Here the control of the means of violence makes good the lack of political coherence and the absence of vision. The *coup d'état* is a straightforward seizure of power within the state, the replacement of some rulers by others. It is the clearest proof that counter-hegemonic politics are aimed at the control of the state rather than at changing policies.

What of revolution in Africa? There are in many African countries overtly revolutionary political movements which dispute the legitimacy of the existing political order and seek its overthrow.[74] However, there have been in Africa very few sustained armed revolutionary challenges (e.g., Congo, Cameroon, Angola) to the state.[75] Perhaps the fact that none has hitherto succeeded explains why, in truth, there are comparatively few armed insurrections in contemporary Africa – as opposed to, say, Latin America or Asia. Perhaps too, it is because there are very few countries in Africa where conditions are propitious for revolution,[76] that is where sufficiently numerous elements within civil society believe they would benefit more from overthrowing the existing state rather than working through it.

Perhaps, more simply, it is because, at this stage in the evolution of post-colonial Africa, the hegemonic function of the state is still so central that counter-hegemonic élites seldom manage to generate the historical and ideological justification which would legitimise their enterprise. Counter-hegemonic politics often lack committed and coherent 'intellectuals' since many opposition leaders are more concerned to find a way into the state than to further the aim of any revolutionary designs.[77]

They are concerned to position themselves as political challengers within the existing political order rather than offer a vision for a different political order. In Africa, so-called opposition leaders and other critical ideologues are coopted with amazing ease if, at times, little grace. Indeed, the most sustained critique of the existing political order in Africa seems to come from writers and artists who are in no position successfully to construct a counter-hegemonic project.[78]

What this suggests is that the dialectics of the hegemonic drive in contemporary Africa play themselves out through the state. However inefficient and devoid of resources, the state is for the time being (and is likely to remain) at the centre of politics. Because the state is neither monolithic nor stable and above all because it is so porous, the strategy of seeking access to it is (and is likely to remain) the most logical option for individuals. Indeed, it is the very softness and overdevelopment of the state, like a lumbering giant queen bee fulfilling its symbolic and practical function, which enables it to continue both to survive and to service so many in the community.

Put another way, it could be argued that the state has survived as state only insofar as it has been successfully colonised by civil society. In other words, the dialectics of the hegemonic drive have pitted state against civil society in a mock battle, like the ritual contest between males in the animal kingdom, where each in the end has had to make space for the other. If this is true, then the apparent deliquescence of political order in contemporary Africa is in reality the adaptation of the post-colonial state to the realities of civil society. The very weaknesses, ambiguities, disorders and inefficiencies found in the typical African state are not simply signs of its degeneration but an indication of the establishment of a *modus operandi* between state and civil society.

The dialectics of the hegemonic drive reveal a situation in which state and civil society are silent accomplices in the maintenance of a political order which is productive for both. Political analysis must thus seek to move beyond the examination of the way in which state and civil society publicly joust and focus instead on the shadowy world of politics in which the deals between the two are struck.[79]

14 The Politics of Dependence

Perhaps the most widely discussed feature of post-colonial Africa is its dependence.[1] It is certainly the condition that appears most prominently in the analysis of contemporary Africa. Africans, Africanists, observers and inhabitants of Africa all point to the peculiarly debilitating external context within which recently independent nation-states have found themselves right from their inception. Whatever the perspective of the analyst, radical or conservative, particularist or universalist, the inescapable fact that Africa is a continent of dependent countries is invariably the backdrop against which the analysis of its politics proceeds.[2]

This is not altogether surprising for Africa is indeed a continent of dependent countries and the fact of dependence does indeed matter greatly for its politics.[3] This is, however, where the consensus ends. There is little agreement on the precise meaning of dependence or on its implications for the economic and political life of Africa. This too is unsurprising in that, above and beyond the specific analysis associated with underdevelopment theory discussed in Part I, there are divergent views on the relative significance of dependence for Africa.

What is dependence? Here, as before, we must start at the beginning and consider the notion within its appropriate historical context. If the *Ur*-notion of dependence is to be found in general histories of the development of the world capitalist system, the historically closer and more relevant model for Africa derived from the analysis of the process of economic *under*development experienced by Latin American countries in the late nineteenth and twentieth centuries.[4] The relevance of that model lay in the historical similarity between post-colonial countries 'dependent' for their economic 'development' on the capitalist core of which the former colonial countries were the central part.

This original notion of dependence implied in the first instance that post-colonial countries were dependent on outside capital, equipment, personnel and know-how for the development of a capitalist economy. Second, it saw the economic development of the dependent country as 'enclave' capitalist development which, though beneficial for the local (dependent) capitalist class, was economically detrimental to the country as a whole. The hallmark of such development was that, in the long run, it enabled a balance of capital transfer favourable to the advanced countries. Third, it argued that the

233

continued economic development (or rather *under*development) of the dependent country implied greater rather than lesser dependence.[5]

This process became known in Africa as neo-colonialism – that is,
broadly, the continued economic dominance of the former colonial power
after independence. The African variant of dependency theory thus emphasises the continuities with the colonial period and focuses on the links,
institutional and informal, which make this continued dominance possible.[6]
Particular attention is paid to the role of the African ruling classes, the chief
beneficiaries of dependence, sometimes dubbed *comprador bourgeoisie*,
seen as the handmaidens of foreign capital.[7]

To this original conceptualisation of dependence as *under*development
has been added a new notion of dependence as destitution. The realisation
that post-colonial African countries were becoming less and less able to
survive, let alone develop, without foreign aid has led to a fairly apocalyptic
redefinition of the concept of dependence.[8] Whereas the earlier analysis
(*à la* Samir Amin) argued that, with political will, dependence could be
combated, that a strategy of economic self-sufficiency could lead to economic
independence, the later prognosis recognised that many African countries
no longer had any choice about the condition of dependence.[9] Without
outside aid, these countries could not survive.

It is of some importance, therefore, to distinguish between these two
notions when discussing the import of dependence for domestic politics.
The first implies a choice about economic development, a political decision
to follow a course which will make the country more or less dependent on
foreign capital, equipment, personnel and know-how. Whether in reality
there is such a choice is a question to which I return later. The second
implies the inescapable fact that, whatever the choices made, a number of
African countries have been reduced to the condition of mendicant. Whether
such a fate is as inescapable as it appears to be is also a question to which
I will return.[10]

At this stage I merely want to show how the meaning of dependence has
changed over time and how that change is tied to the changing perception
of Africa. While the earlier notion of dependence viewed African states as
independent actors, capable of making economic decisions which would
alter the development orientations of their country, the later took the infinitely more fatalistic view of governments as prisoners of circumstances
beyond their control. The difference between these two notions of dependence
hinges on the question of political choice, or rather the balance of options
on which choice can be exercised.[11]

The issue of political choice is central to political analysis. It matters a
great deal, especially for ordinary men and women, what economic choices

their government makes. It thus matters a great deal what view of dependence is taken. Africanists agree that Africa is 'dependent' but tend to divide on the question of whether or not dependence is or can ever become economically productive for Africans. They differ on their interpretation of the potential long-term benefits of capitalist development. Those who believe that capitalist dependence inevitably fosters underdevelopment argue for self-sustained, non-capitalist development even if such development is slow and modest.[12] Those (including some Marxists) who believe in the historically progressive role of capitalism favour better management of foreign capital and greater freedom for the market.[13]

Given the (perceived) widespread failure of 'socialist' attempts at self-sustained autonomous development and the (perceived) failure of other forms of statist economic strategies, there is now greater consensus among the anti-capitalist faction. But here the call is for true, as opposed to spuriously 'African', revolutions to overthrow the ruling classes bound to foreign capital and permit the rise of regimes truly committed and accountable to the masses of working people.[14]

Paradoxically, the two sides, although ideologically at odds, now share the belief that the exercise of political choice could enable Africa to surmount the present debilitating crisis induced by its economic dependence. Paradoxically, too, both sides now see the salvation of Africa in the liberation of the shackled energy and enterprise of the 'masses', that is, civil society. The widespread recognition that it is African rulers who are responsible for Africa's economic crisis has rekindled the belief that the political solution to the crisis lies in the transformation of the state, either through greater democracy or through revolution.[15] We have thus come full circle. After the long period of despondency which followed the recognition that post-colonial Africa had failed its economic 'take-off', political agency is back at the centre of politics.

Yet, if we are to understand the implications of dependence on the domestic politics of African countries, we need to go beyond the general notions of dependence outlined above. For one thing, there is not 'a' single form of dependence. Each country is tied to the world market and to various national economies by multiple and complex links which are not profitably reduced to a single notion of dependence.[16] The spectacular economic growth of some so-called 'Third World' countries (e.g., the Gulf states, Taiwan, Singapore, Hong Kong, South Korea) is one of many indications that it is pointless to reason in undifferentiated terms. Conversely, the total failure of the (thankfully) few attempts at economic autarchy (e.g., Kampuchea, Burma) shows that the choice is not between dependence and independence but rather of what form of interdependence.

I discussed elsewhere the geographical, ecological, historical and structural constraints on Africa's economies which largely determine the complexion of their economic relation with the outside world.[17] I have shown how limited the economic choices of many African countries are and how many of these choices are determined by the legacy of the colonial economy. Nevertheless, there are in Africa many countries the economies of which are perfectly viable and a few with exceptional economic potential. Furthermore, even where national economies are not (in strict economic terms) viable, African governments are not without choice in the determination of their economic policies. Yet, today they all seem to suffer (albeit in varying degrees) from a profound economic crisis.[18]

Why it is that this economic crisis is almost always necessarily attributed to Africa's dependence cannot simply be taken for granted but needs to be explained.

The facts of dependence are well known and have been widely rehearsed in general terms as well as in country-studies.[19] The raw statistics of the economic relations between African countries and the outside world do not tell us a transparent and objectively simple story. African countries need to export what they produce or extract. The terms of trade of these exportable products are not always favourable and often deteriorate over time. They need to import goods and know-how at relatively higher prices. They also need to allow in foreign capital if they want to spur industrial development. These are the realities of dependence but they are also the realities of interdependence as they apply to most countries.[20] In and of themselves they do little to explain the consequences of dependence.

How does dependence manifest itself in domestic terms? What are the political implications of dependence? Are there different types of dependence? Are there connections between the degree and kind of dependence and the political choices available to governments? What are the primary determinants of political choices in contemporary African countries?[21]

In the first instance, Africa's economic crisis is a crisis of production.[22] Since independence, African countries have tended to produce less, sometimes in absolute terms, sometimes in relation to population growth over the same period. This reduction in (mainly agricultural) production cannot simply be explained in terms of dependence. Dependence on an unfavourable world market, on declining terms of trade for raw material and agricultural products, makes it imperative for both governments and producers to seek to increase production. The fact that most countries have not managed to produce more needs to be explained in terms other than those of dependence.[23]

Africa's economic crisis is, second, a crisis in investment. The exploitation of existing resources (agriculture and raw materials) can only be productive if it is reinvested productively, that is in economic activities which will generate future growth. Here, the (admittedly very different) case of the oil-rich Gulf states provides 'a' model of what investment can mean. The export-led Asian economies provide another model. But there are in Africa very few countries (even oil-rich Nigeria or Gabon) where there has been sufficient productive investment. This, again, is not simply explained by way of dependence.[24]

Finally, Africa's economic crisis is a crisis in management. Whatever the constraints on production, whatever the difficulties of investment, much of what has happened to African economies is directly or indirectly attributable to poor management.[25] Even if 'appropriate' economic policies were devised, their successful implementation would require proper management. Given that education is without doubt the greatest achievement of post-colonial African governments, it is odd that such managerial skills appear to be so scarce. Since this crisis in management is likely to increase the country's dependence (however it is defined), it too needs to be explained rather than simply assumed.

Explaining some of the paradoxes of Africa's economic crisis requires that we look simultaneously outside and inside Africa.[26] Outside, we need to consider whether dependence has changed, whether it is now so different from what it was earlier conceived to be that we fail to see the relation between its effects and the 'crisis'. Internally, we need to ask how the realities of dependence affect the politics of African countries, or rather the political choices of their ruling élites and counter-élites.

Dependence has indeed changed over time. The original underdevelopment theories emphasised on the one hand the development of capitalist enclaves managed by local (dependent) capitalists and on the other the exploitation of the mineral resources of peripheral countries for the development of the core countries.[27] The reality of dependence for African countries today is different. The economic crisis is perceived by most governments to stem (in part at least) from insufficient foreign capital investment and falling demand for their mineral or agricultural products. Because of this, dependence now means increasingly having to rely on foreign aid in order to 'invest in development' or merely to function as a country. The symbol of dependence today is the IMF's structural adjustment programme, not 'cigar-smoking-fat-capitalists'.

Indeed, it is scarcely an exaggeration to say that today many African countries would be bankrupt – i.e., their state could not even finance its own reproduction – without foreign aid. Most African countries are thus dependent on continued IMF/World Bank support for their survival. And IMF conditions have become the *imprimatur* for much bilateral aid. Such dependence implies not only that a significant (and often a growing) proportion of state finance is met by foreign grant but also that economic policy is largely determined by IMF/World Bank *desiderata*. Whether African governments approve of these or not (and few do) they have no choice. Today, without the appropriate structural adjustment programme, there can be no World Bank finance and virtually no bilateral loans.[28]

Other forms of aid, multilateral or bilateral, are not as tightly controlled by the World Bank. UN agencies and charitable aid, for example, aim to provide support to non-state activities and impose few conditions beyond those of accountability and good management. Nor is it dependent on IMF approval.[29] Such aid, however, even when it is massively productive for the local beneficiaries, does not in and of itself affect the national economy more than marginally. It aims to support concrete projects for self-sufficiency and autonomous economic development, usually at local levels.

The dependence of which one speaks nowadays is the dependence of states on outside grants and loans rather than, as underdevelopment theory postulated, the dependence of economies on outside capital. The mark of dependence in Africa today is not the number of foreign firms installed in any country or the extent to which their profits are repatriated outside that country. By that criterion, many African countries would have become less dependent – since multinationals are now less keen than ever to come to Africa.[30] It is rather the dependence of states on foreign aid. In other words, it is states rather than national economies which are bankrupt. Or rather, it is the bankruptcy of the state which has brought about the demise of the (official) economy. Cut state appropriation by, say, fifty per cent and most African economies will suddenly appear viable, if not healthy.[31]

The financial bankruptcy of African states is largely the result of their rulers' hegemonic drive. Where internal revenues no longer suffice, these rulers naturally seek extra resources abroad. Whether they get them or not essentially has to do with international politics. Whether, on the other hand, they use foreign aid productively has to do with domestic politics. How they manage dependence is of vital importance for the continued survival of states even if it is not so readily important for the reduction of the dependence of the economy over which they preside. The readiness of African rulers to accept structural adjustment programmes has more to do with the degree of bankruptcy of the state than with their conversion to the latest IMF policies.[32]

This is important. The reality in Africa today is that dependence is part of the state's economic calculus. The assumption that dependence is nefarious or undesirable for the country's economic health is no longer valid. The question now is not whether countries are dependent on foreign aid but what form this dependence takes. Dependence is one more variable in the economic equation which determines the fate of African countries. Aid is merely one of the sources of budgetary revenues. Expenditures and investments are now budgeted on the assumption that they will partly be financed by the outside. Most African governments expect foreign loans and grants to be forthcoming even if they recognise that they come with strings attached.[33]

It has hitherto been customary to look at this state of affairs with moral indignation and to assume that African governments actually worked, or at least ought to work, to reduce such dependence in the long term. The fact that so far they have not succeeded and that, on balance, dependence is increasing has usually been ascribed to the depth of the economic crisis from which Africa suffers and to the lack of internal resources with which to replace such aid.

It is now time to recognise reality for what it is. Dependence may or may not be morally reprehensible – some now argue that debt defaulting is only the just repayment made by the advanced world which has so benefited from the plunder of Africa – but it is today part of the economic life of African countries.[34] We must thus no longer look at the question of dependence as though it were a temporary aberration but start from the recognition of its central economic role.[35] Only then can we begin to understand the significance of the politics of dependence.

The notion of dependence must be recast. There are not two sets of political actors, aid donors and aid recipients, as is usually believed, but at least three: aid donors, African states, African civil societies. This matters for the understanding of the relations between the international and domestic politics of aid.

Aid donors (multilateral or bilateral) divide into two groups: financial and charitable. The former, best symbolised by the World Bank but reproduced by a multitude of bilateral economic agencies, essentially act as lending or credit institutions. Though the modalities of the credit are many and the conditions attached to lending can also vary infinitely, loans of this type are first and foremost straightforward financial transactions. Where they differ from standard credit is that lender and recipient both know that there is no legally enforceable manner of recovering the 'mortgage' if repayments fall behind or cease. Defaulting countries cannot be punished, only deprived of further credit. Consequently, strict conditions, such as structural adjustment programmes, are imposed before credit is granted.

Although it is expected that the implementation of structural adjustment programmes will make it more, rather than less, likely that African states will be able to repay their debts, the decision on whether to grant credit is political as well as economic. The World Bank is the key to this system.

Where it agrees to finance credit, national and commercial banks follow. There are few straightforward commercial loans made by individual banks to African states which are not underwritten by World Bank credit agreements or conditionalities. But World Bank decisions are made in line with the *desiderata* of its most influential (that is Western) members. In part, credit is given or withdrawn as reward, punishment or encouragement. Thus, for example, socialist countries are usually denied credit unless they agree to radical changes in economic policy or change their foreign policy: Mozambique receives credit but Angola does not.

World Bank finance is usually tied to economic liberalisation, that is a reduction in state expenditures, privatisation, the opening up of the economy to foreign investment and the provision of free market incentives to domestic producers.[36] Nevertheless, however much the World Bank seeks to circumscribe the economic role of the state in Africa, the immediate and even long-term consequence of the credit it grants is to provide additional revenues for the state.[37] Because debt is allowed to grow and debts are rescheduled (when conditionalities are met) even when it is manifest that African exchequers have no conceivable way of repaying their loans other than further borrowing, such credit must ultimately be considered a straightforward grant, rather than a loan, to the state.

If my argument is correct, then the meaning of dependence is indeed different. However disagreeable it may be for state rulers to have to rely on foreign aid, it is still infinitely less disagreeable than not having foreign aid at all.[38] Once the structural adjustment conditions for the grant are met, and since the penalties for default are feeble or non-existent, dependence is rather less onerous for rulers than is habitually imagined. Rulers have at their disposal extra revenues which they would not otherwise have, even if these come with strings attached and even if the social consequences of adjustment are severe.[39] No matter how determined World Bank policymakers are that the conditions for lending strengthen the non-state economic sector, so long as credit is issued to the state, it is the state that it will serve. Indirectly or directly, therefore, dependence buttresses the state in Africa.

Charitable aid, on the other hand, is different. It is usually a straightforward gift and it is channelled directly either to the victims of (man-made or natural) disasters or to those at the local level who will directly benefit from the aid. It is, additionally, independent in that it rarely transits through the state. While it is invariably on a small scale – the philosophy of such aid is that is should be limited and targeted – charitable aid goes straight to the needy, to individuals within civil society.[40]

It is thus a challenge to the state in two ways. First, it bypasses state channels and cannot therefore easily be appropriated by the state. It brings no direct gain to the state or to the ruling élites. Second, it provides means by which individuals, however wretched, can survive and (when the aid is productive) begin to improve their lives independently from any state control. It thus strengthens, however minimally, the most disenfranchised members of civil society, those starving or without resources.

Charitable aid now generally aims at reducing the dependence of recipients, even when those recipients are starving and destitute. It is a move away from an earlier notion of charity which was thought to induce a psychology of aid-dependence.[41] There is today greater agreement and greater determination amongst donors and recipients alike to organise aid productively – to use aid to reduce dependence on further aid. Reducing dependence means, of course, giving individuals greater economic autonomy and thus also reducing their dependence on the state.[42] Hence, the politics of charitable aid are linked to the politics of civil society and are in this way often at odds with those of the state.

The tragic case of Ethiopia illustrates my point.[43] Ethiopia as a socialist state is not granted credit by the World Bank.[44] It must seek aid elsewhere. The catastrophic 1984 famine, even worse than that of 1974, triggered massive humanitarian and charitable aid.[45] After the emergency was over, charitable aid aimed at helping the poor and destitute reconstruct a productive and autonomous life in their own regions. State policy, on the other hand, was to move the inhabitants of the poorest regions to more fertile areas where, with government help (and, inevitably, under government control), they were supposed to be able to start farming more profitably than they ever had a chance to do at home.[46] Many of the charities denounced the government's plan as forced migration.[47] The government then threatened to stop independent charitable aid. Regardless of the merits of the respective arguments, I simply want to emphasise here how the logic of charitable aid clashed with the logic of the state.[48]

It would be tempting to see aid to civil society as a means of undermining state hegemony in Africa. It is indeed useful to understand that there is a fundamental division here between aid to the state and aid to civil society. Both the state and civil society in Africa are now often dependent on aid. Both seek their own channels to outside donors. Nevertheless, it would be naïve to push the dichotomy too far. State and civil society are not simply enemies engaged in a titanic struggle for political supremacy. Rather, they remain indissolubly linked, accomplices as it were in the search for ever greater foreign aid.

The state remains at the centre of Africa's political economy and, for this reason, penetration of the state remains the primary strategy of the hegemonic drive. In this respect, then, dependence (i.e. foreign aid to the state) buttresses the centrality of the state. Paradoxically, therefore, in view of the current fashion against statism, the system of dependence which is underpinned by the World Bank is one of the most significant factors in the survival of the post-colonial state as it emerged after independence. This aid supports the state's hegemony and in this way strengthens its role as patrimonial state.[49]

To conceive such dependence as detrimental to African countries is either to misunderstand the politics of aid or to make a value judgement on the role of the state. Only if it is argued that the state in Africa should wither, so as, for example, to release the productive energy of civil society, is dependence as it exists now counter-productive (in that it sustains the state). Otherwise, dependence in the form of aid is in the interests of all parties.[50] It suits donors who can in this way exercise influence on the politics of African countries. It also suits the recipients (state rulers and their clients) who are able to finance a state apparatus and state expenditures out of all proportion to the country's resources. There is thus a coalition of interests, external and internal, conspiring to keep this system of aid/dependence in place.

It may be asked, however, why donors should be prepared to continue to finance the extravagances of African states. They might well, in principle, prefer not to but international politics dictate that they should do so. In the system of nation-states which emerged in the nineteenth century and was consolidated after the independence of the former colonies, it is in the 'general' interest to maintain a relatively stable system of nation-states. Financing the aid which helps maintain the position of the state system is more profitable for the West (or the East for that matter) than allowing the breakdown of states which may turn domestic unrest into regional or global conflicts.[51] The system of subsidy (or, seen from the other side, of repayment), which is implicit in the inevitable rescheduling and eventual writing-off of state debts, is the price which the richer nations have to pay for the maintenance of a relatively stable international political order.

Dependence is thus hardly dependence at all; rather it is interdependence. If African states are in a position to bargain with donors and if donors feel they must provide the aid which helps maintain those states in place, then recipients are not powerless but have some leverage.[52] Not all states are in a position to bargain and those which can bargain do not all have equal leverage. Nevertheless, a surprisingly large number of African states, even small ones, have managed to exercise such leverage either by playing potential donors one against the other or through the politics of non-alignment.[53] Thus, for example, are votes in the UN negotiated.

So it is not just Zaïre's Mobutu who, though one of the African leaders most often alleged by the press to be corrupt, is still able to command almost total support in the West and whose state continues to receive massive foreign aid. It is also Chad's regimes which get aid because of their anti-Gaddafi stance. It is the former French colonies (Senegal, Côte d'Ivoire, Cameroon, Chad, Gabon) which are indispensable to France's notion of *grandeur*. It is Gabon, which provides the West with uranium, or Botswana, with its diamonds, or Ghana and Mozambique, because their new sense of realism must be rewarded, or Nigeria, which is both a major supplier of oil and a local superpower, etc.[54]

If it is true, then, that the state system in contemporary Africa is 'dependent' in the way discussed above, it is equally true that it is in the interests of state rulers and, more generally, the ruling élites of Africa to be so 'dependent'. It is also in the interests of all those who benefit from what I have called the strategy of state penetration.[55] This amounts to a large number of people, even if they do not all benefit equally from their appurtenance to the state and even if civil society contains yet a larger number of people. In simple terms this means that power in Africa contains a crucially important external dimension which is not easily understood by reference to the orthodox notion of dependence.

Giving an account of politics in Africa today thus demands an analysis of what I call the domestic politics of dependence. Aid has become an integral part of state policy, that is the state takes aid into account when devising and implementing policies. Insofar as it is accountable, then, the state must in part be accountable to outside constituencies (donors). Accountability here means that the state meets the conditions under which aid is delivered. Because dependence (aid) is now so central to the survival and operation of African states, accountability to aid-donors is a priority, even if it is at the expense of accountability to domestic constituencies. Therefore, the politics of dependence means that there is in Africa a system in which state accountability to donors may well (and often does) override accountability to domestic constituents.[56]

This is best illustrated by the effects of the structural adjustment programmes which governments must implement if they are to receive World Bank aid. The same process is replicated on smaller scale in negotiations between African states and other donors. While the World Bank criteria for lending may change (as they reflect donor ideologies) the obligation for recipient states to comply with the conditions imposed on the loan do not.

Current World Bank lending *desiderata* appear to impose conditions which reduce state power and favour civil society. However, the net effect of aid is rather to strengthen some sections of the state (e.g. 'aid bureaucrats') at the expense of others (e.g. civil administration) rather than simply to weaken the state at the expense of civil society. However stringent the current structural adjustment programmes, it would be odd indeed if aid to the state (and administered by the state) were to to be used to undermine the position of ruling élites who control that aid.[57]

Structural adjustment programmes usually have a devastating impact on the lower orders of state dependents and on all those who benefit either from price controls or state subsidies (both being attempts by the state to buy peace within civil society). Governments who agree to World Bank conditions must be mindful of the social and political consequences of the implementation of policies which are inimical to so many. On the other hand, given the acute need of most African states to reduce vastly inflated state expenditures, it is actually convenient for rulers that the blame for austerity be attached to outside villains (IMF) rather than to the state. Structural adjustment programmes may thus help African rulers to implement economic polices for which they have no domestic mandate and which work against the interests of a large proportion of their domestic constituents.

Although a number of governments have been worried about the domestic consequences of structural adjustment programmes, few have, like Tanzania or Zambia, attempted to hold out against the World Bank. Many governments have had to face protest and violence as a result. Whether such opposition (by sections of civil society) is deplored or ignored by state rulers, the consequence of having to repress it cannot be in the interest of greater political accountability, particularly when it leads to permanently greater state coercion. On balance, however, the costs to the state of greater coercion are less than the gains of receiving financial aid.

The ultimate objective of current structural adjustment programmes in Africa is, of course, economic liberalisation – to reduce the economic role of the state and to spur the economic development of the non-state sector. The success of such programmes is judged by standard economic indicators: economic growth, inflation, trade balance, balance of payments, debt, currency levels, etc.. By these measures, there is presently a belief among World Bank officials that the adjustment programmes are working. Macroeconomic data look promising.[59]

Insofar, however, as the economic development of the non-state sector threatens the power of the state (as it necessarily must, though not always in ways which are obvious), it is to be doubted whether the long-term effect of these structural adjustment programmes will be as envisaged. It would not be unreasonable to suppose that the economic development of the non-state sector, if it occurs, will eventually be harnessed by the state – or rather by sections of the ruling classes within the state.[60] For, as I have explained, at the individual level, there is no sharp dichotomy between state and civil society.

This is why it is illusory to conceive of the IMF/World Bank and the African states as adversaries, even if the latter readily charge the former with intolerable interference in their internal affairs. For, in truth, the two are allies – not because they agree on policy but because they need each other. The World Bank as the financial arm of the Western world needs to consider political criteria and because of this it must accept the parameters of state politics, even if its overt economic policies seek to promote the growth of the non-state sector. African states, whatever their political outlook, need the financial support of the World Bank.[61]

Furthermore, it is not in the financial interest of donors and lenders to let African states go bankrupt. If they did, debtor repayments, which (however small) still represent an enormous transfer of funds from debtor to donor, would cease altogether.[62] The paradoxical reality of aid (dependence) is that, within limits, borrower states are in a position to exercise considerable leverage on lending institutions and thus to obtain further aid.[63] It is not entirely surprising, therefore, even if it is a little disquieting, to find out that aid is never entirely suspended, even to countries whose states scarcely deserve recognition.[64]

The case of Equatorial Guinea, where the politics of the state rulers were nothing short of barbaric, is revealing in this respect. While Spain, the former colonial power, could no longer countenance the dire excesses of the Macias Nguema regime and suspended aid, the French were stealthily providing aid so as to position themselves economically in the country. As soon as Macias Nguema was replaced by his equally tyrannical nephew, international lending, which had never entirely ceased, resumed fully.[65]

The question of the morality or instrumentality of aid/dependence is a practical rather than an *a priori* question. If aid is conceived as a crutch which African countries should learn to do without, then their dependence on foreign aid will be seen as alarming. If, on the other hand, aid is conceived merely as an historically justified transfer of resources from the developed to the underdeveloped world, then the continued or even growing reliance of African states on foreign aid will appear justified. Whatever the position taken on this issue, it is important to examine more specifically how the politics of aid work themselves out in the body politic.

At the macro-level, the management of aid is administratively onerous. From the implementation of wholesale structural adjustment programmes to the small-scale (but detailed) work which goes into assessing bilateral aid for local development projects, the machinery of the state is busy working to the *desiderata* of aid-donors. Many countries simply do not possess the trained staff to carry out such tasks. Other countries do but are devoting to it scarce administrative resources which are badly needed elsewhere. Only a few countries in Africa are in a position to make optimum use of aid.[66]

Whatever the level of state competence, dependence means that policies are (in part at least) extraverted. The point here is not simply that African governments would be better employed thinking out their own policies but rather that the extent to which they must accede to the donors' wishes is a function of their need for aid and not of the superior logic of donor policies. Put another way, policy-making becomes subservient to the policy of obtaining aid. The more dependent on aid the state is, the more subservient it becomes – hence, the current conversion of formerly 'radical/socialist' states (e.g. Ghana, Mozambique) to World Bank structural adjustment programmes.[67]

The political consequences of this situation are significant. First, it means that the notion of political accountability must be revised. In a paradoxical continuation of the colonial situation, the African governments are again partly accountable to outside paymasters. Whereas before, colonial governments were mindful of the imperial exchequer, present-day African governments must heed lenders and aid-donors. Their predicament is to balance the cries of their domestic constituents with the whispers of their foreign constituents. This reduces the degree to which governments can meaningfully be accountable to their own subjects.[68]

It means, second, that the nature of state patronage is partly determined by outside considerations. When aid-donors were more state-oriented and readily supported the statist policies of African governments, large networks of state-dependent clients benefited from those policies. Now that aid-donors are resolutely against statism, many of the former clients have dropped through the trapdoors. Producers and the new entrepreneurs are the beneficiaries of current policies.

Where once large-scale education was fashionable, it is now seen as unproductive and aid is more readily channeled towards rural integrated projects. Where once assistance was given for green revolutions, it is now reserved for supporting the local initiatives of small-scale agricultural producers. Although the shift in aid policies has tended to benefit civil society, as is now deemed desirable by aid-donors, it has not seriously reduced state hegemony.

Third, dependence creates new networks of political and economic influence within the state and civil society. Those in charge of managing aid within what are euphemistically called ministries of economic co-operation are in a position to challenge or even undermine the government's economic policies.[69] The very control over the information pertaining to aid is a very precious commodity which can, and is, readily used to gain influence. Further down the system, all the way down to local levels, those who control access to aid are in a position of power. There is thus created a distinct and parallel network of patronage, only partially integrated into the state, with its own principles of political accountability.

Finally, where aid reaches the local level directly, bypassing the state altogether, it impinges directly on existing relations of power. Non-governmental and charitable aid to individual (rural or urban) communities is now much more common in Africa than it was in the heyday of state-centred notions of development. There are thousands of small-scale projects initiated locally and supported by funds from outside which (in part at least) escape the control of the state. Whether these projects can ever succeed if they meet with hostility from the state is open to question.

Their implications for local politics, however, are clear. Those who now have access to outside aid, especially those who manage to employ that aid productively, gain political ascendancy. They are now in a position to resist and to challenge state pressure. Alternatively, they can set up their own networks of patronage. Such aid provides the economic means whereby previously disenfranchised citizens acquire a modicum of power, power to compete with or negotiate entry into state networks or, even, to launch counter-hegemonic politics.

To conclude, though in abstract ideological or moral terms, dependence may not be desirable, in practice it is in the interests of states and individuals alike. Aid is an additional commodity which creates resources for many within and without the state. The politics of aid are thus an integral part of the contemporary politics of Africa. The effects of dependence/aid are to reinforce the state economically and, hence, politically. So long as it is in the interests of lenders and donors, as it is, to maintain a relatively stable international state system, then aid will boost state power over the power of civil society. Or rather it will provide resources to sustain what I call the dialectics of the hegemonic drive.

15 The Reproduction of Power

The question of the reproduction of power is one of the central issues in politics. Since tenure of power is necessarily finite, how power is transmitted from one individual/group to another over time is of some consequence both for the rulers and for the ruled. The nature and practice of the reproduction of power over succeeding political generations is, in all polities, one of the hallmarks of the nature of political order.[1]

The notion of reproduction of power goes beyond that of the transfer of power although the manner in which the two are connected is politically important. The concept of the transfer of power implies the possibility that power might pass from one set of rulers to any other potential set of rulers. The concept of the reproduction of power, on the other hand, implies that power is transmitted within the same set of ruling élites from one political generation to the next. Whether the assumption of continuity is warranted or not is, of course, one of the central questions in political analysis.[2]

However, these simple dichotomies between the notions of transfer and reproduction of power establish a clear conceptual contrast which may fail to reflect political realities.[3] There may, for example, be clear constitutional guidelines about the transfer of power from one government to the next. Governments may indeed follow each other in constitutional tranquillity. Yet, power may be reproduced within a very reduced circle of individuals who may well be closely related by personal, political or economic ties.

Conversely, unconstitutional or even violent seizures of power do not necessarily mean the success of counter-élites. They may merely enable the rise of new rulers who are part of the selfsame small circle of ruling élites. Palace coups, for example, are notorious for ensuring that power is reproduced within a certain military 'club' as it were.[4] The overthrow in Equatorial Guinea of Macias Nguema by his nephew Obiang Nguema is perhaps the most extreme case of such reproduction of power 'within the family' but it is not so unfamiliar in Africa or elsewhere.

On the other hand, both constitutional and unconstitutional transfers of power may bring to the top new élites who, hitherto, had no significant access to power. Whether by elections or less elegant means, it is possible for civil society to sanction the end of one political dynasty and usher in a new one.[5] Revolutions are good at making a clean sweep of ruling élites although here, too, it is well to note the (sometimes considerable) continuities with the old political order.[6]

Although it is common to think that political and economic power are confined to a more narrow group of interconnected ruling élites where power is transferred by undemocratic means, this is not always the case. Where economic and political power is the preserve of a small group (e.g. Burundi, Swaziland), a constitutional transfer of power will merely continue to reproduce power within that small élite. Only a complete revolution, that is unconstitutional politics, would dislodge them. Where economic and political power is more widely dispersed in social and geographical terms (e.g. Nigeria, Cameroon) both constitutional and unconstitutional transfers of power may throw up surprises.[7]

The question of whether power is reproduced within a given family, kin or social group, class, etc, is thus not one which is easily settled by a simple examination of constitutional practices. Nor can it be determined by an analysis of the modalities of the transfer of power, whether legal or illegal. Or rather, the examination of the mechanics of the transfer of power is only one element in the process by which power passes from one political generation to the next. The more important question concerns the relationship between the hegemonic drive and the reproduction of power, for the reproduction of power is nothing but the working out of the hegemonic drive over time.[8]

It is customary to think that the issue of the reproduction of power derives from class analysis. This is true only insofar as liberal analysis is primarily concerned with the relation between the individual and society whereas class analysis emphasises that between social group (class) and society.[9] Focus on the individual *ipso facto* pre–empts discussion of the transfer of power between and within classes just as focus on class *ipso facto* pre-empts discussion of the transmission of power from one individual to the next. Each acknowledges the conceptual reality of the other's analytical category (individual or class) but rejects its causal primacy.

Liberal analysis is thus wont to look at the transfer of power in terms of the elections of representatives by individuals and to ignore the class or other corporate links between them. Class analysis interprets the electoral basis for the transfer of power from the perspective of the socio-economic interests which individuals are seen to represent.[10] At their opposite extremes, liberal analysis denies the reality of the reproduction of power while class analysis rejects the hypothesis that power can be reproduced other than in class terms. These pristine positions of principle, however, are of little practical use in the analysis of the real world. In Africa, perhaps even more than elsewhere, there is no simple and edifying definition of either individual or class reproduction.[11]

Two caveats are in order. First, post-colonial Africa is, at most, thirty years old. Some countries have been independent for a decade or even less. There is little historical depth to justify a long-term analysis of the post-colonial reproduction of power over generations. Although it is true that political generations may be short lived, what matters most for political analysis is the transmission of power over biological generations (twenty to thirty years).

Second, the question of the reproduction of power since independence cannot be properly assessed without taking into account its colonial antecedents. Here, as before, I cannot emphasise too strongly the limitations of a political analysis which takes independence as its starting point. The realities of the reproduction of power within individual African countries are likely to derive as much from their pre-colonial and colonial history as from the vagaries of post-colonial politics. What is of interest, therefore, is not simply the record of regime and government changes since independence but the more subterranean movements of power within and between various social groups over time: the continuities and the ruptures with the colonial and pre-colonial past.[12]

How profound a rupture was independence for the reproduction of power in Africa? I have already explained why I believe that independence was a political revolution. A political revolution, however, is not a complete revolution in the sense that the political rupture at the top is not the outcome of a socio-economic explosion below. Nor does it lead to the radical socio-economic transformations brought about by full-scale revolutions.[13] Political revolutions are essentially radical changes in the complexion and personnel of the centres of political power. They are consequential indeed but they are not as consequential for the societies which experience them as full-scale revolutions.

It is often argued that independence marked a fundamental rather than a superficial break in the continuities of power. Whereas colonial rule most often sought collaborators among 'traditional' political élites, nationalism made it possible for modern élites to rise to the top.[14] Independence, the triumph of nationalism, is seen as the victory of the 'verandah boys' over the 'chiefs'. In this view, independence broke the hold of tradition and prevented the reproduction of the power of the established élites into the post-colonial era. Such a view of independence is easily fashioned by the symbolic significance of Nkrumah's mass politics or Sékou Touré's systematic political destruction of his country's chiefdoms. Nevertheless, the reality of independence is considerably more complex than these *images taillées* would suggest.[15]

Although it is true that in some countries (and Guinea is the most extreme case) the chiefs were smashed by the new boys, the socio-economic and political importance of 'traditional' élites was rarely destroyed.[16] What happened is that a new political superstructure was erected upon the colonial and pre-colonial political structure. Where, as in Ghana, the 'traditional' élites were denied access to the state, they joined, or more frequently established, counter-hegemonic projects.[17] Where, as in Guinea, the war between the state and those élites was total, they avoided frontal confrontation and took refuge elsewhere. Now that Sékou Touré is gone it will be interesting to see whether they, or their successors, re-emerge.[18]

In most other countries, the dichotomies between old (ie. colonial or even pre-colonial) and new (ie. nationalist) élites were not as sharp. In a number of countries (e.g. Mauritania, Sierra Leone, Nigeria, Burundi, Swaziland, Malawi, Botswana, Lesotho) the post-colonial rulers issued from pre-existing (sometimes pre-colonial) élites. In other countries (e.g., Senegal, Upper Volta, Mali, Dahomey, Chad, Kenya, Congo, Zaïre), the new boys had links with (even if they did not always represent the interests of) old and established élites. Even where there were no obvious connections (e.g., Cameroon, Tanzania, Togo, Dahomey, Central African Republic) the strength of the new élites rested as much on their nationalist success as on their accommodation with pre-existing established élites.[19]

This ought not to be surprising for one of the surest indications that a given political order has run its course is the readiness of established élites to support revolution.[20] In the fifties and sixties, few doubted that colonial rule would end soon. Realism alone dictated that the established colonial élites should support nationalism, even if they did not always like the manners of the nationalists. Only where the nationalists deliberately and systematically set out to eliminate them did the old élites organise politically against the new boys.

Because nationalism was a political revolution rarely committed to the total subversion of the existing hegemonic order, the established élites could be persuaded to support it.[21] The nationalists curtailed their revolutionary ambitions in exchange for (symbolic and financial) support from the 'establishment'. In turn, the 'establishment' could be persuaded to withdraw from the open political stage so long as they maintained political influence. There are few better examples of this *quid pro quo* than the case of Kenyatta, taken by the British to be the leader of a 'revolutionary' Mau Mau but looked upon by the Mau Mau radicals as a member of the 'establishment'.[22] Nationalist leaders like Senghor, Ahidjo, Ould Dadah, Houphouët-Boigny, Banda, etc., were from the same mould.

In this respect, therefore, the nationalist revolution was not often the break which it is frequently assumed to be. The continuities with the colonial period were strong even if they were obscured by the pageantry of the transfer of power.[23] The glitter of a truly African government often gave the wrong impression that the social order over which it now presided had been altered.

The African colonial 'establishment' was itself already the product of the transformation of the African social order by colonial rule.[24] It was those new colonial élites (teachers, clerks, bureaucrats, traders, merchants, catechists, etc.), the economic and social pillars of the new African communities, who were prepared to support nationalism, even if sometimes it meant conceding centre stage to the new boys. It was up to the younger generation to take the risks which nationalism entailed and to prove themselves in the contest with the colonial masters. Nationalist success did eventually give that younger generation a unique opportunity to gain undreamt-of power over their elders but they rarely broke from the socioeconomic order which had made their rise to power possible.[25]

How, then, was power transmitted during the nationalist revolution? What were the consequences for the reproduction of power of the creation of the post-colonial order?

Regardless of whether the nationalist counter-élites swept away the old establishment (which was rare) or whether they accommodated them (which was common), the single most important aspect of the nationalist revolution was generational rather than social.[26] The nationalist campaign, decolonisation and the transfer of power upset the incremental process by which generations normally follow each other and power from one generation is passed to the next. It enabled the swift and sudden rise of a young generation of politicians who seized this unique chance to reach the top.

Whereas the colonial order had, for reasons of expediency, broadly favoured the maintenance of the generational hierarchy, the nationalist movement which colonial rule spawned cut right through the generations. For the first time in Africa 'youngsters' were in a position to assert themselves politically in relation to their 'elders' – bypassing the social and economic constraints which in 'traditional' African society check the political ambitions of the younger generation. Nationalist agitation, mass politics, the tactics of the 'verandah boys' were not just means of putting pressure on the colonial state. They were also attempts by the younger generation to build an organisation and to gather support for themselves outside the existing 'traditional' networks of power and patronage controlled by the 'elders'.

If Nkrumah's Convention People's Party (CPP) was the clearest example of such political strategy, similar processes took place in virtually all African colonies.[27] The example of Balante support for the *Partido Africano da Independência da Guiné e Cabo Verde* (PAIGC), the nationalist movement in Portuguese Guinea, is typical. There, the cause of the PAIGC was embraced by the Balante youth with such enthusiasm that the party lost control of the guerrilla war which it had initiated. It emerged that many young Balante had in fact hijacked the PAIGC and were seeking to overthrow their elders by force of arms. As a result, the elders rejected the PAIGC. The party only managed to re-establish control by integrating the elders into the new party political structure.[28] With greater subtlety and less violence, this too is a process which was repeated throughout colonial Africa.

The hallmark of the nationalist revolution, then, was that, with some important exceptions, the young generation took power at independence, before their time as it were. Whether they were radical or conservative was often less significant than the fact that they were young. In generational terms, independence provoked a fracture in the process by which power was hitherto transmitted in Africa.[29] It is this which gave the colonial transfer of power a revolutionary aura, a portent of great deeds to come. The fiery rhetoric of a younger generation enjoying massive political success was frequently mistaken for a true commitment to change.

Independence was also mistaken for a radical break in the continuity of power. The nationalist leadership was in fact often composed of the progeny of the colonial African establishment (churchmen, businessmen, chiefs, clerks, traders, teachers, etc.). They belonged to the generation of young Africans whose parents had had the foresight and/or the means to provide (missionary or state) education for them.[30] Though it is true that some of the established élites, chiefly the Muslims of West Africa, had eschewed Western education for their sons, most others had eagerly sought it. Their sons, unlike the sons of the Muslim aristocrats, immediately benefitted from being educated.[31]

Education was the means by which colonial élites sought to ensure that their power was transmitted to their descendents. At the time, when the proportion of Africans who were educated was still small, education was clearly a passport to success. Independence merely confirmed the political dominance of the newly educated younger generation. The swiftness with which this younger generation came to power was perhaps unexpected, for until it happened no-one knew how long the transfer of power would last. Nevertheless, those who had been able to educate their children in colonial times had clearly intended them to gain in power.[32]

Independence was followed by rapid Africanisation. Within a few years, Africans had replaced Europeans in most state, public and private organisations. This process, in which education was often the key to the top, made it possible for a very large number of young people swiftly to reach positions usually only filled by far more senior and experienced staff. In this respect too the transfer of power was truly a generational revolution.[33] Unsurprisingly, it was plain to this generation that they were the beneficiaries of unique circumstances and that they must consolidate their power quickly.

The nationalist revolution thus gave the impression that in post-colonial Africa power would be reproduced quickly, that young people could expect to rise to the top faster than ever had been possible in 'traditional' or colonial society. It also encouraged many to believe that the constraints of 'traditional' society had been broken once and for all. In hindsight, it is easy to see that these impressions were illusory.[34] What is more interesting for political analysis is to understand the implications of the nationalist revolution for the reproduction of power in post-colonial Africa.

The gains made by the young generation who took power at independence and by all those who benefited from rapid Africanisation were, of course, at the expense of the generations which followed them. The younger those in place were, the longer was their potential tenure of office, implying a concomitant and proportional delay in the putative rise to the top of the next generation. The dynamics of rapid political change so forcefully implied in the nationalist revolution were now invalidated by the fact that political mobility was at a standstill. This inevitably tended to induce the next generations to resort to extra-systemic, illegal, means of displacing the ruling élites.[35]

This generational discrepancy engendered instability within the political system. It was a powerful force against the political order instituted at independence. The necessity for the younger generations to bide their time was exacerbated by the realisation that those holding power had no intention of abiding by the constitutional procedures which made political competition possible. Conversely, the knowledge by those in power that the frustrated younger generations would seek to oust them in order to reach the top made them suspicious and militated in favour of state repression.[36]

The greater illusion, however, was the assumption (shared by nationalists and Africanists alike) that the nationalist revolution had erased prior (colonial and pre-colonial) categories of political obligation and had created new practices for the reproduction of power. Although those in power appeared free from the constraints of prior 'traditional' political obligation, the legitimacy of their power was tied to the legitimacy of nationalism. Thus, to pursue the example given above, traditional 'elders' in the Balante villages of Portuguese Guinea recognised the historical legitimacy of the power of the young party cadres not because they recognised the legitimacy of the power of the young *per se* but because they understood the necessity for a nationalist struggle led by the young.[37]

The nationalist revolution was but one brief episode in the long history of Africa. As, in the years following independence, the nationalist legitimation of power dissipated, so did the legitimacy of the political process which had validated the rise to the top of a generation so 'young'. Shorn of its nationalist credentials, the legitimacy of the rulership of young politicians was now often questioned. Over time, the notion of rulership was politically Africanised: it was re-appropriated by the 'traditional' African political order in which the notion of elder was again relevant.[38] It meant, *inter alia*, that the 'traditional' concepts of political hierarchy, which had merely been put in abeyance by the nationalist illusion, began to re-assert themselves.

At the same time, the rulers of the independent African states discovered that the viability of their regimes depended partly on legitimating the new political order in terms of the 'old' – sinking roots in the 'traditional' practices of African communities.[39] While they themselves had readily usurped the position of their 'elders', they now wanted to legitimate their rulership by assuming the mantle of 'new elders'. The widespread practice by these rulers of conferring upon themselves titles which implied experience, wisdom, authenticity, strength and primacy (e.g., teacher, lion, chief, father, elder, old man) is a reflection of their need to reinvent for themselves the trappings of 'traditional' rulership.[40]

Like all *nouveaux puissants*, the new rulers needed to legitimate their power by reference to the ideology and beliefs of the preceding ('traditional') political order – even revolutionaries cannot ignore the 'Mandate from Heaven'.[41] The paternalistic discourse of so many contemporary African leaders (of which Mobutu is one possible extreme) is, of course, an attempt at justifying their refusal to relinquish power.[42] It is a sleight of hand to prevent succeeding generations from claiming a right to the power which they, as 'new elders', now have. Nevertheless, and this is significant, it is also an attempt to do so in the 'traditional' language of power legitimation.[43]

The consequences of the nationalist revolution for the reproduction of power were thus severe in generational terms. A generation of young people took power, appropriated all positions of leadership and, in good 'traditional' fashion, sought to remain in place for the term of their natural life. Whether they succeeded or not, their seizure of power totally disrupted the 'natural' process by which power had 'traditionally' been transmitted from generation to generation. It led to the virtual political elimination of the older generation and to the monopolisation of power by a historically privileged younger generation.

The prospect that the same generation would remain in power for two, three or four decades, was not one which could leave the following political generations indifferent. One of the chief reasons for potential or actual political instability in Africa lies in the attempt by younger competitors to remove the seemingly immovable 'new leaders' who thus monopolise power. This can easily degenerate, as when there is a succession of *coups d'état*. Witness the fact that coup plotters are often younger and of more junior ranks than those they seek to overthrow.[44]

Nevertheless, despite the picture of political chaos usually associated with Africa, a surprisingly large number of leaders have managed to remain in power for a very long time – far longer than in the West – even if they have not always seen out the rest of their natural political life. A short list of the most successful would include: Nyerere, Kenyatta, Kaunda, Banda, Houphouët-Boigny, Ould Dadah, Jawara, Senghor, Sékou Touré, Pereira, Tolbert, Ahidjo and Mobutu. Contrary to established myths, longevity can be one of the characteristics of leadership in Africa.[45]

Where the historic nationalist leaders were able to stay in power until the end of their political career, they also in the process contributed to the re-legitimation of age as an attribute of power. Paradoxically, then, the process by which the 'young Turks', who had themselves usurped the power of their 'elders', were allowed to mature in power and in turn to become 'elders' themselves, was a factor in the successful Africanisation of politics.[46] To the young generations of the eighties, the historic nationalist generation is indeed a generation of 'elders'. The completion of their tenure of power as 'elders' has helped to legitimise the political system, institutionalise new mechanisms of rulership and reconnect the political order with its African roots.[47]

The analysis of contemporary African politics must thus take into account the fact that the practice of rulership has been Africanised. In particular, it is important to recognise that the notion of political maturity, a quality necessary to rulers the world over, has today a more strongly generational quality in Africa than it had two decades back. This does not mean that, in future, power in Africa will return to the hands of the 'elders' but it does mean that, for some time to come at least, it is likely to reincorporate a degree of deference to 'traditional' attributes of rulership which seemed to have disappeared in the first decade of independence.[48]

Where younger challengers were successful in displacing the historic nationalist leadership, they unleashed a process of instability difficult to control. Once they had committed the crime of *lèse majesté*, they could expect little favour from other competitors. It is thus easy to understand why, in post-colonial Africa, there was either great stability or great instability of leadership. Unless succession to the nationalist generation was orderly, as it was in a few countries (e.g., Senegal, Cameroon, Kenya, Tanzania), the legitimacy of state power was very seriously eroded by the unconstitutional removal of that generation. Coup often prompted coup.[49]

Where instability of leadership developed as a result of coups and other illegal seizures of power, the process of political routinisation and institutionalisation simply did not occur. Instability disrupted the legitimation of the post-colonial order and retarded its necessary re-Africanisaton. So, where the likes of Master-Sergeant Doe, Flight-Lieutenant Rawlings, Captain Sankara, Captain Campaoré, etc., fail to manage an orderly transition of power to their successors, they eventually suffer the fate of those they removed from power. Where the process of rulership fails to mature, it delays the return to a more consistent generational pattern to the reproduction of power.

To summarise, then, the nationalist revolution catapulted to power a generation of young politicians and, in so doing, sacrificed the generations which followed. Once in power that nationalist generation sought to legitimise their rule, and thereby legitimise the post-colonial order, by a gradual process of re-Africanisation. Where they succeeded, and retired as the 'elders' of the community, they contributed significantly to the institutionalisation and ritualisation of a process of reproduction of power consonant with the norms of a newly Africanised political order.[50] Where they failed, where generational turmoil followed the instability of leadership, there is as yet no formalised or ritualised reproduction of power. The process of African institutionalisation is deferred. There remains a vacuum at the centre of politics.

What of the second aspect of the reproduction of power– the consolidation of political and economic hegemony over time? By what means do political and economic élites seek to reproduce themselves in contemporary Africa? Do they succeed? Why?

Placed in the appropriate historical perspective, the question is more complex than it often appears to be. The most common argument is that the nationalist élites were essentially new élites, that they had little control over the productive sector of the economy when they came to power, that statism was the means by which they sought to gain that control and that power was the instrument of their economic hegemony.[51] There is, of course, much that is accurate in this image of the hegemonic drive of the new post-colonial élites. The simplifications which it contains, however, obscure a number of factors which are relevant to the understanding of the reproduction of power in contemporary Africa.

First, as we have already seen, the nationalist élites were rarely 'new' élites as such, even if they did displace their elders.[52] They often issued from economically well-established families. They were usually highly educated and they frequently had good careers. They not infrequently possessed land or at least drew revenues from the exploitation of land, just as they often were involved in business or trade. Even when they themselves were not directly active in economic activities, they were usually part of communities which were. Few, in other words, were without access to the productive sector of the economy which could help finance their political activities. Many were successful entrepreneurs by the time they came to power and most became so after they came to power.

Second, although it is in every sense true that political power enabled the post-colonial élites considerably to advance their hegemonic drive, it is not similarly true that their economic success was wholly dependent on their tenure of power. Power was the means by which they became, and expanded as, entrepreneurs but many rulers ensured that the fruit of their entrepreneurship would survive their fall from power. For every well-publicised story of a 'corrupt' leader held to account for his venality after being deposed, there are hundreds of untold stories of continued profitable entrepreneurship.[53] Indeed, the punishment of those whose greed was unchecked (punishment which is still rare) merely confirms the success with which rulers become entrepreneurs.

Third, the standard analysis assumes a distinction between the private and the public which, though conventional, can be misleading in the context of the African post-colonial order.[54] The patrimonial notion of power and the relation of the individual to the community which obtain in contemporary Africa do not lend themselves so readily to a distinction between public office and private gain.[55] African political practices do not frown on the overlapping of the two as does political morality in the West today. Indeed,it is well understood that political prominence carries with it economic privileges, now as before. Just as, for example, elders in parts of East Africa appropriated a proportion of the cattle rustled by the young, so it is understood in Africa today that power brings profit.[56]

The key question in contemporary Africa is not so much whether rulership enables personal accumulation – it patently does – but how much it is legitimate for those in power to appropriate in this way. Outside observers, who have no very good answer to that question, tend to extremes. They either take the view that appropriation by public officials is wrong and conclude that Africa is corrupt to the core, or they assume that the 'African' way sets no limits to the greed of politicians.[57]

A more careful observation of the realities of African politics reveals that, while the private and public overlap, thus allowing private gain from public office, there are limits which are well understood (even if not explicitly stated) by rulers and ruled alike. The line between what is and what is not acceptable may not always be neat and it may change according to circumstances but is is real enough. Where an Houphouët-Boigny has hitherto been able safely to boast of his millions in the knowledge that it would do his political reputation no harm, and Afrifa was put to death and others have been jailed for their excessive greed.[58]

The causal link between power and wealth is clear enough in Africa, as it is in many other parts of the world. Is there, however, as clear a pattern between appropriation and the reproduction of power? Is there, in particular, a connection between power and the formation of a ruling class? Has power enabled rulers to form as a class?

It is of course early in the history of the post-colonial Africa to judge about the formation of identifiable classes – even considering the strong lines of continuity from colonial and even pre-colonial times.[59] At this stage, we can only make preliminary remarks. Broadly, there are in Africa today three different situations: the first, where state appropriation dominates the economy of a potentially productive country; the second, where the private sector is alive if not flourishing and the third, where the economy is moribund and the potential for economic progress is severely constrained.

To take the last situation first, there is in such countries (e.g. Burkina Faso, Mali, Niger, Chad, Cape Verde, Lesotho) so little potential for large-scale productive accumulation that there is very little prospect for collective accumulation, even less class formation. The politics of scarcity do not lend themselves so readily to the patterns of accumulation which would make it possible for a political class fully to ensure its reproduction.[60] Although some individuals always manage to enrich themselves in situations of great scarcity, they are too few and isolated to be conceived as a class, even if they manage to pass on their wealth to their offspring.

In those countries, competition for scarce resources is too fierce, politics is too unstable and production too fickle to provide a basis for the stable prosperity of ruling élites.[61] State power is savagely contested because it brings with it one of the only guaranteed sources of revenues. No ruler, let alone ruling group, is allowed to enjoy the fruits of power for long. Stability, where it endures (e.g. Cape Verde) – which is rare – is the result of a form of economic management which does not sacrifice the population to the accumulation of ruling élites.[62] This, in and of itself, makes it difficult for a ruling élite to become a class, although it does not preclude its reproduction as an elite.

Paradoxically, the communities most able to survive and to reproduce themselves are those which operate outside the formal economy. Cattle-owners, traders, smugglers, religious-community leaders, etc., can all maintain some autonomy from the state and thus continue to function as they did before independence. Not all, however, survive unscathed the ravage of drought, famine and war but where they do survive, they survive in greater continuity than those who rely on access to the state. Here too, however, the limits on resources and the difficulties of accumulation usually rule out the possibility of these communities becoming established classes.[63]

There is in this group of countries very little chance that ruling élites can reproduce themselves into viable and productive ruling classes. There are too few resources available for power to be productively transformed into class accumulation. The economy is so feeble that the extent to which it can be plundered is limited. The politics of individual greed or of austerity (i.e., limiting private gain for the sake of the community) are more likely to be the norms than the sustained development of a ruling class.[64]

The set of countries (e.g. Guinea, Ghana, Benin, Congo, Zaïre, Tanzania, Angola, Mozambique), where the state dominates (or has dominated for long periods) the economy, contains a wide range of political practices. There are in this group, countries of different sizes, population, resources and economic potential. What they all share is the potential for a relatively prosperous economy: they possess a potentially strong agriculture and/or a potential for manufacturing and industrial development. They may in addition be mineral rich or be endowed with a large population – hence a large internal market.

What these countries have in common is an active, hegemonic (sometimes predatory) state which seeks to maintain maximum control over the economy. Such statist economic policies entail some form of primitive accumulation, some form of industrial planning and a system of licences for domestic and foreign trade. Whether they succeed or not – whether they can succeed or not – is of course related to the way in which power is reproduced in this system. At best, assuming that primitive accumulation and foreign aid were sufficient to sustain a degree of industrial development, a 'new ruling class' (in the Eastern European sense) might emerge.[65]

It is too early to say whether this is a realistic hypothesis for Africa, given that so far no country has managed sufficient accumulation of resources to sustain large-scale industrial development. Without the development of a manufacturing industry which the state can control, there is little realistic prospect of the emergence of a 'new ruling class'. No ruling class dependent for its reproduction on agriculture in Africa can be secure, for no ruling class has hitherto managed to control the agricultural sector.[66]

What we have witnessed so far is the predatory, rather than productive, aspect of statism. In other words, the ruling élites have been more concerned to accumulate than to invest.[67] Without investment, however, the long-term future of these ruling élites is collectively, if not individually, precarious, for, in order to sustain the reproduction of ruling élites into a 'new ruling class', it is necessary to develop an economy which a ruling class can control. So far, there is little evidence of this happening in statist African countries.

There are several factors which militate against the formation of such a 'new ruling class'. The first is the relationship of the individual to the community which leads to significant redistribution of wealth from the successful patron to a large number of clients.[68] Whether this is a 'pre-capitalist' practice or not, it certainly reduces the potential development of state capitalism. Second, there is among many (though not all) ruling élites a frenzied need to hoard and/or consume. Again, both are understandable in the African context. The conspicuous display of wealth is a *sine qua non* of power. In addition, the probability that they will lose power is high enough to induce them to hoard.

Third, there is little evidence yet that African rulers have managed to invest productively in the political and economic future of their progeny.[69] While in the Indian subcontinent and elsewhere, there are now well-established dynasties of rulers and tycoons, no such pattern has emerged in Africa – other than in those few cases (e.g., Swaziland, Lesotho) where the rulers belong to a royal family. Whether this is due to the fact that Africans are singularly resistant to dynasties – witness the relatively 'democratic' selection of chiefs and even kings in pre-colonial Africa – we do not know. Nor do we know whether it is because the progeny of African rulers have proved to be particularly inept. Where there has been continuity of power, it has lain in the ruler's community rather than in his individual family. Whether this constitutes a 'new ruling class' is debatable.

Finally, insofar as statism stifles capitalism, the rulers of these countries do not have the option of private entrepreneurship (other than the parallel market) which would help to transform power into class hegemony. Statist economies do favour those who control the state but they do not constitute secure enough foundations for sustained class development. While the incumbents of state power maximise their short-term returns, they rarely possess the independent economic instruments of class reproduction.[70] Their progeny, though clearly privileged within the system, thus rarely inherit the independent economic means of class dominance.

In economically statist countries (still the majority in Africa), there is little indication that the processes by which power is reproduced amount to the reproduction of a ruling class. It may be that statism is so inefficient as to prevent such class reproduction. Or it may be that statism generates a proliferation of patrimonial networks which result in a fairly wide redistribution of resources. Whatever the case, because of the nature of the hegemonic drive in contemporary Africa, it is difficult to imagine that statism will diminish significantly in the future.[71]

There remains however, the final set of African countries (e.g., Senegal, Liberia, Nigeria, Cameroon, Côte d'Ivoire, Kenya, Zimbabwe), where the private economic sector is strong, if not actually thriving. In those countries, capitalism is allowed to flourish within the limits imposed by the state – which still remains the dominant economic actor. There are no stifling constraints on indigenous capitalist development nor on foreign investment. As a result, domestic entrepreneurs and foreign investors compete on a relatively open market.[72]

Yet, there are limits to how 'free' the market is. The state remains paramount. First, the state retains the ability to control the market so that, ultimately, the private sector must divert some of its resources to 'buying off' (through a properly regulated system of taxation or licences or through a more informal system of 'kickbacks') its freedom from the state. Second, with very few exceptions, the rulers themselves are active participants in the private sector. Presidents, ministers, bureaucrats (high and low), invest their (proper or ill-gotten) gain in the private sector. This in itself ensures that the private sector remains relatively safe from the predatory instincts of the state but it does mean that state power gives an advantage to budding capitalists.

Nevertheless, it is in those countries that power and wealth are most easily reproduced over time, for it is there that the relation between power and wealth is most productive. Wealth is an important political asset in that it facilitates access to power. Power facilitates private entrepreneurship. This complementarity between wealth and power is, politically, a stabilising force. It is possible for rulers to amass wealth and to invest it productively in the economy. Losing power does not automatically mean losing wealth. Conversely, entrepreneurs can profitably carry out their trade without fear of excessive state appropriation. They, in turn, know that accumulated wealth can purchase power.

It is, of course, this productive relation between wealth and power, between the public and private sectors, which produces the most congenial environment for the reproduction of power. Power is most easily transmitted from generation to generation when it can transit through wealth. It is, therefore, in the so-called 'state capitalist' countries of Africa with relatively healthy economies that the ruling élites are most likely to be able to reproduce themselves as ruling classes.[73] Whether they do so or not, however, is not a straight forward matter because this putatively productive relationship between power and wealth remains precarious.

First, some countries with good economic potential (e.g., Liberia, Zambia, Uganda, Zaïre, Ghana, Nigeria) are either severely mismanaged or else ruthlessly plundered by their rulers. Where that happens, capitalist development is seriously curtailed and the parallel economies which develop are not so conducive to a productive relationship between wealth and power.[74] Second, some countries with successful capitalist economies are heavily dependent on the exports of agricultural or mineral products (e.g. Senegal, Nigeria, Côte d'Ivoire, Kenya, Zambia, Botswana), the world price of which they do not control. Sudden, or even gradual, changes in the value of their exports (as has happened with oil, copper, coffee, cocoa and tea) can cripple their economy.[75]

Third, few of these countries are immune from political crises – the evidence so far does not suggest that these countries are any less prone to political disorder than their more statist or more destitute counterparts. Where the question of the leadership succession has not been settled, where the armed forces have already taken power before, where specific (ethnic, religious, regional, racial) communities are excluded from the political arena, where there are regional conflicts, where drought threatens, etc., there is always the risk that civil wars, coups, violence or other challenges to the state will lead to the collapse of the political order. When that occurs, the mechanisms by which power is reproduced through wealth are damaged, if not destroyed. The ensuing reshuffling of the cards impinges on the processes by which power was being reproduced into class.

While it is clearly in this group of countries that the formation and reproduction of ruling élites are most discernible and most advanced, their history so far does not yet support the thesis that these élites are reproducing as classes. Where there has been relative political stability since independence (e.g. Senegal, Côte d'Ivoire, Cameroon, Kenya), there is some discernible pattern in the reproduction of power. Elsewhere, as for example in Nigeria, the evidence is not as clear.

Yet, there remains, even in the most stable and prosperous of these countries, a need to balance so many political factors that the reproduction of ruling élites into ruling classes cannot proceed unhindered. Their continued tenure of power and accumulation of wealth depends on their ability to hold the political community together. This in turn demands that they redistribute a significant proportion of their wealth.

There are in Africa very few countries which are both economically prosperous and free from the threat of political disorder. There are thus few candidate cases for the study of the reproduction of power over generations. While it is no doubt true that some among the élites will prosper whatever the circumstances, it remains undeniable that prosperity is greater and the reproduction of power easier in conditions of relative social and political peace.

Thus, the complexion of the reproduction of power in contemporary Africa is still uncertain. It is too early to say with any confidence whether definable social classes are going to emerge from the present socio-economic magma. Whether they do will depend in large measure on whether present ruling élites manage to devise more effective mechanisms for reproducing themselves into ruling classes.

Notes

PART I: THE MEANINGS OF POLITICAL INTERPRETATION

Introduction

1. P. Marnham, 'A continent that was forgotten by the twentieth century', *Independent on Sunday*, 16 September 1990 p. 20.
2. For Marnham what is wrong with Africa is, in effect, its 'Africanness', now resurfacing in the post-colonial era. In a glorious display of most prejudices extant about Africa, he writes:

   > Little is known of the pre-colonial era in Africa but there is evidence to suggest that it was for much of the time characterised by ignorance, slavery and ritual murder. Colonisation was marked by mechanised warfare, forced labour and brutal exploitation. De-colonisation to date has often been worse . . .

   See also Andreski, 1968.
3. For a useful discussion, see Martin Staniland, 'Democracy and Ethnocentrism', in Chabal, 1986.
4. See 'Thinking about Politics in Africa', in Chabal, 1986.
5. A point also implicitly made by Douglas Rimmer in his reply to Marnham:

   > Patrick Marnham presents a selection of information to illustrate the contention that nowhere in Africa is there a flicker of hope. An equally dispiriting account of the condition of Britain could be rendered by concentrating attention on the current reports of homelessness, deterioration in public services, drug addiction, child abuse, street hooliganism, satanic cults, begging and the like.

   Letter to *Independent on Sunday*, 23 September 1990, p. 18.
6. Bayart, 1989, p. 19.
7. Lonsdale, 1989.
8. Hodder-Williams, 1984.
9. Lonsdale, 1981.
10. See Donal Cruise O'Brien, 'Modernization, Order and the Erosion of a Democratic Ideal: American Political Science, 1960–1970', *Journal of Development Studies*, 8 (1972).
11. See, among many, Rothchild and Chazan, 1988.
12. For a useful economic summary, see Fieldhouse, 1986.
13. See here Jewsiewicki and Newbury, 1986.
14. As background, see Gann and Duignan, 1969.
15. For a summary, see here Chazan *et al.*, 1988, pp. 1–32.
16. Discussed in Staniland, 1985.
17. For a macro-picture, see Rimmer, 1984. For a micro-picture, see Richards, 1985.

18. World Bank, *Accelerated Development in Sub-Saharan Africa* (Washington DC: World Bank, 1981): *Toward Sustained Development in Sub-Saharan Africa* (Washington, DC: World Bank, 1984): *Financing Development with Growth in Sub-Saharan Africa, 1986–1990* (Washington DC: World Bank, 1986). See also Gerald Helleiner, *The IMF and Africa in the 1980s* (Princeton: Princeton Essays in International Finance No. 152, July 1983).
19. Among many possible examples, see: Wilks, 1975; Iliffe, 1979; Cooper, 1980; Peel, 1983.
20. For an example, see Harrison, 1984. For a rebuttal, see Hill, 1986. pp. 171–4.
21. One useful summary is Bénot, 1968.
22. For the critical view, see: Ake, 1979; L.A. Jinadu, 'Some Reflections on African Political Scientists and African Politics', *West African Journal of Sociology and Political Science*, 1, 3 (1978).
23. For some contrasting critical works on African literature, see, *inter alia*: Innes, 1990; Amuta, 1990; Achebe, 1975; Ngugi wa Thiong'o, 1982 and 1985; Emmanuel Obiechina, *Culture, Tradition and Society in the West African Novel* (Cambridge: Cambridge University Press, 1975); Soyinka, 1976.
24. For African views see here, among others: Barongo, 1983; Anyang' Nyong'o, 1987; Oyugi *et al.*, 1988
25. Compare and contrast here Anderson, 1983, and Mudimbe, 1988.
26. See Staniland, 1985.
27. Maimire Mennasemay, 'Political Theory, Political Science and African Development', *Canadian Journal of African Studies*, 16, 2 (1982).
28. Although even here there are limits, as is evident in Iliffe, 1987. For a trenchant critique of *The African Poor*, see Achille Mbembe's review in *Politique africaine*, 37 (1990), pp. 138–9.
29. As is evident in Chazan *et al.*, 1988 – otherwise one of the most useful books on African politics published recently.
30. This is important. *Power in Africa* is a reflection, an argument, a polemic even and not a history. It assumes broad knowledge of contemporary African history.

Chapter 1   Paradigms Lost

Development theory
1. The classics of this literature would include: Huntington, 1968; Apter, 1985; Binder *et al.*, 1971. For an overview see: Samuel Huntington, 'The Change to Change: Modernization, Development and Politics', *Comparative Politics*, 4, 3 (1971): Higgott, 1983; Richard Sandbrook, 'The Crisis in Political Development Theory', *Journal of Development Studies*, 12, 2 (1976).
2. See: Almond and Coleman, 1960; Almond and Powell, 1966.
3. Karl Deutsch, *The Nerves of Government* (London: The Free Press of Glencoe, 1963), and 'Social Mobilization and Political Development', *American Political Science Review*, 55, 3 (1961).
4. See David Easton, *The Political System* (New York: Knopf, 1953). See also: Robert Merton, *Social Theory and Social Structure* (Glencoe, Illinois: The Free Press, 1957); E. Rostow, *The Stages of Economic Growth: a non-Communist Manifesto* (Cambridge: Cambridge University Press, 1960).

5. See Ted Robert Gurr, *Why Men Rebel* (Princeton: Princeton University Press, 1970).
6. Among the best were Apter, 1955 and 1961.
7. This is most clearly developed in Huntington, 1968.
8. On the concept of political culture, see: Gabriel Almond and Sydney Verba, *The Civic Culture* (Boston: Little, Brown & Co., 1965); Lucian Pye and Sydney Verba (eds), *Political Culture and Political Development* (Princeton: Princeton University Press, 1965).
9. The most useful summary of this argument is Zolberg, 1966.
10. For an illustration, see Coleman, 1963.
11. See here, among many: Apter, 1955; Bienen, 1967.
12. On leadership, see Wilner, 1968. On the single-party state, see Zolberg, 1966.
13. Put in its proper perspective by Christopher Clapham, 'The Context of African Political Thought', *Journal of Modern African Studies*, 8, 1 (1970).
14. On ethnicity, see Enloe, 1973. The most useful such 'revisionist' book was perhaps Kasfir, 1976.
15. By the seventies, fewer political scientists wrote on Africa.
16. Most notable among political scientists who did continue to publish on Africa were Crawford Young and René Lemarchand. See: Young, 1976 and 1982; René Lemarchand 'African Power through the Looking Glass', *Journal of Modern African Studies*, 11, 2 (1973). For a reflection on what this section has been about, see James Coleman and C.R.D. Halisi, 'American Political Science and Tropical Africa', *African Studies Review*, 26 (1983).

Class theory

17. For a summary of some of the key issues, see: Stephen Katz, *Marxism, Africa and Social Class: a Critique of Relevant Theories* (Montreal: McGill University, 1980); Peter Gutkind and Peter Waterman (eds), *African Social Studies: a Radical Reader* (London: Heinemann, 1977).
18. See David Seddon (ed.), *Relations of Production: Marxist Approaches to Economic Anthropology* (London: Cass 1978).
19. See, among many, Saul, 1979.
20. The most influential statement was perhaps Coquery-Vidrovitch, 1969. See also Donald Crummey and C. Stewart, 1981. For a wider discussion of the issues, see: Hindess and Hirst, 1975; Aidan Foster-Carter, 'The Modes of Production Controversy', *New Left Review*, 107 (1978).
21. See here Suret-Canale, 1988.
22. For the classic Marxist statement, see Warren, 1980. For the differing view, see Rodney, 1972.
23. See, for example, Rey, 1971.
24. See here, for example: Claude Meillassoux, *Anthropologie économique des Gouro de Côte d'Ivoire* (Paris: Mouton, 1964); Terray, 1972; Maurice Bloch (ed.), *Marxist Analysis and Social Anthropology* (London: Malaby, 1975).
25. Jack Goody, 'Feudalism in Africa', *Journal of African History*, 4, 1 (1963) and *Technology, Tradition and the State in Africa* (London: Oxford University Press, 1971). See also Ernest Gellner, 'Class before State: the Soviet Treatment of African Feudalism', *Archives européennes de sociologie*, 28 (1977).
26. Jean Suret-Canale, 'Traditional Societies in Tropical Africa and the Concept of

the "Asiatic Mode of Production": Marxism and the Study of African Societies', in Suret-Canale, 1988.
27. See, for example, Emmanuel Terray (ed.), *L'esclavage en Afrique précoloniale* (Paris: Maspéro, 1975).
28. For one example of a fairly orthodox treatment, see Jean Suret-Canale, *French Colonialism in Tropical Africa* (London: C. Hurst, 1971).
29. For a case study of how the notion of dual economy was thought to apply in practice, see G. Arrighi, 'Labour Supplies in Historical Perspective: a Study of the Proletarianization of the African Peasantry in Rhodesia', *Journal of Development Studies*, 6, 3 (1970). For a discussion of how the concept might apply to Mozambique, see First, 1983.
30. See here, *inter alia*: Sandbrook and Cohen, 1975; R. Cohen, 'Classes in Africa: Analytical Problems and Perspectives', *The Socialist Register 1972* (London: Merlin Press, 1972); John Saul and R. Woods, 'African Peasantries', in T. Shanin (ed.), *Peasants and Peasant Societies* (Harmondsworth: Penguin, 1971); Ken Post, '"Peasantization" and Rural Political Movements in Western Africa'. *Archives européennes de sociologie*, 13, 3 (1972). For a more general treatment, see Markovitz, 1977
31. On the notion of classless socialism, see Chabal, 1988
32. For a class analysis of Uganda, see Mamdani, 1976.
33. For a useful case study of the extent to which they do, see Jeffries, 1978. For a different case study, see Jeanne Penvenne, 'A History of African Labor in Lourenço Marques, Mozambique, 1877 to 1950', PhD Thesis, Boston University, 1982.
34. See text Part IV, Chapters 2 and 4.
35. See Kitching, 1980.

Underdevelopment theory
36. Some of the classic works would include: Frank, 1967; Theotonio dos Santos, 'The Structure of Dependence' in Charles Wilbert (ed.), *The Political Economy of Development and Underdevelopment* (New York: Random House, 1973); Immanuel Wallerstein, 'Dependence in an Interdependent World', *African Studies Review*, 17, 1 (1974). For a review of the literature, see: Tony Smith, 'The Underdevelopment of Development Literature', *World Politics*, 31, 2 (1979); Staniland, 1985. For underdevelopment theory as it applies to Africa, see: Rodney, 1972; Amin, 1972.
37. Here, see for example, Harry Johnson, *Economic Policies Toward Less Developed Countries* (New York: Praeger, 1967).
38. See here Celso Furtado, *Development and Stagnation in Latin America: a Structural Approach* (New Haven: Yale University Press, 1965).
39. See, among others: F.H. Cardoso and E. Faletto, *Dependencia y Desarrollo en America Latina* (Santiago: ILPES, 1967); Frank 1967; Furtado *op. cit.*
40. For a review of the literature, see Ian Roxborough, *Theories of Underdevelopment* (London: Macmillan, 1979).
41. See here Christian Palloix, *Problémes de la croissance en économie ouverte* (Paris: Maspéro, 1969).
42. See here: Rodney, 1972; Fanon, 1965.
43. For Africa, see here Ruth First, *The Barrel of a Gun* (New York: Pantheon Books, 1970) and, *inter alia*, Decalo, 1976.

44. Samir Amin, *L'Accumulation à l'échelle mondiale* (Paris: Anthropos, 1971); *Le d'éveloppement inégal* (Paris: Editions de Minuit, 1973); *L'Afrique de l'Ouest bloquée* (Paris: Editions de Minuit, 1971); *L'économie du Maghreb* (Paris: Editions de Minuit, 1966); *Le Maghreb moderne* (Paris: Editions de Minuit, 1970); *Le monde des affaires sénégalais* (Paris: Editions de Minuit, 1969); *Le développement du capitalisme en Côte d'Ivoire* (Paris: PUF, 1967); *Trois expériences africaines de développement: la Mali, la Guinée et le Ghana* (Paris: PUF, 1965) and (with Catherine Coquery-Vidrovitch) *Histoire économique du Congo, 1880–1968* (Paris: Anthropos, 1967). Rodney, 1972.

45. See here, *inter alia*: Rey, 1971; R. Cohen, 'Classes in Africa: Analytical Problems and Perspectives', *The Socialist Register 1972* (London: Merlin Press, 1972).

46. Emmanuel Arghiri, *L'Echange inégal* (Paris: Maspéro, 1969). See also Thomas Balogh, *Partenaires inégaux dans l'échange international* (Paris: Dunod, 1971).

47. For case studies, see: Mamdani, 1976; Shivji, 1973.

48. See Wallerstein, 1976.

49. Samir Amin, *Le développement inégal*, pp. 325–40.

50. Fanon, 1965.

51. Whereas Samir Amin's economic analysis of unequal development is sharp and well informed, his class analysis of individual countries (e.g. Senegal, Côte d'Ivoire, Mali, Guinea, Ghana) is less convincing.

52. See, for an example, Shivji, 1976.

53. 'Analysis of African politics in terms of dependency is out of fashion now', write the editors of a recent volume on West Africa (Cruise O'Brien *et al.*, 1989, p. 10).

Revolutionary theory

54. A selection of the relevant literature, both conceptual works and country studies, would include: Munslow, 1986; James Mittelman, *Underdevelopment and the Transition to Socialism: Mozambique and Tanzania* (New York: Academic Press, 1981); Chabal, 'People's War, State Formation and Revolution in Africa', in Kasfir, 1984; Chabal, 'Revolutionary Democracy in Africa: the Case of Guinea-Bissau', in Chabal, 1986; Lars Rudebeck, *Guinea-Bissau: a Study of Political Mobilisation* (Uppsala: Scandinavian Institute of African Studies, 1974) and *Guinea-Bissau: folket, partiet och staten* (Uppsala: Scandinavian Institute of African Studies, 1977); P. Aaby, *The State of Guinea-Bissau: African Socialism or Socialism in Africa?* (Uppsala: Scandinavian Institute of African Studies, 1978); Carlos Lopes, *Etnia, Estado e Relações de Poder na Guiné-Bissau* (Lisbon: Edições 70, 1982); Munslow, 1983; Saul, 1979 and 1985. For a perceptive discussion of socialism in Africa, see David and Marina Ottaway, *Afrocommunism* (New York: Holmes & Meier, 1981). For a contrasting view, see Thomas Henriksen, 'Lusophone Africa' in Duignan & Jackson, 1986.

55. See here Munslow, 1986. More generally on twentieth-century revolutions: Wolf, 1969; Dunn, 1972.

56. For a summary of these arguments, see Chabal, 1988.

57. See here Zolberg, 1966.

58. On the early socialist experiments, see Rosberg and Callaghy, 1979.

59. See here, for example, Crummey and Stewart, 1981.

60. See here Gérard Chaliand, *Mythes révolutionnaires du Tiers Monde* (Paris: Seuil, 1976). Contrast with his later book, *Contre l'ordre du monde: les rebelles* (Paris: Seuil, 1983).
61. See my 'People's War', in Kasfir, 1984.
62. For some interesting research about the socio-economic effects of people's war in the liberated areas, see *A Situação nas Antigas Zonas Libertadas de Cabo Delgado*, Centro dos Estudos Africanos (CEA), Universidade Eduardo Mondlane, 1983. See also the University Eduardo Mondlane Department of History's *História de Moçambique*, particularly vols 2 and 3. For similar evidence in Guinea-Bissau, see Jocelyn Jones, 'The Peasantry, the Party and the State in Guinea-Bissau', Oxford, D.Phil. thesis, 1987.
63. On the history of Ethiopia see, *inter alia*: Markakis, 1974; Clapham, 1988; Lefort, 1980.
64. Two of the most revealing books on the nationalist war in Zimbabwe are: Lan, 1985; Ranger, 1985a.
65. See here my argument in 'People's War' in Kasfir, 1984.
66. This is perhaps best seen in the post-colonial experience of Mozambique; see: Munslow, 1986; Saul, 1985.
67. The weaknesses of revolutionary theory were exposed early on by David and Marina Ottaway *op. cit.*

Democratic Theory

68. Among important recent statements are: Richard Sklar, 'Democracy in Africa', in Chabal, 1986, and 'Developmental Democracy', *Comparative Studies in Society and History*, 29, 4 (1987); Oyugi *et al.*, 1988; Anyang' Nyong'o, 1987. For a more general background, see: Samuel Huntington, 'Will more Countries Become Democratic?' *Political Science Quarterly*, 99, 2 (1984); Robert Jackson and Carl Rosberg, 'Democracy in Tropical Africa: Democracy versus Autocracy in African Politics', *Journal of International Affairs*, 38, 2 (1985). For the conceptual background, see: Roland Pennock, *Democratic Political Theory* (Princeton: Princeton University Press, 1979); Robert Dahl, *Polyarchy: Participation and Opposition* (New Haven: Yale University Press, 1971); Arend Lijphart, *Democracies* (New Haven: Yale University Press, 1984); Barrington Moore, 1966 and 1979; C.B. Macpherson, *The Real World of Democracy* (Oxford: Oxford University Press, 1966); John Dunn, 'Democratic Theory', in Dunn, 1979.
69. See what Sklar writes in 'Developmental Democracy', op.cit. p. 714.
70. See Francis Fukuyama's 'end of history' concept, note 84 below.
71. This is one of Sklar's main arguments in 'Democracy in Africa', op.cit.
72. See examples in Staniland, 'Democracy and Ethnocentrism', in Chabal, 1986.
73. Sklar writes: 'But democracy dies hard. Its vital force is the accountability of rulers to their subjects' – 'Democracy in Africa', op.cit., p. 17. On political accountability, see Part II, Chapter 3.
74. For the notion of 'capture', see Hyden, 1980.
75. For a case study on the second economy, see MacGaffey, 1987.
76. On the state, see Part II, Chapter 4.
77. See here, *inter alia*, Steven Lukes, *Individualism* (Oxford: Oxford University Press, 1973).
78. On elections in Africa, see Hayward, 1986.

79. This is a point I examine in detail in Part IV, Chapter 12.
80. See here Pateman, 1970.
81. A useful example of such an approach is Bayart, 1979.
82. A danger which can be avoided by the use of the concept of good government. See John Dunn, 'The Politics of Representation and Good Government in Post-colonial Africa', in Chabal, 1986. See below, Part III, Chapter 10.
83. See Richard Sklar's discussion of electoral democracy in 'Developmental Democracy', op. cit., pp. 691–4.
84. F. Fukuyama, 'The End of History', *National Interest*, 16, 1989.

PART II CONCEPTS FOR THE ANALYSIS OF POWER IN AFRICA

Chapter 2 The Political Community

1. On the model of Edward Saïd, *Orientalism* (London: Routledge & Kegan Paul, 1978).
2. Controversy still surrounds Conrad's *Heart of Darkness*.
3. One interesting case is the history of French missionaries in Basutoland. See here, *inter alia:* Leonard Thomson, *Survival in Two Worlds: Moshoeshoe of Lesotho, 1786–1870* (Oxford: Clarendon Press, 1975); Victor Ellenberger, *A Century of missionary Work in Basutoland (1833–1933)* (Morija: Sesuto Book Depot, 1938).
4. See Roland Oliver, *The Missionary Factor in East Africa* (London: Longman, 1952).
5. Well illustrated by the accounts of missionaries in Lesotho.
6. On a rapidly changing pre-colonial society, see Wilks, 1975.
7. The epitome of the British colonial mind was Lord Lugard. See Margery Perham, *Lugard*, 2 vols (London: Collins, 1956 and 1960).
8. For a comparison with the French see: W. Cohen, 1971; Gifford and Louis, 1982. For a more general treatment, see Wesseling, 1978.
9. On the 'invention' of communities, see: Anderson, 1983; Hobsbawn & Ranger, 1983.
10. On what Lonsdale calls the colonial civilising mission, see his 'Political Accountability in African History', in Chabal, 1986.
11. For a revealing account of this process, see Kenyatta, 1938.
12. As one example, see Liebenow, 1986, pp. 1–12.
13. As counterpoint, see Clifford Geertz (ed.), *Old Societies and New States* (Glencoe, Illinois: The Free Press, 1963).
14. See, *inter alia*, Lucy Mair, *Primitive Government* (Bloomington: Indiana University Press, 1977).
15. See Meyer Fortes and E.E. Evans Pritchard (eds), *African Political Systems* (Oxford: Oxford University Press, 1940).
16. *Facing Mount Kenya* (Kenyatta, 1938) is instructive both as a commentary on early anthropology and on Kenyatta's creative use of the discipline.
17. The notion of 'primitive society' contained an argument about why such societies had not 'modernised' in the first place.
18. See *inter alia*, Robinson & Gallagher, 1961.

19. For some nationalist notions, see: Kwame Nkrumah, *Consciencism* (New York: Monthly Review Press, 1964); Léopold Sédar Senghor, *On African Socialism* (New York: Praeger, 1964).
20. A good illustration of this process will be found in Amílcar Cabral, 'Libération nationale et culture', in Cabral, 1975.
21. See Hobsbawn and Ranger, 1983.
22. Kenyatta, op.cit.
23. For a 'nationalist' view, see Cheikh Anta Diop, *Antériorité des civilisations nègres* (Paris: Présence Africaine, 1967).
24. See here Lonsdale's notion of the nationalists' 'civilising mission' in 'Political Accountability', op.cit.
25. For one example, see Pratt, 1976.
26. See: Anderson, 1983; Hobsbawn and Ranger, 1983; Gellner, 1983; Mudimbe, 1988; Mbembe, 1988.
27. On the state see here: Claessen and Skalnik, 1981; Londsdale, 1981. On the notion of 'nation', see, *inter alia*: Ali Mazrui & Michael Tidy, *Nationalism and New States in Africa* (London: Heinemann, 1984); Ronald Cohen and John Middleton (eds), *From Tribe to Nation in Africa* (Scranton: Chandler Publishing, 1970).
28. For a good summary of this process, see Zolberg, 1966.
29. One will compare profitably Cabral and Nyerere here. Amilcar Cabral, 1975; Julius Nyerere, *Freedom and Unity* (Dar es Salaam: Oxford University Press,1966).
30. Yves Bénot, 1968.
31. Lonsdale writes of Kenyatta:

> He saw . . . that men cannot look forward with responsibility to their posterity unless they can also, not in mere imagination but in an imagination which takes the measure of power, look back to their ancestors. Kenyatta imagined that he was preserving his Kikuyu people in print; in fact he was creating them.

John Lonsdale, 'Political Accountability' op.cit. p. 142.
32. Where large numbers did not recognise themselves in the nationalist myth, problems could arise. For the case of Angola, see Marcum,1969 and 1978.
33. English-speaking Africans, for example, found it difficult to appreciate the need for French-speaking Africans to build a nationalist discourse on a prior negritude discourse.
34. See here a classic: Hodgkin, 1956.
35. For a comparative summary see, for example, Ruth Schachter Morgenthau, *Political Parties in French-Speaking Africa* (London: Oxford University Press, 1964).
36. Angola and the (former Belgian) Congo are among the two foremost examples of colonies where this question of identity was never satisfactorily settled. On Angola, see Marcum, 1969 and 1978. On the Congo, see, *inter alia*: Callaghy, 1984; Crawford Young, *Politics in the Congo* (Princeton: Princeton University Press, 1965).
37. See Crawford Young's discussion of *authenticité* in his 'Zaire and Cameroon', in Duignan & Jackson, 1986. See also Willame, 1972. On Nyerere's thought, see: William Duggan & John Civille, *Tazania and Nyerere: a Study of Ujaama and Nationalism* (New York: Orbis Books, 1976); Bienen, 1967.

38. An argument to be found in Anyang' Nyong'o, 1987.
39. Compare here the nature of the nationalist part in, say Côte d'Ivoire and Guinea in the immediate post-colonial period. See the chapters on Guinea and Côte d'Ivoire in Dunn, 1978.
40. On Sékou Touré's Guinea, see R.W. Johnson, 'Sékou Touré and the Guinean Revolution', *African Affairs*, 69, vol. 277 (1970). See also Ladipo Adamolekun, *Sekou Toure's Guinea* (London: Methuen,1976). On Senghor, see Irving Leonard Markovitz, *Leopold Sedar Senghor and the Politics of Negritude* (New York: Atheneum, 1969).
41. On some poorly plausible national constructions in East Africa, see Markakis, 1987.
42. Contrast Tangri, 1985, chapter 1, and Liebenow, 1986, chapter 3.
43. For example, the attempt by the PAIGC to create a binational state by joining Guinea-Bissau and Cape Verde was not rooted in a very secure notion of political community and did not survive long after independence. See Chabal, 1983.

Chapter 3   Political Accountability

1. I have been inspired by Lonsdale, 'Political Accountability in African History', in Chabal, 1986.
2. See Dunn, 1980.
3. Chabal, in Chabal, 1986, pp. 11–12.
4. Lonsdale, 'Political Accountability' op.cit., p. 128.
5. By sharing I mean that the rulers' legitimacy is accepted.
6. Lonsdale writes:

    Accountability is, quite simply, the problem of power. All power is, and must be, a scarce resource which is unequally shared.

    Lonsdale, 'Political Accountability' . . . op.cit., p. 128.
7. For a case study of a largely egalitarian society. See R. Lee, *The !Kung San* (Cambridge: Cambridge University Press, 1979).
8. For a study of power relations in Nigeria, see Joseph, 1987.
9. Lonsdale, 'Political Accountability' op.cit., pp. 146–57.
10. L. de Heusch, *The Drunken King or the Origin of the State* (Bloomington: University of Indiana Press, 1982).
11. On the 'rice' coup in Guinea-Bissau in 1980: Chabal, in *West Africa*, 15 December 1980, pp. 2554–6; 22/29 December 1980, pp. 2593–4 and 12 January 1981, pp. 62–3.
12. On representation: Pitkin, 1972. On Marx: Draper, 1977.
13. See Collier, 1982.
14. A point sometimes missed by exponents of democratic theory. See, for example, Callaghy, 'Politics and Vision in Africa: the Interplay of Domination, Equality and Liberty', in Chabal, 1986.
15. On the Chinese political culture: J. Levenson, *Lian Ch'i-Ch'ao and the Mind of Modern China* (Berkeley: University of California Press,1959); J. Fairbank (ed.), *The Chinese World Order* (Cambridge, Mass.: Harvard University Press, 1968).
16. L. Bianco, *Origins of the Chinese Revolution, 1914–1959* (Stanford: Stanford University Press, 1971).

17. A useful comparative analysis is Dunn, 1972.
18. J. Lonsdale, 'The European Scramble and Conquest in African History', in R. Oliver and G. Sanderson (eds), *The Cambridge History of Africa*, vol. 6 (Cambridge: Cambridge University Press, 1985).
19. For an African perspective, see J.F.A. Ajayi, 'African on the Eve of the European Conquest', in J.F.A. Ajayi (ed.), *General History of Africa*, vol. 6 (London: Heinemann and UNESCO, 1989).
20. See Crummey, 1986.
21. Hill, 1963.
22. On the Kenyan case, see Kitching, 1980.
23. Isaacman, 1972. On political Africanisation see Part IV, Chapter 12.
24. Lord Lugard, *Dual Mandate in British Tropical Africa* (Edinburgh, 1952).
25. For one telling example, see Cruise O'Brien, 1971.
26. For one possible example, see Ranger, 1985b.
27. M. Chanock, *Law, Custom and Social Order* (Cambridge: Cambridge University Press,1985); S.F. Moore, *Social Facts and Fabrications* (Cambridge: Cambridge University Press, 1986).
28. For the earliest such interpretation, see Fanon,1967.
29. T. Smith, 'A Comparative Study of French and British Decolonization', *Comparative Studies in Society and History*, 20, 1 (1978).
30. The myth was strongest in those countries which had achieved independence through armed struggle. See Chabal, 1983, chapter 7.
31. Lonsdale, 'Political Accountability', op.cit., p. 146.
32. Lonsdale, 'The European Scramble', op.cit.
33. Lonsdale, 'Political Accountability', op.cit., p. 146.
34. It was difficult as it involved overcoming prejudices which clouded the official mind. One example: C. Harrison, *France and Islam in West Africa* (Cambridge: Cambridge University Press, 1988), p. 147.
35. See Lee, 1967.
36. On Portuguese colonialism: Newitt, 1981; on French colonialism: Cohen, 1971.
37. R. Robinson, 'The Moral Disarmament of African Empire', *Journal of Imperial and Commonwealth History*, 8 (1979).
38. Lord Lugard: [We need] 'a class who in a crisis can be relied on to stand by us, and whose interests are wholly identified with ours'. Quoted in Wesseling, 1978, p. 159.
39. On the legitimacy of spirit mediums, see Lan, 1985.
40. Contrast Hodgkin, 1956, and Freund, 1984.
41. On the economics of decolonisation: Fieldhouse, 1986, chapters 1 and 2.
42. Gellner calls nationalism a 'theory of political legitimacy'. Gellner, 1983, p. 1.
43. Lonsdale writes: 'Almost everybody at the time [of independence], even colonial officials, dared to believe that with the new accountability of politics . . . economic and social progress would together thrive' ('Political Accountability', op.cit, p. 153).
44. The contradictions are most visible in the former Portuguese colonies where post-colonial support for the nationalists was quickly dissipated. For an interesting case study, see Galli and Jones, 1987.
45. For one comparative account, see W.H. Morris Jones and G. Fisher (eds), *Decolonization and After* (London: Cass, 1978).

46. See: Hodder-Williams, 1984; Tordoff, 1984.
47. See, for example, R. Crook, 'Bureaucracy and Politics in Ghana: a Comparative Perspective', in P. Lyon and J. Manor (eds), *Transfer and Transformation: Political Institutions in the New Commonwealth* (Leicester: Leicester University Press, 1983).
48. Hyden, 1980.
49. Anyang' Nyong'o writes: 'At the centre of the failure of African states to chart viable paths for domestic accumulation is the problem of accountability, the lack of democracy'. (Anyang' Nyong'o 1987, p. 19).

Chapter 4   The State

1. Probably the two most useful discussions of the state in Africa are Bayart, 1989, and Lonsdale, 1981. Others include: J.P. Nettl, 'The State as Conceptual Variable', *World Politics*, 20, 4 (1968); Peter Anyang' Nyong'o, 'The Economic Foundations of the State in Contemporary Africa', *Présence Africaine*, 127/8 (1983); Claude Ake, *A Political Economy of Africa* (London: Longman, 1981); Issa Shivji, 'The State in the Dominated Social Formations of Africa: some Theoretical Issues', *Social Sciences Journal*, 32, 4 (1980); Peter Evans *et al.*(eds), *Bringing the State Back In* (Cambridge: Cambridge University Press, 1985); Theda Skocpol, *The State and Social Revolutions* (Cambridge: Cambridge University Press, 1980); R. Fossaert, *La Société. Les États* (Paris: Seuil, 1985); B. Badie and P. Birnbaum, *Sociologie de l'État* (Paris: Grasset, 1979); Emmanuel Terray (ed.), *L'État contemporain en Afrique* (Paris: L'Harmattan, 1987); Hamza Alavi, 'The State in Post-Colonial Societies', *New Left Review*, 74 (1972); Rothchild and Chazan, 1988.
2. See Claessen and Skalnik, 1978. For a case study, see J. Miller, *Kings and Kinsmen* (Oxford: Oxford University Press, 1970).
3. Lonsdale, 1981, p. 154.
4. Illustrated by the attempts to use N. Poulantzas, *Political Power and Social Classes* (London: New Left Books, 1973) and *State, Power, Socialism* (London: New Left Books, 1978).
5. See Collier, 1982.
6. On the historical perspective, Bayart, 1989, pp. 19–64.
7. For a more sensitive approach, Chazan *et al.*, 1988, pp. 35–66.
8. For an overview, see E. Service, *Origins of the State and Civilization* (New York: Norton, 1975).
9. M. Weiner and S. Huntington (eds), *Understanding Political Development* (Boston: Little, Brown, 1987).
10. For one example on parties, Liebenow, 1986, pp. 204–36.
11. Bayart, 'Les sociétés africaines face à l'État', *Pouvoirs*, 25 (1983).
12. For a comparative perspective, Z. Ergas (ed.), *The African State in Transition* (London: Macmillan, 1987).
13. Shivji, *op.cit.*
14. R. Sklar, 'The Nature of Class Domination in Africa', *Journal of Modern African Studies*, 17, 4 (1979).
15. G. Mathias and P. Salama, *L'État surdéveloppé* (Paris: Maspéro, 1983); Colin Leys, 'The "Overdeveloped" Colonial State: a Re-Evaluation', *Review of African Political Economy* 5 (1976).

16. For two class analyses: Shivji, 1976; Mamdani, 1976.
17. G. Williams, 'There is no Theory of Petit-Bourgeois Politics', *Review of African Political Economy*, 6 (1976).
18. See A. Gramsci, *Selections from the Prison Notebooks* (New York: International Publishers, 1971) and *The Modern Prince* (New York: International Publishers, 1972).
19. See Note 16 above; see also Leys, 1975.
20. See Note 15 above.
21. On the state: Bayart in Chabal, 1986, pp. 111–16.
22. As Callaghy writes: '[T]he African centralising patrimonial state is a Leviathan, but a lame one', in Chabal, 1986, p. 36.
23. Bayart, in Chabal, 1986, p. 112.
24. In France the state was instrumental in creating the nation; E. Weber, *Peasants into Frenchmen* (London: Chatto & Windus, 1977).
25. On the notion of hegemonic drive: Part IV, Chapter 12.
26. See Callaghy, 1984.
27. J. Lonsdale, 'The Conquest State of Kenya', in J.A. de Moor and H. Wesseling (eds), *Colonial Warfare*, (Leiden: Brill,1990).
28. R. Robinson, 'Non-European Foundations of European Imperialism', in R. Owen and B. Sutcliffe (eds), *Studies in the Theory of Imperialism* (London: Longman, 1972).
29. Which theories of collaboration were adept at disguising. One example: J. Gallagher *et al.*, *Locality, Province and Nation: Essays on Indian Politics, 1870 to 1940* (Cambridge: Cambridge University Press, 1973).
30. See Kitching, 1980.
31. On Weber, see Mommsen, 1974.
32. B. Berman, 'Structure and Process in the Bureaucratic States of Colonial Africa', *Development and Change*, 15 (1984).
33. For Lonsdale (1981, p. 190) the colonial state is 'Bonapartist'.
34. For one case study, see Iliffe, 1979.
35. Lonsdale, in Chabal, 1986, p. 146.
36. M. Chanock, *Law, Custom and Social Order* (Cambridge: Cambridge University Press, 1985).
37. See, as one example, R. Crook, 'Legitimacy, Authority and the Transfer of Power in Ghana', *Political Studies*, 35 (1987).
38. Cabral advocated complete decentralisation: see B. Davidson, *The Liberation of Guiné* (Harmondsworth, Penguin, 1969), p. 137.
39. R. Price, *Society and Bureaucracy in Contemporary Ghana* (Berkeley: University of California Press, 1975).
40. Bayart, in Chabal, 1986, p. 117.
41. This is particularly true of countries like Mozambique where social integration under colonial rule was poor. See Saul,1985.
42. Bayart quotes: 'Partout le plein fait le visible de la structure mais le vide structure l'usage'. Bayart, 1989, p. 7.
43. On the role of the military in 1966: Luckham, 1971. On the Nigeria constructed after the civil war: Joseph, 1987; Diamond, 1988.
44. On Guinea-Bissau, see Chabal, 'Revolutionary Democracy in Africa', in Chabal, 1986, and Galli and Jones, 1987.
45. Mugabe's electoral victory was indeed largely the result of his party being seen as the nationalist victor.

46. The 'honeymoon' period between rulers and citizens did not last long. Lonsdale in Chabal, 1986, p. 155.
47. See Fieldhouse, 1986 and Marseille, 1984.
48. As the French-speaking countries did successfully. See Olivier Vallée, *Le prix de l'argent CFA* (Paris: Karthala, 1989).
49. On this issue, see Part IV, Chapter 15.
50. Hill, 1963.
51. See Part IV, Chapter 12.
52. See Bayart in Chabal, 1986, pp. 115–16.

Chapter 5   Civil Society

1. In this chapter I am inspired by Bayart's work: Bayart, 1979 and 1989; 'La politique par le bas en Afrique noire', *Politique africaine*, 1 (1981); 'La revanche des sociétés africaines', *Politique africaine*, 11 (1983); 'Les sociétés africaines face à l'État', *Pouvoirs*, 25 (1983); 'La société politique camerounaise (1982–1986)', *Politique africaine*, 22 (1986); 'L'hypothése totalitaire dans le Tiers Monde', in G. Hermet (ed.), *Totalitarismes* (Paris: Economica, 1984); and, of course, 'Civil Society in Africa', in Chabal 1986.
2. On civil society: P. Clastres, *La société contre l'État* (Paris: Editions de Minuit, 1974); C. Lefort, *L'invention démocratique* (Paris: Fayard, 1981); M. Foucault, *La volonté de savoir* (Paris: Gallimard, 1976); M. de Certeau, *L'invention du quotidien* (Paris: UGE, 1980); G. Althabe, *Oppression et libération dans l'imaginaire* (Paris: Maspéro, 1969); M. Augé, *Théorie des pouvoirs et idéologie* (Paris: Hermann, 1975); Coulon, 1981.
3. Bayart, 'La Politique par le bas', op.cit.
4. On an African tyranny, see Liniger-Goumaz, 1989.
5. Bayart in Chabal, 1986, p. 112.
6. Chabal, in Chabal, 1986, p. 15.
7. Chabal, 'Revolutionary Democracy in Africa', in Chabal, 1986.
8. As is well illustrated in Bayart, 1979.
9. See the case of rural dwellers in Hyden, 1980.
10. On counter-hegemonic politics, see Part IV, Chapter 13.
11. See Bayart, in Chabal, 1986, pp. 111–16.
12. For a neat example of stealth, see Hill, 1986, pp. 1–5.
13. Here one will read with profit Richards, 1985.
14. J.-F. Bayart, 'L'Enonciation du politique', *Revue française de science politique*, 35, 3 (1985).
15. On high politics, see Lonsdale in Chabal, 1986, p. 130.
16. On 'delinquency' in Cameroon: Bayart, 1979, p. 136.
17. On what civil society is: Bayart, in Chabal, 1986, p. 112.
18. On political accountability, see Part II, Chapter 3.
19. There is some similarity here with the situation in Eastern Europe before 1990: on how *Solidarity* became the voice of civil society, see Lech Wałesa, *Un chemin d'espoir* (Paris: Fayard, 1987).
20. On students' political role: W. Hanna, *University Students and African Politics* (New York: Africans, 1975); Mbembe, 1985.
21. By 'traditional' I imply no value judgement but only chronology.
22. On tradition and modernity, see Rajni Kothari, 'Tradition and Modernity Revisited', *Government and Opposition*, 3, 3 (1968).

23. See how traditional and modern relate in Kenyatta, 1938.
24. I. Kopytoff (ed.), *The African Frontier* (Bloomington: Indiana University Press, 1987).
25. For an interesting case study, see Wilks, 1975.
26. Particularly ethnicity. See Ranger, 1985b.
27. Mau-Mau is a clear example: R. Buijtenhuijs, *Le mouvement 'Mau-Mau': une révolte paysanne et anticoloniale en Afrique noire* (The Hague: Mouton, 1971); D.L. Barnett and K. Njama, *Mau Mau from Within* (New York: Modern Reader, 1970); C. Rosberg and J. Nottingham, *The Myth of Mau Mau: Nationalism in Kenya* (New York: Praeger, 1966); D. Throup, *Economic and Social Origins of Mau-Mau, 1945–1953* (London: Currey,1987); T. Kanogo, *Squatters and the Roots of Mau-Mau, 1905–1963* (London: Currey, 1987).
28. See here Cabral's comments in 'Resistência Cultural', in *Analise de Alguns Tipos de Resistência* (Lisbon: Seara Nova, 1974).
29. For a useful discussion of the 'traditional', see Mbembe, 1988, particularly his reading of witchcraft, pp. 64–5.
30. On India: L. and S. Rudolph, *The Modernity of Tradition* (Chicago: University of Chicago Press, 1967); E. Shils, *The Indian Intellectual between Tradition and Modernity* (The Hague: Mouton, 1961); M. Singer, *When a Great Tradition Modernizes* (London: Pall Mall, 1972).
31. See in this respect Apter, 1965.
32. I develop this point in Part IV, Chapter 12.
33. Hence the overreaction today when commentators decry the 'backward' quality of African politics. See Notes, Part I, Introduction, n. 1.
34. See Part II, Chapter 4.
35. See Lloyd, 1966.
36. See Kasfir, 1976; Ranger, 'The Invention of Tradition in Colonial Africa', in Hobsbawn and Ranger, 1983; Vail, 1989.
37. See Hyden, 1980.
38. Bayart in Chabal, 1986, p. 111.
39. Ibid.
40. Hence, the resort to 'traditional ideologies'. One case: J.T.V.M. de Jong, 'Jangue Jangue', *Politique africaine*, 28 (1987).
41. On the state's economic power in Zaïre: MacGaffey,1987.
42. In Equatorial Guinea production virtually ceased: Liniger-Goumaz, 1989.
43. N. Kasfir, 'State, Magendo and Class Formation in Uganda', in Kasfir, 1984.
44. See MacGaffey,1987.
45. R. Jeffries, 'Ghana', in Cruise O'Brien *et al.*, 1989, and a special issue on Guinea: *Politique africaine*, 36 (1989).
46. See Munslow, 1986.
47. See J. Lonsdale (ed.), *South Africa in Question* (London: Currey, 1988).
48. Bayart in Chabal, 1986, p. 119.
49. See Markovitz, 1987.
50. As Chazan *et al.*, 1988, have done.
51. As Bayart, 1979, chapter 7, does with profit.
52. See M. Watts, *Silent Violence* (Berkeley: University of California Press, 1983).
53. Iliffe, 1987; Polly Hill, *Dry Grain Farming Families* (Cambridge: Cambridge University Press, 1982).
54. Hill, 1986, chapter 8.

55. Ibid., p. 1.
56. Lan, 1985.
57. Ranger, 1985a.
58. See Note 51.
59. See Crummey, 1986.
60. I discuss production in Part II, Chapter 6.
61. See Bayart's 'Cameroon', in Cruise O'Brien *et al.*, 1989.
62. Bayart, 'La Revanche des sociétés africaines', *op.cit.*
63. Mbembe, 1988, chapter 6.
64. For a case study of 'corruption', see Le Vine, 1975.

Chapter 6   Production

1. Lonsdale in Chabal 1986, pp.126–7.
2. Crummey & Stewart, 1981; Hindess & Hirst, 1975; A. Foster-Carter, 'The Modes of Production Controversy', *New Left Review*, 107 (1978).
3. This chapter is partly an attempt to discuss production other than in Marxist terms. See Part I, Chapter 1. Section 2.
4. Bayart also emphasises the importance of physical geography for political analysis, in Chabal, 1986, p. 114.
5. For definitions, see Paul Sweezy, *The Theory of Capitalist Development* (New York: Modern Reader,1968), chapters 2 and 3.
6. On exchange, trade and imperialism, ibid, part IV.
7. On technology and ecology: J. Goody, *Technology, Tradition and the State in Africa* (Oxford: Oxford University Press,1971); J. Ford, *The Role of the Trypanosomiases in African Ecology* (Oxford: Oxford University Press, 1971).
8. D. Seddon (ed.), *Relations of Production* (London: Cass, 1978); R. Law, 'Slaves, Trade and Taxes: the Material Base of Political Power in Precolonial Africa', *Research in Economic Anthropology*, 1 (1978).
9. For one case study: Curtin, 1975.
10. For one case study, see Richard Waller, 'The Lords of East Africa: The Maasai in the mid-nineteenth century, c. 1840–1885' (Cambridge University, PhD Thesis, 1978).
11. C. Meillassoux (ed.), *The Development of Indigenous Trade and Markets in West Africa* (Oxford: Oxford University Press, 1971) and *L'esclavage en Afrique précoloniale* (Paris: Maspéro. 1975).
12. See Wallerstein, 1976.
13. Fernand Braudel, *The Mediterranean and the Mediterranean World in the Age of Philip II* (2 vols, London: Collins, 1972 and 1973) and *Capitalism and Material Life, 1400–1800* (London: Fontana, 1974).
14. On Asante, see: Wilks, 1975; T.C. McCaskie, 'Accumulation, Wealth and Belief in Asante History', *Africa*, 53 (1983).
15. Ibid.
16. Goody, op.cit.
17. On Science in China, see the excellent *Science and Civilisation in China* series published by Cambridge University Press.
18. See Hill, 1963.
19. For the background to one part of Africa, see Hopkins, 1973.
20. See, for example, Richards, 1985.

21. J. Lonsdale, 'The European Scramble and Conquest in African History', in R. Oliver and G.N. Sanderson (eds), *The Cambridge History of Africa*, vol. 6 (Cambridge: Cambridge University Press, 1985).
22. See Rey, 1971.
23. On labour policies and taxation: B. Fetter, *Colonial Rule and Regional Imbalance in Central Africa* (Boulder: Westview, 1983).
24. Hopkins, 1973.
25. See Gellner, 1983.
26. See Note 2 above.
27. Suret-Canale, 1988, pp. 1–24; Coquery-Vidrovitch, 1969.
28. See Hopkins' argument here (Hopkins, 1973).
29. On this, see Wallerstein, 1974 and 1980. Two cases: A. Latham, *Old Calabar, 1600–1891* (Oxford: Clarendon Press, 1973) and R. Law, *The Oyo Empire c.1600–c.1836* (Oxford: Clarendon Press, 1977).
30. On slavery, see Lovejoy, 1983.
31. For one example, see McCaskie, op.cit.
32. Particularly *vis-à-vis* their 'barons'. See L.A. Fallers, *The King's Men* (Oxford: Oxford University Press, 1964).
33. See Iliffe, 1987.
34. For a most instructive case study, see Iliffe, 1979.
35. See here Lonsdale, 1981, pp. 189–91.
36. For an area affected by migrant labour, see First, 1983.
37. For a case study of Kenya, see Kitching, 1980.
38. On migrant labour and bride-price, see First, 1983.
39. On the sale of land, see Hill, 1986, chapter 13. Also B. Freund, 'Labor and Labor History in Africa: a Review of the Literature', *African Studies Review*, 27, 2 (1984).
40. See the illuminating case study of Kenya in Kitching, 1980.
41. See my discussion of class theory in Part I, Chapter 1, 'Paradigms Lost', section 2.
42. See here Robin Cohen, 'From Peasants to Workers', in Gutkind and Wallerstein, (eds), *The Political Economy of Contemporary Africa* (Beverley Hills: Sage, 1976); Sandbrook and Cohen, 1975.
43. For an interesting, if untypical, case study, see Vail & White, 1980. For another example, see Bruce Berman and John Lonsdale, 'Crisis of Accumulation, Coercion and the Colonial State', *Canadian Journal of African Studies*, 14, 1 (1980).
44. For one example see Colin Leys, *European Politics in Southern Rhodesia* (Oxford: Oxford University Press, 1959).
45. Contrast Kitching, 1980, and Leys, 1975.
46. Hopkins, 1973; Rimmer, 1984.
47. See John Tosh, 'The Cash Crop Revolution in Tropical Africa: an Agricultural Reappraisal', *African Affairs*, 79, vol 314 (1980).
48. Hill, 1963.
49. On France's colonies, see: Hopkins, 1973; Marseille, 1984.
50. For a general overview, see Fieldhouse, 1986.
51. On Zambia, see D. Philip, *Africanisation, Nationalisation and Inequality* (Cambridge: Department of Applied Economics, 1979).
52. Unless, that is, emigration is seen as production. For Mozambique, contrast

António Rita-Ferreira, *O Movimento Migratório de Trabalhadores entre Moçambique e a África do Sul* (Lisbon: Junta de Investigações do Ultramar, 1963) and First, 1983.

53. Ben Turok, *Development in Zambia* (London: Zed Press, 1979).
54. Here, Nigeria provides perhaps the most striking example. See, J.K. Onoh, *The Nigerian Oil Economy* (London: Croom Helm, 1983).
55. Compare Hopkins, 1973, and Samir Amin, *L'Afrique de l'Ouest bloquée* (Paris: Editions de Minuit, 1971).
56. On the case of Ghana, see Beckman, 1976.
57. On Ghana: Hill, 1963. On the Ivory Coast: R. Hecht, 'Cocoa and the Dynamics of Socio-Economic Change in Southern Ivory Coast', Cambridge University, Ph.D. thesis, 1981. On São Tomé: Clarence-Smith, 1985.
58. Here, see Fieldhouse, 1986, chapter 2.
59. Fieldhouse argues that, on balance, it is the policies of post-colonial African governments rather than their weaknesses within the international economy which explain their 'arrested development'.
60. See Bates, 1981 and 1983.
61. There is still debate on how successful green revolutions in fact were in Asia. On Africa, see Richards, 1985.
62. Amilcar Cabral, 1980, pp. 125–6.

PART III   THE CONSTRUCTION OF THE AFRICAN POST-COLONIAL ORDER

Chapter 7   The Crisis of Nationality and Sovereignty

1. Different from L. Binder *et al.*, 1971.
2. Anderson, 1983; Hobsbawn and Ranger, 1983.
3. See also: F.H. Hinsley, *Nationalism and the International System* (London: Hodder & Stoughton, 1973); Mudimbe, 1988.
4. Which Marxism failed to recognise. See: Ronaldo Munck, *The Difficult Dialogue: Marxism and Nationalism* (London: Zed Press, 1986); J. Breuilly, *Nationalism and the State* (Manchester: Manchester University Press, 1982); H.B. Davis, *Toward a Marxist Theory of Nationalism* (New York: Monthly Review Press, 1978).
5. A revisionist view: Seal in J. Gallagher *et al.*, *Locality, Province and Nation* (Cambridge: Cambridge University Press, 1973).
6. For a comparative analysis, see Munck, op.cit., chapter 6.
7. Anderson, 1983.
8. See Part II, Chapter 4.
9. J. Breuilly, op.cit.; Gellner, 1983.
10. A. Smith, *State and Nation in the Third World* (Brighton: Wheatsheaf Books, 1983).
11. Hinsley, op.cit.; Gellner, 1983.
12. E. Saïd, *The Question of Palestine* (London: RKP, 1980).
13. J. Lonsdale (ed.), *South Africa in Question* (London: Currey, 1988).
14. True even of Liberia which never was a colony *stricto sensu*.

15. Nationalities which were viable, as shown in Wilks, 1975.
16. O. Aluko, *The Foreign Policies of African States* (London: Hodder & Stoughton, 1977).
17. T. Shaw and O. Aluko (eds), *Nigerian Foreign Policy* (New York: St. Martin's Press, 1984).
18. Tony Hodges, *Sahara Occidental* (Paris: L'Harmattan, 1987); Markakis, 1987; Buijtenhuijs, 1987.
19. See for Kenya, Kenyatta's seminal *Facing Mount Kenya* (1938).
20. Yves Person, 'Samori and Resistance to the French', in R. Rotberg and A. Mazrui (eds), *Protest and Power in Black Africa* (New York: Oxford University Press, 1972). On Mozambique: Isaacman, 1976.
21. Donal Cruise O'Brien, 1971.
22. N. Chazan 'Ethnicity and Politics in Ghana', *Political Science Quarterly*, 47, 3 (1982); Ben Amonoo, *Ghana 1957–1966* (London: Allen & Unwin, 1981). On Guinea: Suret-Canale, 1988, pp. 148–78.
23. D. Low, *Baganda in Modern History* (London: Weidenfeld, 1971).
24. See here, for example, Joseph, 1987
25. Duignan and Jackson, 1986; Foy, 1988.
26. A. Cabral, *Analise de Alguns Tipos de Resistência* (Lisbon: Seara Nova, 1974).
27. W. Whiteley, 'Language Policies of Independent African States', in T. Sebeok (ed.), *Current Trends in Linguistics*, vol. 7 (The Hague: Mouton, 1971).
28. A. Lestage, *Literacy and Illiteracy* (Paris: UNESCO, 1982).
29. E. Lisboa, 'Education in Angola and Mozambique', in Brian Rose (ed.), *Education in Southern Africa* (London: Macmillan, 1970).
30. With the exception of Swahili in Tanzania and Kenya.
31. A process in which Angola's Pepetela, for example, is actively engaged. See his *A Revolta da Casa dos Ídolos* (Lisbon: Edições 70, 1980) and *Mayombe* (Lisbon: Edições 70, 1979).
32. Russell Hamilton, *Literature Africana: Literature Necesária*, vol. 1 (Lisbon: Edições 70, 1981), introduction.
33. Ngugi wa Thiongo, 1982 and 1985 and 'The Language of African Literature', *New Left Review*, 125 (1985).
34. For a Marxist perspective on Ngugi, see Amuta, 1990.
35. D. Martin, *L'héritage de Kenyatta* (Paris: L'Harmattan, 1985).
36. On South Africa, see: Lonsdale, *op. cit.*; H. Adam and K. Moodley, *South Africa without Apartheid* (Berkeley: University of California Press, 1986); R. Price and C. Rosberg (eds), *The Apartheid Regime* (Berkeley: International Studies, 1980).
37. Anderson, 1983.
38. T. Nairn, *The Break-Up of Britain* (London: New Left, 1977).
39. A heavily overworked area of African politics. For one example, see D. Smock and K. Bentsi-Enchill (eds), *The Search for National Integration in Africa* (New York: Free Press, 1975).
40. For a coherent approach, see Naomi Chazan *et al.*, 1988.
41. See: Foy, 1988; D. Meintel, *Race, Culture and Portuguese Colonialism in Cabo Verde* (Syracuse: Syracuse University, 1984).
42. Here see Crawford Young, 1976.
43. In this connection, see Rothchild and Chazan, 1988.
44. Also neglected by the editors (Cruise O'Brien *et al.*, 1989).

45. M. Crowder (ed.), *The Cambridge History of Africa*, vol. 8 (Cambridge: Cambridge University Press, 1984).
46. H. Kohn, *Nationalism: its Meaning and History* (New York: Van Nostrand, 1955).
47. A. Mazrui and M. Tidy, *Nationalism and New States in Africa* (London: Heinemann, 1984).
48. J. Ajayi and M. Crowder, *History of West Africa*, vol. 2 (London: Longman, 1988).
49. See the need in post-communist Eastern Europe and the Soviet Union to reconnect with the pre-communist, nationalist, period.
50. On 'civilising missions', see Lonsdale in Chabal, 1986.
51. For a revealing discussion, see Kasfir, 1976.
52. Nowhere more dramatically than in Angola. See Marcum, 1969 and 1978.
53. For a study of the possible meaning of divide and rule in India, see Farzana Shaikh, *Community and Consensus in Islam* (Cambridge: Cambridge University Press, 1989).
54. Presented with clarity in Chazan *et al.*, 1988.
55. See Part II, Chapter 3.
56. Donald Rothchild, 'State-Ethnic Relation in Middle Africa', in G. Carter and P. O'Meara (eds), *African Independence: the First Twenty-Five Years* (Bloomington: Indiana University Press, 1985).
57. On this instrumental notion of ethnicity, see Enloe, 1973.
58. As Anderson, 1983, shows.
59. Hinsley, op cit.
60. John Markakis, 1987. Although, following the collapse of the Ethiopian regime in 1991, Eritrea may become independent.
61. Spanish Sahara, Sudan, Ethiopia and Somalia – all cases of very peculiar colonial circumstances.
62. Despite strong ethnic divisions, none of the contenders for power in Liberia has suggested partitioning the country.
63. Regime opposition is in part protest against such rigidities.
64. Anderson, 1983.
65. Bayart, in Chabal, 1986.

Chapter 8   the Crisis of Legitimacy and Representation

1. Gifford and Louis, 1982.
2. On the relation between power and nationalism, see Anderson, 1983; Hobsbawn & Ranger, 1983 and Gellner, 1983.
3. For two different views on the relationship between representation and legitimacy, see: Jürgen Habermas, *Legitimation Crisis* (Boston: Beacon Press 1975); Pitkin, 1972.
4. For one example of this process, in the Portuguese colonies of Guinea and Cape Verde, see Chabal, 1983.
5. In Angola, the fact that Portugal had to hand over the power to the Movimento de la Libertação de Angola (MPLA) meant that the MPLA became the 'legitimate' inheritor of the colonial state – even if that was contested by its competitors and some foreign countries. Revealing about this transfer of power is Ryszard Kapuscinski, *Another Day of Life* (London: Picador, 1987).

6. See Côte d'Ivoire's decolonisation in Zolberg, 1964.
7. The nationalist parties from the Portuguese African colonies which eventually emerged as the 'legitimate' governments were those which were diplomatically most successful. See here Chabal, 1983.
8. See the case of French Guinea in, for example, B. Ameillon, *La Guinée: bilan d'une indépendance* (Paris: Maspéro, 1964).
9. A process particularly well illustrated by Sékou Touré's behaviour in the years after independence. See here Ladipo Adamolekun, *Sékou Touré's Guinea* (London: Methuen, 1976).
10. See Theda Skocpol, *States and Social Revolutions* (Cambridge: Cambridge University Press, 1979).
11. Notions which are rarely discussed in what are otherwise useful books on African politics: Tangri, 1985; Chazan *et al.*, 1988.
12. See Part II, Chapter 3.
13. As Lonsdale does in 'Political Accountability in African History', in Chabal, 1986.
14. Nor did it have deep roots in what is called, for lack of a more useful expression, the political 'traditions' of Africa.
15. And eventually closer to what was, dismissively, referred to as the practices of 'traditional Africa'.
16. The extent to which the so-called politics of patrimonialism are in fact expressions of what I call the Africanisation of politics is crucial. See Part IV, Chapter 12, and Mbembe, 1988.
17. See, for Cameroon, Bayart, 1979.
18. Lonsdale, 'Political Accountability' op.cit.
19. Claiming that particularistic representation would mean the break-up of the nation. On the Mozambican case, see Geffray,1990.
20. Seen in the increasing frequency of coups. Decalo,1976.
21. For a comparative examination, see Rosberg & Callaghy,1979.
22. The case of Nigeria epitomises the process by which military (political) power is generated. See Luckham, 1971.
23. Although at the time the militarisation of politics was seen by some as evidence of 'modernisation'. See Huntington, 1968.
24. The two arguments combined in notions such as 'democratic representation within the one-party state'. See Zolberg, 1966.
25. On patrimonialism and prebendalism, see Joseph, 1987.
26. On clientelism, see René Lemarchand, 'Political Clientelism and Ethnicity in Tropical Africa: Competing Solidarities in Nation Building', *American Political Science Review*, 76, 1 (1972).
27. For one interesting case-study of these linkages, see John Dunn and A.F. Robertson, *Dependence and Opportunity: Political Change in Ahafo* (Cambridge: Cambridge University Press, 1973).
28. See, for example, Baynham, 1986.
29. For an overview, see Sandbrook, 1985.
30. On the meanings of civil society, see Part II, Chapter 5.
31. McGaffey, 1987.
32. I emphasise again that these dichotomies between state and civil society only apply in a formal, conceptual sense. In real life, individuals straddle the two. See Part IV, Chapter 13.

33. Jean-François Bayart, 'La revanche des sociétés africaines', *Politique africaine*, 11 (1983).
34. The moves towards multi-party democracy are, of course, also a consequence of the recent events in Eastern Europe.
35. See Richard Sklar, 'Democracy in Africa', in Chabal, 1986.
36. Richard Sklar, 'Developmental Democracy', *Comparative Studies in Society and History*, 29, 4 (1987).
37. World Bank, *Financing Development with Growth in Sub-Saharan Africa, 1986–1990* (Washington DC: World Bank, 1986).
38. The moves towards multi-party democracy in countries like, say, Cape Verde and Zaïre are totally different. One cannot conceive that Mobutu would allow the defeat of his ruling party.
39. Achebe is particularly interesting in this respect. See Carroll, 1990 and Innes, 1990.
40. Ngugi wa Thiong'o, 1982 and 1985.
41. See the continued importance of the notion of the 'traditional' Russian political community in the political debate (e.g., Solzhenitsyn) now taking place in the Soviet Union.
42. See Sklar, 'Democracy in Africa', op.cit. Traditional here means nothing other than 'grounded in the deep history of the political community'.
43. John Dunn, 'The Politics of Representation and Good Government in Post-colonial Africa', in Chabal, 1986.
44. I develop this point further in Part IV, Chapter 12.
45. Which is what Callaghy attempts to do in his 'Politics and Vision in Africa', in Chabal, 1986.
46. See here a similar plea, Achille Mbembe, 'Pouvoir, violence et accumulation', *Politique africaine*, 39 (1990).
47. By which I also mean formal aspects of political legitimacy losing ground to informal ones.
48. A good example of this is the reascendancy of so-called traditional chiefs in Mozambique. See Geffray,1990.
49. The most useful study on representation is Pitkin, 1972.
50. See here my discussion in Part II, Chapter 2.
51. See: A.H. Birch, *Representation* (London: Pall Mall, 1971); Pateman, 1970; Dunn, 1979; Young, 1976.
52. See: Hal Draper, *Karl Marx's Theory of Revolution* (New York: Monthly Review Press, 1977); Avineri, 1971.
53. See Dunn, 1979.
54. This finds an echo in the limited and limiting notions of identity which a focus on ethnicity imposes. See Kasfir, 1976.
55. For one well-illustrated example of how little it managed to achieve in this respect, see Lan, 1985.

Chapter 9   The Crisis of Accumulation and Inequality

1. Sara Berry, 'The Food Crisis and Agrarian Change in Africa', *African Studies Review*, 26, 2 (1983); Ravenhill, 1986; S. Commins *et al.*, *Africa's Agrarian Crisis; the Roots of Famine* (Boulder: Westview Press, 1986); M. Glantz (ed.),

Famine in Africa (Cambridge: Cambridge University Press, 1987). See also the various World Bank reports.

2. Jacques Giri, *L'Afrique en panne* (Paris: Karthala, 1988) and, for a very revealing African view, Tidiane Diakité, *L'Afrique malade d'elle même* (Paris: Karthala, 1986). On famine, see Sen, 1981.

3. Rimmer, 1984; Bates, 1981 and 1983; Austen, 1987.

4. John Dunn, 'The Politics of Representation and Good Government in Post-colonial Africa', in Chabal, 1986.

5. For some recent books: Foy, 1988; Contamin and Fauré, 1990.

6. For a provocative view, see Achille Mbembe, 'Pouvoir, violence et accumulation', *Politique africaine*, 39 (1990).

7. On the link between ideology and 'development', Young, 1982. On that between inequality and injustice, Barrington Moore, 1979.

8. For the Marxist perspective, Paul Baran, *The Political Economy of Growth* (New York: Modern Reader, 1957). For a masterly account of inequality, see Gunnar Myrdal, *Asian Drama*, vol. 1 (New York: Pantheon, 1968), chapter 12.

9. See Note 1; Martin Fransman (ed.), *Industry and Accumulation in Africa* (London: Heinemann, 1982); Hart, 1980; Tore Rose (ed.), *Crisis and Recovery in Sub-Saharan Africa* (Paris: OECD, 1985).

10. On the former, Chazan *et al.*, 1988; on the latter, Fieldhouse, 1986.

11. For the 'nationalist' perspective, Rodney, 1972.

12. On the imperialism of the weak, Clarence-Smith, 1985.

13. For two views: Hopkins, 1973; Frederick Cooper, 'Africa and the World Economy', *African Studies Review*, 25, 2/3 (1981).

14. How limited is debatable. Fieldhouse, 1986; Amin, 1972.

15. For a summary of such arguments, see Fieldhouse, 1986.

16. Compare the economies of settler and non-settler colonies.

17. An analysis increasingly common among Africans: Anyang' Nyong'o, 1987; Oyugi *et al.*, 1988; Mbembe, 1988.

18. In relation to agriculture, see Bates, 1983.

19. For one recent view, see J.-F. Médard, 'L'État patrimonialisé', in *Politique africaine*, 39 (1990).

20. World Bank, *Financing Development with Growth in Sub-Saharan Africa, 1986–1990* (Washington DC: World Bank, 1986).

21. On the impact of structural adjustment, Duruflé, 1988.

22. René Dumont and Marie-France Mottin, *L'Afrique étranglée* (Paris: Seuil, 1980).

23. Richard Sklar, 'Democracy in Africa', in Chabal, 1986.

24. It is debatable whether any African régime has ever seriously contemplated primitive accumulation. See Munslow, 1986.

25. On Ghana, Beckman, 1976.

26. See here, for example, Bates, 1983.

27. Fieldhouse, 1986, p. 242.

28. Ghana is interesting: Naomi Chazan, *The Anatomy of Ghanaian Politics* (Boulder: Westview Press, 1983); E. Rado, 'Notes towards a Political Economy of Ghana today', *African Affairs*, 85, vol. 341 (1986).

29. For some background, Fieldhouse, 1986, chapter 3.

30. Dumont & Mottin, op.cit., pp. 234–47; A. Coulson, *Tanzania: a Political economy* (Oxford: Oxford University Press, 1982).

31. On Ghana: Chazan, op.cit., R. Jeffries, 'Ghana', in Cruise O'Brien *et al.*, 1989.

On Guinea: A. Morice, 'Guinée 1985: État, corruption et trafics', *Temps Modernes*, February 1987.

32. J. Rweyemanu, *Underdevelopment and Industrialization in Tanzania* (Nairobi, 1973). See also, Coulson, op.cit.
33. In this connexion, see Ajit Singh, 'Industrialization in Africa: a Structuralist View', in Martin Fransman, op.cit.
34. See here, on the Côte d'Ivoire, Contamin and Fauré, 1990.
35. For a summary of the argument, Fieldhouse, 1986.
36. For an example of this argument, Bates, 1981 and 1983.
37. Observe the change in the World Bank position.
38. Bates, 1983.
39. *Guardian*, 3 January 1989.
40. For one example, see John Vidal, 'Losing Confidence in the Aid Trick', *Guardian*, 21 September 1990.
41. On our fears, see Francis Gendreau and Émile Le Bris, 'Les grandes peurs de l'an 2000', *Politique africaine*, 39 (1990).
42. See Sandbrook,1985.
43. On an exceedingly poor if not unviable, country: Claudette Savonnet-Guyot, *État et sociétés au Burkina* (Paris: Karthala, 1986).
44. For a case study of such 'resolution', Bayart, 1979.
45. See the connection between my notion of the productive use of inequality and Lonsdale's notion of 'civilising mission'.
46. O. Hirschman, *The Strategy of Economic Development* (New Haven: Yale University Press, 1958).
47. Achieved by peaceful or violent means. See Warren, 1980.
48. For a historian's view, Iliffe, 1983.
49. Contrast Iliffe, 1983 and 1987.
50. Compare Fieldhouse, 1986, chapter 2, and Amin, 1973.
51. One of the most useful comparative books is Barrington Moore, 1966. See also Skocpol,1979.
52. See above, Part II, Chapter 6.
53. See Iliffe, 1983.
54. See Lloyd, 1966.
55. Frantz Fanon, 1965 and 1967.
56. On the Côte d'Ivoire, see Y.-A. Fauré & J.-F. Médard (eds), *État et bourgeoisie en Côte d'Ivoire* (Paris: Karthala, 1982).
57. On, for example, Tanzania, see Coulson, op.cit.
58. While this gap grew sharper, new strategies were devised to allow civil society to penetrate the state. See Part IV, Chapter 13.
59. See here P. Duignan and L.H. Gann (eds), *Colonialism in Africa*, vol. 4 (Cambridge: Cambridge University Press, 1975).
60. Fieldhouse, 1986, would probably disagree here.
61. For the French case, see Marseille, 1984.
62. Compare D. Fieldhouse, *Unilever Overseas* (London: Allen & Unwin, 1978) with C. Coquery-Vidrovitch, 'SCOA et CFAO dans l'Ouest Africain, 1910–1965', *Journal of African History*, 16, 4 (1975).
63. For an overview, see Fieldhouse, 1986, chapter 1.
64. An illusion of post-war social policies in Western Europe.
65. A process neatly summarised in Duruflé, 1988, pp. 7–9.

66. G.-F. Gakosso, *La réalité congolaise* (Paris: La Pensée universelle, 1983); B. Hughes, *Le Congo* (Paris: Maspéro, 1975).
67. On the instructive Kenyan case, Kitching, 1980.
68. A point lost on those who advocate state-led development.

Chapter 10   The Crisis of Good Government and Political Morality

1. The question of the morality of politics ought not to be confined to the 'Third World'; it applies to all polities.
2. R. Sklar, 'Democracy in Africa' and M. Staniland 'Democracy and Ethnocentrism', in Chabal, 1986.
3. S. Hamsphire (ed.), *Public and Private Morality* (Cambridge: Cambridge University Press, 1975); A. Sen and B. Williams (eds), *Utilitarianism and Beyond* (Cambridge: Cambridge University Press, 1982).
4. Up to the early seventies, the study of African politics in France was often limited to the study of constitutionalist politics.
5. For one possible example, see Amnesty International, 'Mozambique: the Human Rights Record, 1975–1989: Recent Government Measures', AI Index: AFR 41/01/89 (London, 1989).
6. For example, corruption. See V. Le Vine.
7. Remember General Westmoreland saying that killing Vietnamese was 'acceptable' because they had a different notion of life.
8. One must include Chomsky's obfuscations on the Khmer Rouge.
9. For a truly appalling case, see Liniger-Goumaz, 1989.
10. D. Parfit, *Reasons and Persons* (Oxford: Clarendon Press, 1984).
11. J. Dunn, 'The Politics of Representation and Good Government in Post-colonial Africa', in Chabal, 1986, p. 169.
12. Ibid.
13. Op.cit.
14. Here see J. Dunn, 1984.
15. World Bank, *Financing Development with Growth in Sub-Saharan Africa, 1986–1990* (Washington DC: World Bank, 1986).
16. Young, 1982, was hampered by definitional problems.
17. J. Dunn, 'The Politics of Representation', op.cit., p. 173.
18. For an uneven summary of the governmental performance of many of these countries, see Duignan and Jackson, 1986. For a more useful comparative survey, see Collier, 1982.
19. 'Third World' countries have not had the same continuity of political independence as European and North American states.
20. Anderson, 1983; Gellner, 1983.
21. Lee, 1967.
22. For an overview of Portuguese colonial rule, Newitt, 1981.
23. T Smith, 'A Comparative Study of French and British Decolonization', *Comparative Studies in Society and History*, 20, 1 (1978).
24. Fieldhouse, 1986.
25. On various forms of colonial rule: Hodgkin,1956.
26. France had no settler colonies in Black Africa; the relevant comparison with the British settler colonies would be Algeria.
27. See here P. Duignan and L.H. Gann (eds), *Colonialism in Africa*, vol. 4 (Cambridge: Cambridge University Press, 1975).

28. On colonial and post-colonial economic policy, Fieldhouse, 1988, p. 245.
29. A. Lestage, *Literacy and Illiteracy* (Paris: UNESCO, 1982).
30. The importance of middle-ranking managers to good government is nowhere better illustrated than in Cape Verde: Foy, 1988.
31. For a comparative overview, Duignan and Jackson, 1986.
32. Guinea-Bissau is a clear illustration of this proposition: Chabal, 'Revolutionary Democracy in Africa' in Chabal, 1986.
33. See Part II, Chapter 4.
34. J. Dunn, 'The Politics of Representation' op.cit.
35. W. Cohen, 1971.
36. Lee, 1967.
37. Hodgkin, 1956.
38. For the colonial period: Robinson and Gallagher, 1961. For the post-colonial period: C. Clapham (ed.), *Private Patronage and Public Power* (London: Pinter, 1983).
39. For an overview, M. Crowder (ed.), *The Cambridge History of Africa*, vol. 8 (Cambridge: Cambridge University Press, 1984).
40. Bayart, 'Civil Society in Africa', in Chabal, 1986, p.113.
41. In, say, the Gold Coast and Côte d'Ivoire, colonial government found it expedient to jail the nationalist leaders before acknowledging the depth of their support in the country.
42. See above, Part II, Chapter 4.
43. The record of Côte d'Ivoire is in this respect interesting because it is so ambiguous: Y. Fauré and J.-F. Médard (eds), *État et bourgeoisie en Côte d'Ivoire* (Paris: Karthala, 1982).
44. See Part II, Chapter 4.
45. Among one of the most perverse examples of the utilisation of the colonial inheritance was the decision by the Frelimo government in Mozambique to transform the Portuguese 'strategic hamlets' into model 'cooperative' villages. Geffray, 1990.
46. The reasons why this occurred are important and should be examined in detail. For a discussion of the relevance of what I call political Africanisation, see Part IV, Chapter 12.
47. On one case of administration weakness: Galli & Jones, 1987.
48. In Senegal, white civil servants served under Senghor and even Diouf. G. Hesseling, *Histoire politique du Sénégal: institutions, droit et société* (Paris: Karthala, 1985).
49. Ghana illustrates the problem: R. Price, *Society and Bureaucracy in Contemporary Ghana* (Berkeley and Los Angeles: University of California Press, 1975).
50. See a recent biography of Lumumba: J.-C. Willame, *Patrice Lumumba: la crise congolaise revisitée* (Paris: Karthala, 1990).
51. See J. Dunn, 'The Politics of Representation', op.cit.
52. On the demands placed on socialist regimes, Dunn, 1984.
53. On this issue, Bates, 1981.
54. One should not be too naïve here. Now that even a country like Côte d'Ivoire is in deep trouble, it is easy to see how poor government at times has been. Contamin and Fauré, 1990.
55. On the prebendal dimension, Joseph, 1987.
56. The most extreme form of such developments can be found in countries like Angola and Mozambique (Geffray, 1990; Cahen, 1987).

57. Newitt, 1981.
58. On how patronage, corruption, forms an important cement between the state and civil society, see Part IV, Chapter 13.
59. J. Dunn, 'The Politics of Representation' op.cit., p. 174.

Chapter 11   The Crisis of Violence and Survival

1. For a debatable view on the misery of the 'Third World', P. Harrison, *Inside the Third World* (Harmondsworth: Penguin, 1984).
2. Sen, 1981, and 'The Standard of Living', in *The Tanner Lectures, 1985* (Cambridge: Cambridge University Press, 1987).
3. A legacy of the notion of Africa as the 'dark continent'?
4. See particularly, Mbembe, 1985 and 1988.
5. It is well here not to forget the violence unleashed by decolonisation, nor that the most violent state in Africa has long been South Africa, a state run entirely by whites.
6. A belief held by those who think that Africans are 'culturally' violent and also implicit in teleological views of evolution.
7. For an economic overview, Hopkins, 1973.
8. Fieldhouse, 1986.
9. M. Staniland, in Chabal, 1986.
10. Some liberals who earlier justified the excesses of African governments now see in the African 'crisis' a fulfilment of their newly held view that Africa is inherently incapable of developing.
11. The idea that India was somehow more 'civilised' than Africa is breaking down in the face of communal violence, showing how illusory it is to explain violence in 'relativist' cultural terms.
12. Barrington Moore, *Reflections on the Causes of Human Misery* (Boston: Beacon Press, 1970).
13. See Part II, Chapter 6, and Part IV, Chapter 14.
14. On the Zaïrean economy: W. Leslie, *The World Bank and Structural Transformation in Developing Countries: the Case of Zaïre* (Boulder: Rienner, 1987); World Bank, *Zaïre: Current Economic Situation and Constraints* (Washington DC, 1980).
15. On Africa's dependence, see Part IV, Chapter 14.
16. For a sharp view of Africa's constraints, Fieldhouse, 1986.
17. Duruflé, 1988.
18. For a provocative view on aid, see K. Borgin and K. Corbett, *The Destruction of a Continent* (New York: Harcourt, 1982).
19. Chabal, 'Revolutionary Democracy in Africa: the Case of Guinea-Bissau', in Chabal, 1986; Galli and Jones, 1987.
20. Sen, 1981.
21. Part IV, Chapter 14.
22. Duruflé, 1988.
23. In Ghana, Rawlings embraced structural adjustment: R. Jeffries, 'Ghana', in Cruise O'Brien *et al.*, 1989.
24. The riots and demonstrations which follow the implementation of structural adjustment suggest opposition.
25. On political accountability, see Part II, Chapter 3.

26. On the role of the state, see Part II, Chapter 4.
27. Paul Richards, 'Ecological Change and the Politics of African Land Use', *African Studies Review*, 26, 2 (1983).
28. S. Berry, 'The Food Crisis and Agrarian Change in Africa', *African Studies Review*, 27, 2 (1984); D. Requier-Desjardins, *L'alimentation en Afrique* (Paris: Karthala, 1989).
29. For an historical overview, Iliffe, 1987.
30. G. Myrdal, *Asian Drama*, vol. 1 (New York: Pantheon, 1968), chapters 10 and 12.
31. Iliffe, 1987.
32. With some exceptions, like Cape Verde: Foy, 1988.
33. Sen, 1981.
34. Richards, op.cit.
35. As, say, in Kenya, Zimbabwe and to some extent Lesotho.
36. Hopkins, 1973; Rimmer,1984.
37. See L.H. Genn & P. Duignan, 'Namibia, Botswana, Lesotho and Swaziland', in Duignan & Jackson,1986.
38. See Note 32 above.
39. Clapham, 1988.
40. Markakis, 1987.
41. Geffray, 1990.
42. T. Hodges, *Angola to the 1990s* (London: Economist Intelligence Unit Special Report 1079, 1987).
43. R. Buijtenhuijs, *Le Frolinat et les guerres civiles du Tchad: 1977–1984* (Paris: Karthala, 1987); with reservation, A. Dadi, *Tchad: l'État retrouvé*(Paris: L'Harmattan, 1987).
44. Sen, 1981.
45. Iliffe, 1987.
46. On Liberia and Ghana, see Cruise O'Brien *et al.*, 1989.
47. On the Horn: Markakis, 1974 and 1987. On South Africa: J. Lonsdale (ed.), *South Africa in Question*; H. Adam and K. Moddley, *South Africa without Apartheid* (Berkeley: University of California Press, 1986); T. Callaghy (ed.), *South Africa* (New York: Praeger, 1983); R. Price and C. Rosberg (eds), *The Apartheid Regime* (Berkeley: Institute of International Studies, 1980); T. Lodge, *Black Politics in South Africa since 1945* (London: Longman, 1983).
48. T. Hodges, *Sahara Occidental* (Paris: L'Harmattan, 1987).
49. Markakis, 1987.
50. D. Austin, 'Pax Africana', in Baynham, 1986.
51. On the process of sedimentation, see Anderson, 1983.
52. Or rather to construct a political analysis on the notion of atavistic hostility is to surrender to a primitive explanation.
53. On the nation-state, see Part III, Chapter 7.
54. The analogy also stresses the impossibility of speeding the process of the formation of nation-states. Gellner, 1983.
55. By ascriptive I mean all forms of objective and subjective self-identification and not just, or even primarily, ethnicity.
56. In Mozambique, neither the Portuguese nor the successor state managed to construct a coherent country. To date Mozambique is largely unformed as a nation-state. Geffray, 1990, Cahen, 1987.

57. Lebanon and Sri Lanka were long regarded as paragons of democratic stability. Enloe, 1973.
58. For an African perspective, Mbembe, 1988, pp.142–52.
59. Haile Selassie's government shared the same callous attitude towards famine as the regime which followed, Clapham, 1988.
60. Nguema's bloody tyranny was state terrorism rather than totalitarianism. Liniger-Goumaz, 1989.
61. Mbembe, 1988, focuses too little on passive violence.
62. See here, on good government, Part III, Chapter 10.
63. The process of sedimentation in Africa is easily as 'advanced' as in some East European countries (Yugoslavia, Bulgaria).
64. Luckham, 1971.
65. Diamond, 1988.

PART IV   POLITICAL CHANGE AND CONTINUITY IN CONTEM-PORARY AFRICA

Chapter 12   The Dynamics of Political Africanisation

1. Huntington, 1968.
2. Kasfir, 1976.
3. Hobsbawn and Ranger, 1983; R. Bendix, 'Tradition and modernity reconsidered', *Comparative Studies in Society and History*, IX, 3 (1967); R. Kothari, 'Tradition and Modernity Revisited', *Government and Opposition*, III, 3 (Summer 1968).
4. Perhaps best illustrated in African literature; for example, Pepetela, *Yaka* (Lisbon: Dom Quixote, 1984).
5. A promising start has been made by Chazan *et al.*, 1988.
6. My definition of Africanisation is not Africa focused: it is the universal *process* by which political culture impinges on political change. So that, for example, analysts of Japan could legitimately be interested in the process of 'Nipponification'.
7. Bayart, 1989, pp. 19–61.
8. Isaacman, 1972; M. Newitt, *Portuguese Settlement on the Zambesi* (London: Longman 1973).
9. See D. Birmingham, *The Portuguese Conquest of Angola* (London: Oxford University Press, 1965).
10. A. Hastings, *A History of African Christianity* (Cambridge: Cambridge University Press,1979); M. Fortes & G. Dieterlen (eds), *African Systems of Thought* (London: IAI, 1965).
11. Islam was more easily appropriated by Africans: J.S. Trimingham, *Islam in West Africa* (London: Oxford University Press, 1959); P. Clarke, *West Africa and Islam* (London: Arnold, 1982); M. Hiskett, *The Development of Islam in West Africa* (London: Longman, 1984); C. Coulon, *Les Musulmans et le pouvoir en Afrique* (Paris: Karthala, 1983).
12. On the Japanese 'model': G. L. Bernstein (ed.), *Japan and the World* (London: Macmillan, 1988).

13. Similarly on nationalism: Anderson, 1983.
14. Dunn, 1979, chapter 1. On some notions of the individuai: C. Piault *et al.*, *Prophétisme et thérapeutique* (Paris: Hermann, 1975); L. Dumont, *Homo hierarchicus* (Paris: Gallimard, 1966).
15. Dunn, 1979, chapter 4.
16. Well illustrated by Kenyatta, 1938.
17. G. Balandier, *Anthropologie politique* (Paris: PUF, 1967) and *Sens et puissance. Les dynamiques sociales* (Paris, PUF,1971).
18. Hodder-Williams, 1984; Chazan *et al.*, 1988, chapter 7.
19. On Mobutu's Zaïre: Callaghy, 1984; M. Schatzberg, *Politics and Class in Zaïre* (New York: Africana Publishing Co., 1980); C. Young and T. Turner, *The Rise and Decline of the Zaïrian State* (Madison: University of Madison Press, 1985); N. Karl-i-Bond, *Mobutu ou l'incarnation du mal* (London: Rex Collings, 1982). On Houphouët-Boigny's Ivory Coast: Y. Fauré and J.-F. Médard, *État et bourgeoisie en Côte d'Ivoire* (Paris: Karthala, 1982); J. Bauli, *La politique intérieure d'Houphouët-Boigny* (Paris: Eurafor Press, 1982); Brigitte Masquet, 'Côte d'Ivoire: pouvoir présidentiel, palabre et démocratie', *Afrique contemporaine*, 114 (1981).
20. Houphouët-Boigny is a master; one example: Parti Democratique de la Côte d'Ivoire (PDCI), *Séminaires d'information et de formation des secrétaires généraux* (Abidjan: Fraternité Hebdo, 1985), pp. 8–10, 11–14.
21. J.-F. Bayart, 'La Politique par le bas en Afrique noire', *Politique africaine*, 1 (1981).
22. Sklar, 'Democracy in Africa', in Chabal, 1986; Barongo, 1983; Oyugi *et al.*, 1988.
23. Zolberg, 1966.
24. On high and low politics: Lonsdale, 'Political Accountability in African History', in Chabal, 1986.
25. Pitkin, 1972; Pateman, 1970.
26. Dunn, 'From Democracy to Representation' in Dunn, 1980.
27. Illustrated in Bayart,1979.
28. On elections: Collier, 1982; Hayward, 1986.
29. J. Dunn and A.F. Robertson, *Dependence and Opportunity* (Cambridge: Cambridge University Press,1973).
30. Le Vine, 1975; M. Ekpo (ed.), *Bureaucratic Corruption in Sub-Saharan Africa* (Washington: University Press of America, 1979).
31. As is evidenced in Jomo Kenyatta, 1938.
32. On wealth and politics:, Bayart, in Chabal 1986, p. 123.
33. On political leadership: Cartwright, 1983; Jackson & Rosberg, 1982; V. Le Vine, 'Leadership Transition in Black Africa', *Munger Africana Library Notes*, 30 (1975); Lancine Sylla, 'Succession of the Charismatic Leader', *Daedalus*, 111, 2 (1982).
34. On legitimacy: Lonsdale, in Chabal, 1986, p. 129.
35. Jackson and Rosberg, 1982.
36. On one case of tyranny: Liniger-Goumaz, 1989.
37. See Notes 30 and 31, pending a real political biography.
38. Such discourses abound. On Zaïre, Schatzberg, *op.cit.*
39. T. Shaw and N. Chazan, 'The Limits of Leadership: Africa in Contemporary World Politics', *International Journal*, 37, 4 (1982).

40. Although it probably has a lot to do with good government.
41. In Ghana in 1971, during a period of conflict between unions and government, commercial workers wore badges displaying: 'Monkey De Work, Baboon De Chop' (small men do the work, big men eat) – quoted in Tangri, 1985, p. 89.
42. Sklar, 'Democratic Theory' in Dunn, 1979; Pateman, 1970.
43. R. Dahl, *A Preface to Democratic Theory* (Chicago: Chicago University Press, 1956) and *Polyarchy* (New Haven: Yale University Press, 1971).
44. On witchcraft and greed, Bayart, 'Civil society in Africa', in Chabal, 1986, p. 123.
45. J. Dunn, 'The Politics of Representation and Good Government in Post-colonial Africa', in Chabal, 1986.
46. Quoted in *Fraternité-Matin*, 29 April 1983, p. 17.
47. Ibid.
48. On Mobutu's wealth, see: Young & Turner, op.cit., pp. 178ff; Callaghy, op.cit., p.179; Schatzberg, op.cit., pp.136ff.
49. Bayart, 1989, pp. 119–22.

Chapter 13   The Dialectics of the Hegemonic Drive

1. On hegemony: A. Gramsci, *Selections from the Prison Notebooks* (London: Lawrence & Wishart, 1971), *The Modern Prince* (New York: International Publishers, 1972); *Note sul Machiavelli, sulla Politica e sullo Stato Moderno* (Turin: Einaudi, 1966).
2. On class analysis, see Part I, Chapter 1, 'Paradigms Lost'.
3. On Gramsci's hegemony and passive revolution: C. Buci-Glucksmann, *Gramsci et l'État* (Paris: Fayard, 1975); P. Ginsborg,'Gramsci and the Era of Bourgeois Revolution', in J.A. Davis (ed.), *Gramsci and Italy's Passive Revolution* (London: Croom Helm, 1979); J. Femia, *Gramsci's Political Thought* (Oxford: Clarendon Press, 1981)
4. As Bayart (1989, p. 227 and *passim*) has also pointed out.
5. See Femia, op.cit.
6. Bayart, 1979, p. 19.
7. Bayart, 1989, pp.146–7.
8. My review of Bayart, 1989: *International Affairs*, 66, 3 (1990), pp. 626–7.
9. See Part II, Chapter 4.
10. Lonsdale, 1981.
11. More orthodox: Chazan *et al.*, 1988, chapter 2.
12. These dichotomies were introduced for conceptual clarity, see Part II, Chapters 3 and 4.
13. Bayart, 1989, p. 260, my italics.
14. Mbembe (1985 and 1988) shows why dichotomies are misleading.
15. See above, Part II, Chapters 3 and 4.
16. At the micro-level, individuals straddle the two.
17. H. Alavi, 'The State in Post-Colonial Societies'; G. Mathias and P. Salama, *L'État surdéveloppé* (Paris: Maspéro, 1983); C. Leys, 'The "Overdeveloped" Colonial State', *Review of African Political Economy*, 5 (1976).
18. Chazan *et al.*, 1988, pp. 45–8.
19. R. Lemarchand, in Rothschild and Chazan, 1988.

20. A zero-sum game is not a realistic model but it does illustrate the dilemmas for patronage systems once resources run out.
21. Leading partly to its overdevelopment. See Note 17 above.
22. See here, for example, D. Court, 'The Education System as a Response to Inequality', in J. Barkan and J. Okumu (eds), *Politics and Public Policy in Kenya and Tanzania* (New York: Praeger, 1979).,
23. Mbembe, 1985.
24. On nationalisations in Africa: F.N. Burton and H. Inoue, 'Expropriations of Foreign-Owned Firms in Developing Countries', *Journal of World Trade Law*, 18, 5 (1984).
25. M. Adejugbe, 'The Myths and Realities of Nigeria's Business Indigenization', *Development and Change*, 15, 4 (1984).
26. Fieldhouse, 1986, particularly chapters 4 and 9.
27. On Senegal: D. Cruise O'Brien, *Saints and Politicians* (Cambridge: Cambridge University Press,1975); J. Copans, *Les marabouts de l'arachide* (Paris: Le Sycomore, 1980); Coulon, 1981.
28. Bayart's 'L'État rhizome', Bayart, 1989, pp. 270–80.
29. The notion of 'consummation' flows from pre-colonial notions.
30. On Weber, Mommsen, 1974.
31. See above, Part II, Chapter 5.
32. Gramsci's writings are relevant to Africa: Femia, *op.cit.*
33. Bayart, 'La revanche des société africaines', *Politique africaine*, 11 (1983).
34. On Africa's ensuing economic crisis: Ravenhill, 1986.
35. Duruflé, 1988.
36. I am talking here of the balance between state and society.
37. See here as a summary, Chazan *et al.*, 1988, pp. 229–35.
38. Mbembe, 1985.
39. Bayart, 1989, chapter 9.
40. See Part II, Chapter 4.
41. On 'traditional' power: see Bayart, 1989, chapter 5.
42. 'The End of Chieftaincy in Guinea', in Suret-Canale, 1988.
43. See Part II, Chapter 5.
44. Hodgkin, 1956, for how important they already were.
45. Mbembe, 1988, chapter 4.
46. Coleman & Rosberg, 1966.
47. Bayart, 'Civil Society in Africa', in Chabal,1986.
48. The longevity of East European socialist states was partly due to the inability of society to organise against the state.
49. Where the economic crisis has now eroded the state's power.
50. Zaïre may be the most extreme such case: MacGaffey,1987.
51. See here Part II, Chapter 6.
52. Sandbrook, 1985.
53. See Part III, Chapter 11.
54. Which Bayart (1979), for example, does.
55. On the reproduction of power: see Part IV, Chapter 15.
56. Mommsen, 1974; S. Krasner, *Structural Conflict* (Berkeley: University of California Press, 1985).
57. N. Karl-i-Bond, *Mobutu ou l'incarnation du mal* (London: Rex Collings, 1982).
58. Which process is sustaining state preponderance.

59. On youth politics: Bayart, in Chabal, 1986, p. 119.
60. Baynham, 1986.
61. For one example of this, MacGaffey,1987.
62. Chazan *et al.*, 1988, chapter 7.
63. One aspect of political Africanisation has been the fraying of the boundaries between state and civil society.
64. On Zaïre's parallel economy, MacGaffey, 1987.
65. One will reread with profit A. de Tocqueville, *Democracy in America* (New York: Harper & Row, 1966).
66. As in Uganda, Chad, Equatorial Guinea, Mozambique, etc.
67. R. Lemarchand, *Rwanda and Burundi* (London: Pall Mall, 1970).
68. On the Horn of Africa: Markakis, 1987.
69. Ch. Becker & A. Lericollais, 'Le problème frontalier dans le conflit sénégalo-mauritanien', *Politique africaine*, 35 (1989).
70. For a relevant background: Crummey,1986.
71. For Senegal: Cruise O'Brien, op.cit., Coulon, op.cit.
72. On Rwanda and Burundi: R. Lemarchand, *Rwanda and Burundi*, op.cit.
73. Most spectacularly, the Biafra secession.
74. Anyang' Nyong'o, 1987.
75. On the early case of Cameroon: Joseph, 1977.
76. For what I mean by propitious: Chabal in Kasfir, 1984.
77. A. Gramsci, *Gli Intellettuali e l' Organizzazione della Culture* (Turin: Einaudi, 1949).
78. Ngugi wa Thiong'o, 1982 and 1985.
79. MacGaffey, 1987, illustrates the processes discussed here.

Chapter 14   The Politics of Dependence

1. Frank, 1967; C. Wilbert (ed.), *The Political Economy of Development and Underdevelopment* (New York: Random House, 1973); I. Wallerstein, 1976, and 'Dependence in an Interdependent World', *African Studies Review*, 17, 1 (1974); T. Smith, 'The Underdevelopment of Development Literature', *World Politics*, 31, 2 (1979); Staniland, 1985; Rodney, 1972; Amin, 1972; D. Cohen and J. Daniel (eds), *Political Economy of Africa* (London: Longman, 1981).
2. On underdevelopment theory see Part I, 'Paradigms Lost' Section 3.
3. For how it matters to Africa's violence: Part III, Chapter 11.
4. Frank, 1967; Wallerstein, 1976.
5. C. Furtado, *Development and Stagnation in Latin America* (New Haven: Yale University Press, 1965).
6. Wallerstein, 1976; Rodney, 1972.
7. Mamdani, 1976; Shivji, 1973.
8. Harrison, 1984; K. Borgin and K. Corbett, *The Destruction of a Continent* (New York: Harcourt Brace Jovanovich, 1982).
9. See Notes, Part I, Chapter 1, n. 62.
10. For a critique of Harrison (1984), see Hill, 1986, pp. 171–4.
11. On agency and good government: Dunn, in Chabal, 1986.
12. C. Diaz-Alejandro in A. Fishlow *et al.*, *Rich and Poor Nations in the World Economy* (New York: McGraw Hill, 1978).

13. Warren, 1980.
14. Anyang' Nyong'o, 1987.
15. Fieldhouse, 1986.
16. The level of generalisation in dependency theory has always been one of its fundamental weaknesses: Staniland, 1985.
17. See Part II, Chapter 5, and Part III, Chapter 9.
18. Ravenhill,1986.
19. Rodney, 1972; Amin, *Le Développement inégal* (Paris: Editions de Minuit, 1973).
20. For a non-dependency perspective, Fieldhouse, 1986.
21. Dunn, 1980.
22. For a more general discussion: Part II, Chapter 6.
23. For alternative explanations: Richards, 1985; Bates, 1981 and 1983; Hart, 1982.
24. On the post-colonial consumption logic: Duruflé, 1988.
25. Fieldhouse, 1986, part III.
26. For an 'orthodox' view: Chazan *et al.*, 1988, chapters 9 and 10.
27. see Note 1.
28. Duruflé, 1988, conclusion.
29. World Bank, *Financing Development with Growth in Sub-Saharan Africa, 1986–1990* (Washington DC: World Bank, 1986).
30. T. Moran, *Multinational Corporations and the Politics of Dependence* (Princeton: Princeton University Press, 1974).
31. Bates, 1983; Hart, 1980.
32. There are some exceptions, such as Rawlings: R. Jeffries, 'Ghana', in Donal Cruise O'Brien *et al.*, 1989.
33. Few governments are explicit or realistic about this form of dependence; on the Cape Verde exception: Foy, 1988.
34. For an interesting case: T. Callaghy, 'The Political Economy of African Debt: the Case of Zaire' in Ravenhill, 1986.
35. See Hill,1986, pp. 83–94, on indebtedness.
36. P. Guillaumont, *Croissance et ajustement* (Paris: Economica, 1985).
37. Duruflé,1988.
38. As those (Nyerere, Kaunda, etc.) whose politics set them against structural adjustment have found out to their cost.
39. The key question for rulers is whether they can get away with the social consequences of structural adjustment.
40. One case: J. Quan, *Mozambique: a Cry for Peace* (Oxford: Oxfam, 1987).
41. For background on domestic charity in Africa: Iliffe, 1987.
42. Charities do not formulate their aid policies in such terms.
43. Lefort, 1983.
44. R. Hirsch, 'Ajustement structurel et politiques alimentaires en Afrique subsaharienne', *Politique africaine*, 37 (1990).
45. *The Challenge of Drought: Ethiopia's Decade of Relief and Rehabilitation* (Addis Ababa: Relief and Rehabilitation Commission, 1985).
46. G. Vivini, 'Famine and the Resettlement Programme in Ethiopia', *Africa* (Rome), 2 (1986).
47. Most hysterical was A. Glucksmann and T. Wolton, *Silence, on tue* (Paris: Grasset, 1986).

48. G. Prunier, '"Il faut savoir terminer une révolution": l'Éthiopie depuis 1984', *Politique africaine*, 33 (1989).
49. It is difficult to believe that the World Bank and the IMF are not aware of the effects of foreign aid on the survival of the state.
50. See my argument in Part II, Chapter 3.
51. T. Shaw and O. Aluko (eds), *The Political Economy of African Foreign Policy* (New York: St. Martin's Press, 1983).
52. O. Aluko, *The Foreign Policies of African States* (London: Hodder & Stoughton, 1977).
53. W. Scott Thomson, *Ghana's Foreign Policy,1957–1966* (Princeton: Princeton University Press, 1969).
54. Shaw and Aluko, op.cit.
55. R. Lemarchand, 'The State, the Parallel Economy and the Changing Structure of Patronage Systems in Africa' in Rothchild and Chazan, 1988.
56. Perhaps an extreme case of such predicament was Guinea-Bissau under Luiz Cabral's presidency (1975–80): R. Dumont and M.-F. Mottin, *L'Afrique étranglée* (Paris: Seuil, 1982), pp. 236–7.
57. On Guinea-Bissau: Galli and Jones, 1987. On Ghana, another interesting case, see Jeffries, op.cit.
58. Duruflé, 1988.
59. For a more sceptical view, ibid.
60. Largely for the reasons outlined in Part IV, Chapter 13.
61. For example, the conversion of Mozambique to a multi-party democracy derives in part from its need for World Bank support.
62. Africa's debt is astronomical (relative to income): World Bank, *World Debt Tables, 1989–90* (Washington DC: World Bank, 1990).
63. As the largest debtor nations (Latin America) have shown.
64. Callaghy,'The Political Economy of African Debt', op.cit.
65. Liniger-Goumaz, 1988.
66. See Part III, Chapter 9.
67. The story of Guinea-Bissau is also instructive.
68. On political accountability, see Part II, Chapter 3.
69. There ought to be a Ministry of Aid in every country.

Chapter 15   The Reproduction of Power

1. Reproduction of power is a deeper and more extensive notion than leadership change. Huntington, 1968; Jackson and Rosberg, 1984.
2. Transfer of power assumes a 'political free market'; see R. Dahl, *Polyarchy* (New Haven: Yale University Press, 1971).
3. C. Clapham, *Third World Politics* (Madison: University of Madison Press, 1985).
4. For one interesting overview: Decalo,1975.
5. Hayward, 1986; Collier, 1982.
6. B. Salert, *Revolutions and Revolutionaries* (New York: Elsevier, 1976); Wilner, 1968.
7. Jackson and Rosberg, 1982; M. Doro and N. Stultz (eds), *Governing in Black Africa* (Englewood Cliffs: Prentice-Hall, 1970).
8. On the notion of hegemonic drive, see Part IV, Chapter 13.

9. Dunn, 1984; Avineri,1968, especially pp. 17–40.

10. Dunn, 1979, chapters 2 and 4.

11. V. Le Vine 'Leadership Transition in Black Africa', *Munger Africana Library Notes*, 30 (1975).

12. A. Mazrui, 'The Resurrection of the Warrior Tradition in African Political Culture', *Journal of Modern African Studies*, 13, 1 (1975).

13. For an overview of fully-fledged revolutions, Dunn 1972.

14. On the meaning of independence, Tangri, 1985, chapter 1.

15. On the image of charisma: Apter, 1955; Wilner, 1968.

16. Suret-Canale,'The End of Chieftaincy in Guinea', in Suret-Canale, 1988.

17. B. Amonoo, *Ghana, 1957–1966* (London: Allen & Unwin, 1981).

18. On post-Touré's Guinea: *Politique africaine*, 36 (1989).

19. Bayart, 1989, chapter 5.

20. Barrington Moore,1966.

21. An enduring nationalist myth, debunked early by Fanon, 1967a.

22. J. Lonsdale, 'La pensée politique Kikuyu et les idéologies du mouvement Mau-Mau', *Cahiers d'études africaines*, 27, 3/4 (1987).

23. Fanon, 1967a.

24. Lloyd, 1966.

25. See my discussion in Part III, Chapter 7.

26. On the generational variable: Lonsdale in Chabal, 1986.

27. On Ghana, Amonoo, op.cit.

28. Chabal, 1983, chapter 3.

29. A fracture more consequential than was realised.

30. Protestant missionaries were often charged with inculcating 'disrespect' for elders.

31. P. Foster, *Education and Social Change in Ghana* (Chicago: University of Chicago Press, 1965).

32. R. Clignet, 'Education and Elite Formation', in J. Paden and E. Soja (eds), *The African Experience*, vol. 1 (Evanston: Northwestern University Press, 1970).

33. Chazan *et al*, 1988, pp. 48–9.

34. Achebe's *Anthills of the Savanna* (London: Heinemann, 1987) shows how youth in power feels threatened by 'traditional' power.

35. Mbembe, 1985.

36. A. Zolberg, 'The Structure of Conflict in the New States of Tropical Africa', *American Political Science Review* 62, 1 (1968).

37. Chabal,1983, chapter 3; and privately from J. Cunningham.

38. See Part IV, Chapter 12.

39. I refer to the values and virtues of the pre-colonial order as transformed by the colonial experience; a dynamic process, not timeless dichotomies between a notional 'new' and a notional 'old'.

40. Best-known is perhaps Nyerere's *mwalimu* (teacher).

41. On how Mao coped with this argument: F. Wakeman Jr (ed.), *History and Will* (Berkeley: University of California Press, 1975).

42. T. Callaghy, 'State-Subject Communication in Zaire', *Journal of Modern African Studies*, 17, 3 (1980).

43. On a Zaïrian example: Callaghy, 1984.

44. R. Charlton, 'Plus ça change?', *Cultures et développement*, 13, 1/2 (1981).

45. And becomes a factor legitimising political leadership.

46. See Part IV, Chapter 12.
47. On age and legitimacy: Jackson & Rosberg, 1982.
48. Young coup leaders do not often 'mature' in power.
49. R. Jackman, 'The Predictability of Coups d'État: a Model with African Data', *American Political Science Review*, 72, 4 (1978).
50. A. Mazrui in M. Doro and N. Stulz (eds), op.cit.
51. An argument which I present in Part I, 'Paradigms Lost', Section 2.
52. Lloyd, 1966.
53. S. Othman, 'Nigeria', in Cruise O'Brien *et al.*, 1989.
54. A. Cohen, 1981.
55. Bayart, in Chabal, 1986, pp. 99–114.
56. One case: D. Anderson, 'A History of the Peoples of the Baringo Plains, 1890–1940', Cambridge University, PhD thesis, 1982.
57. Le Vine, 1975.
58. The construction of the world's largest cathedral in Yamassoukro may well have taken Houphouët-Boigny beyond the pale.
59. On classes in Africa, see Part I, 'Paradigms Lost', Section 2.
60. D. Rothchild & R. Curry, *Scarcity, Choice and Public Policy in Middle Africa* (Berkeley: University of California Press, 1978).
61. Special issue on Niger: *Politique africaine*, 38 (1990).
62. Foy, 1988.
63. Still on Niger: S. Abba, 'La Chefferie traditionnelle en question', *Politique africaine*, 38 (1990).
64. One example of austerity: P. Labazée, 'Discours et contrôle politique: les avatars du sankarisme', *Politique africaine*, 33 (1989).
65. For a fascinating illustration: MacGaffey, 1987.
66. R. Sklar, 'The Nature of Class Domination in Africa', *Journal of Modern African Studies*, 17, 4 (1979).
67. MacGaffey, 1987.
68. R. Lemarchand, in Rothchild and Chazan, 1988.
69. Exchange is preferred to production. Bayart, 1989, p. 138.
69. Anyang' Nyong'o, 1987, particularly chapter 4.
70. R. Lemarchand, 'Political Exchange, Clientelism and Development in Tropical Africa', *Cultures et développement*, 4, 3 (1972).
71. Swainson, 1980.
72. On Kenya, see G. Dauch and D. Martin, *L'héritage de Kenyatta* (Paris: L'Harmattan, 1985).
73. The only orderly transfer of power from long-established leaders to their chosen successors has occurred among these countries.
74. As in Nigeria, for example. S. Othman, op.cit.
75. On Zambia and Zaïre: Chazan *et al.*, 1988, pp. 284–5.

Select bibliography

Achebe, C. *Morning Yet on Creation Day*. London: Heinemann, 1975.

Ake, C. *Social Science as Imperialism*. Ibadan: Ibadan University Press, 1979.

Almond, G. and Coleman, J. *The Politics of the Developing Areas*. Princeton: Princeton University Press, 1960.

Almond, G. and Powell, J. *Comparative Politics: a Developmental Approach*. Princeton: Princeton University Press, 1966.

Amin, S. 'Underdevelopment and Dependence in Black Africa', *Journal of Modern African Studies*, 10, 4 (1972).

Amin, S. *Neo-Colonialism in West Africa*. Harmondsworth: Penguin, 1973.

Amuta, C. *The Theory of African Literature*. London: Zed Press, 1990.

Anderson, B. *Imagined Communities*. London: New Left, 1983.

Andreski, S. *The African Predicament*. London: Michael Joseph, 1968.

Anyang' Nyong'o, P. (ed.) *Popular Struggles for Democracy in Africa*. London: Zed Press, 1987.

Apter, D. *The Gold Coast in Transition*. Princeton: Princeton University Press, 1955.

Apter, D. *The Political Kingdom in Uganda*. Princeton: Princeton University Press, 1961.

Apter, D. *The Politics of Modernization*. New Haven: Yale University Press, 1965.

Austen, R. *African Economic History*. London: Currey, 1987.

Avineri, S. *The Social and Political Thought of Karl Marx*. Cambridge: Cambridge University Press, 1968.

Barongo, Y. *Political Science in Africa*. London: Zed Press, 1983.

Barrington Moore. *Social Origins of Dictatorship and Democracy*. Boston: Beacon Press, 1966.

Barrington Moore. *Injustice*. London: Macmillan, 1979.

Bates, R. *Markets and States in Tropical Africa*. Berkeley: University of California Press, 1981.

Bates, R. *Essays on the Political Economy of Rural Africa*. Cambridge: Cambridge University Press, 1983.

Bayart, J.-F. *L'État au Cameroun*. Paris: Presses de la Fondation Nationale des Sciences Politiques, 1979.

Bayart, J.-F. *L'État en Afrique*. Paris: Fayard, 1989.

Baynham, S. *Military Power and Politics in Black Africa*. London: Croom Helm, 1986.

Beckman, B. *Organizing the Farmers*. Uppsala: SIAS, 1976.

Bénot, Y. *Idéologies des indépendances africaines*. Paris: Maspéro, 1968.

Berry, S. *Fathers Work for their Sons*. Berkeley: University of California Press, 1985.

Bienen, H. *Tanzania: Party Transformation and Economic Development*. Princeton: Princeton University Press, 1971.

Binder, L. *et al. Crises and Sequences in Political Development*. Princeton: Princeton University Press, 1971.

Buijtenhuijs, R. *Le Frolinat et les guerres civiles du Tchad*. Paris: Karthala, 1987.

Cabral, A. *Unité et lutte*. Paris: Maspéro, 1975.

Cabral, A. *Unity and Struggle*. London: Heinemann, 1980.

Cahen, M. *Mozambique: la révolution implosée*. Paris: l'Harmattan, 1987.

Callaghy, T. *The State–Society Struggle*. New York: Columbia University Press, 1984.

Carroll, D. *Chinua Achebe*. London: Macmillan, 1990.

Cartwright, J. *Political Leadership in Africa*. London: Croom Helm, 1983.

Chabal, P. *Amílcar Cabral*. Cambridge: Cambridge University Press, 1983.

Chabal, P. (ed.), *Political Domination in Africa*. Cambridge: Cambridge University Press, 1986.

Chabal, P. 'Historia y Praxis en El Uso y El Abuso de La Noción de Socialismo Africano', in Luis Castro Leiva (ed.), *Usos y Abusos de La Historia en Teoría y en La Práctica Política*. Caracas: IDEA, 1988.

Chazan, N. *et al. Politics and Society in Contemporary Africa*. London:Macmillan, 1988.

Claessen H. and Skalnik, P. *The Study of the State*. The Hague: Mouton, 1981.

Clapham, C. *Transformation and Continuity in Revolutionary Ethiopia*. Cambridge: Cambridge University Press,1988.

Clarence-Smith. G. *The Third Portuguese Empire*. Manchester: Manchester University Press, 1985.

Cohen, A. *The Politics of Elite Culture*. Berkeley: University of California Press, 1981.

Cohen, W. *Rulers of Empire*. Stanford: Hoover Institution Press, 1971.

Coleman, J. *Nigeria:: Background to Nationalism*. Berkeley: University of California Press, 1963.

Coleman J. and Rosberg, C. *Political Parties and National Integration in Tropical Africa*. Berkeley: University of California Press, 1966.

Collier, R. B. *Regimes in Tropical Africa*. Berkeley: University of California Press, 1982.

Contamin, B and Fauré, J.-Y. *La bataille des entreprises publiques en Côte d'Ivoire*. Paris: Karthala, 1990.

Cooper, F. *From Slaves to Squatters*. New Haven: Yale University Press, 1980.

Coquery-Vidrovitch, C. 'Recherches sur un mode de production africain', *La Pensée*, 144, 1969.

Coulon, C. *Le marabout et le prince*. Paris: Pedone, 1981.

Cruise O'Brien, D. *The Mourides of Senegal*. Oxford: Oxford University Press, 1971.

Cruise O'Brien, D. *et al. Contemporary West African States*. Cambridge: Cambridge University Press,1989.

Crummey, D. *Banditry, Rebellion and Social Protest in Africa*. London: Currey, 1986.

Crummey, D. and Stewart, C. *Modes of Production in Africa*. London: Sage,1981.

Curtin, P. *Economic Change in Precolonial Africa*. Madison: University of Wisconsin Press, 1975.

Decalo, S. *Coups and Army Rule in Africa*. New Haven: Yale University Press, 1976.

Diamond, L. *Ethnicity and Democracy in Nigeria*. London: Macmillan, 1988.

Draper, H. *Karl Marx's Theory of Revolution*. New York: Monthly Review Press, 1977.

Duignan, P. and Jackson, R. (eds), *Politics and Government in African States*. London: Croom Helm, 1986.

Dunn, J. *Modern Revolutions*. Cambridge: Cambridge University Press, 1972.

Dunn, J. *West African States.* Cambridge: Cambridge University Press, 1978.

Dunn, J. *Western Political Theory in the Face of the Future.* Cambridge: Cambridge University Press, 1979.

Dunn, J. *Political Obligation in its Historical Context.* Cambridge: Cambridge University Press, 1980.

Dunn, J. *The Politics of Socialism.* Cambridge: Cambridge University Press, 1984.

Duruflé, G. *L'ajustement structurel en Afrique.* Paris: Karthala, 1988.

Enloe, C. *Ethnic Conflict and Political Development.* Boston: Little, Brown & Co., 1973.

Fanon, F. *The Wretched of the Earth.* London: McGibbon & Kee, 1965.

Fanon, F. *Black Skin, White Masks.* New York: Grove Press, 1967a.

Fanon, F. *Towards the African Revolution.* New York: Monthly Review Press, 1967b.

Fieldhouse, D. *Black Africa, 1945–1980.* London: Allen & Unwin, 1986.

First, R. *Black Gold.* Brighton: Harvester Press, 1983.

Foy, C. *Cape Verde.* London: Pinter, 1988.

Frank, A. *Capitalism and Underdevelopment in Latin America.* New York: Monthly Review Press, 1967.

Freund, B. *The Making of Contemporary Africa.* London: Macmillan, 1984.

Galli, R. and Jones, J. *Guinea-Bissau.* London: Pinter, 1987.

Gann, L.H. and Duignan, P. *Colonialism in Africa, 1870–1960.* Cambridge: Cambridge University Press, 1969.

Geffray, C. *La cause des armes au Mozambique.* Paris: Karthala, 1990.

Gellner, E. *Nations and Nationalism.* Oxford: Blackwell, 1983.

Gifford, P. and Louis, W. *The Transfer of Power in Africa.* New Haven: Yale University Press, 1982.

Harrison, P. *Inside the Third World.* Hardmondsworth: Penguin, 1984.

Hart, K. *The Political Economy of West African Agriculture.* Cambridge: Cambridge University Press, 1980.

Hayward, F. *Elections in Independent Africa.* Boulder: Westview Press, 1986.

Higgott, R. *Political Development Theory.* London: Croom Helm, 1983.

Hill, P. *The Migrant Cocoa Farmers of Southern Ghana.* Cambridge: Cambridge University Press, 1963.

Hill, P. *Development Economics on Trial.* Cambridge: Cambridge University Press, 1986.

Hindess, B. & Hirst, P. *Pre-Capitalist Modes of Production.* London: Routledge, 1975.

Hobsbawn, E. and Ranger. T. *The Invention of Tradition.* Cambridge: Cambridge University Press, 1983.

Hodder-Williams, R. *An Introduction to the Politics of Tropical Africa.* London: Allen & Unwin, 1984.

Hodgkin, T. *Nationalism in Colonial Africa.* London: Muller, 1956.

Hopkins, A.G. *An Economic History of West Africa.* London: Longman, 1973.

Huntington, S. *Political Order in Changing Societies.* New Haven: Yale University Press, 1968.

Hyden, G. *Beyond Ujamaa in Tanzania.* London: Heinemann, 1980.

Iliffe, J. *A Modern History of Tanganyika.* Cambridge: Cambridge University Press, 1979.

Iliffe, J. *The Emergence of African Capitalism.* London: Macmillan, 1983.

Iliffe, J. *The African Poor.* Cambridge: Cambridge University Press, 1987.

Innes, C.L. *Chinua Achebe*. Cambridge: Cambridge University Press, 1990.

Isaacman, A. *Mozambique: the Africanization of a European Institution*. Madison: University of Wisconsin Press, 1972.

Isaacman, A. *The Tradition of Resistance in Mozambique*. Berkeley: University of California Press, 1976.

Jackson, R. and Rosberg, C. *Personal Rule in Black Africa*. Berkeley: University of California, 1982.

Jeffries, R. *Power and Ideology in Ghana*. Cambridge: Cambridge University Press, 1978.

Jewsiewicki, B. and Newbury, D. *African Historiographies*. Beverly Hills: Sage Publications, 1986.

Joseph, R. *Radical Nationalism in Cameroun*. Oxford: Clarendon Press, 1977.

Joseph, R. *Democracy and Prebendal Politics in Nigeria*. Cambridge: Cambridge University Press,1987.

Kasfir, N. *The Shrinking Political Arena*. Berkeley: University of California Press, 1967.

Kasfir, N. (ed.), *State and Class in Africa*. London: Cass, 1984.

Kenyatta, J. *Facing Mount Kenya*. London: Secker and Warburg, 1938.

Kitching, G. *Class and Economic Change in Kenya*. New Haven: Yale University Press, 1980.

Lan, D. *Guns and Rain*. London: Currey,1985.

Lee, J.M. *Colonial Development and Good Government*. Oxford: Clarendon Press, 1967.

Lefort, R. *Ethiopia: an Heretical Revolution?*. London: Zed Press, 1980.

Le Vine, V. *Political Corruption: the Ghana Case*. Stanford: Hoover Institution Press, 1975.

Leys, C. *Underdevelopment in Kenya*. London: Heinemann, 1975.

Liebenow, J.G. *African Politics*. Bloomington: Indiana University Press, 1986.

Liniger-Goumaz, M. *Small is not Always Beautiful*. London: Hurst, 1989.

Lloyd, P. *The New Elites of Tropical Africa*. Oxford: Oxford University Press, 1966.

Lonsdale, J. 'States and social processes in Africa', *African Studies Review*, 24, 2–3, 1981.

Lonsdale, J 'Africa's Pasts in Africa's Future', *Canadian Journal of African Studies*, 23, 1, 1989.

Lovejoy, P. *Transformations in Slavery*. Cambridge: Cambridge University Press, 1983.

Luckham, R. *The Nigerian Military*. Cambridge: Cambridge University Press, 1971.

MacGaffey, J. *Entrepreneurs and Parasites*. Cambridge: Cambridge University Press,1987.

Mamdani, M. *Politics and Class Formation in Uganda*. London: Heinemann, 1976.

Marcum, J. *The Angolan Revolution*. 2 vols. Cambridge: MIT Press, 1969 and 1978.

Markakis, J. *Ethiopia: Anatomy of a Traditional Polity*. Oxford: Oxford University Press,1974.

Markakis, J. *National and Class Conflict in the Horn of Africa*. Cambridge: Cambridge University Press, 1987.

Markovitz, I. *Power and Class in Africa*. Englewood Cliffs: Prentice-Hall, 1977.

Markovitz, I. *Studies in Power and Class in Africa*. Oxford: Oxford University Press,1987.

Marseille, J. *Empire colonial et capitalisme français*. Paris: Albin Michel, 1984.

Mbembe, A. *Les jeunes et l'ordre politique en Afrique noire*. Paris: l'Harmattan, 1985.

Mbembe, A. *Afriques indociles*. Paris: Karthala, 1988.

Mommsen, W. *The Age of Bureaucracy*. Oxford: Oxford University Press, 1974.

Mudimbe, V. *The Invention of Africa*. Bloomington: Indiana University Press, 1988.

Munslow, B. *Mozambique*. London: Longman, 1983.

Munslow, B. *Africa: Problems in the Transition to Socialism*. London: Zed Press, 1986.

Newitt, M. *Portugal in Africa*. London: Hurst, 1981.

Ngugi wa Thiong'o. *Writers in Politics*. London: Heinemann, 1982.

Ngugi wa Thiong'o. *Barrel of a Pen*. London: New Beacon, 1985.

Oyugi, W. *et al. Democratic Theory and Practice in Africa*. London: Currey, 1988.

Pateman, C. *Participation and Democratic Theory*. Cambridge: Cambridge University Press, 1970.

Peel, J. *Ijeshas and Nigerians*. Cambridge: Cambridge University Press, 1983.

Pitkin, H. *The Concept of Representation*. Berkeley: University of California Press, 1972.

Pratt, C. *The Critical Phase in Tanzania*. Cambridge: Cambridge University Press, 1976.

Ranger, T. *Peasant Consciousness and Guerrilla War in Zimbabwe*. London: Currey, 1985a.

Ranger. T. *The Invention of Tribalism in Zimbabwe*. Gweru: Mambo Press, 1985b.

Ravenhill, J. *Africa in Economic Crisis*. New York: Columbia University Press, 1986.

Rey, J-P. *Colonialisme, néo-colonialisme et transition au capitalisme*. Paris: Maspéro, 1971.

Richards, P. *Indigenous Agricultural Revolution*. London: Allen & Unwin, 1985.

Rimmer, D. *The Economies of West Africa*. London: Weidenfeld & Nicolson, 1984.

Robinson, R. and Gallagher, T. *Africa and the Victorians*. London: Macmillan, 1961.

Rodney, W. *How Europe Underdeveloped Africa*. London: Bogle l'Overture, 1972.

Rosberg, C. and Callaghy, T. *Socialism in Sub-Saharan Africa*. Berkeley: Institute of International Studies, 1979.

Rothchild, D. and Chazan, N. (eds). *The Precarious Balance*. Boulder: Westview Press, 1988.

Sandbrook, R. *The Politics of Africa's Economic Stagnation*. Cambridge: Cambridge University Press, 1985.

Sandbrook, R. and Cohen R. *The Development of an African Working Class*. London: Longman, 1975.

Saul, J. *The State and Revolution in Eastern Africa*. London: Heinemann, 1979.

Saul, J. *A Difficult Road*. New York: Monthly Review Press, 1985.

Sen, A. *Poverty and Famines*. Oxford: Oxford University Press, 1981.

Shivji, I. *The Silent Class Struggle*. Dar es Salaam: Tanzania Publishing House, 1973.

Shivji, I. *Class Struggles in Tanzania*. London: Heinemann, 1976.

Skocpol, T. *States and Social Revolutions*. Cambridge: Cambridge University Press, 1979.

Soyinka, W. *Myth, Literature and the African World*. Cambridge: Cambridge University Press, 1976.

Staniland, M. *What is Political Economy?* New Haven: Yale University Press, 1985.

Suret-Canale, J. *Essays on African History*. London: Hurst, 1988.

Swainson, N. *The Development of Corporate Capitalism in Kenya*. Berkeley: University of California Press, 1980.

Tangri, R. *Politics in Sub-Saharan Africa*. London: Currey, 1985.

Terray, E. *Marxism and 'Primitive' Societies*. New York: Monthly Review Press, 1972.

Tordoff, W. *Government and Politics in Africa*. Bloomington: Indiana University Press, 1984.

Vail, L. *The Creation of Tribalism in Southern Africa*. London: Currey,1989.

Vail, L. and White, L. *Capitalism and Colonialism in Mozambique*. London: Heinemann, 1980.

Wallerstein, I. *The Modern World System*. 2 vols. New York: Academic Press, 1974 and 1980.

Wallerstein, I. 'The Three Stages of African Involvement in the World Economy', in P.C. Gutkind & I. Wallerstein, *The Political Economy of Contemporary Africa*. Beverley Hills: Sage, 1976.

Warren, B. *Imperialism: Pioneer of Capitalism*. London: New Left Books, 1980.

Wesseling, H. *Expansion and Reaction*. Leiden: Leiden University Press, 1978.

Wilks, I. *Asante in the Nineteenth Century*. Cambridge: Cambridge University Press,1975.

Willame, J.C. *Patrimonialism and Political Change in the Congo*. Princeton: Princeton University Press, 1972.

Wilner, R. *Charismatic Political Leadership*. Princeton: Princeton University Press, 1968.

Wolf, E. *Peasant Wars of the Twentieth Century*. New York: Harper & Row, 1969.

Young, C. *The Politics of Cultural Pluralism*. Madison: University of Wisconsin Press, 1976.

Young, C. *Ideology and Development*. New Haven: Yale University Press, 1982.

Zolberg, A. *One Party Government in the Ivory Coast*. Princeton: Princeton University Press, 1964.

Zolberg, A. *Creating Political Order*. Chicago: Rand McNally, 1966.

Index